# BAD KARMA™

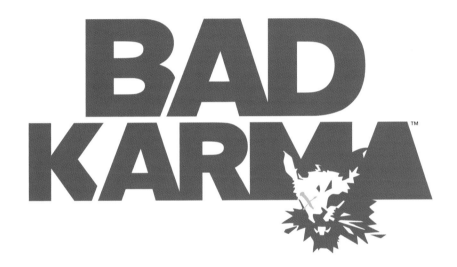

Bad Karma

Alex Grecian
Jeremy Haun
B. Clay Moore
Seth Peck

cover art **Jeremy Haun**
cover colors **John Rauch**
logo **Jonathan Hickman**
book design **Fonografiks**
additonal design **Neil Hicks**
production **Thomas Mauer**

Pin-ups




PRINTED IN CHINA

3

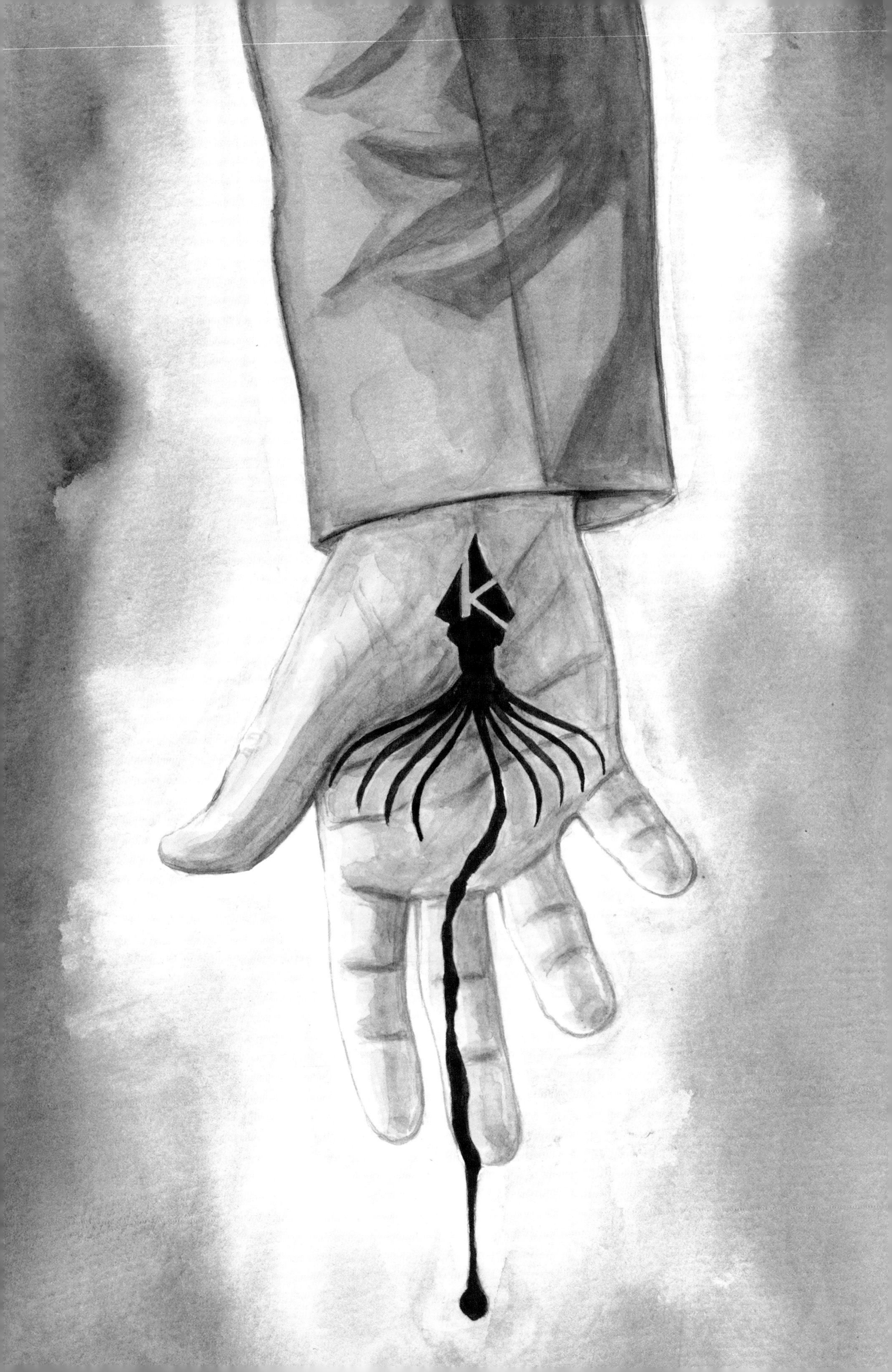

*Below the thunders of the upper deep,*
*Far, far beneath in the abysmal sea,*
*His ancient, dreamless, uninvaded sleep*
*The Kraken sleepeth: faintest sunlights flee*
*About his shadowy sides; above him swell*
*Huge sponges of millennial growth and height;*
*And far away into the sickly light,*
*From many a wondrous grot and secret cell*
*Unnumber'd and enormous polypi*
*Winnow with giant arms the slumbering green.*
*There hath he lain for ages, and will lie*
*Battening upon huge sea-worms in his sleep,*
*Until the latter fire shall heat the deep;*
*Then once by man and angels to be seen,*
*In roaring he shall rise and on the surface die.*

THE KRAKEN
Alfred, Lord Tennyson

# THE ARTIST

story    Jeremy Haun
art      Shane White
colors   Nolan Woodard
letters  Troy Peteri

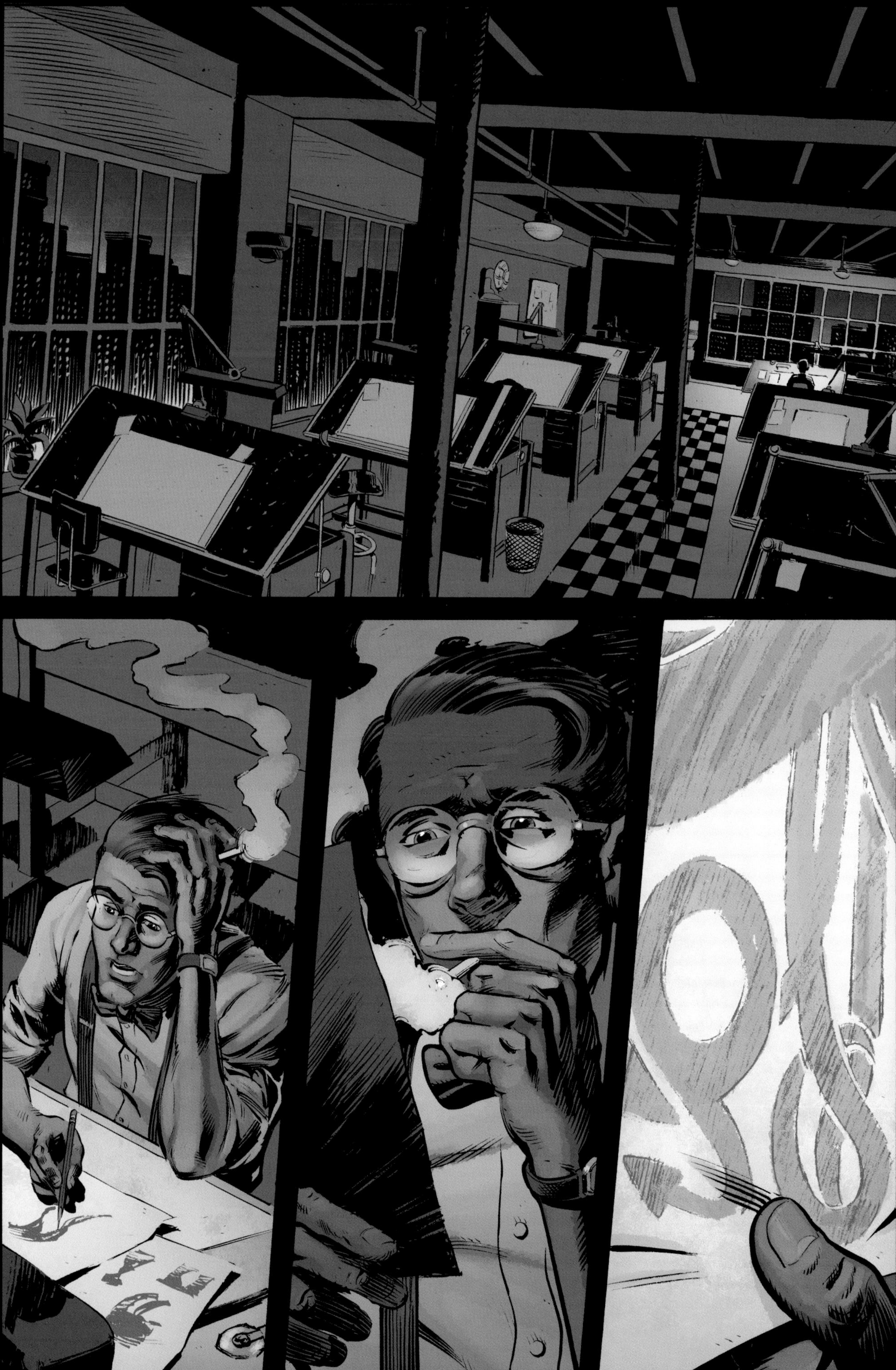

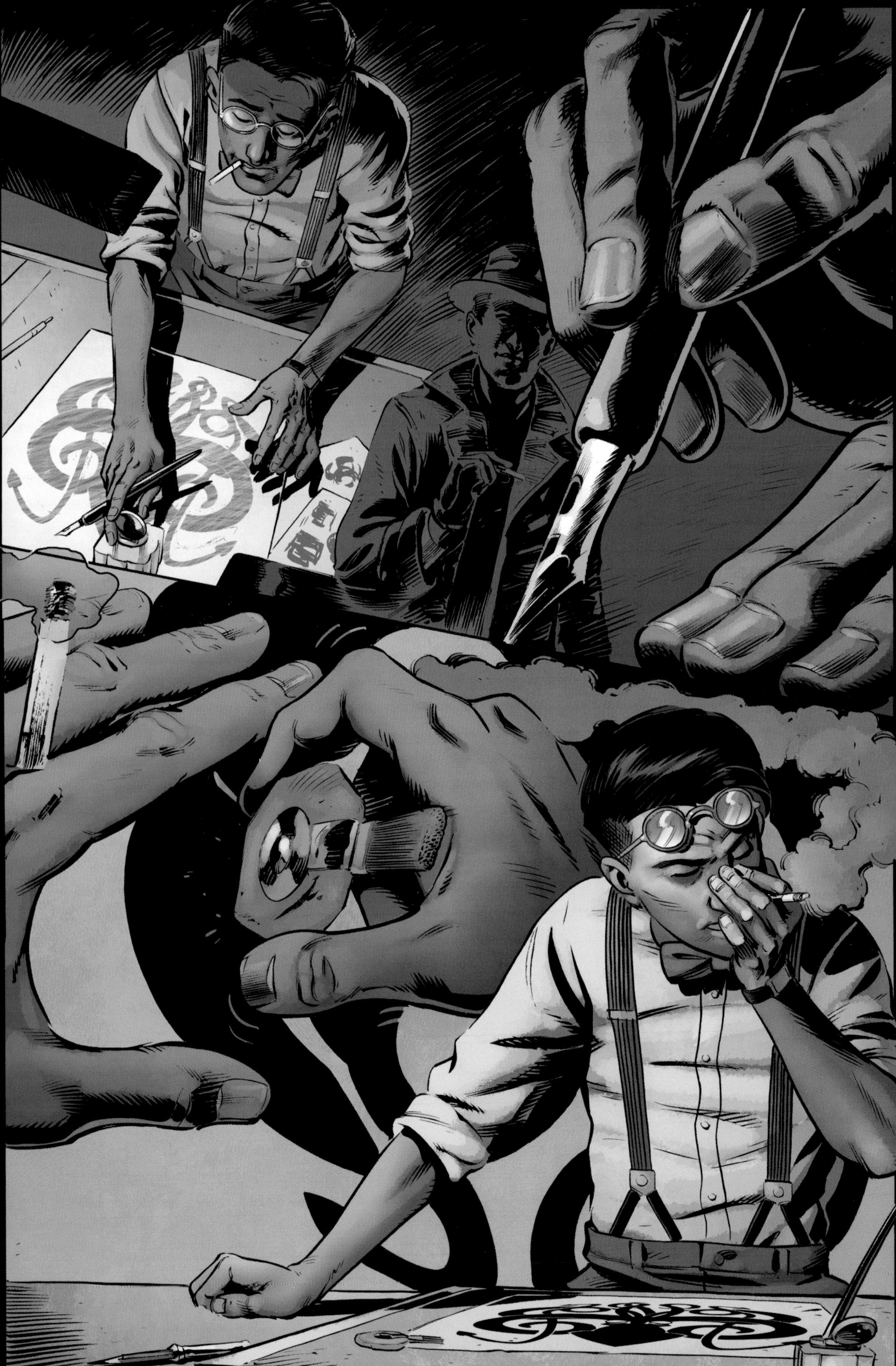

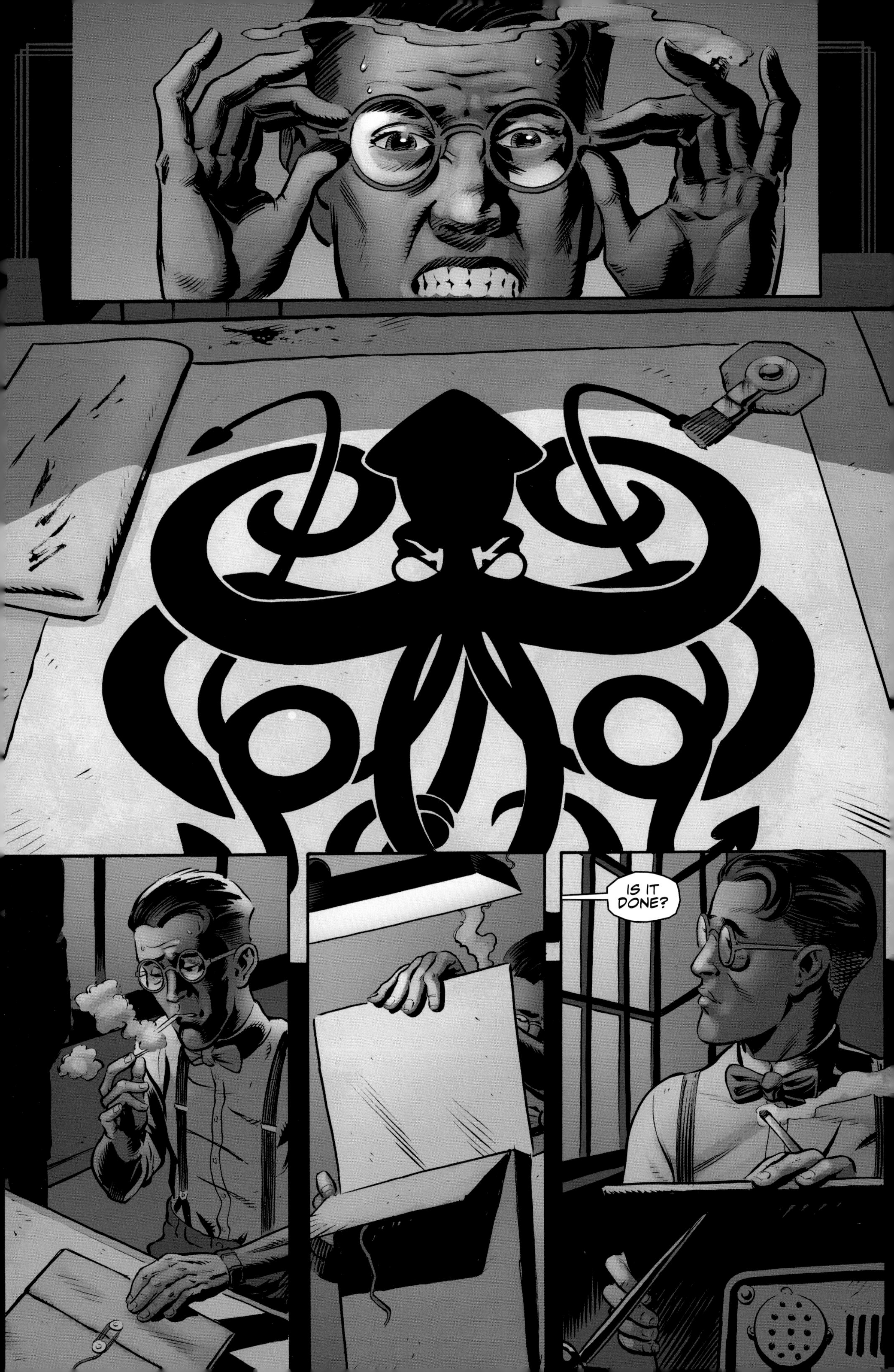
IS IT DONE?

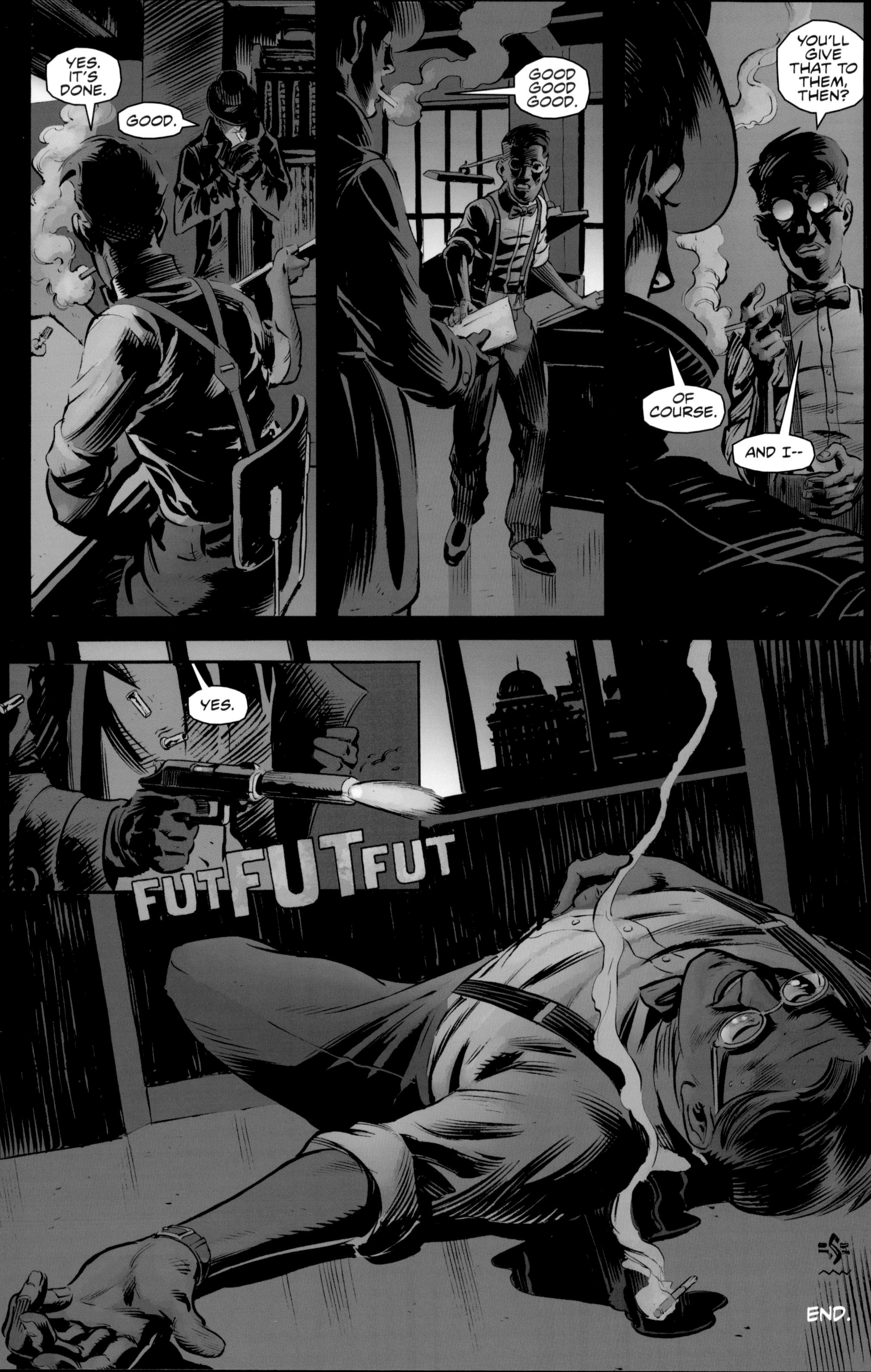
YES. IT'S DONE.
GOOD.
GOOD GOOD GOOD.
YOU'LL GIVE THAT TO THEM, THEN?
OF COURSE.
AND I--
YES.
FUTFUTFUT
END.

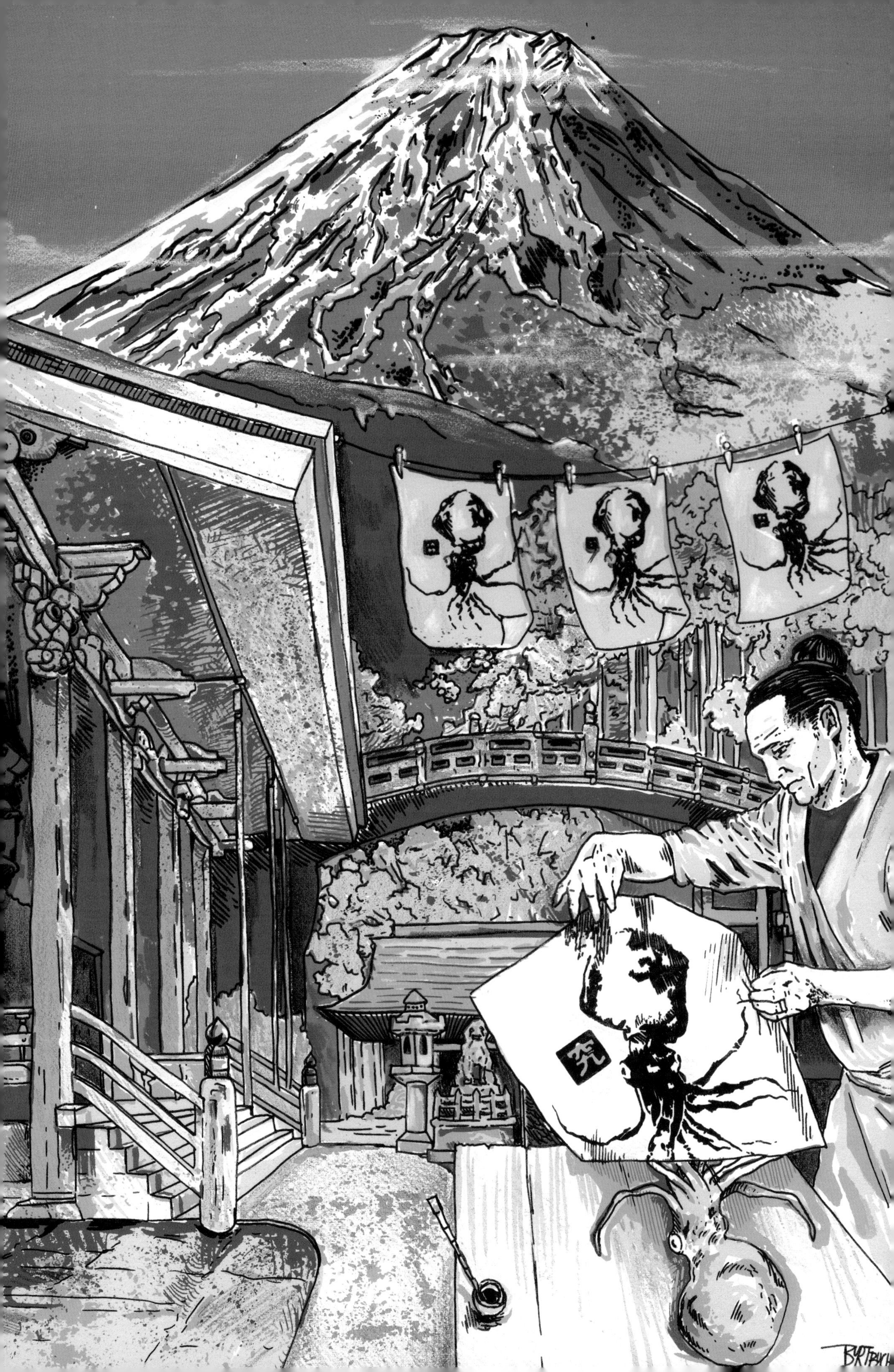

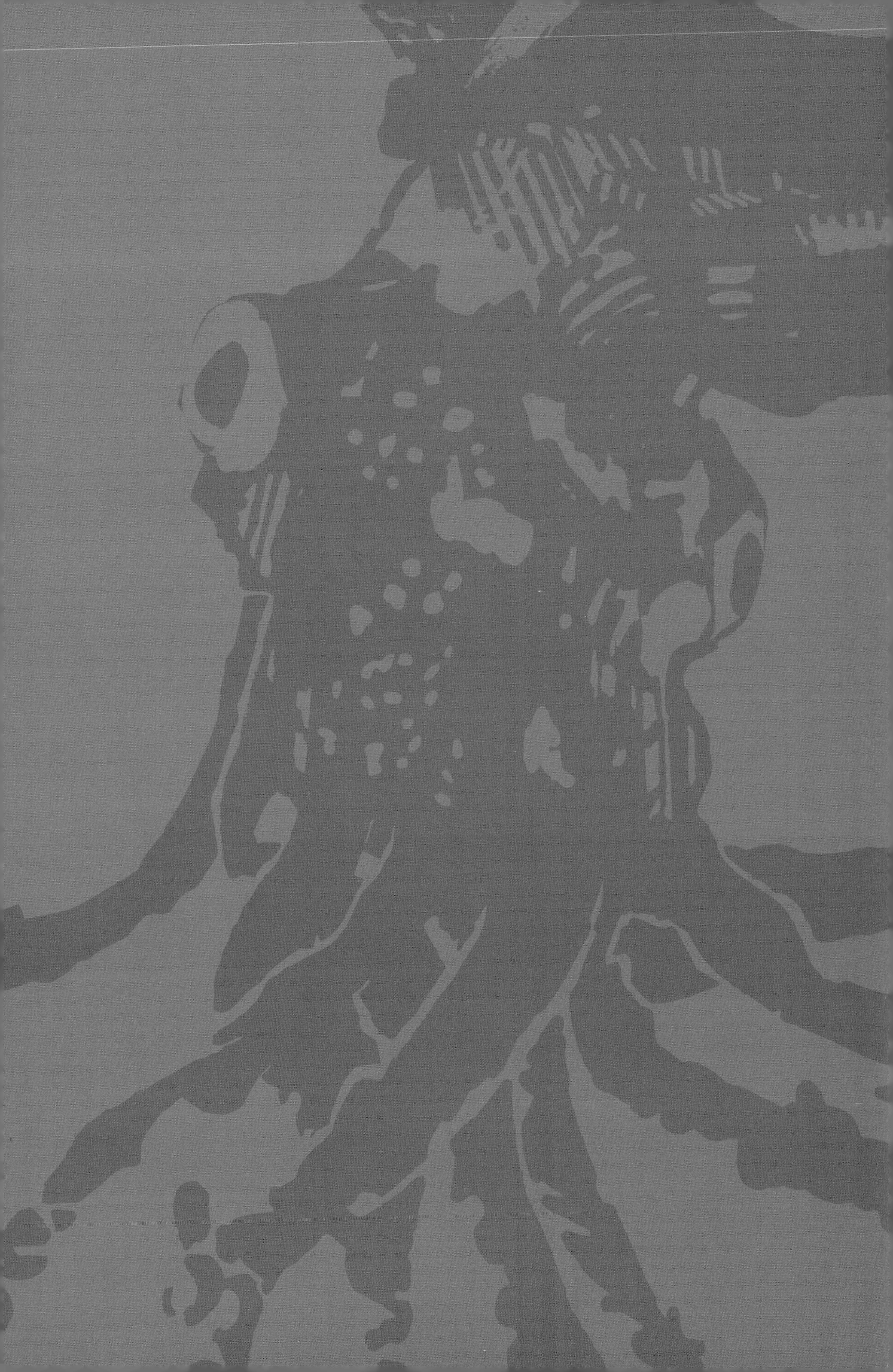

# THE 9TH LIFE OF SOLOMON GUNN™

Collaboration can be a tricky business.

BAD KARMA seemed like a good idea on paper, but the reality of getting four people who are all busy and opinionated creators to work together on such an ambitious project... well, it seemed unlikely. Maybe even impossible.

But it happened.

Alex, Jeremy, Clay and Seth each brought a concept into the fold and we all worked on those projects largely independently of each other. We gave input, but we didn't meddle. But those projects (*Chaos Agent*, *Middleton*, *Old Dog*, and *Hellbent*) didn't give us the opportunity we wanted to actually work together. We wanted to create something from the ground up, something covered with our fingerprints, all of us. So Solomon Gunn was born.

THE NINTH LIFE OF SOLOMON GUNN was, and is, the cornerstone of this entire book. We planned to write it, draw it, and somehow maintain a friendship through the process. Each of us would have a hand in creating this one character. A character who is forced to collaborate with himself! A grand, but impossible experiment.

And yet it worked.

The four of us brainstormed this story together over lunch at a barbecue joint. Clay, Seth and Alex wrote it in stages, passing it around and giving each other notes. Then Jeremy drew it all. Of course, John Rauch colored it and Rus Wooton lettered it, and it wouldn't look as good as it does if they hadn't. (Thanks, guys!)

But this was a Bad Karma project from the beginning. And somehow our luck held out.

Bad Karma
March 2013

| | |
|---|---|
| story | Alex Grecian |
| | Jeremy Haun |
| | B. Clay Moore |
| | Seth Peck |
| art | Jeremy Haun |
| colors | John Rauch |
| letters | Rus Wooton |

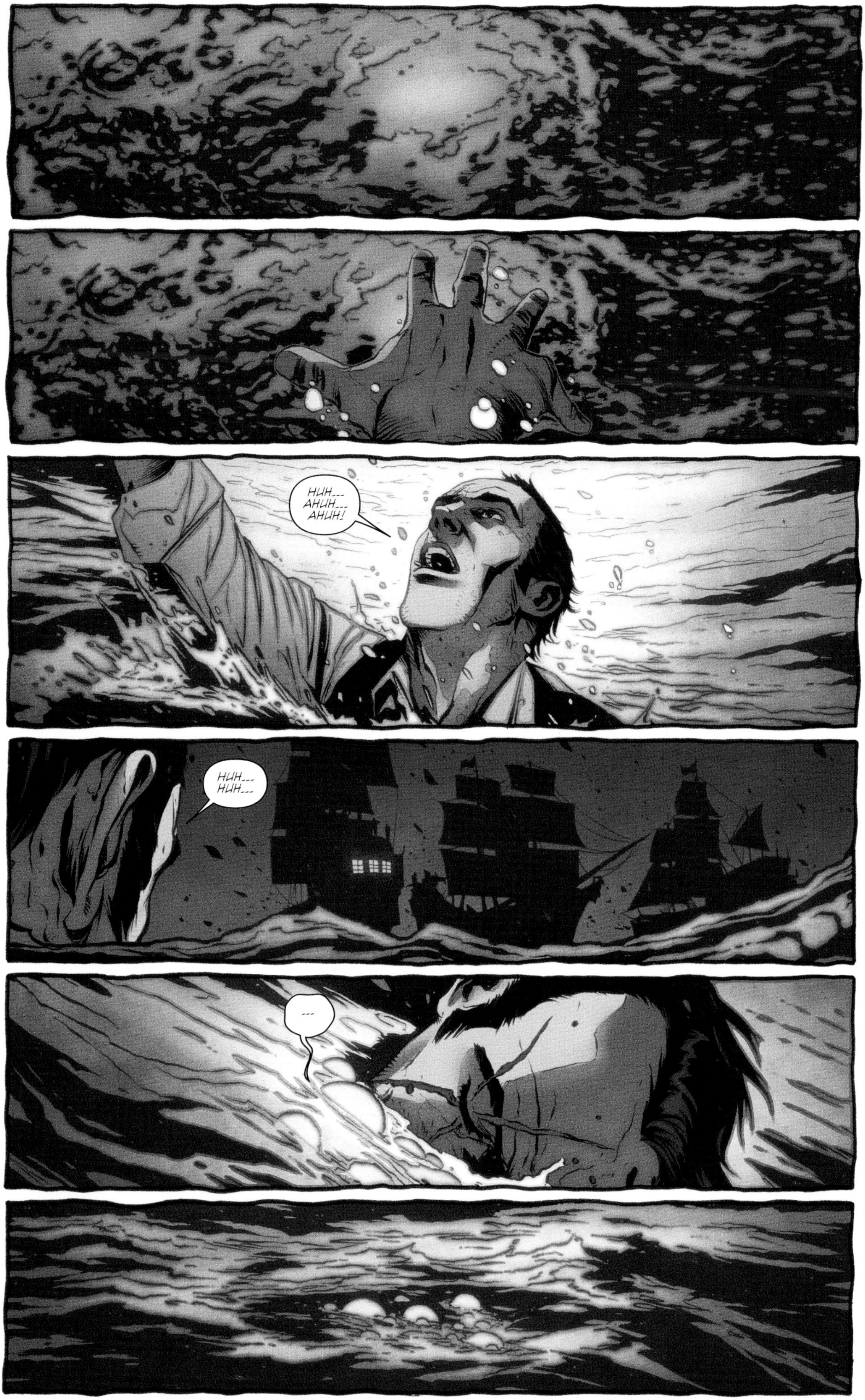
HUH...
AHUH...
AHUH!
HUH...
HUH...
...

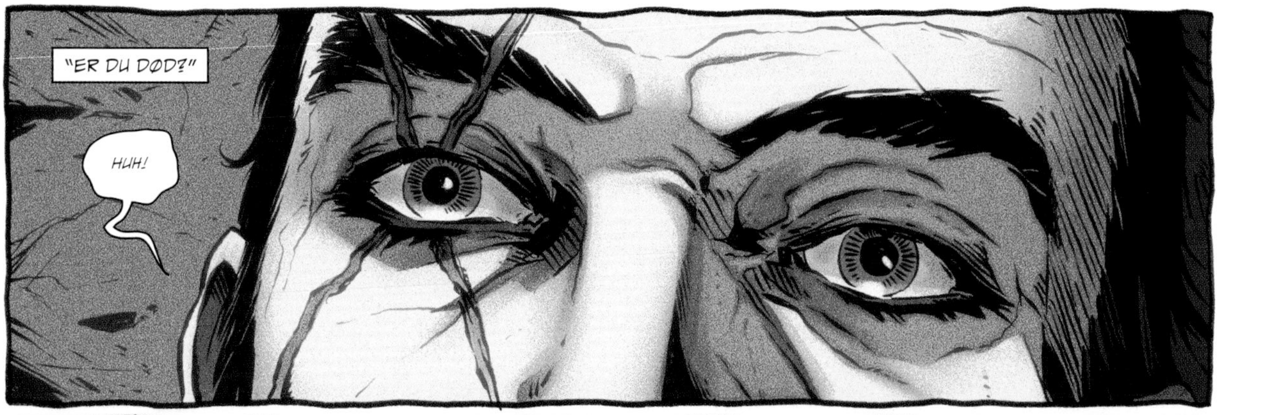
"ER DU DØD?"
HUH!

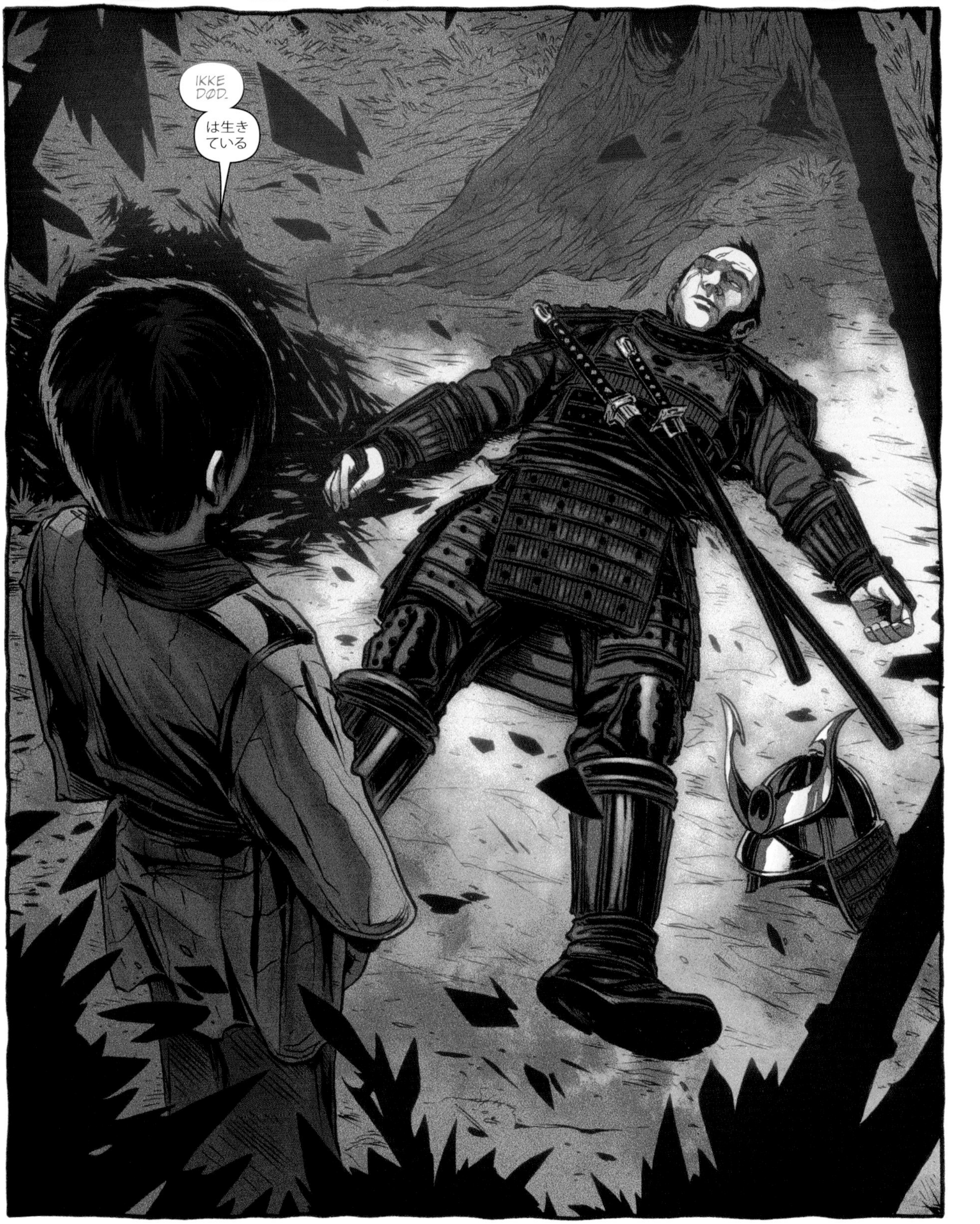
IKKE DØD.
は生きている

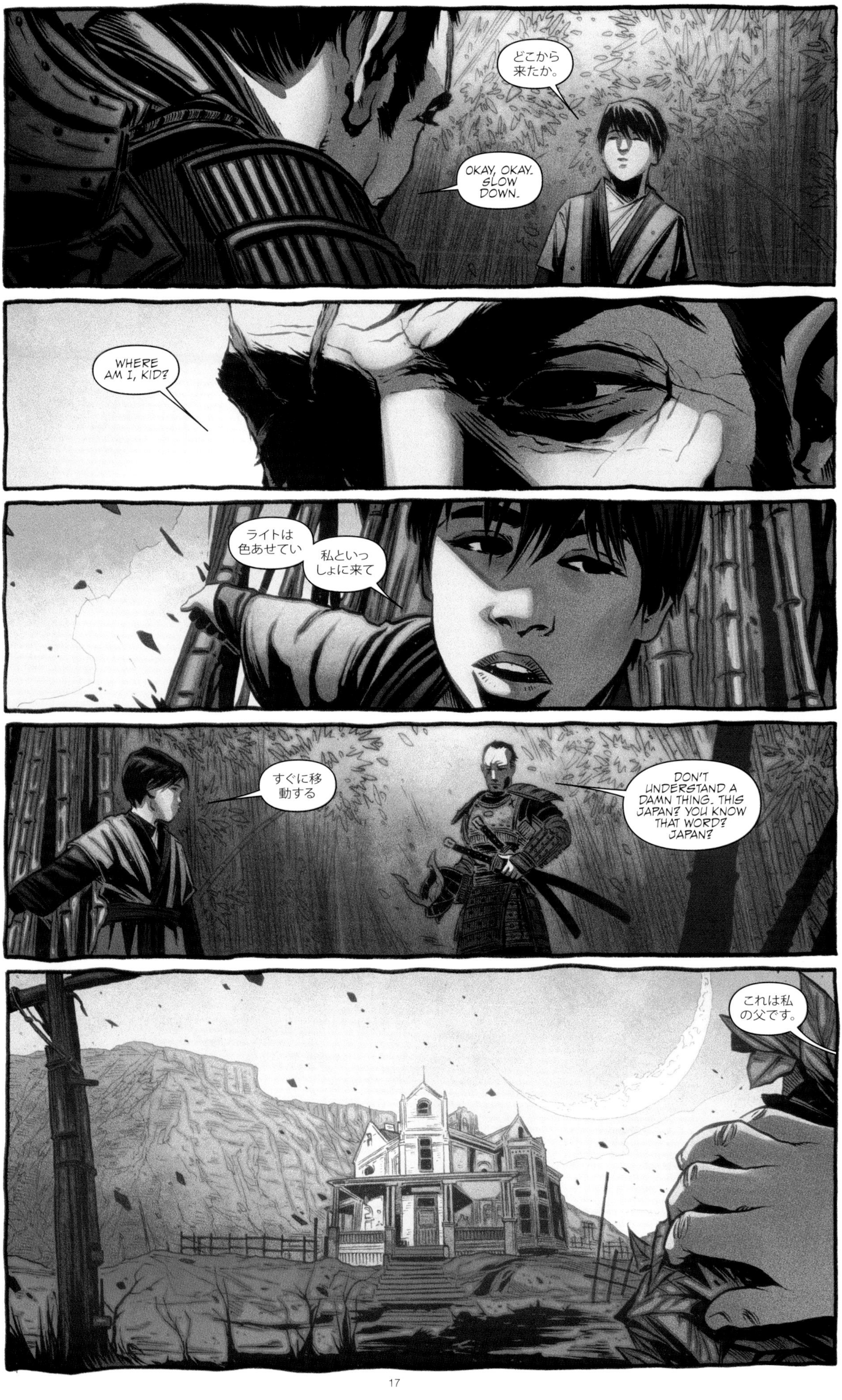
どこから
来たか。
OKAY, OKAY. SLOW DOWN.
WHERE AM I, KID?
ライトは
色あせてい
私といっ
しょに来て
すぐに移
動する
DON'T UNDERSTAND A DAMN THING. THIS JAPAN? YOU KNOW THAT WORD? JAPAN?
これは私
の父です。

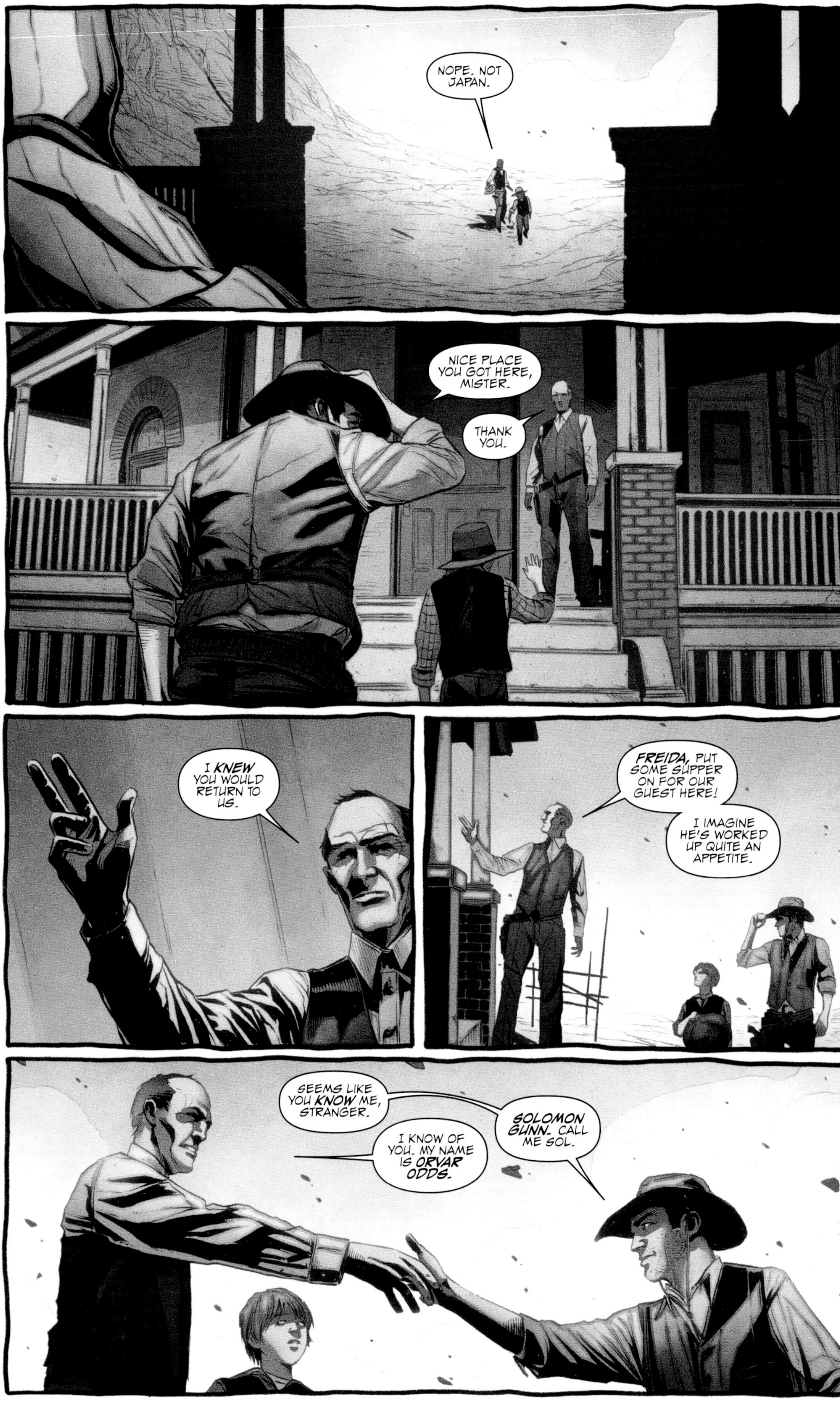
NOPE. NOT JAPAN.
NICE PLACE YOU GOT HERE, MISTER.
THANK YOU.
I KNEW YOU WOULD RETURN TO US.
FREIDA, PUT SOME SUPPER ON FOR OUR GUEST HERE!
I IMAGINE HE'S WORKED UP QUITE AN APPETITE.
SEEMS LIKE YOU KNOW ME, STRANGER.
I KNOW OF YOU. MY NAME IS ORVAR ODDS.
SOLOMON GUNN. CALL ME SOL.

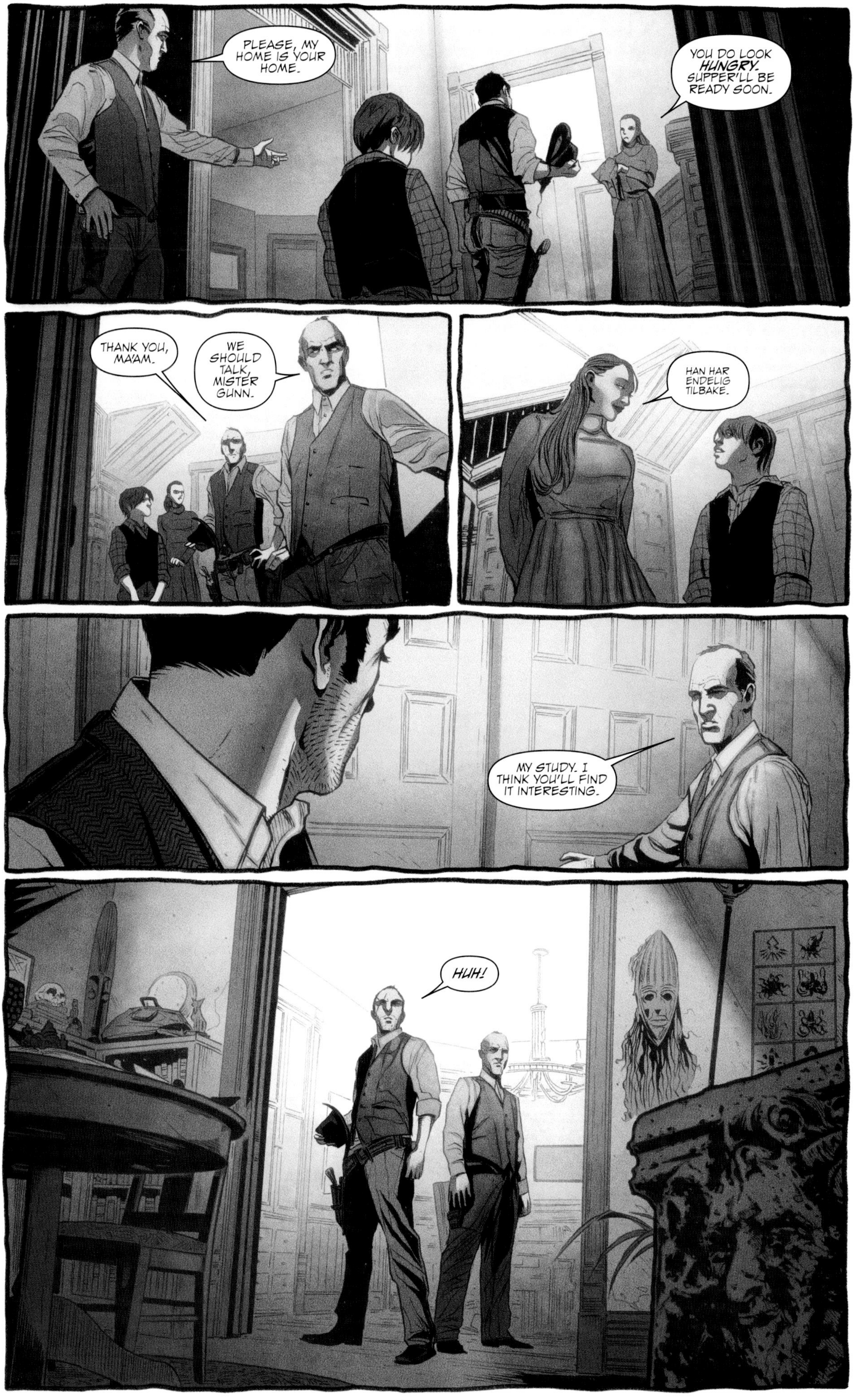
PLEASE, MY HOME IS YOUR HOME.
YOU DO LOOK HUNGRY. SUPPER'LL BE READY SOON.
THANK YOU, MA'AM.
WE SHOULD TALK, MISTER GUNN.
HAN HAR ENDELIG TILBAKE.
MY STUDY. I THINK YOU'LL FIND IT INTERESTING.
HUH!

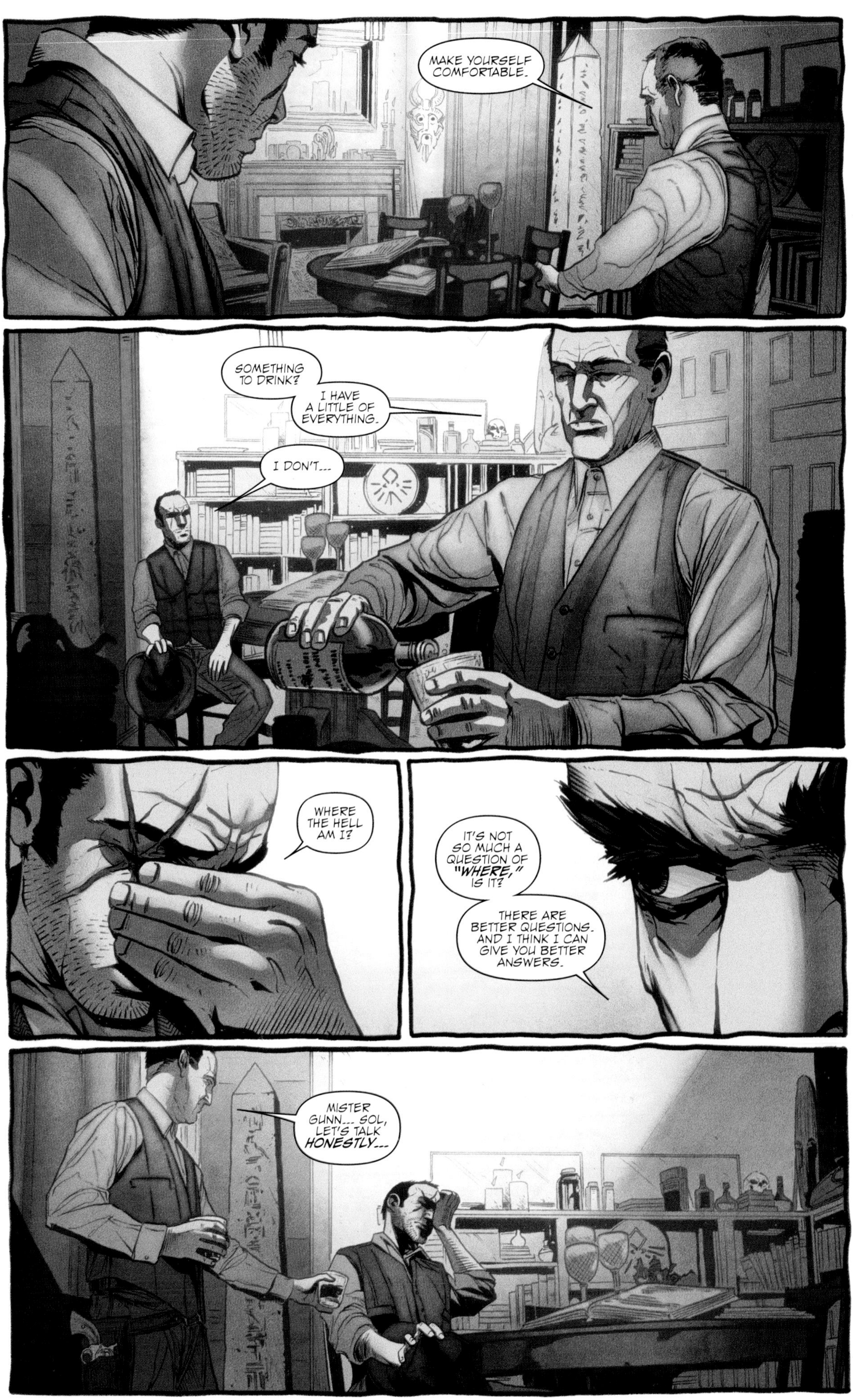
MAKE YOURSELF COMFORTABLE.
SOMETHING TO DRINK?
I HAVE A LITTLE OF EVERYTHING.
I DON'T...
WHERE THE HELL AM I?
IT'S NOT SO MUCH A QUESTION OF "WHERE," IS IT?
THERE ARE BETTER QUESTIONS. AND I THINK I CAN GIVE YOU BETTER ANSWERS.
MISTER GUNN... SOL, LET'S TALK HONESTLY...

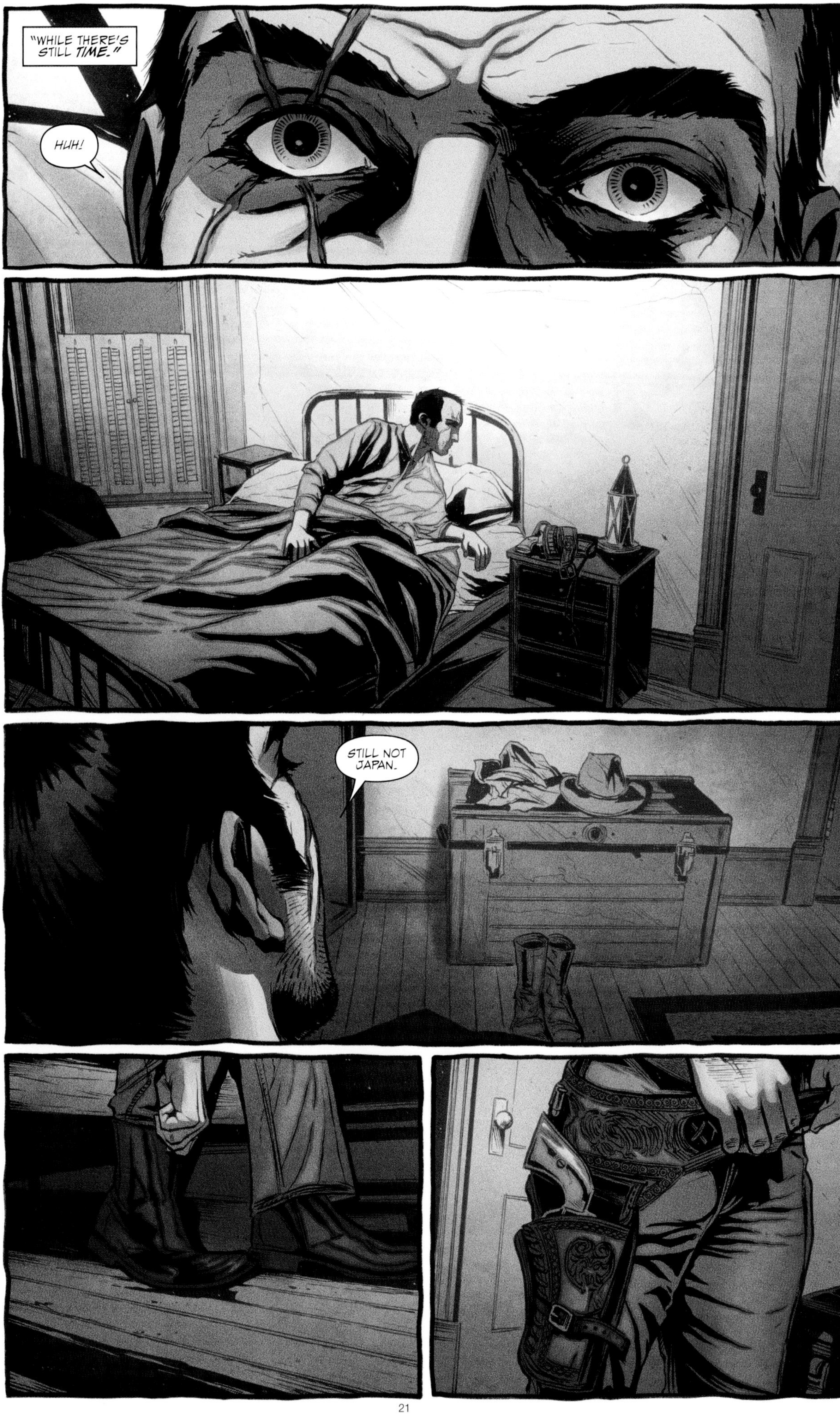
"WHILE THERE'S STILL TIME."
HUH!
STILL NOT JAPAN.

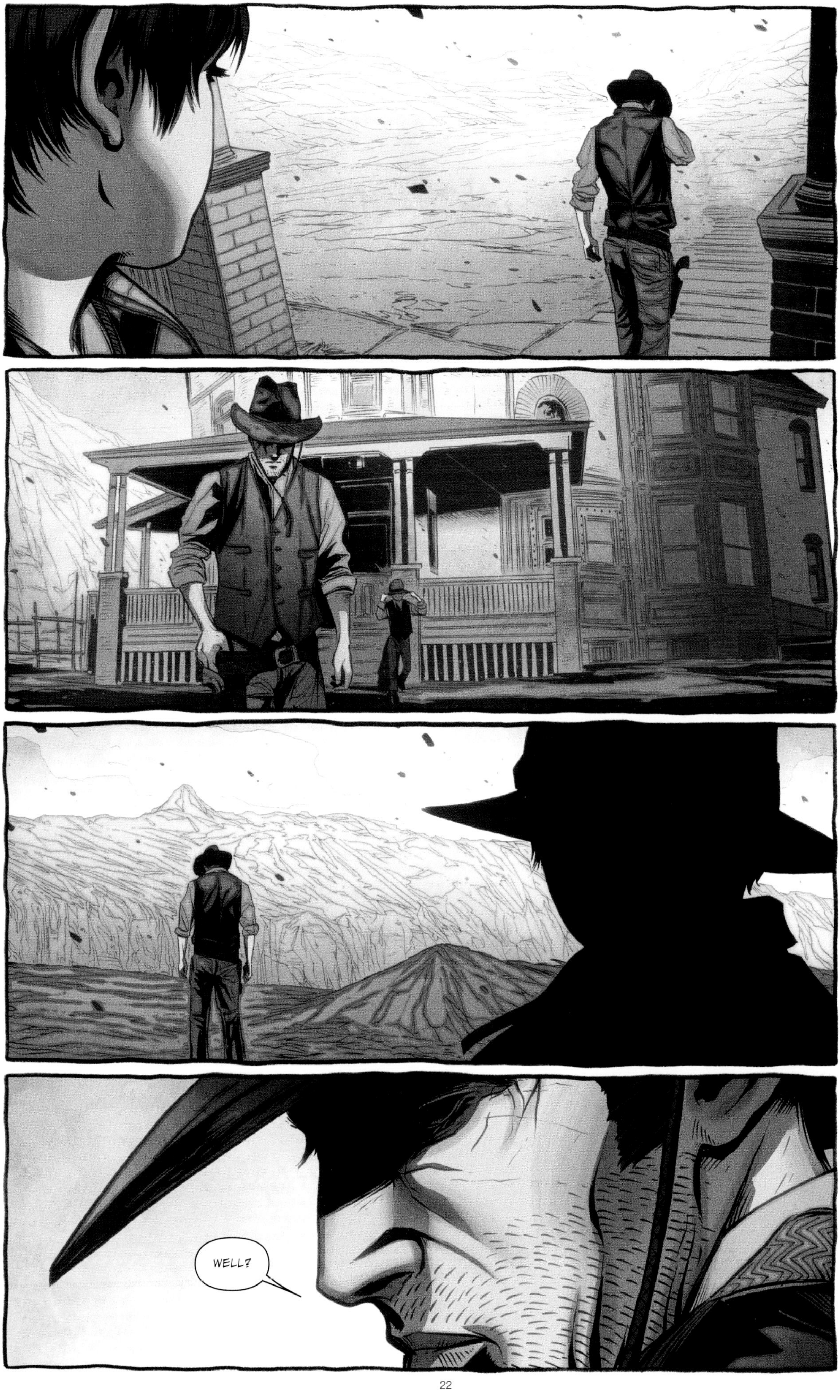
WELL?

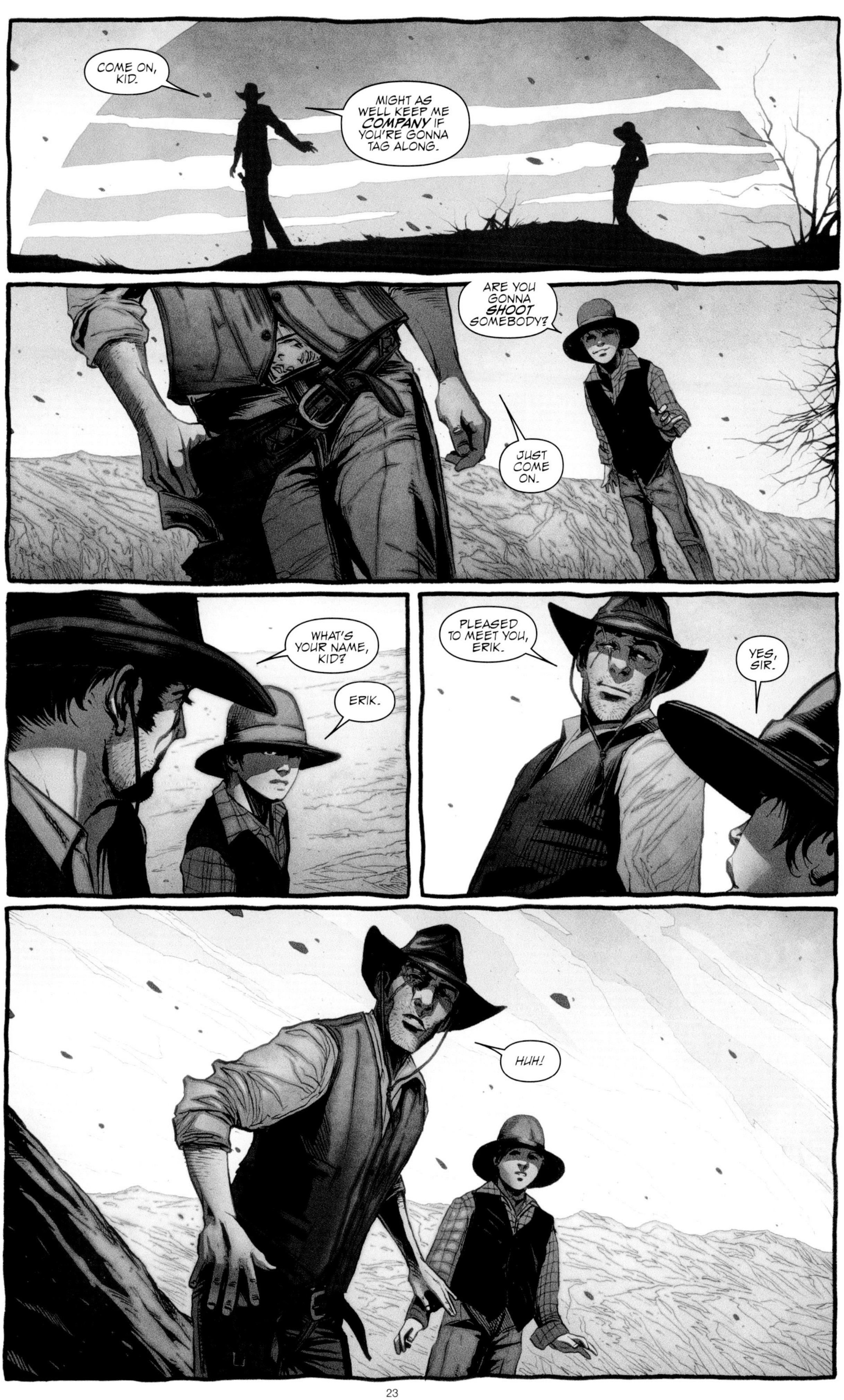
COME ON, KID.
MIGHT AS WELL KEEP ME COMPANY IF YOU'RE GONNA TAG ALONG.
ARE YOU GONNA SHOOT SOMEBODY?
JUST COME ON.
WHAT'S YOUR NAME, KID?
ERIK.
PLEASED TO MEET YOU, ERIK.
YES, SIR.
HUH!

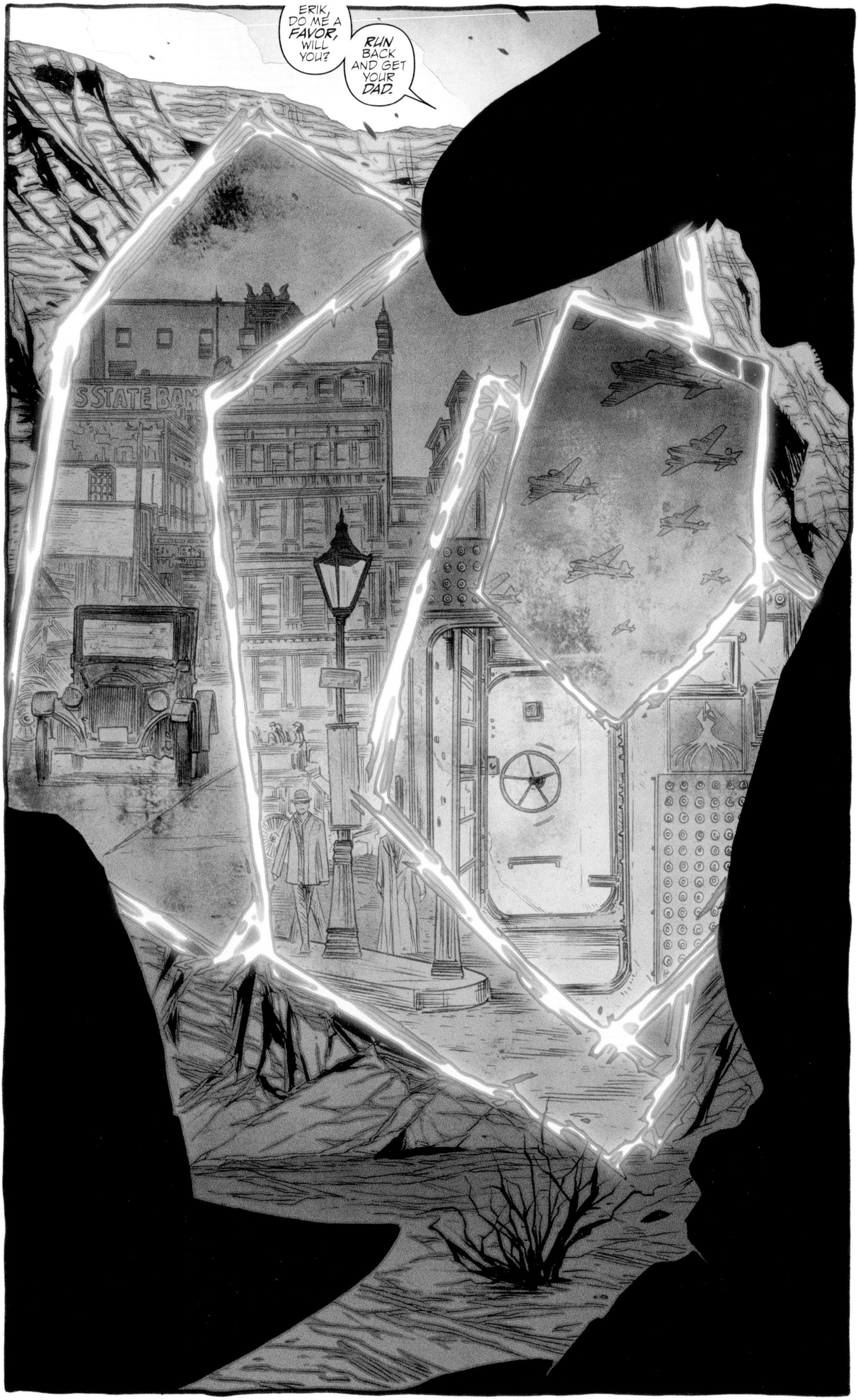
ERIK, DO ME A FAVOR, WILL YOU?
RUN BACK AND GET YOUR DAD.
S STATE BAN

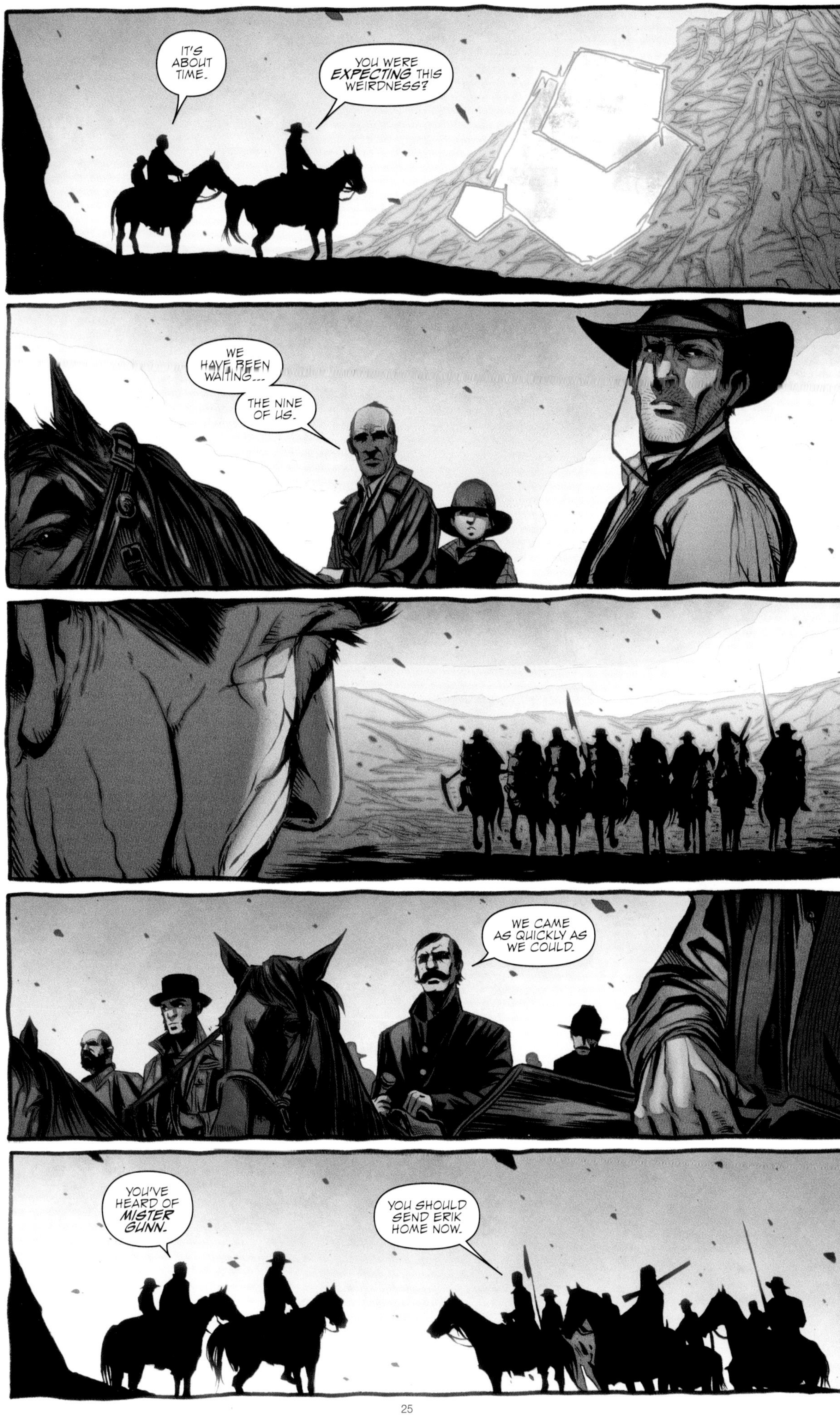
IT'S ABOUT TIME.
YOU WERE EXPECTING THIS WEIRDNESS?
WE HAVE BEEN WAITING...
THE NINE OF US.
WE CAME AS QUICKLY AS WE COULD.
YOU'VE HEARD OF MISTER GUNN.
YOU SHOULD SEND ERIK HOME NOW.

THE BOY IS *OLD ENOUGH* TO LEARN ABOUT WHAT WE DO.

TO LEARN HIS EVENTUAL *ROLE* IN THIS DRAMA.

SPEAKING OF DRAMA, IT'D BE OKAY WITH ME IF SOMEONE WANTED TO *EXPLAIN* A THING OR TWO.

HE DOESN'T *KNOW?*

HOW MUCH DID YOU TELL HIM ORVAR? HE'S NO GOOD TO US IF HE CAN'T--

MIGHT AS WELL SEND HIM BACK HOME WITH THE BOY.

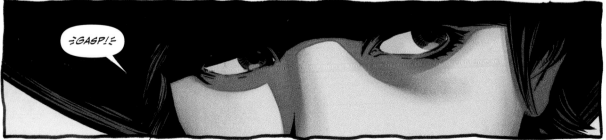

≥GASP!≤

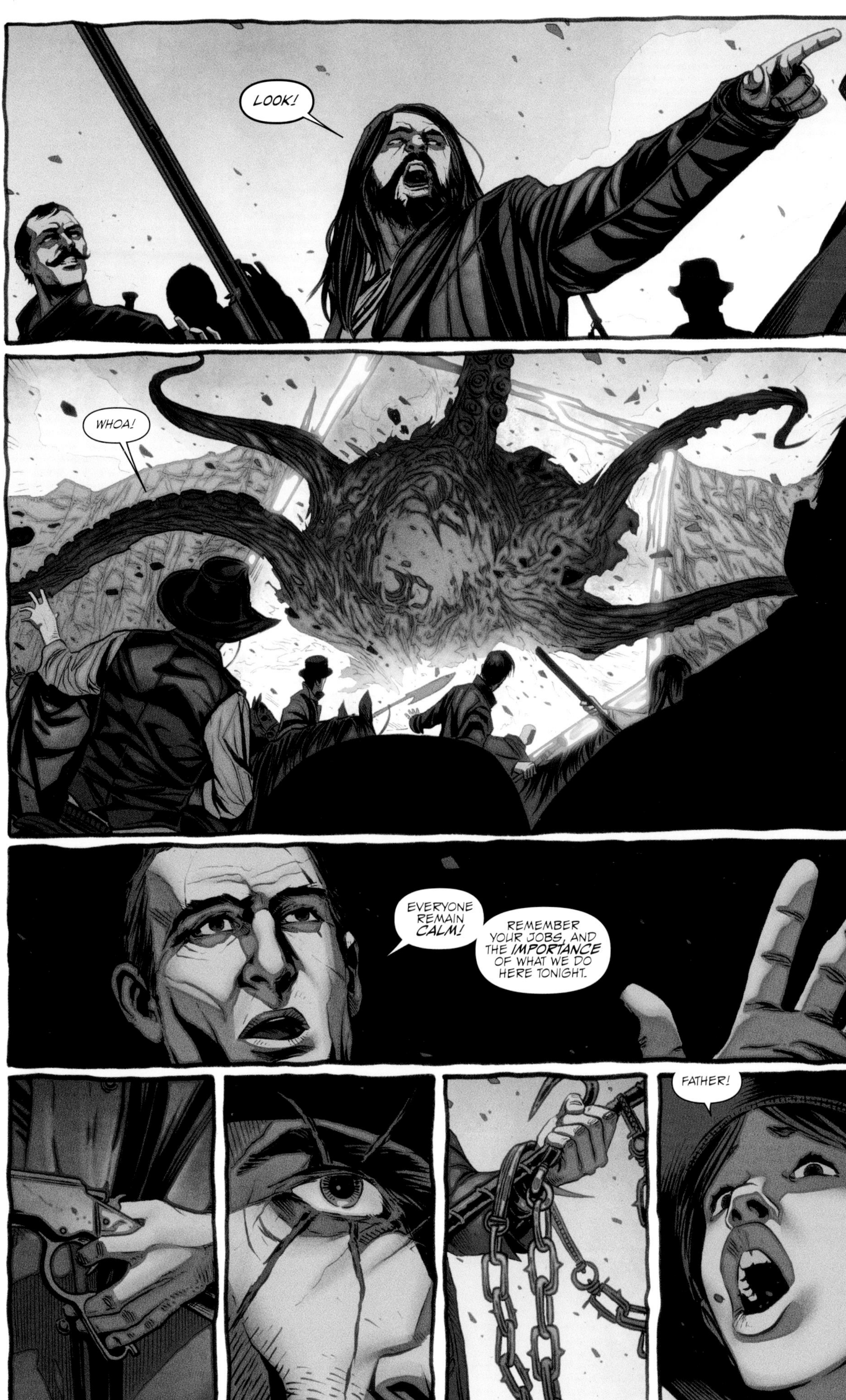
LOOK!
WHOA!
EVERYONE REMAIN CALM!
REMEMBER YOUR JOBS, AND THE IMPORTANCE OF WHAT WE DO HERE TONIGHT.
FATHER!

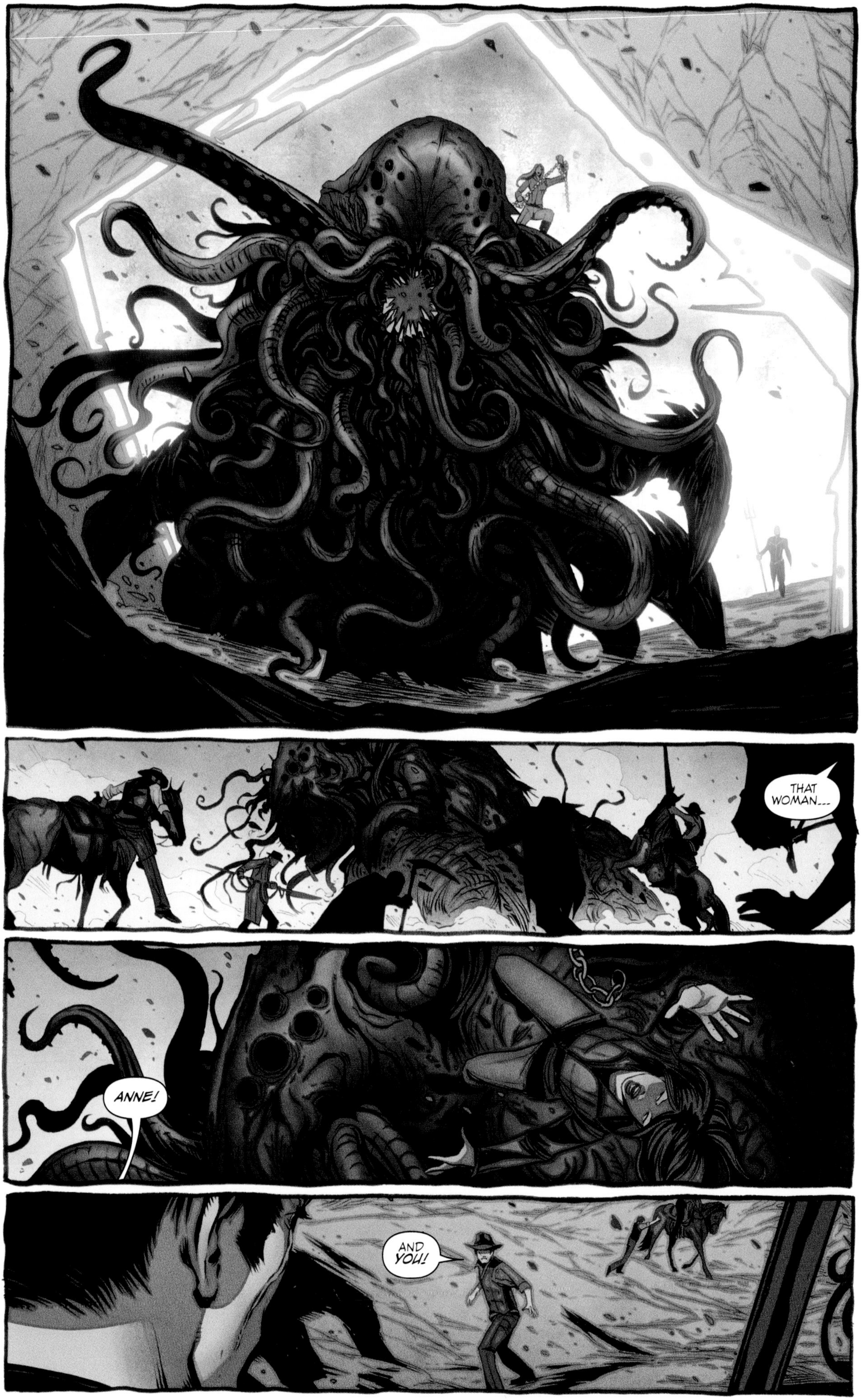
THAT WOMAN...
ANNE!
AND YOU!

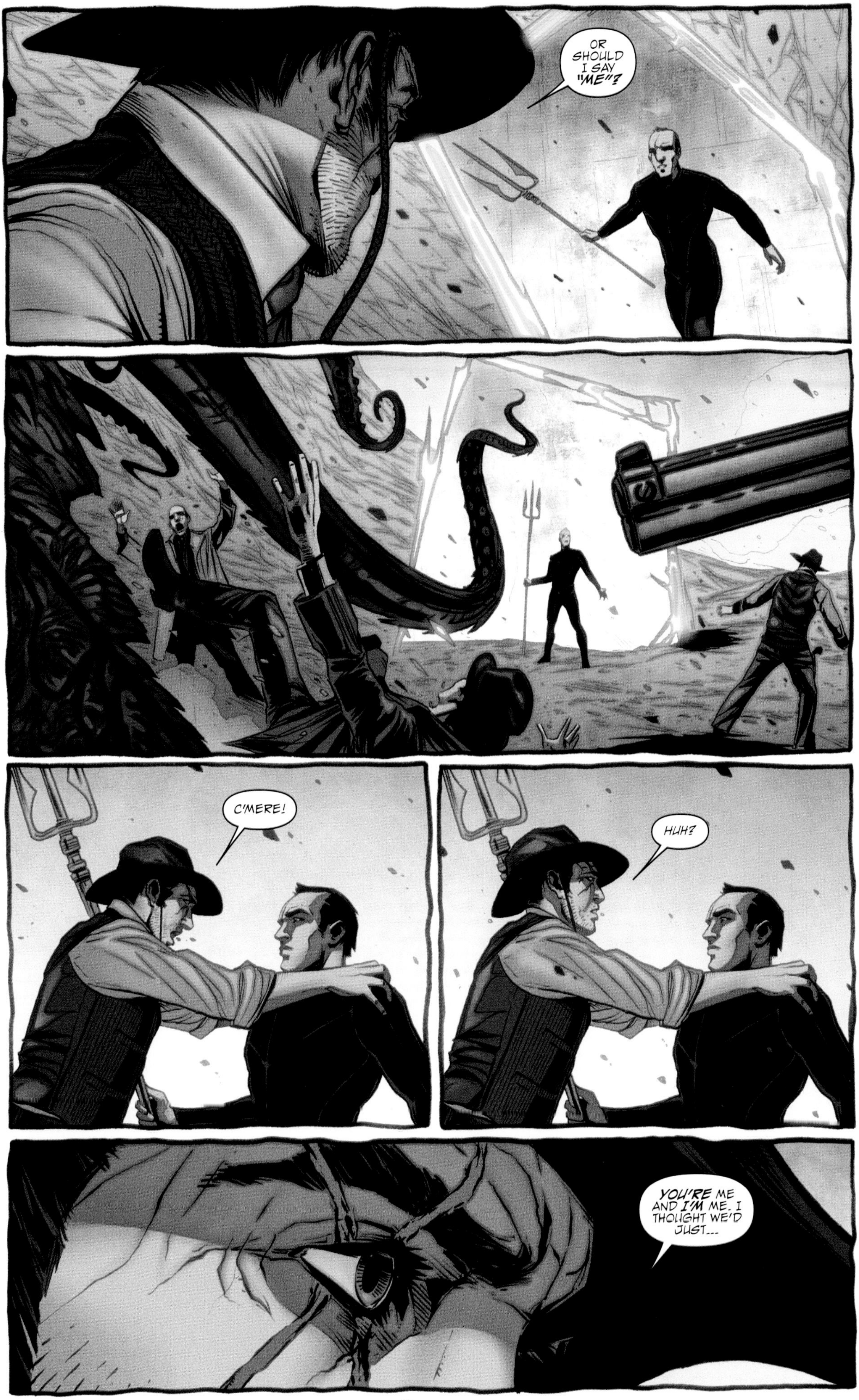
OR SHOULD I SAY "ME"?
C'MERE!
HUH?
YOU'RE ME AND I'M ME. I THOUGHT WE'D JUST...

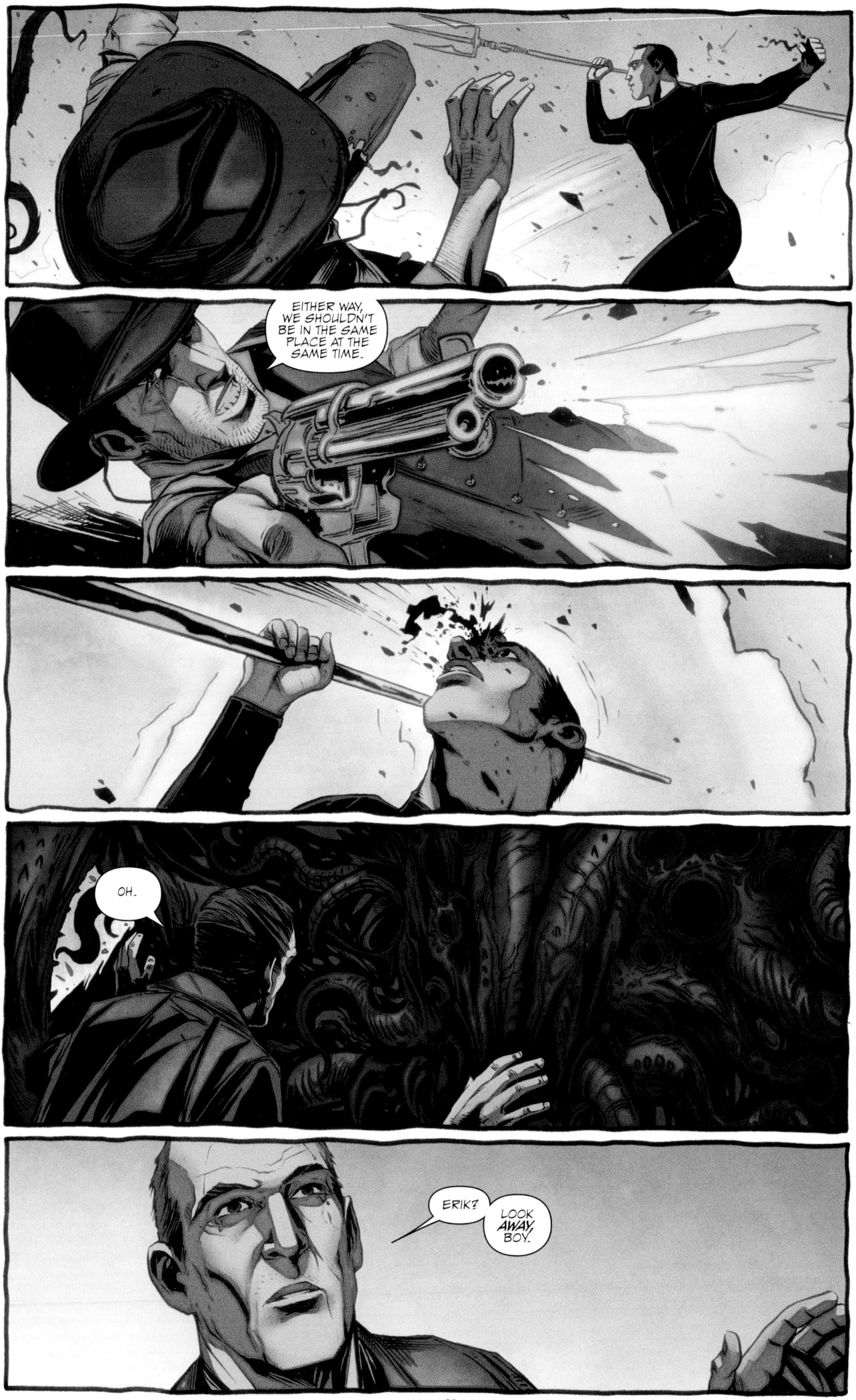
EITHER WAY, WE SHOULDN'T BE IN THE SAME PLACE AT THE SAME TIME.
OH.
ERIK?
LOOK AWAY, BOY.

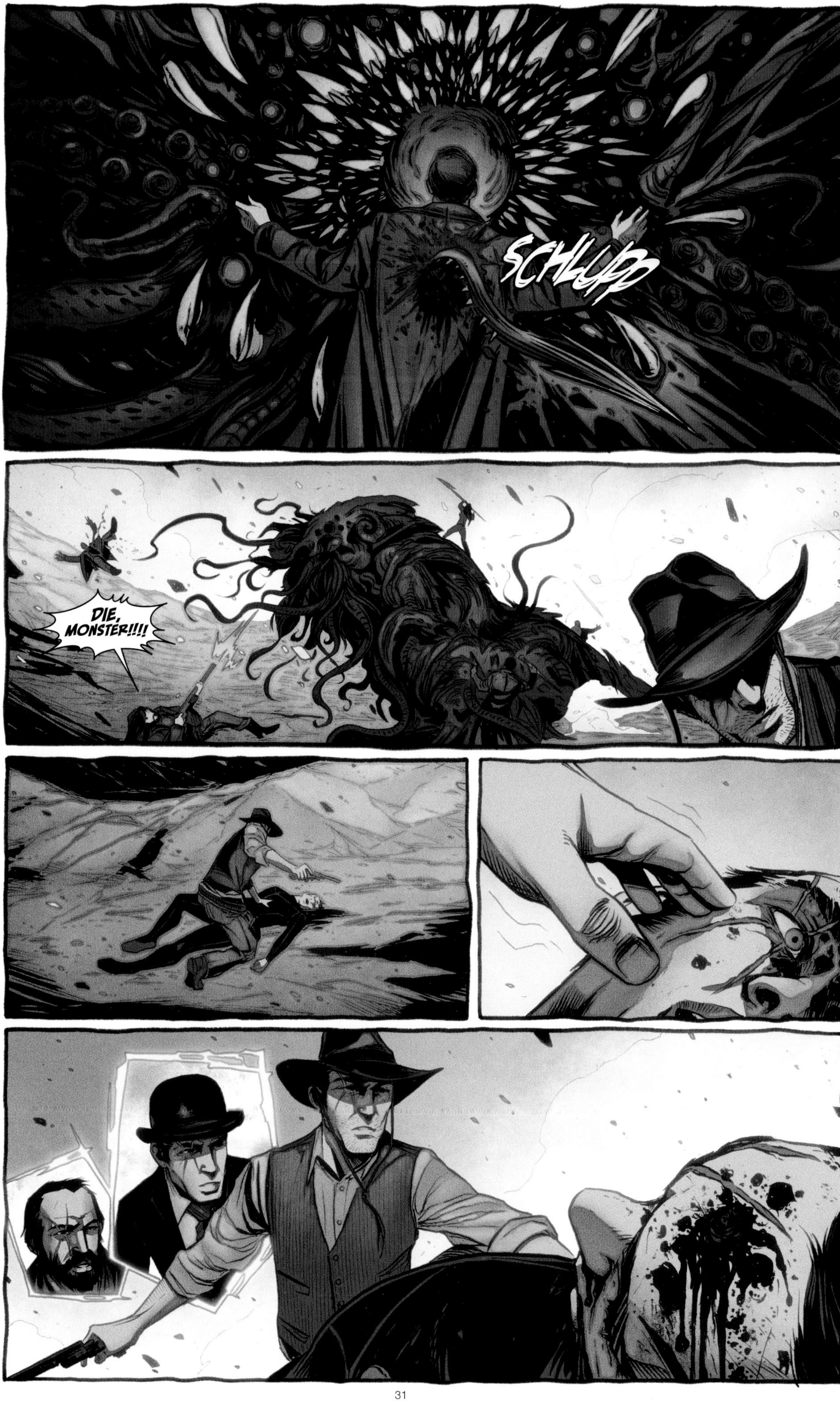
SCHLUPP
DIE, MONSTER!!!!

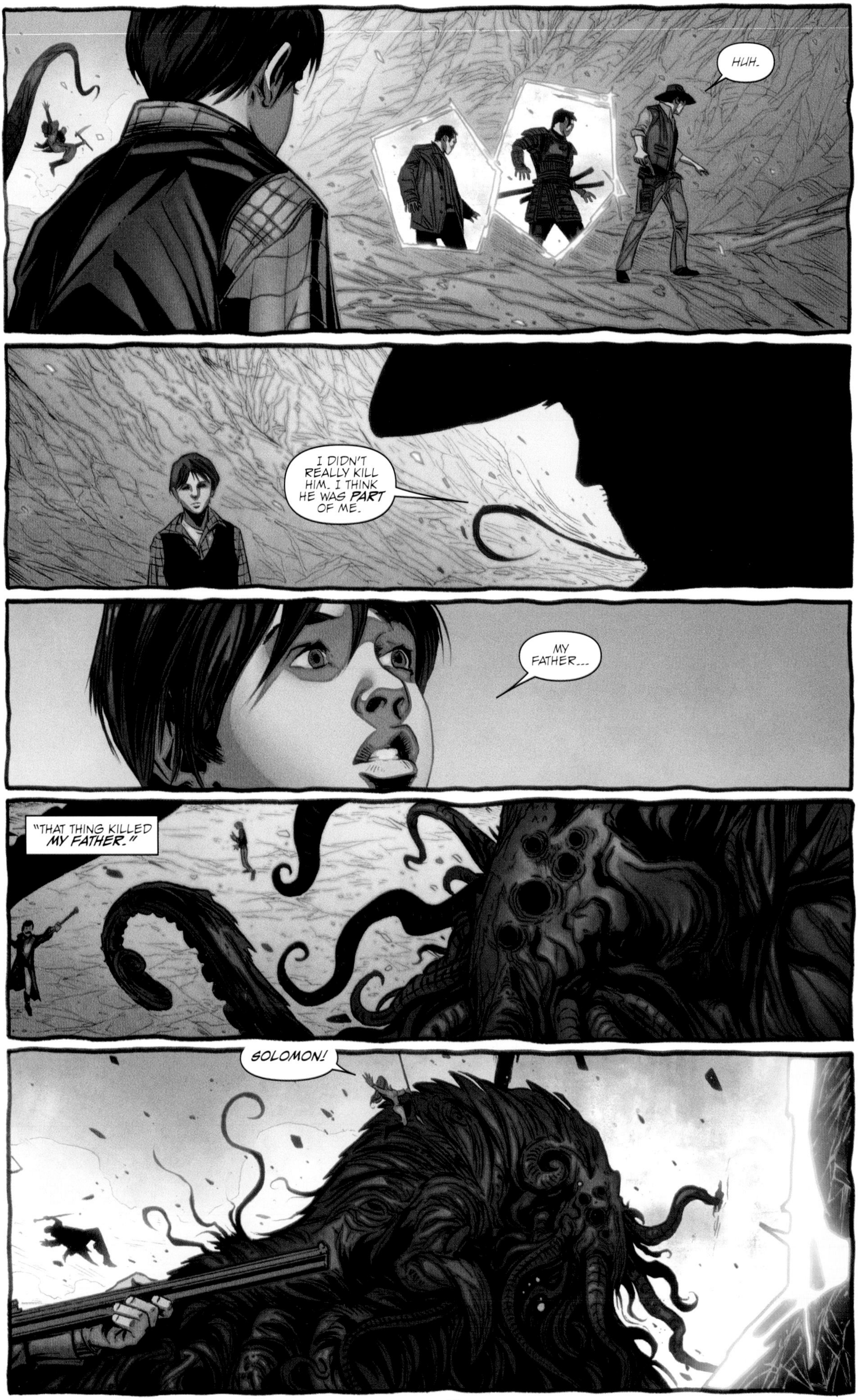
HUH.
I DIDN'T REALLY KILL HIM. I THINK HE WAS PART OF ME.
MY FATHER...
"THAT THING KILLED MY FATHER."
SOLOMON!

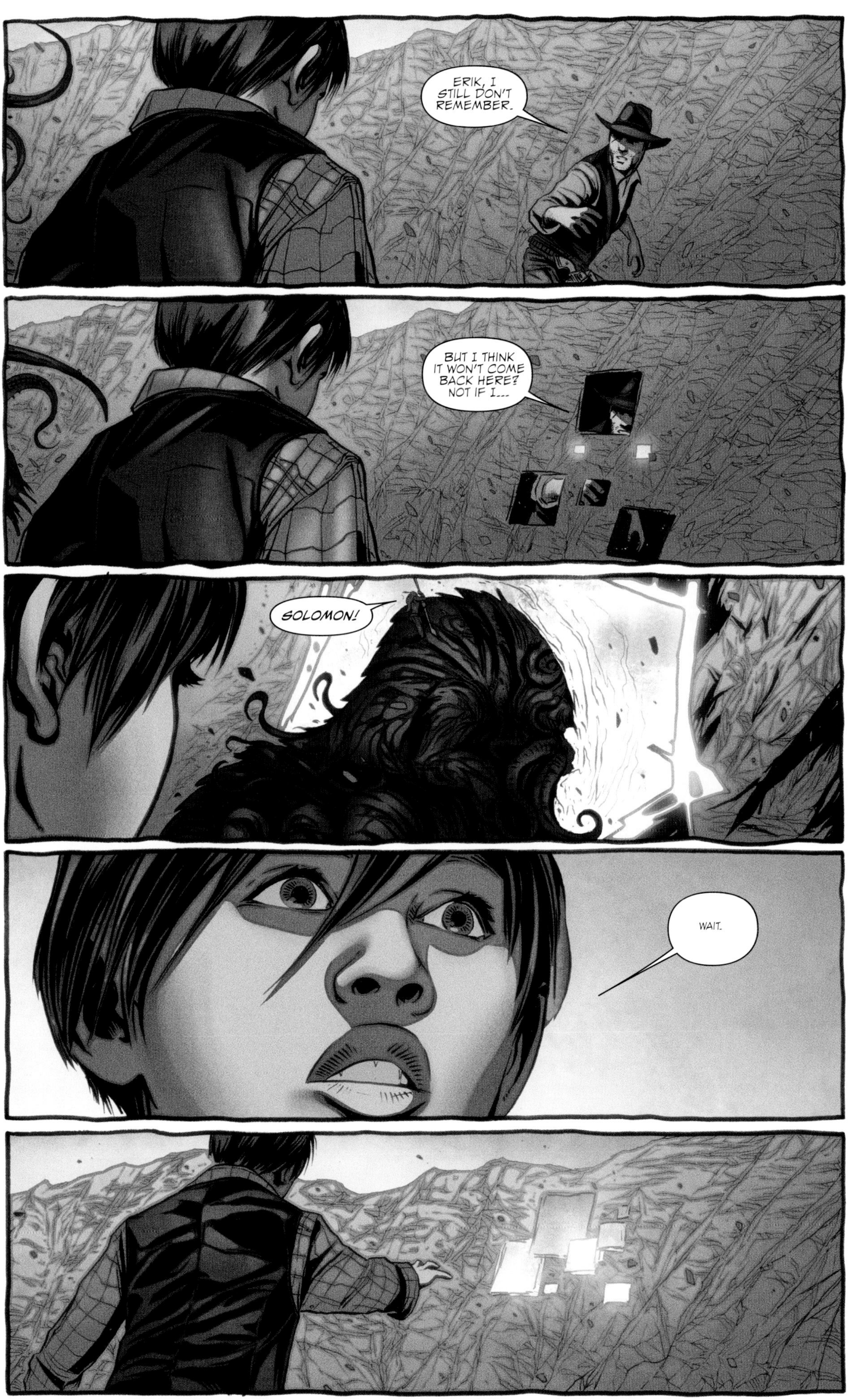
ERIK, I STILL DON'T REMEMBER.
BUT I THINK IT WON'T COME BACK HERE? NOT IF I...
SOLOMON!
WAIT.

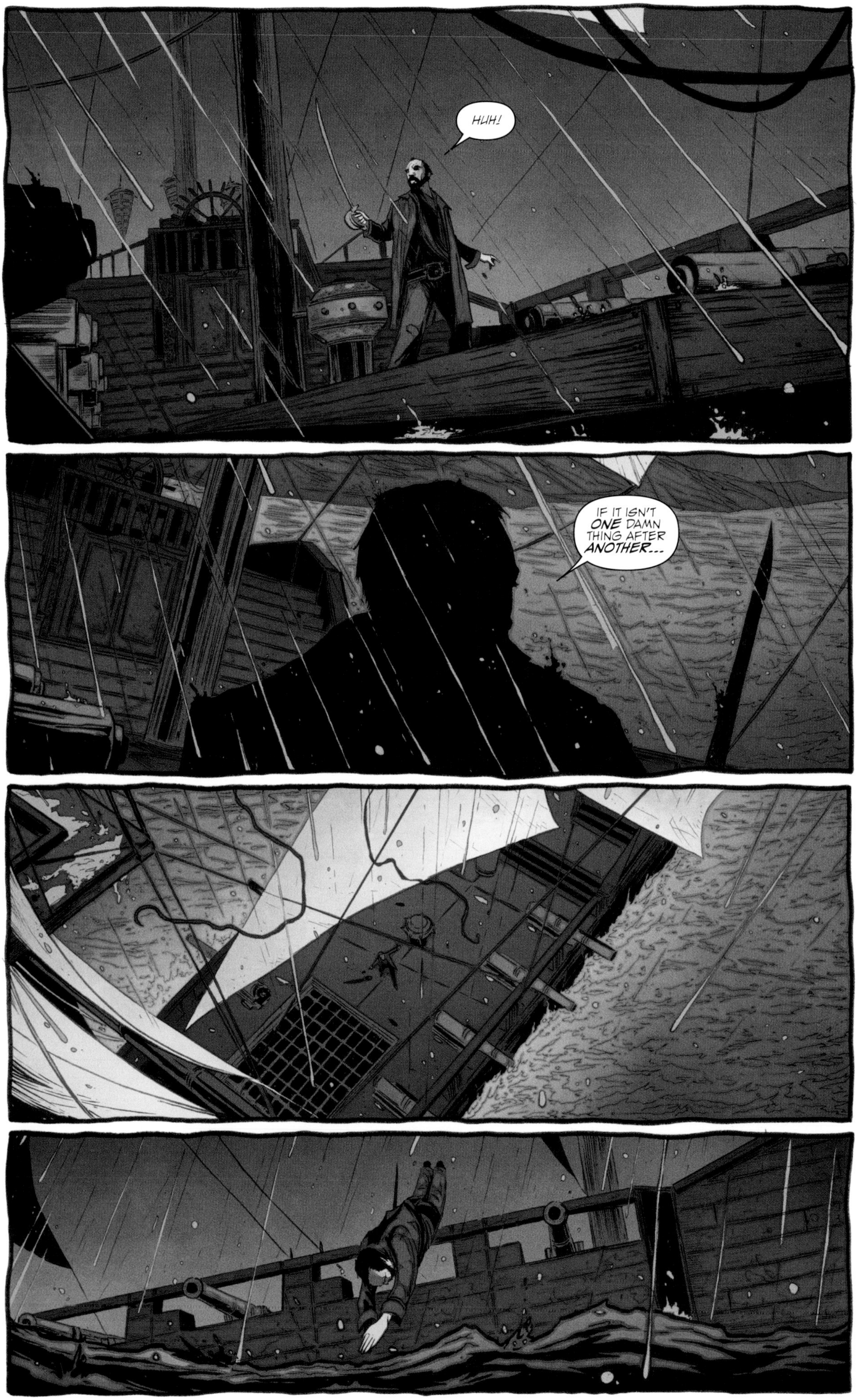
HUH!
IF IT ISN'T ONE DAMN THING AFTER ANOTHER...

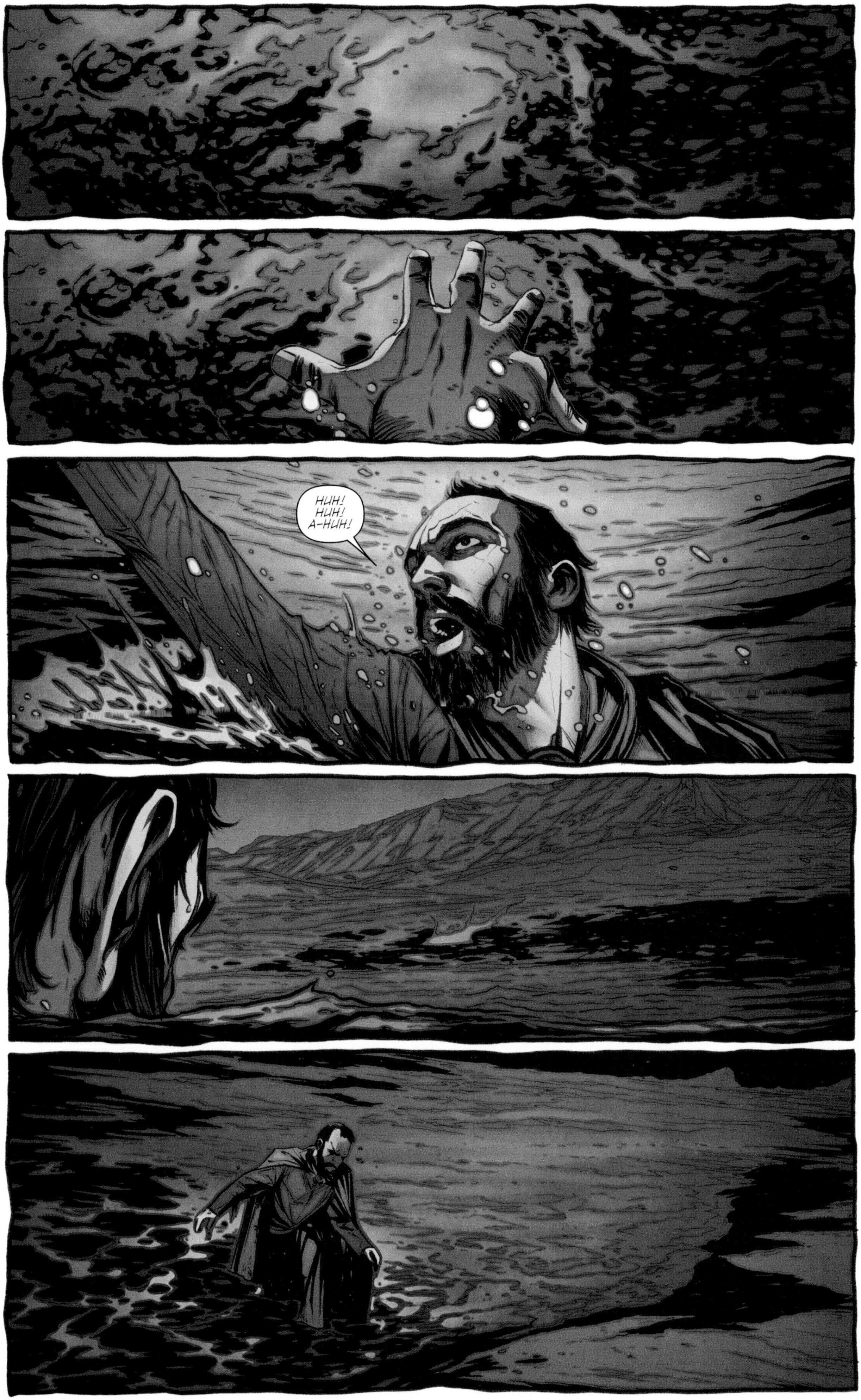
HUH! HUH! A-HUH!

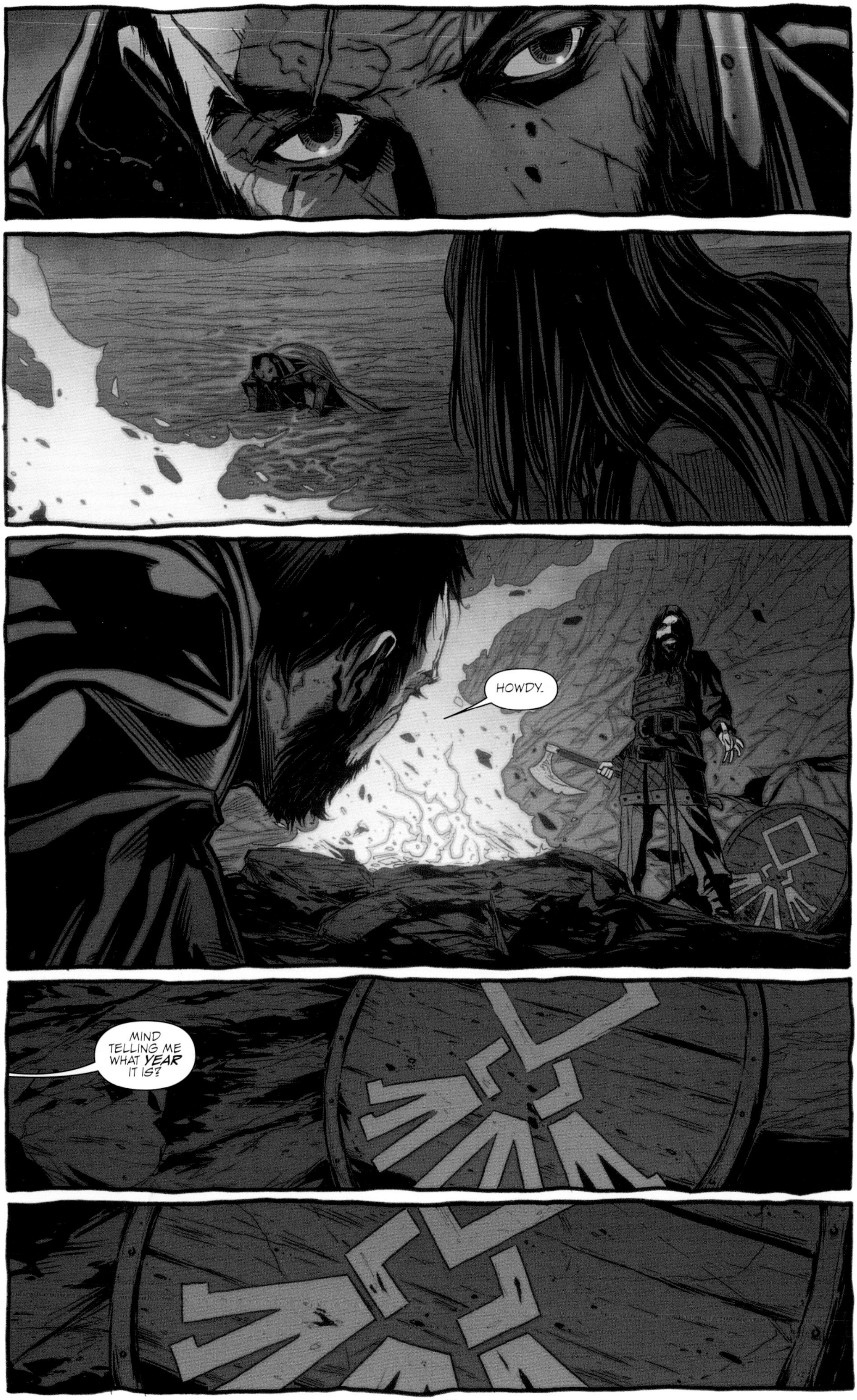
HOWDY.
MIND TELLING ME WHAT *YEAR* IT IS?

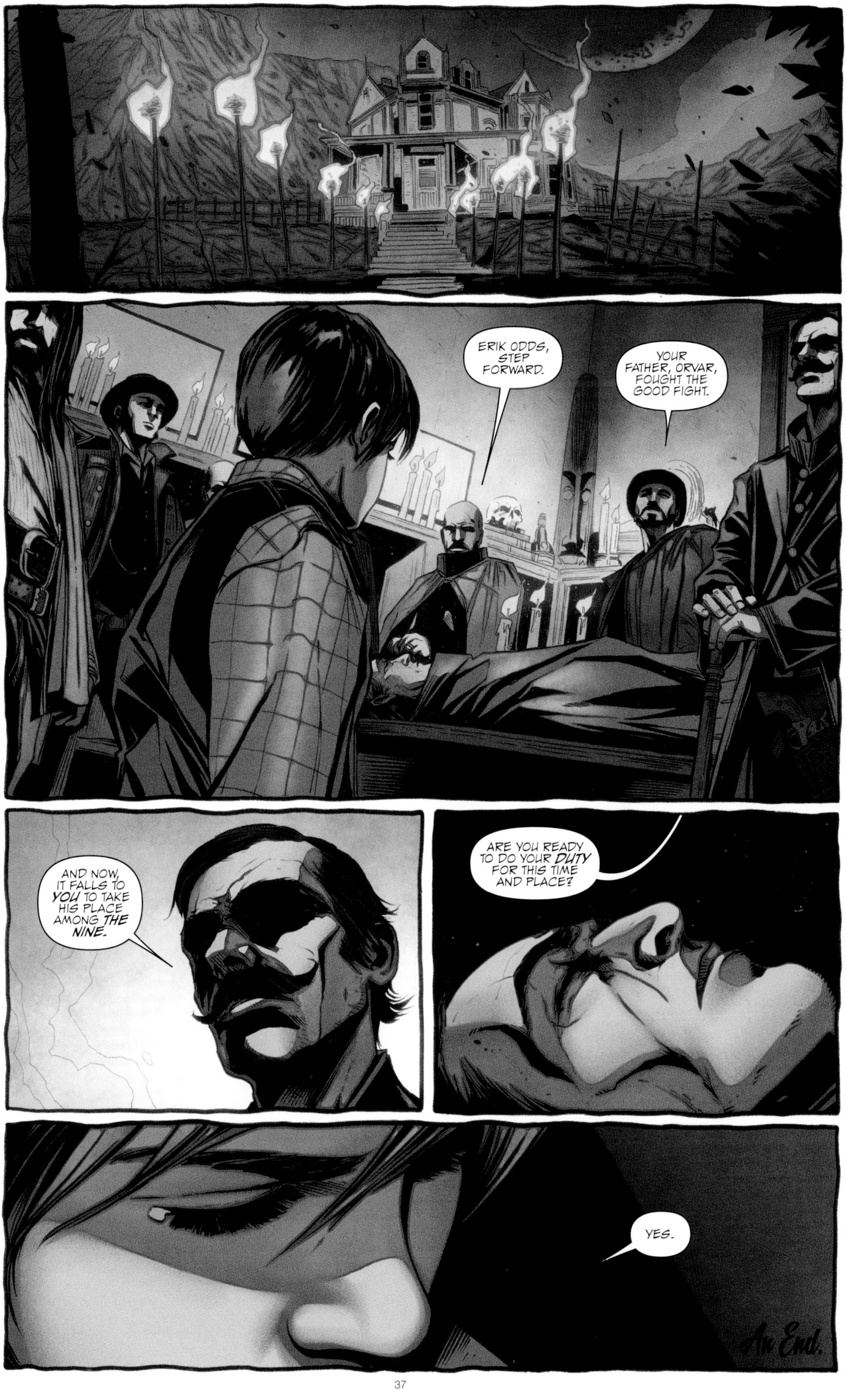
ERIK ODDS, STEP FORWARD.
YOUR FATHER, ORVAR, FOUGHT THE GOOD FIGHT.
AND NOW, IT FALLS TO *YOU* TO TAKE HIS PLACE AMONG *THE NINE*.
ARE YOU READY TO DO YOUR *DUTY* FOR THIS TIME AND PLACE?
YES.
An End.

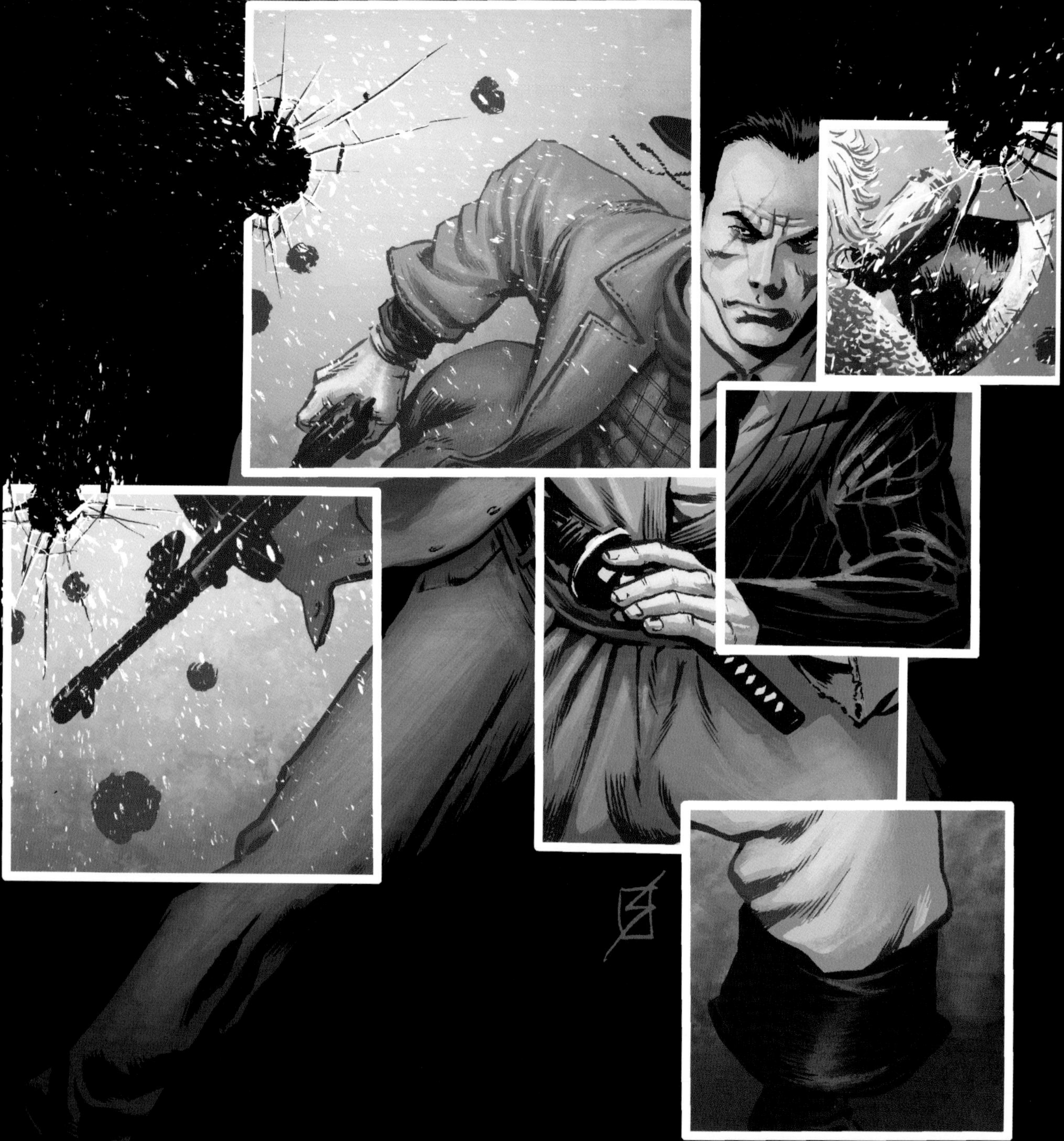

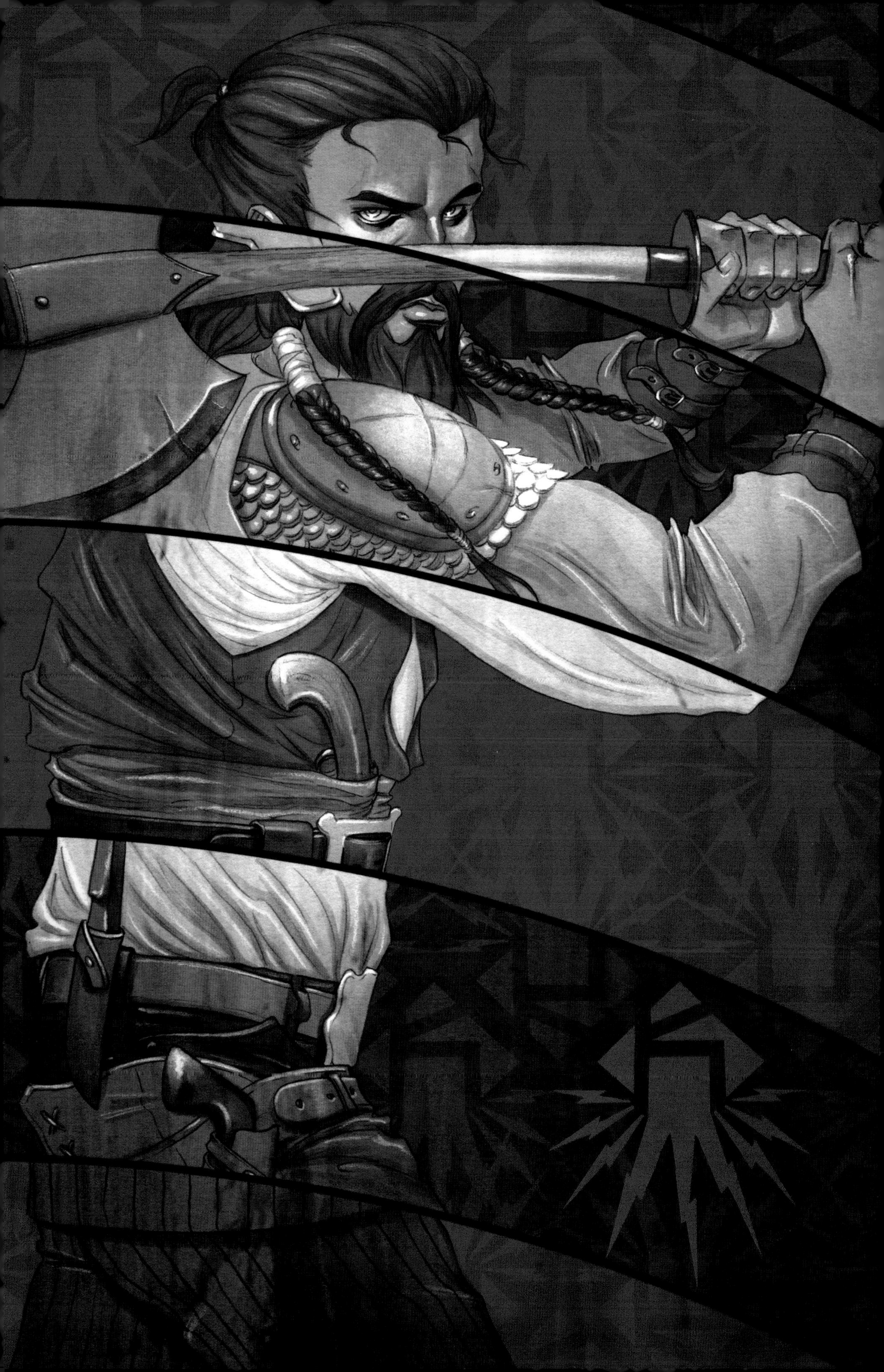

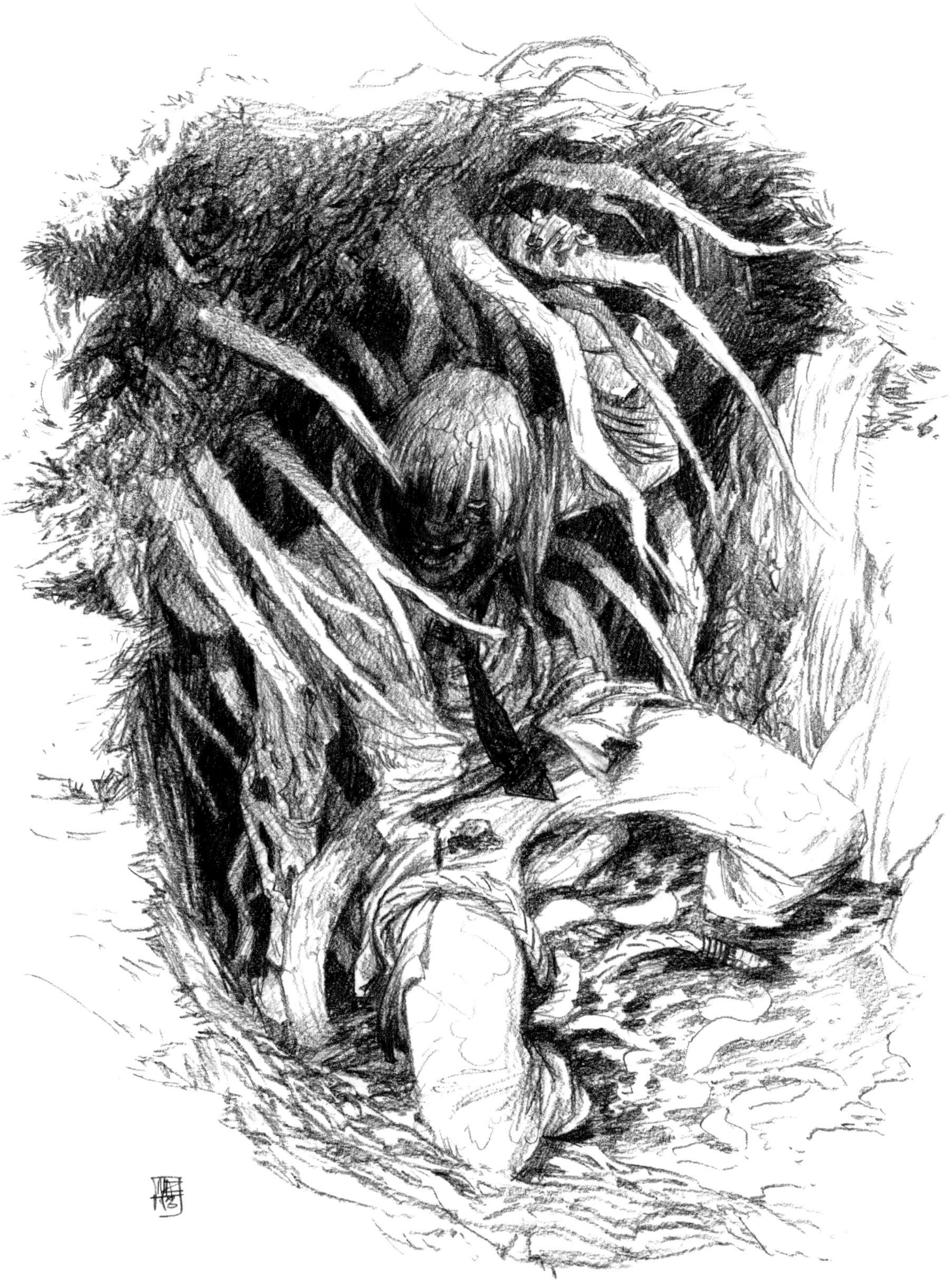

# HUNGRY STEVE
## Alex Grecian

ILLUSTRATIONS Nathan Fox

I know what you're thinking, but everything's fine. Trust me, I got it under control. It was Billy that messed it up, but that was totally an accident and not his fault.

See, that thing we found in the woods last summer was always hungry.

Billy, Evan and me found it. The month school let out, we rode our bikes all through the woods north of town. At first we stuck to the trails, but after awhile we could ride them with our eyes closed. So we started out into the high grass and before we knew it we were all up and down through there where the trees are so thick and close together you could hardly get a bike between them and I tore my shirt on a branch and got in trouble. There's a factory up there with a picture of a big red octopus on the fence and some of the buildings kind of ride the creek and ooze stuff out that makes the water look like a rainbow. But we didn't get too close to it because where the trees touch the fence they're all dead, so we could tell the fence was the kind that would shock you if you touched it.

We went away from there, out where the trees got toppled down in that mudslide last year. There's a sort of a little shack out there, but it's a ways into the woods and you can't see it from where people usually go. It must've been there since my dad was a kid 'cause it's real old and the floor's rotten and there's bird shit all over the floor, but we kind of fixed it up a little bit after we found it. I wouldn't wanna spend the night in there, but it's not too bad for pretending you're a bank robber that's hiding from the cops and paintball and stuff like that.

It was probably the second week we were out there looking for wood we could nail on our clubhouse and right before we headed back to the trail to go home, Billy heard something scuffling behind the bushes over in a clearing. There was a big old tree that'd fallen down and made a giant hole in the ground where its roots used to be. We left our bikes and creeped up close to the hole, thinking it was a deer in there or a 'possum. It was hard to see into that hole at first 'cause it was a black sort of dark and it rained the night before so it was wet and muddy. We gave it a minute and our eyes got used to trying to see in the dark and we got so the sunlight glinting off the little pools of light around the shallow end of the hole didn't bother us so much and, when we could see it, we saw it was a guy. At least, I think it used to be a guy.

Evan never did agree with Billy and me about what it was. He thinks it was a troll, but his parents don't let him watch TV, so what does he know? Billy and me got enough culture we knew right off the bat it was a zombie mucking around down in that hole.

It only had one eye, so it didn't see us right away 'cause we were on the side of it where there was just the socket and you could see a muscle working in there where it kept trying to move that missing eye around. Its right arm was up close to its body and didn't move much, so we figured that arm was probably busted. It was dressed up like my dad when he goes to work, with a tie and all. It had a pair of glasses, but the lenses were gone and they dangled from one ear. I don't know how they didn't fall off already before we came along. Its clothes were muddy and gray 'cause the zombie kept falling down and standing up and shuffling into the side of the hole and falling down again. It was so stupid it couldn't figure out to turn around and climb out the shallow end of the hole, but it didn't help that it was wearing some kind of thin coat like doctors wear and the coat kept getting hooked on the leftover tree roots down in there. Every time it fell down, it would act all surprised and mad and start yelling, but it didn't make any sense 'cause it wasn't using words, just kind of spitting.

Evan got all worried and said something like "Hey, mister, you need some help?" Well, that made the zombie turn around real fast and it came at us, but we were up high where it couldn't reach so it just stood there and kept waving like it wanted us to come down in there with it. No way, José.

Billy and me kidded with Evan quite a bit after that, saying "Hey, mister" in a high-pitched voice like a girl. Evan took it pretty well, though, so we got bored of that and started throwing rocks at the thing in the hole instead.

It was pretty late in the day and we needed to get home, but we didn't want the zombie to be gone by the time we came back the next day. We kind of felt like it was ours since we found it, but if we took it home we'd have to keep it hidden and there's no way we could do that with it growling and hissing all the time. We were also scared it might figure out how to get out of the hole and then we'd come back the next day and it would be waiting in the woods and it'd eat our brains.

Billy said he would stay out in the woods that night and keep an eye on it. Mostly I think he didn't want to go home. Things hadn't been so hot for him since his dad moved out and his mom had different boyfriends around all the time. She probably wouldn't have minded if Billy didn't show up for dinner, but it sounded way too scary leaving him alone at night with a zombie and Evan said we couldn't do that. It looked like we'd have to take our chances on that thing getting out of the hole until I went to get on my bike and my foot got caught in the chain looped around under the seat. That gave me a pretty good idea about how to keep Steve where he was.

Evan used to get a ride to school from his mom, but Billy and me rode our bikes. We had these plastic-covered chains so we could lock them onto the metal rack by the playground. Billy had a padlock, but I have a Kryptonite, so we decided to use that. Billy used to play soccer and he took gymnastics for a while when we were kids, so he climbed up on the old tree roots above the hole. Evan and me threw more rocks at the zombie to get its attention while Billy hung upside-down with his legs hooked over the biggest root. When the zombie wasn't looking, he looped the chain from my bike around its broken arm and locked it to the tree. That made the zombie mad and it spit and roared and tried to claw at Billy, but Billy was pretty fast and he was already out of reach.

We looked the situation over and felt pretty good about it. That zombie wasn't going anywhere. It tugged and pulled, but just got more twisted up in the chain and couldn't go more than about two steps in any direction. After that, we weren't scared of it at all and Evan said we should give it a name. He wanted to give it some dumb troll name, like Zork or something, but I said we should name it after Steve Yount, this creepy older guy who we really hated 'cause he was always hanging around our school even though he didn't go there, and Billy and Evan liked that idea, so we did.

On our way out of the woods Billy hollered "Goodnight, Steve! Sleep tight!" And that made Evan and me laugh 'cause we were still thinking about the real Steve. He has a stupid moustache and he smells bad, which was another reason to name our zombie after him.

We were gonna go back first thing the next day, but Billy had to watch his little sister Megan. She was only six so she was boring and always in the way, but I liked her anyway even though Billy said he didn't. When he finally got free of her, Megan wanted to come and she followed us on her bike, so we rode around until we lost her.

We could smell the dead skunk before we got anywhere near the hole in the woods. I don't mind skunk smell so bad, but most people, including Billy and Evan, can't stand it, so I went up closer than they did. Steve was still down there and he looked real happy. His glasses were gone and we never did find them, so I don't know what happened that night, but Steve had caught a skunk and he was sitting back under the far edge, munching away. When he saw me poke my head over the side of the hole, he didn't try to get me or anything. He smiled and held up a wet gob of skunk fur to show me. I was pretty proud of him and felt like giving him a pat on the head. But I didn't.

After they got used to the stink, Billy and Evan came over to the hole with their shirts pulled up over their noses. Evan almost puked when he saw all the skunk bits, but Billy got excited. He waved at Steve and Steve waved back at him and used his teeth to tear a gray chunk of meat out of what looked like part of the tail. Steve was a sloppy eater and I noticed some of the skunk's guts were inside his shirt pocket, spilling out like they dropped in there while he was chewing.

"He was hungry is all," Billy said. "That's why he was all mad and trying to get us yesterday. Let's feed him some more."

Evan and me weren't so sure about that, but Billy told us to wait by the hole while he ran home. We watched Steve for a while and then we got a little bit bored and climbed a big pine tree. We couldn't see Steve from the tree, but we could hear him smacking his lips and making yummy noises like that skunk was the best thing he ever tasted in his life. When Billy came back he had a package of bologna and three cold hotdogs in a plastic sandwich bag, plus some Oreos and a little bag of chips. The skunk was gone and Steve was starting to look grumpy again, so we opened everything up and threw it all down in the hole. We figured Steve couldn't get grossed out about dirt on his food if he already ate a raw skunk.

Steve picked up the bologna and took a big bite, but spit it back out. He sniffed one of the Oreos and got real mad all of a sudden. He looked at us like we'd done something bad to him on purpose and he tried to throw the cookie at us, but missed. It hit the side of the hole and bounced back at him. That made him even madder and he was starting to really jerk against the chain which made us worry about how strong the tree root was, but then he noticed the skunk guts in his shirt pocket and got happy again.

Once Steve settled down and started eating again, Billy grabbed Evan and my elbows and we all walked a few steps away so Steve wouldn't see us argue.

"We gotta keep feeding him so he'll be tame," Billy said.

Evan rolled his eyes. "Yeah, that worked out so far," he said. He can be negative sometimes.

"I think maybe he only likes meat," Billy said.

"He didn't like the bologna," Evan said.

"A lot of people don't like bologna," I said. I don't like bologna that much unless my mom fries it and puts some ketchup on it.

"I think maybe he likes stuff that's still alive," Billy said. "At least not as dead as bologna."

"Where are we gonna get alive stuff?"

"I have an idea," Billy said. His dad still had his shotgun at Billy's house. Billy's dad left a lot of stuff at Billy's house when he moved out and he kept coming back all the time to get it, one thing at a time, like maybe he wasn't ever gonna move all the way out. Billy kept saying he thought his dad would move back pretty soon and make his mom stop bringing those other guys home, but Evan and me never said anything because we both knew lots of people who got divorced and usually they didn't get back together like Billy wanted. You never know, though, so we didn't wanna say he was wrong. Besides, he was just a kid and we didn't wanna hurt his feelings.

Billy rode home again to get the shotgun and Evan and me climbed back up in that pine tree to wait for him. We couldn't hear Steve munching anymore, but we didn't feel like checking on him. He was starting to seem like he was Billy's pet not ours, and anyway it didn't seem like he ever did much except eat and get mad. He was kind of dumb, really.

We saw Billy coming back, but he had to sort of zigzag around because Megan was riding her bike near the edge of the woods like she was looking for us again. By the time Evan and me got down from the tree and over to the hole, Billy was there. It turned out his dad's shotgun was locked up, so Billy brought his BB gun instead. We didn't mess around with Billy's BB gun very often. Billy and me used to go out to the woods with it, right after he got it for his birthday, and I got so I was pretty good with it, but he accidentally shot one of the tires on his bike and had to get it fixed and got in trouble from his dad. Evan's parents don't let him play with guns, not even squirt guns.

Anyway, Billy gave me the BB gun and I snuck a little way into the trees and shot a squirrel and Billy grabbed it while it was still dragging itself around in a circle and threw the squirrel down in Steve's hole. Steve looked kind of sleepy at first, but when the squirrel flopped around in front of him, Steve hooted and grunted like a gorilla at the zoo. He grabbed the squirrel with his good hand and tore it in half with his teeth so fast that the back half of the squirrel was still moving.

So that was cool to watch for a while, but squirrels are smaller than skunks. It didn't take long for Steve to finish and he looked like he was gonna get mad again so I went back out in the woods with the BB gun. By the time I got back to the hole, Billy and Evan were on their stomachs looking in at Steve. Billy was talking to him like how your mom talks when she's trying to get you to fall asleep. Steve really seemed like he was listening. He had his head cocked to one side and looked like he was concentrating, trying to figure out what Billy was saying.

The sun was already going down, so I'd been gone longer than I thought, but I had three birds and a rabbit. At first Billy said not to feed him the birds because Steve might choke on a bone, but Evan just went ahead while Billy and me were arguing and chucked one of the birds in there. Steve handled it all right, so we gave him the rest. He really liked the rabbit, which I thought he would.

We had to head home, but this time Billy said goodnight for real. He was getting pretty attached to Steve. He said the next day we should bring a blanket in case Steve got cold at night. Evan rolled his eyes.

That night I had a lousy dream and the next morning was gray and drizzly. Evan came over to my house and we watched cartoons for a while. Neither one of us wanted to go out to the hole in the woods, but we figured we had to. It's like when my mom and dad got me a lizard, I had to make all kinds of promises about how I was gonna take care of it. We were responsible for Steve, and anyway we didn't want Billy to be out there alone.

Sure enough, he was already kneeling by the hole when we got there and he had a copy paper box sitting in the mud next to him. The box was wrapped all around with thick clear tape and there were holes poked in the top of it.

"What's in the box, Billy?"

"Zoë."

Zoë was Billy and Megan's cat. Billy's dad always hated Zoë and wanted to get rid of her, but Billy and Megan wouldn't let him. After his dad moved away, Billy started hating the cat too.

I looked down in the hole and Steve waved at me. He was eating a little garden snake I figured Billy caught for him. I didn't really want Billy to feed Zoë to Steve. Snakes and birds and squirrels were okay 'cause they were wild, but Zoë had a food bowl and a litter box. It wasn't the same thing, but I couldn't figure out what to say to Billy without him getting mad.

It turned out I didn't have to say anything because we weren't careful enough when we went out to the woods that morning. We heard sticks breaking and Megan yelped a little before she wheeled her bike into the clearing. She ran right to the box.

"You suck, Billy," she said. "You guys suck too." She was looking at Evan and me when she said that and I thought she was probably right that we sucked if you looked at it from her point of view. "You can't let Zoë go in the woods. She's mine too."

Then she shut up 'cause Steve finished his snake and grunted. Megan looked down in the hole and started crying out of the blue. Steve couldn't figure out what was going on and shuffled over to the wall to try and see us better.

That's when I noticed he wasn't chained up anymore.

"Billy, what did you do?" I said.

"It's okay," Billy said. "Steve's cool now. He's tame. I gave him that snake and he didn't try to get me when I went down there."

"You went down there?" Evan said. He had a look on his face like somebody just puked all over his shirt, he couldn't believe it.

"He didn't even try to get me," Billy said again.

While we were talking and trying to figure out why Billy was being so crazy, Megan kept crying, but then

she grabbed the box with the cat in it and started trying to rip it open. It was a pretty strong box, so mostly she was making the cat mad, jouncing it around in there, but then she got a rock and stuck it under the lid of the box and pulled up on it. The box stayed together where the tape was, but Megan tore a big enough hole that Zoë stuck her head out and yowled. Right then, Billy figured out what Megan was doing and kind of dived at her. He said something like "I wasn't gonna hurt her," but things were moving pretty fast all of a sudden and I didn't hear him very well and anyway he was probably lying. The cat saw him coming and squeezed her way out of the opening in the box. She pushed off with her back legs against Megan and jumped into the hole with Steve.

Like I say, things were moving fast and when Megan saw the cat go down the hole and Billy coming at her, she lost her balance and went down the hole too. Billy almost fell in, but he caught himself on a tree root and stopped at the edge at the same time the cat jumped up on the other side of the hole and Megan started screaming. Evan and me ran over there, but we were too late.

Steve moved slow most of the time, but we noticed that right after he ate he could go pretty fast. I guess that snake was enough meat to get him going 'cause he must have caught Megan before she even hit the ground. By the time Evan and me got over and looked down, Megan's pink sweatshirt and jeans were so wet and slippery with blood she was sliding around in Steve's arms. Before long, she stopped screaming and got this look on her face like she felt sick. When Steve pulled off her other arm, Megan closed her eyes and kind of went to sleep. We could still see her breathing for a while, but she didn't wake up when Steve put his hand inside her stomach. After that, her chest stopped moving and we knew she was dead.

Things got real quiet in the woods and Steve smiled up at us like he was proud. He had some of Megan's hair hanging out of his mouth. Billy's face was gray. He said "Tell my dad he should find Zoë. She's an inside cat." Then Billy climbed down in the hole. Evan turned around and ran, but I stayed for a little while, even though there wasn't anything I could do. Then I went home.

I stayed in the house most of the rest of that day. I didn't do much, just sat on my bed and looked at the wall. I don't know what Evan did 'cause I've only seen him one time since that day and he didn't talk much to me then.

That night I went over to Billy's house. Billy's dad was there and he and Billy's mom were talking when I got there. They asked me where Billy was and I told them everything that happened. Billy's dad frowned and said "You mean Steve Yount? I told Billy to stay away from that pervert."

I told him no it was a zombie we named after Steve Yount, but Billy's dad already had his shotgun from out of the safe. He loaded it and asked me where in the woods and when I told him he went outside and got in his car and drove away. I waited with Billy's mom until she asked me to go home.

I hung around outside Billy's house the next day, waiting for something to happen. In the afternoon, some men came in a van that had the factory logo on it, the big red octopus thing with nine legs. They went inside and later they came out with Billy's mom between them and she got in the van and it drove away. She didn't come back for almost a week, but when she did my parents told me that Billy's dad had kidnapped his kids and the police were looking for him 'cause he didn't have custody.

I tried to talk to Billy's mom about it, but she acted like she didn't even recognize me, even though Billy and me were friends since we first started school. She moved away before the end of the summer and Billy's house still has a For Sale sign out front.

Zoë came back last week. I've been feeding her and she seems okay.

I went to therapy because my parents said I wasn't dealing with the loss of my friend, who supposedly ran away with his dad and sister. My therapist Dr. Levin is pretty much of a dick.

I don't ride my bike in the woods anymore because I don't know if those men from the factory got Hungry Steve or if he's still out there waiting for me to give him a pat on the head. Besides, who would I go with? Evan acts like he believes our parents' story. I guess that's probably the smart thing to do, but I hate him anyway.

Last night when I went outside to feed Zoë I saw Megan. I'm pretty sure it was her even though it was dark. I'm not as scared of her 'cause she's little and she only has one arm anyway. I've got my Kryptonite and my bike chain and I asked my mom if I could camp in the backyard tonight and she said yes so I'm gonna see if Megan comes back again. If she does I'm gonna show everybody and they won't make me go see Dr. Levin anymore.

Don't worry about me. I'll be way more careful than Billy was.

# CHAOS AGENT

story    Seth Peck
art    Andy MacDonald
colors    Jean-Paul Csuka
letters    Dave Lanphear

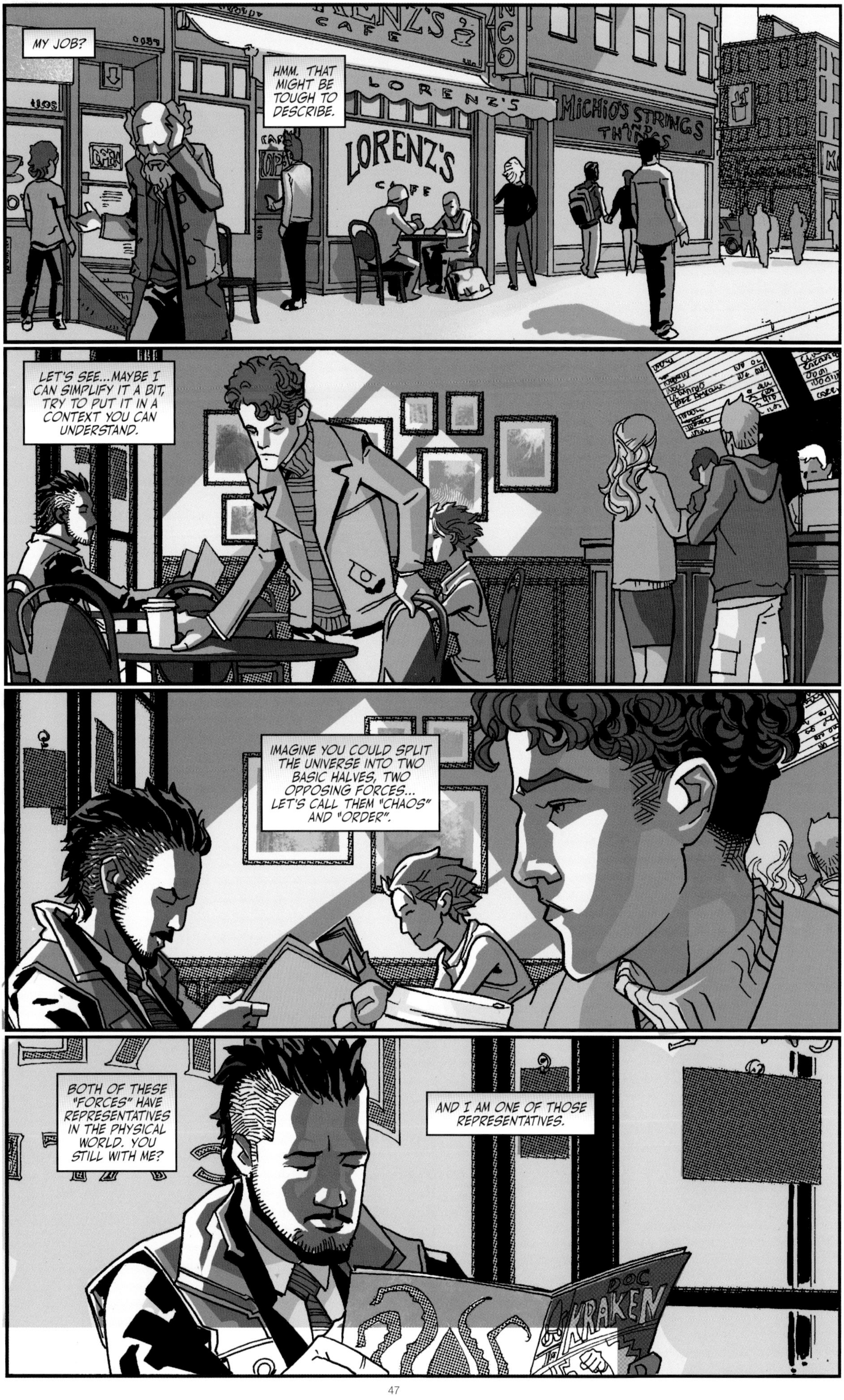
MY JOB?
HMM. THAT MIGHT BE TOUGH TO DESCRIBE.
LORENZ'S CAFE
LORENZ'S
MICHIO'S STRINGS AND THINGS
LET'S SEE...MAYBE I CAN SIMPLIFY IT A BIT, TRY TO PUT IT IN A CONTEXT YOU CAN UNDERSTAND.
IMAGINE YOU COULD SPLIT THE UNIVERSE INTO TWO BASIC HALVES, TWO OPPOSING FORCES... LET'S CALL THEM "CHAOS" AND "ORDER".
BOTH OF THESE "FORCES" HAVE REPRESENTATIVES IN THE PHYSICAL WORLD. YOU STILL WITH ME?
AND I AM ONE OF THOSE REPRESENTATIVES.
DOC KRAKEN

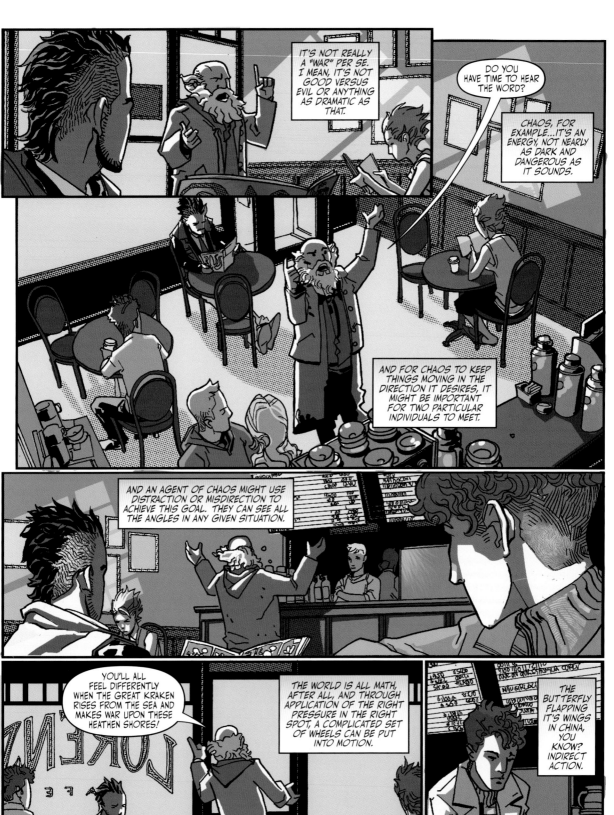

IT'S NOT REALLY A "WAR" PER SE. I MEAN, IT'S NOT GOOD VERSUS EVIL OR ANYTHING AS DRAMATIC AS THAT.

DO YOU HAVE TIME TO HEAR THE WORD?

CHAOS, FOR EXAMPLE...IT'S AN ENERGY, NOT NEARLY AS DARK AND DANGEROUS AS IT SOUNDS.

AND FOR CHAOS TO KEEP THINGS MOVING IN THE DIRECTION IT DESIRES, IT MIGHT BE IMPORTANT FOR TWO PARTICULAR INDIVIDUALS TO MEET.

AND AN AGENT OF CHAOS MIGHT USE DISTRACTION OR MISDIRECTION TO ACHIEVE THIS GOAL. THEY CAN SEE ALL THE ANGLES IN ANY GIVEN SITUATION.

YOU'LL ALL FEEL DIFFERENTLY WHEN THE GREAT KRAKEN RISES FROM THE SEA AND MAKES WAR UPON THESE HEATHEN SHORES!

THE WORLD IS ALL MATH, AFTER ALL, AND THROUGH APPLICATION OF THE RIGHT PRESSURE IN THE RIGHT SPOT, A COMPLICATED SET OF WHEELS CAN BE PUT INTO MOTION.

THE BUTTERFLY FLAPPING IT'S WINGS IN CHINA, YOU KNOW? INDIRECT ACTION.

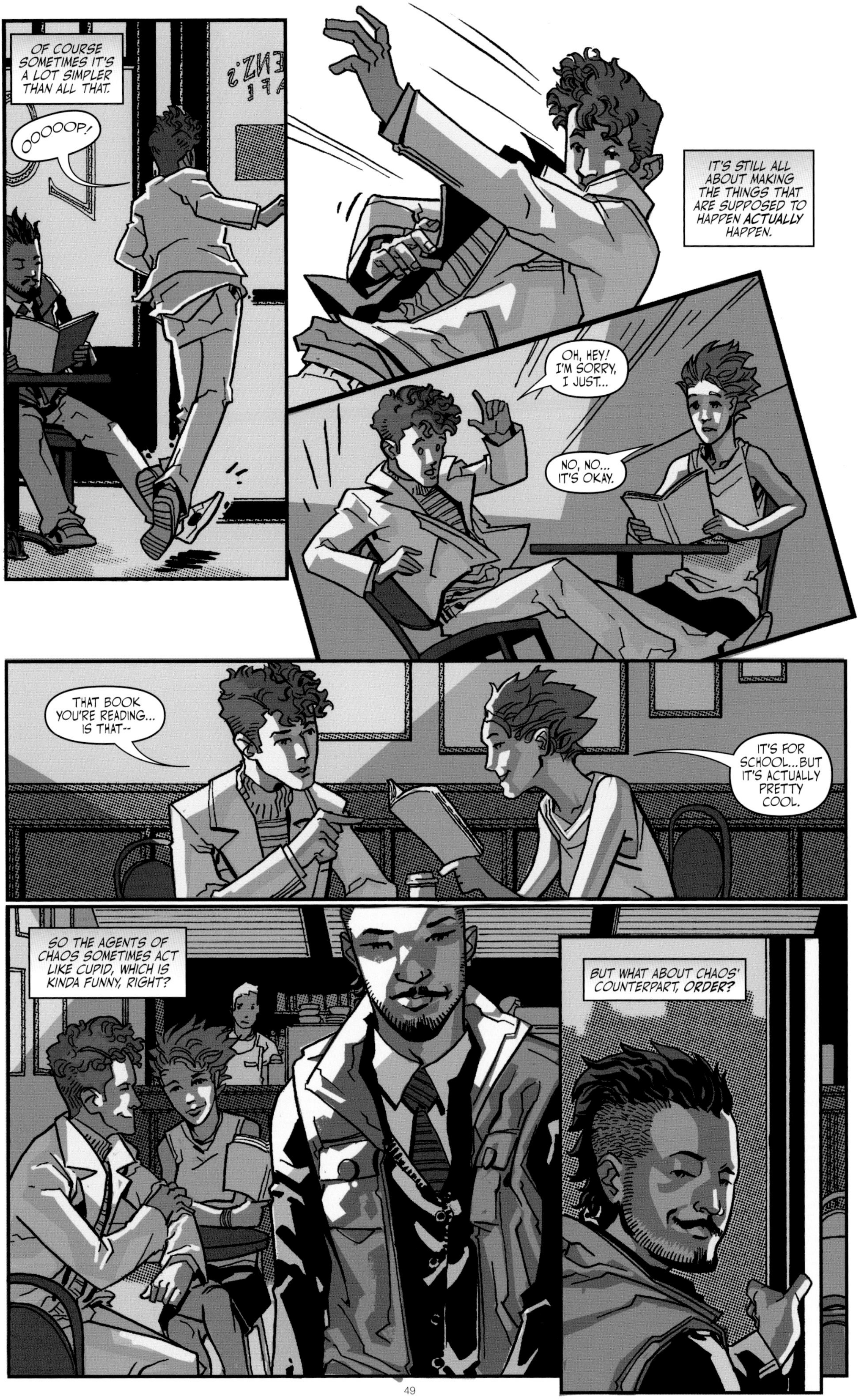
OF COURSE SOMETIMES IT'S A LOT SIMPLER THAN ALL THAT.
OOOOOP!
IT'S STILL ALL ABOUT MAKING THE THINGS THAT ARE SUPPOSED TO HAPPEN ACTUALLY HAPPEN.
OH, HEY! I'M SORRY, I JUST...
NO, NO... IT'S OKAY.
THAT BOOK YOU'RE READING... IS THAT--
IT'S FOR SCHOOL...BUT IT'S ACTUALLY PRETTY COOL.
SO THE AGENTS OF CHAOS SOMETIMES ACT LIKE CUPID, WHICH IS KINDA FUNNY, RIGHT?
BUT WHAT ABOUT CHAOS' COUNTERPART, ORDER?

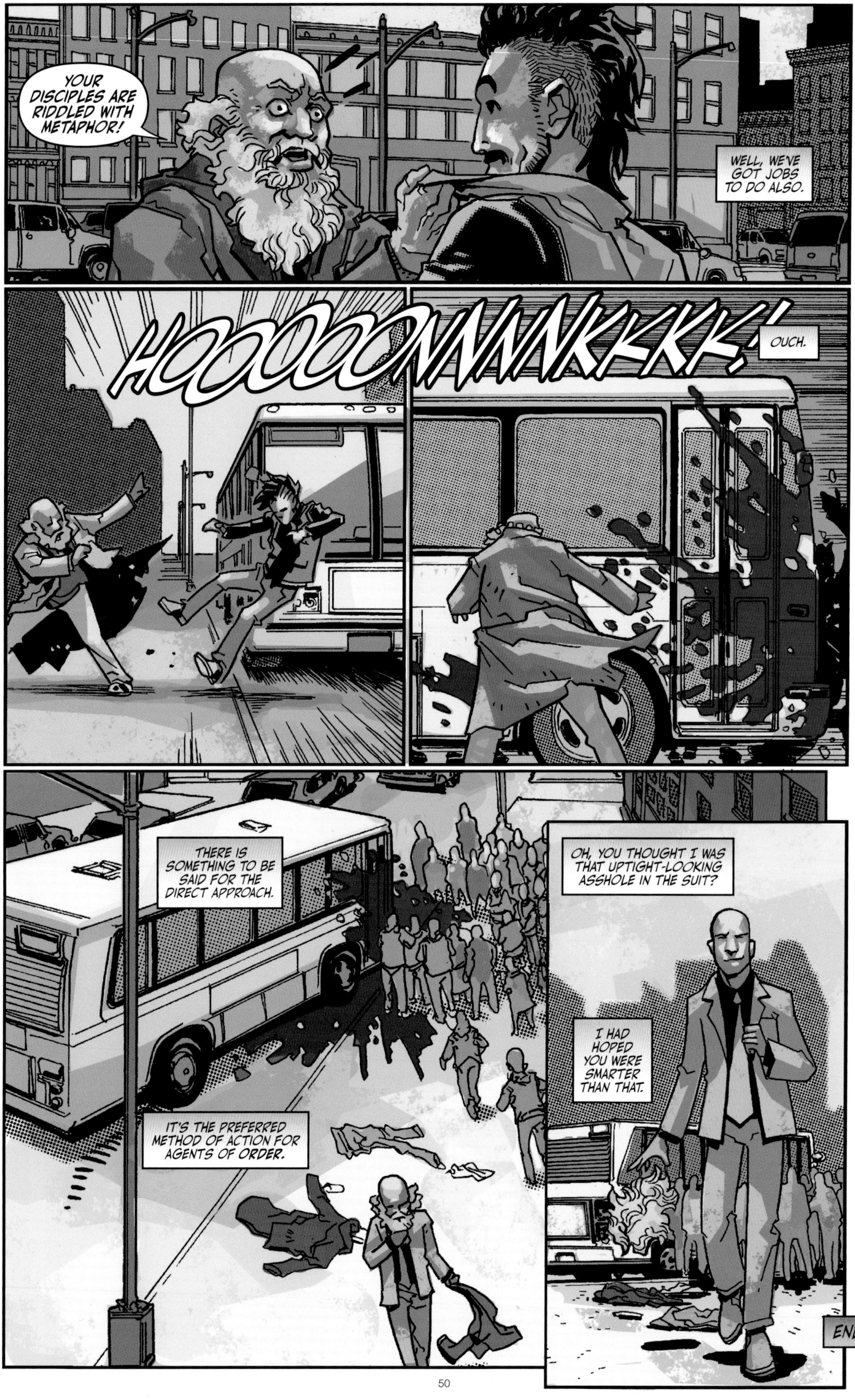
YOUR DISCIPLES ARE RIDDLED WITH METAPHOR!
WELL, WE'VE GOT JOBS TO DO ALSO.
HOOOOONNNNKKKK!
OUCH.
THERE IS SOMETHING TO BE SAID FOR THE DIRECT APPROACH.
IT'S THE PREFERRED METHOD OF ACTION FOR AGENTS OF ORDER.
OH, YOU THOUGHT I WAS THAT UPTIGHT-LOOKING ASSHOLE IN THE SUIT?
I HAD HOPED YOU WERE SMARTER THAN THAT.
END.

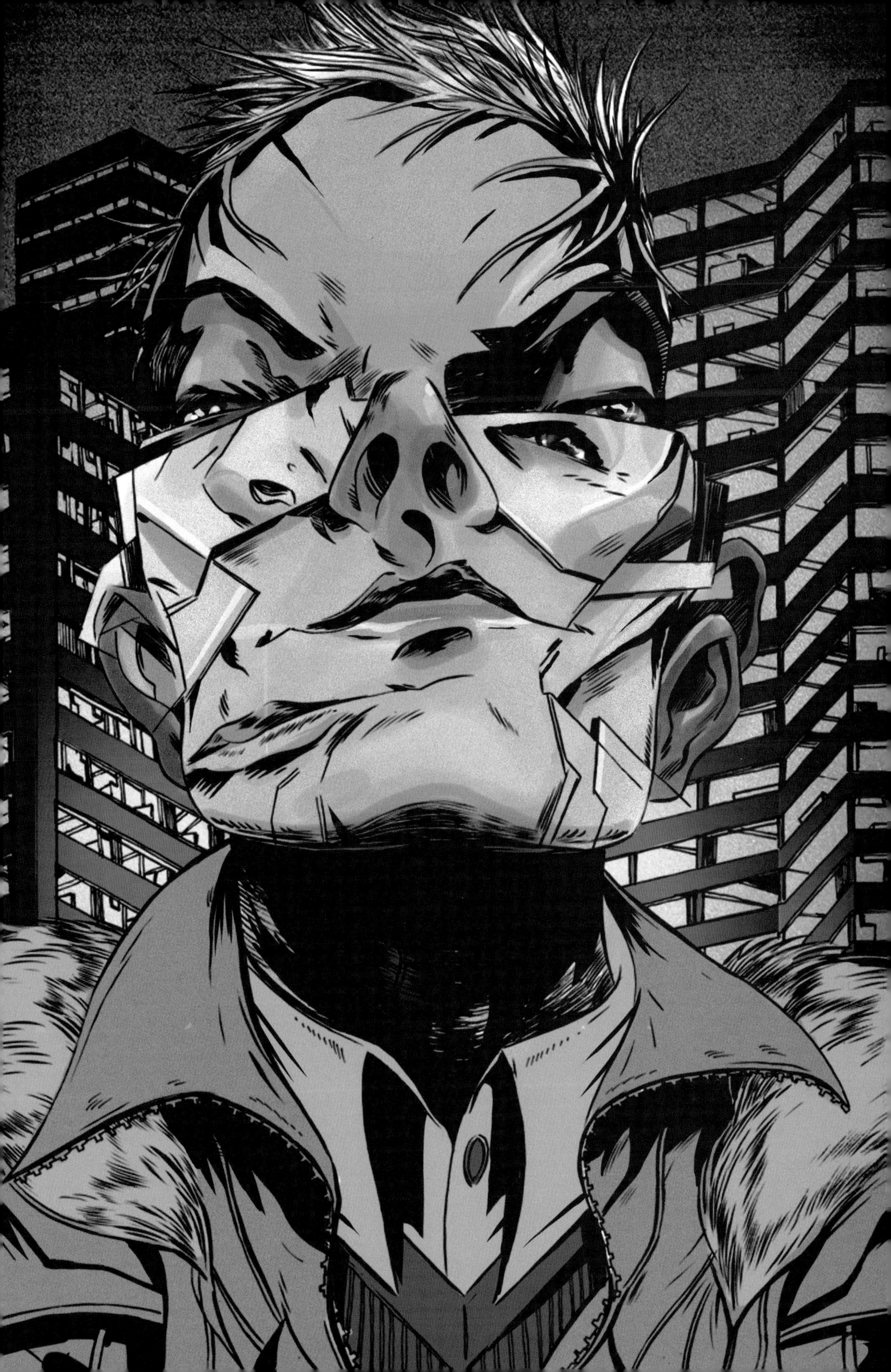

# HELLBENT

James Bentley, the "hero" of HELLBENT, is the worst character I have ever created. He's a violent thug, a vicious bastard—an easy guy to hate.

He's also my favorite.

HELLBENT is, in a way, my love letter to the work of James Ellroy, a novelist well-versed in creating morally-bankrupt characters. I wanted Bentley to echo the hard-boiled men in books like *L.A. Confidential* and *American Tabloid*, guys who were the "hero" by default. The protagonists in those stories are good guys only in the sense that everyone around them is so much worse.

So I created James Bentley; thug, thief, murderer, extortionist… cop. Before I had any idea of the story's setting, I had a very developed picture of Bentley in my mind. I could have dropped him in 1950s L.A., and made it a very obvious Ellroy homage, but I'd also wanted to do something set in Jack the Ripper era London.

Once I made the decision to combine the two concepts, everything fell into place. Almost as fast as I could write it all down, the world of HELLBENT spun itself into existence. I kept a notebook and filled it with bits of Victorian history, H.P. Lovecraft mythology, anything that seemed like a good fit for HELLBENT stories.

For almost a decade this notebook steadily grew, and stretched into other notebooks, just waiting for me to get around to finding it a proper home. My attachment to the concept, to the characters (particularly the crooked copper Bentley) grew deeper.

When the opportunity arose to bring the concept to life in BAD KARMA, I went straight to Tigh Walker, my collaborator on '76. Tigh is a phenomenally talented artist, with an eye for detail and an uncanny ability to breathe life into the environment of the story. He nailed the look and feel of HELLBENT right away, and gave it a dark, moody atmosphere that was absolutely perfect. He got it right from the start, and we hit the ground running, putting together the nasty little bit of Victorian horror-noir you hold in your hands.

So, without further ado, let me introduce you to the inimitable James Bentley.

I hope you hate him as much as I do.

Seth Peck
March 2013

story   Seth Peck
art     Tigh Walker
letters Dave Lanphear

54

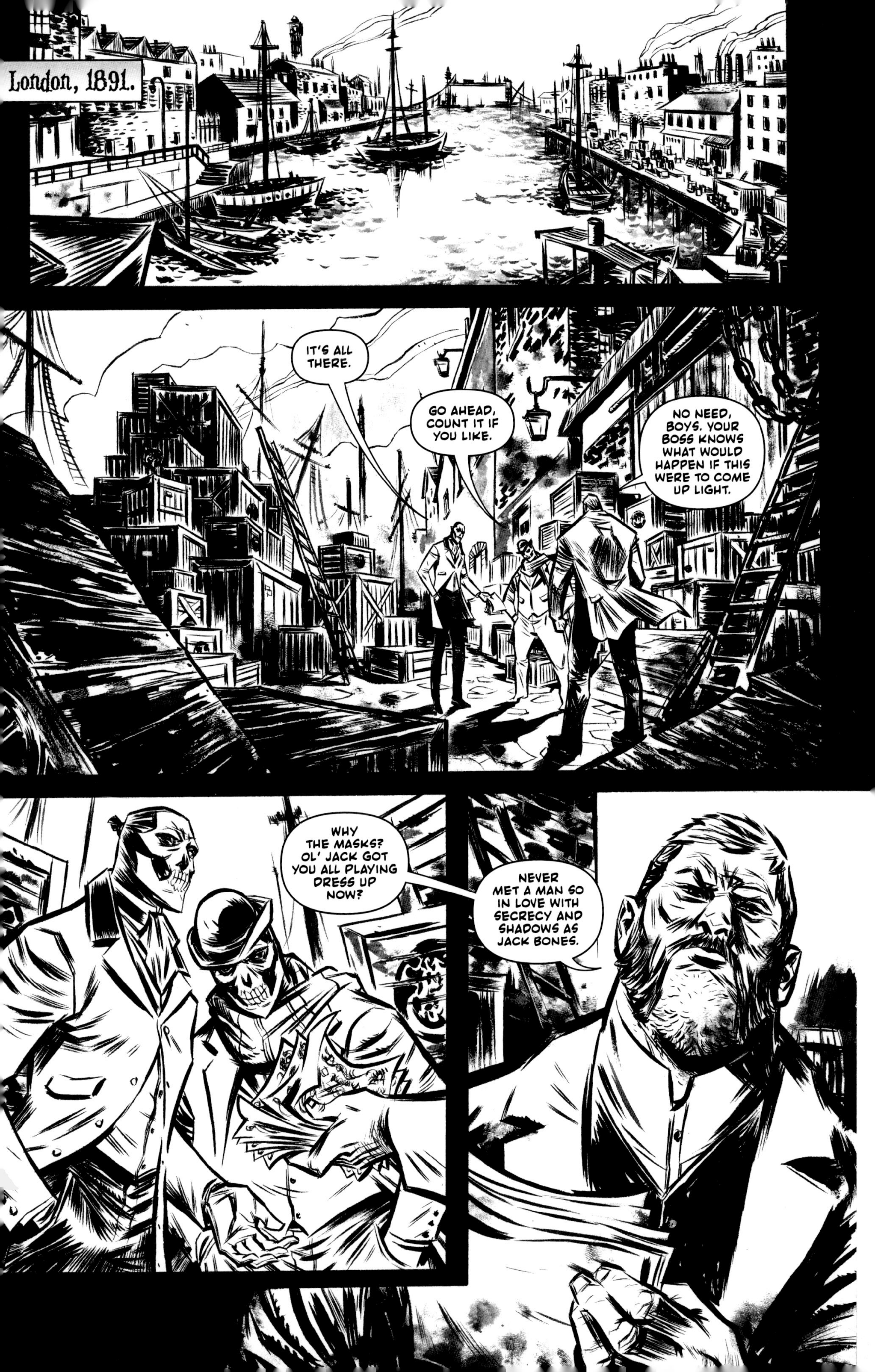
London, 1891.
IT'S ALL THERE.
GO AHEAD, COUNT IT IF YOU LIKE.
NO NEED, BOYS. YOUR BOSS KNOWS WHAT WOULD HAPPEN IF THIS WERE TO COME UP LIGHT.
WHY THE MASKS? OL' JACK GOT YOU ALL PLAYING DRESS UP NOW?
NEVER MET A MAN SO IN LOVE WITH SECRECY AND SHADOWS AS JACK BONES.

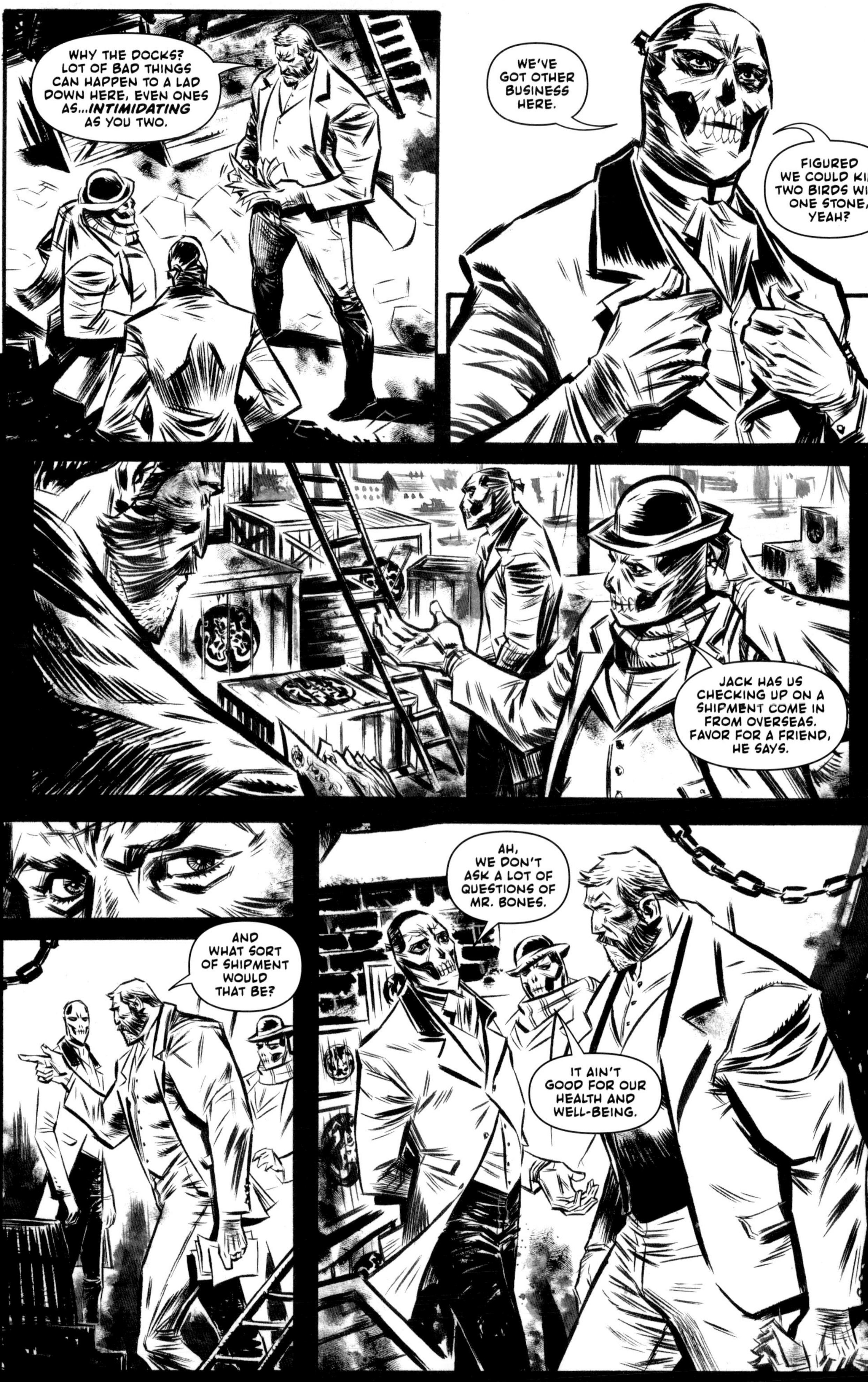

WHY THE DOCKS? LOT OF BAD THINGS CAN HAPPEN TO A LAD DOWN HERE, EVEN ONES AS...*INTIMIDATING* AS YOU TWO.
WE'VE GOT OTHER BUSINESS HERE.
FIGURED WE COULD KILL TWO BIRDS WITH ONE STONE, YEAH?
JACK HAS US CHECKING UP ON A SHIPMENT COME IN FROM OVERSEAS. FAVOR FOR A FRIEND, HE SAYS.
AND WHAT SORT OF SHIPMENT WOULD THAT BE?
AH, WE DON'T ASK A LOT OF QUESTIONS OF MR. BONES.
IT AIN'T GOOD FOR OUR HEALTH AND WELL-BEING.

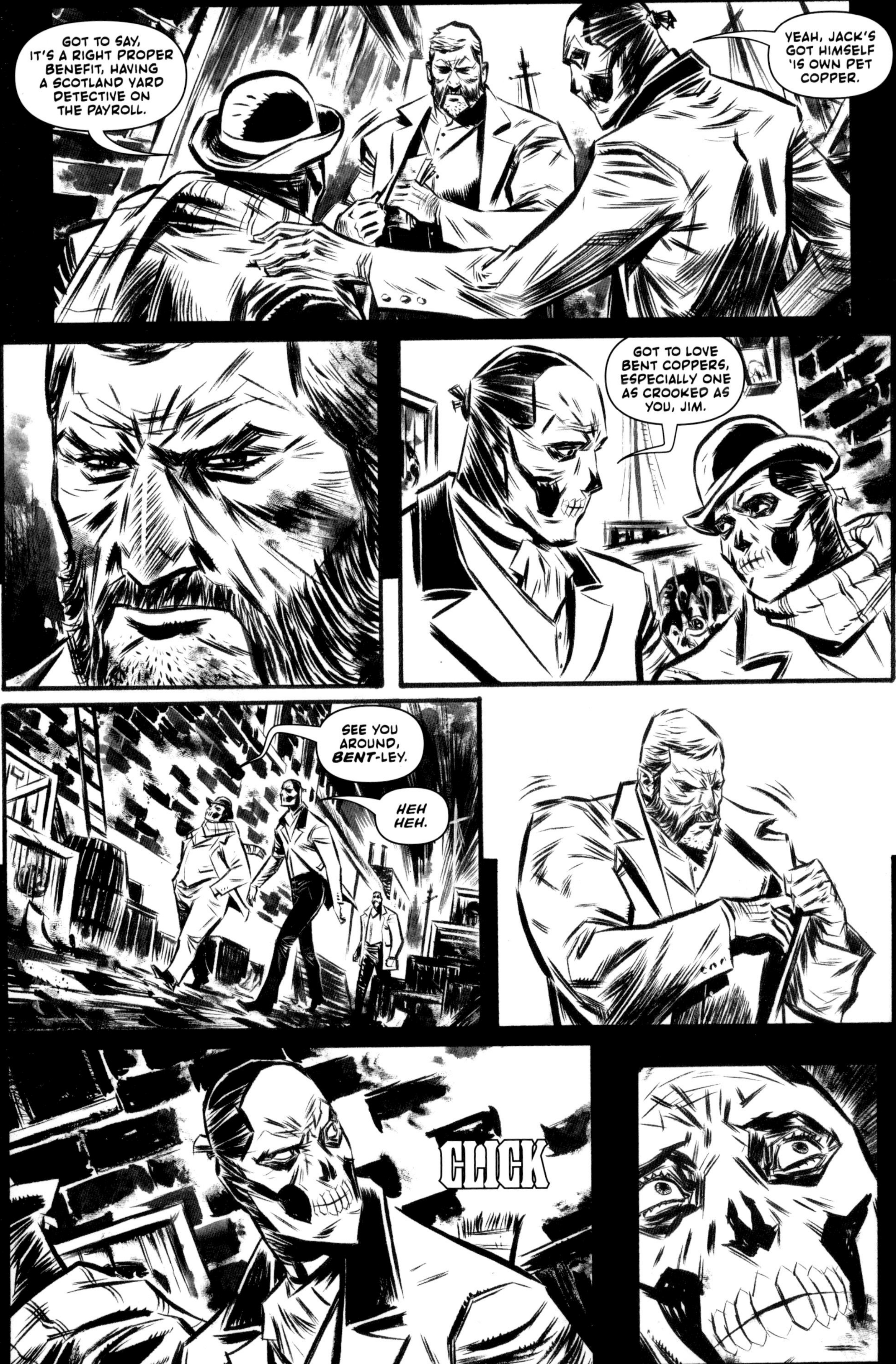
GOT TO SAY, IT'S A RIGHT PROPER BENEFIT, HAVING A SCOTLAND YARD DETECTIVE ON THE PAYROLL.
YEAH, JACK'S GOT HIMSELF 'IS OWN PET COPPER.
GOT TO LOVE BENT COPPERS, ESPECIALLY ONE AS CROOKED AS YOU, JIM.
SEE YOU AROUND, BENT-LEY.
HEH HEH.
CLICK

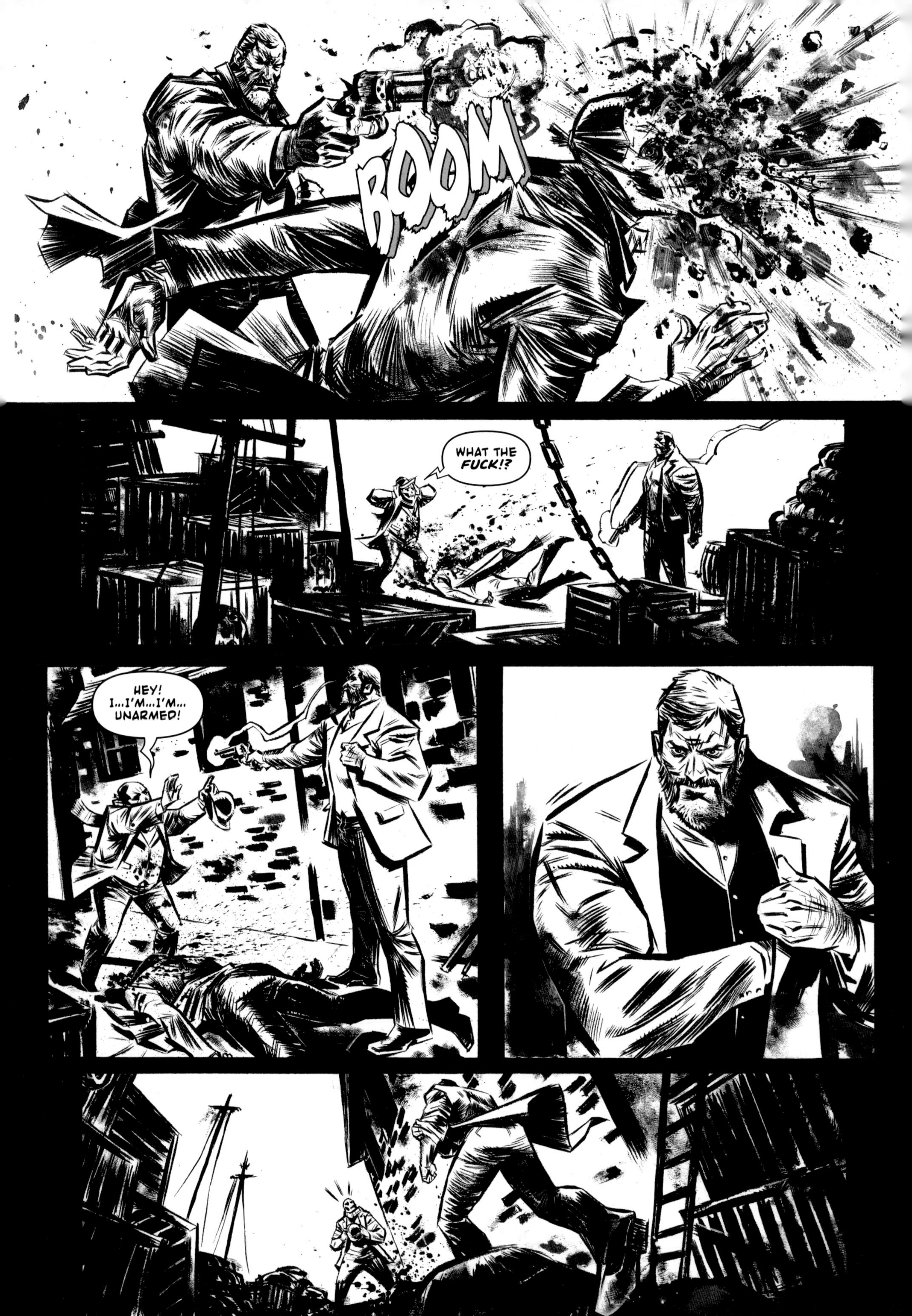
BOOM
WHAT THE FUCK!?
HEY! I...I'M...I'M... UNARMED!

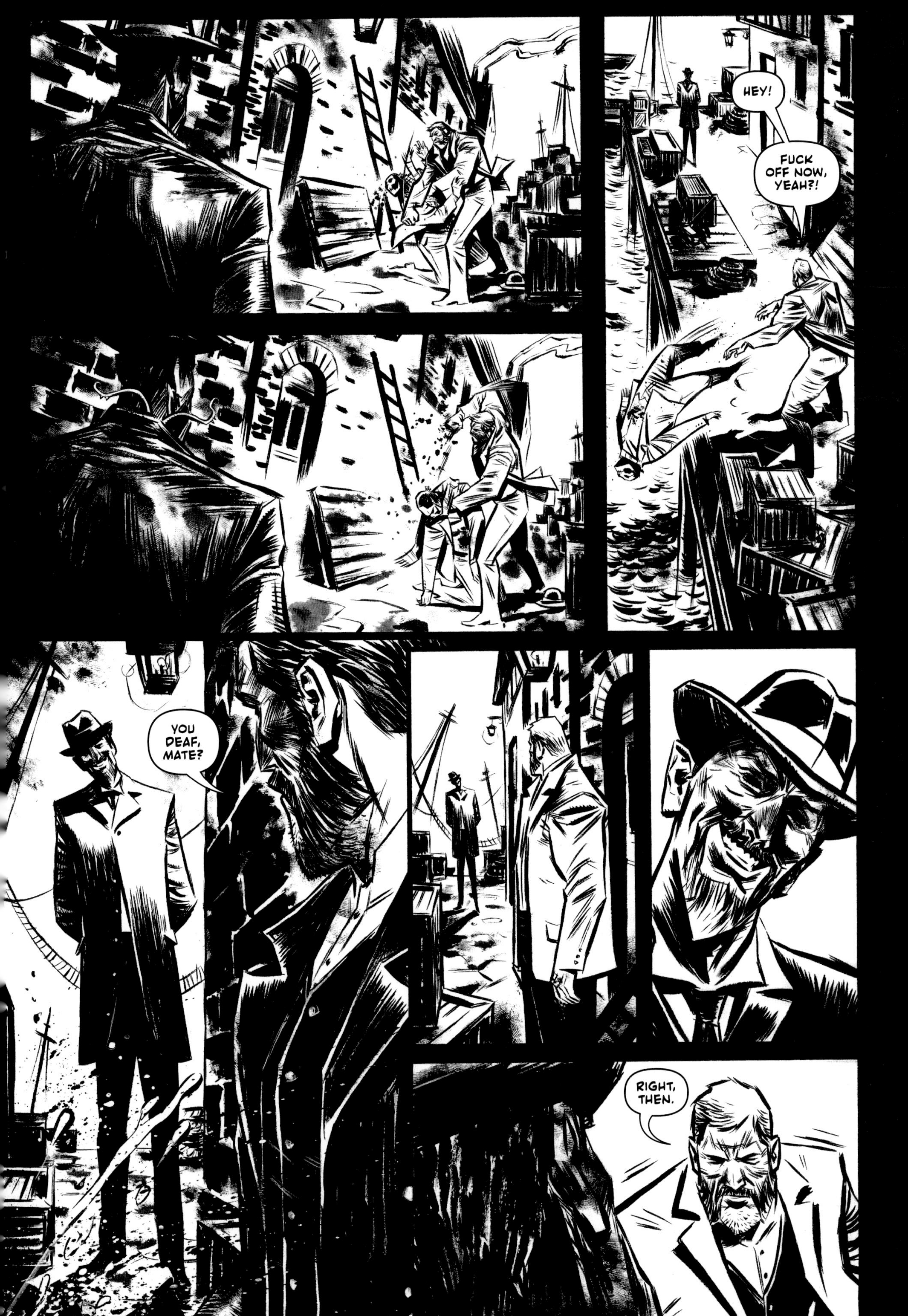
HEY!
FUCK OFF NOW, YEAH?!
YOU DEAF, MATE?
RIGHT, THEN.

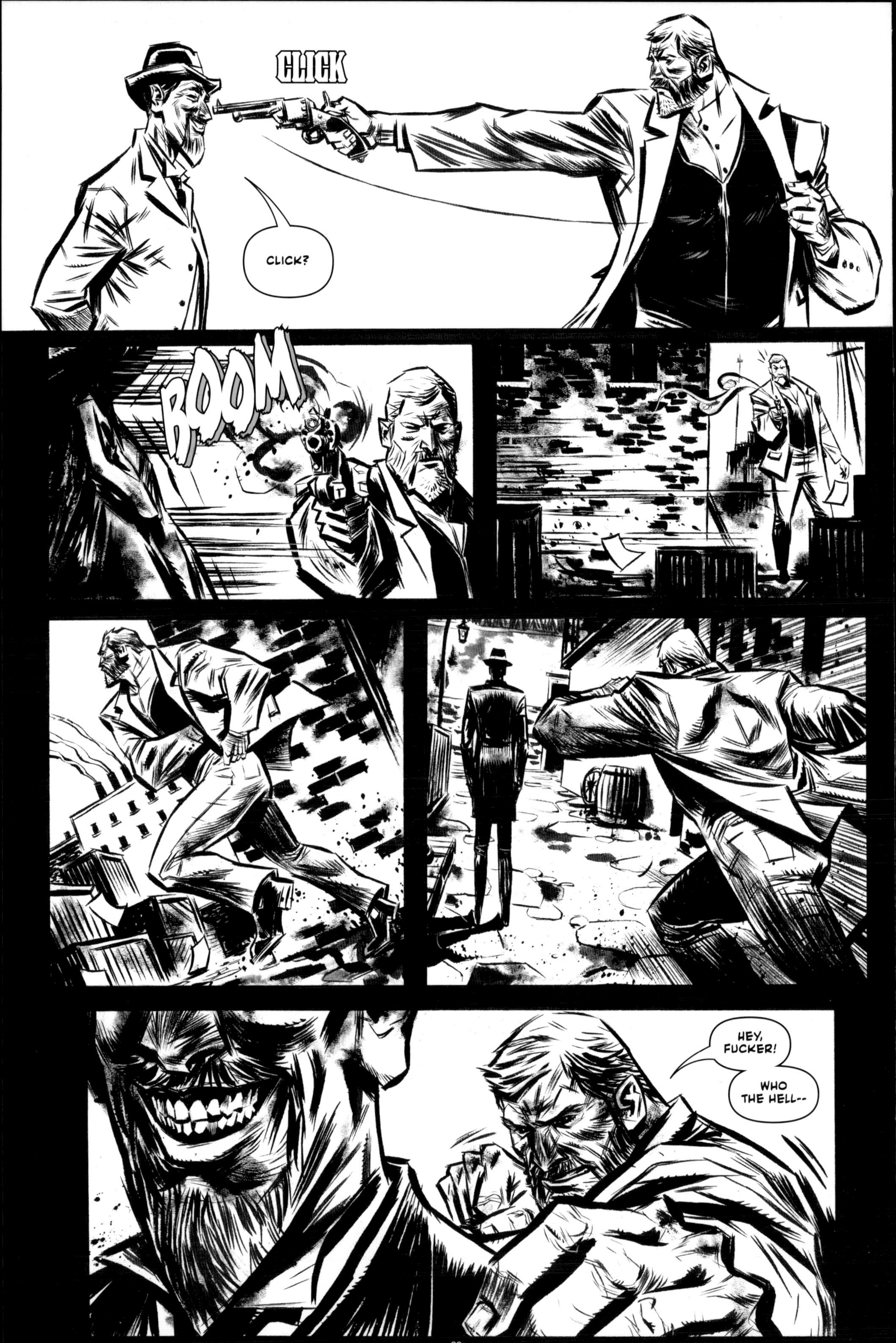
CLICK
CLICK?
BOOM
HEY, FUCKER!
WHO THE HELL--

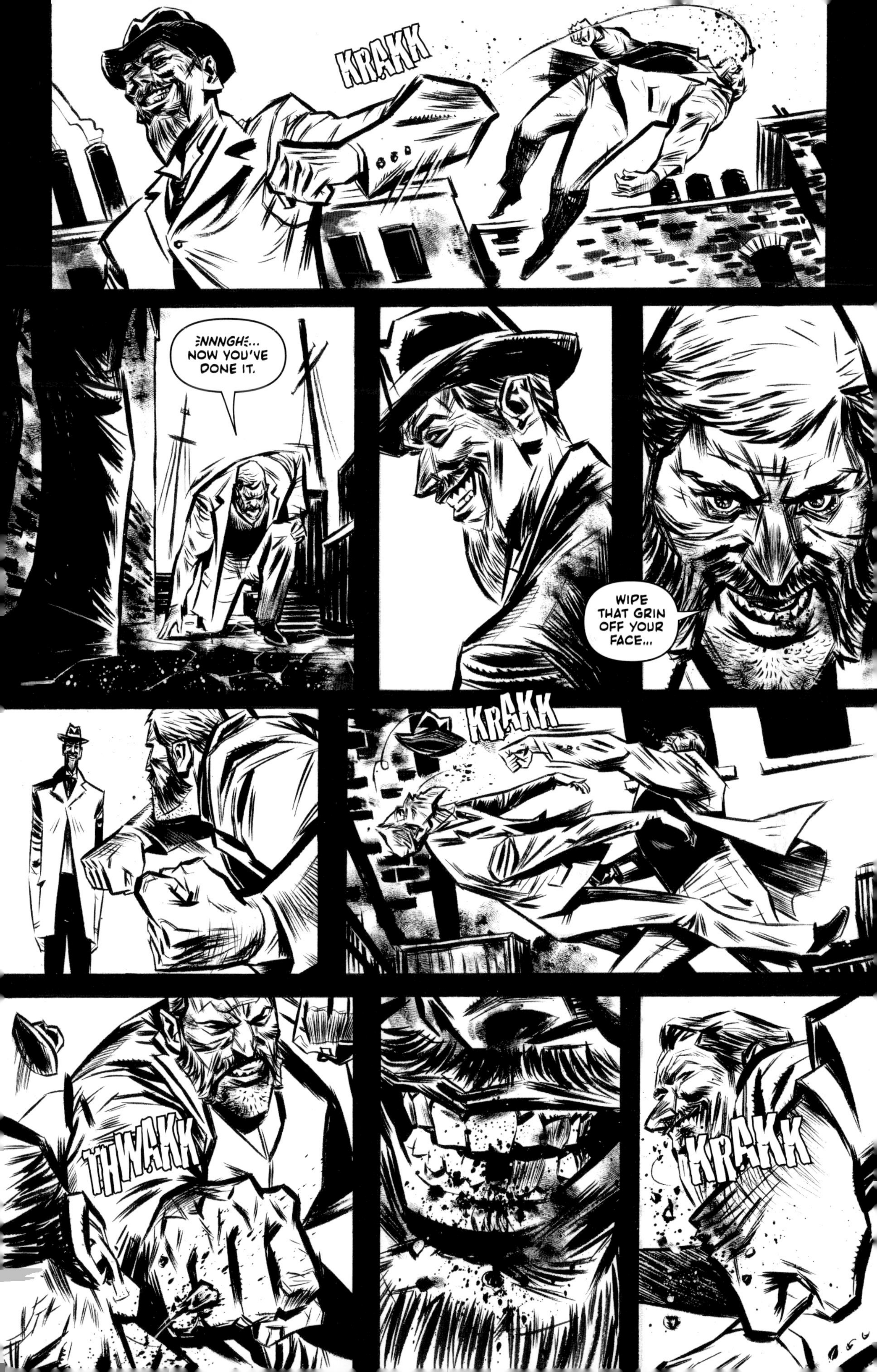
KRAKK
ṄNNNGH... NOW YOU'VE DONE IT.
WIPE THAT GRIN OFF YOUR FACE...
KRAKK
THWAKK
KRAKK

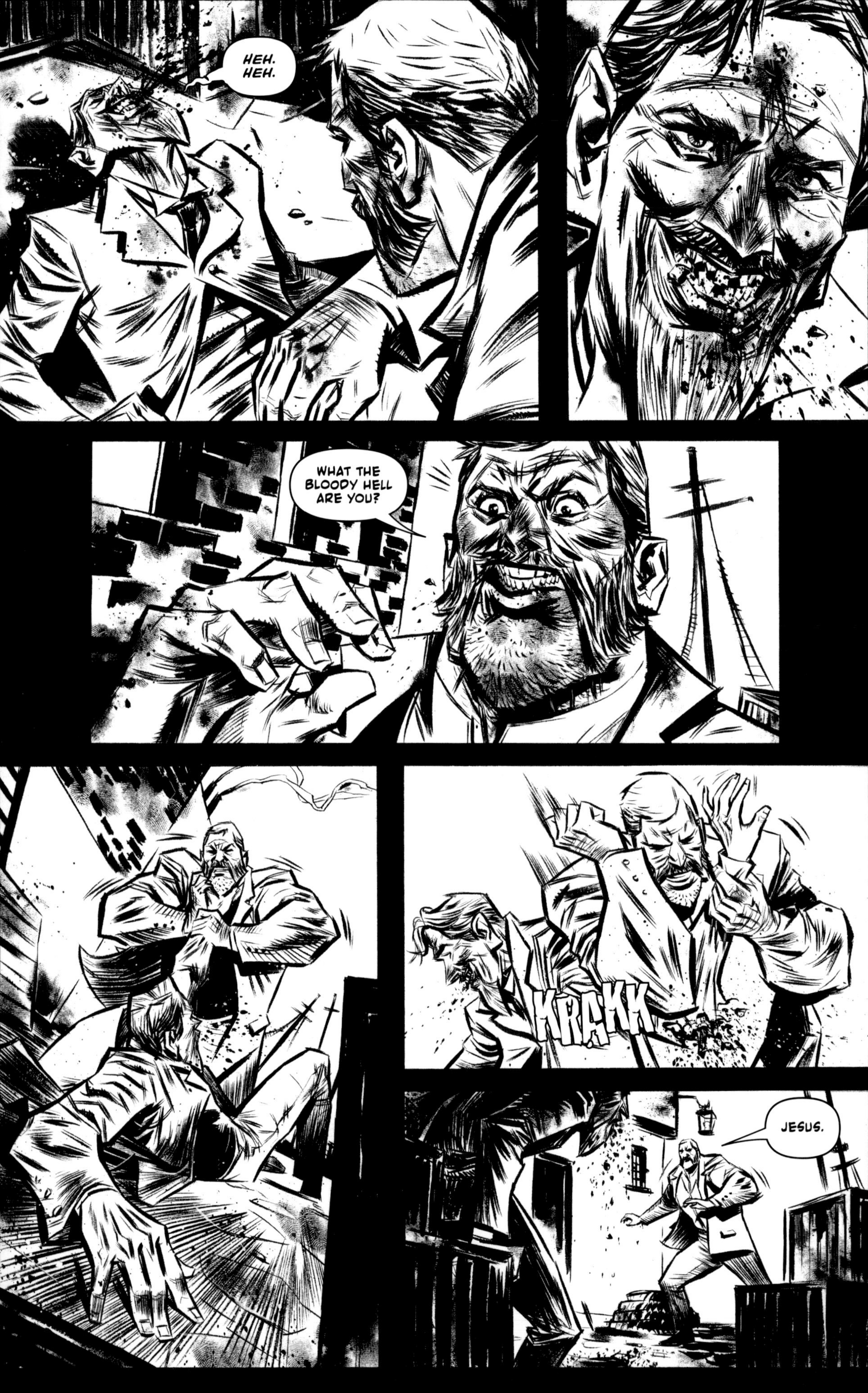
HEH. HEH.
WHAT THE BLOODY HELL ARE YOU?
KRAKK
JESUS.

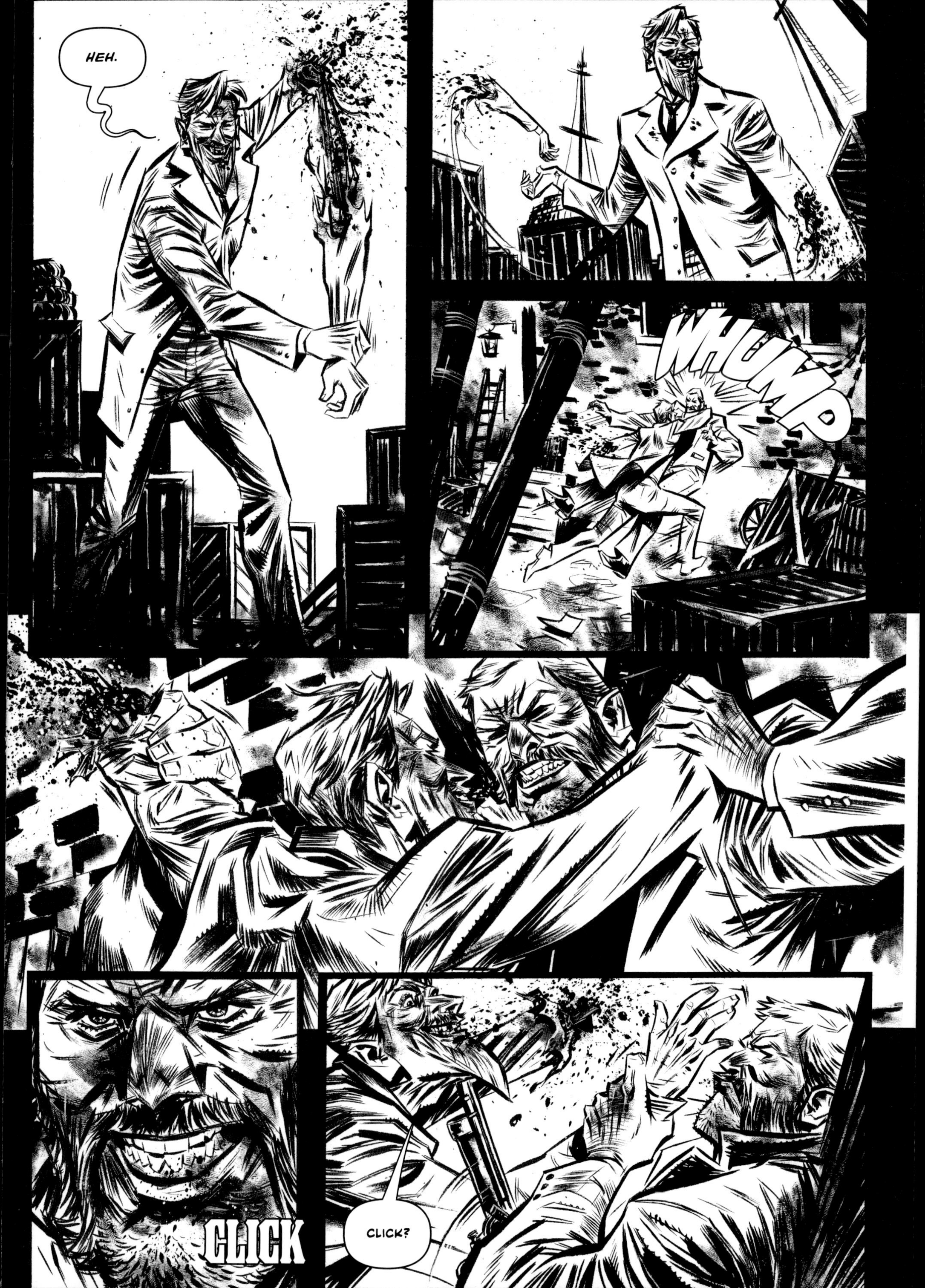
HEH.
WHUMP
CLICK
CLICK?

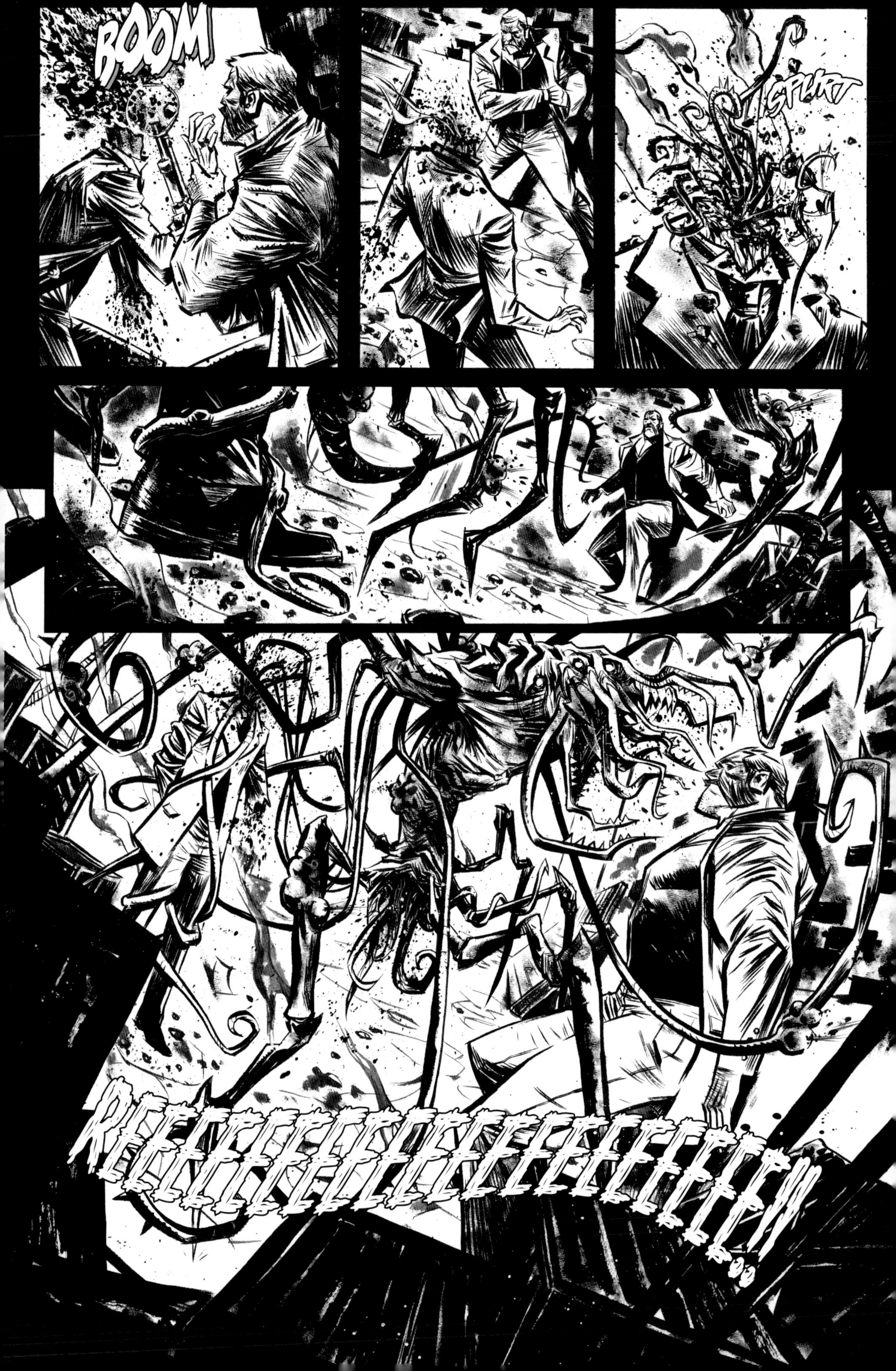
BOOM
SPLURT
REEEEEEEEEEEEEEEEEEEEEEEEEEEEEEEN!!

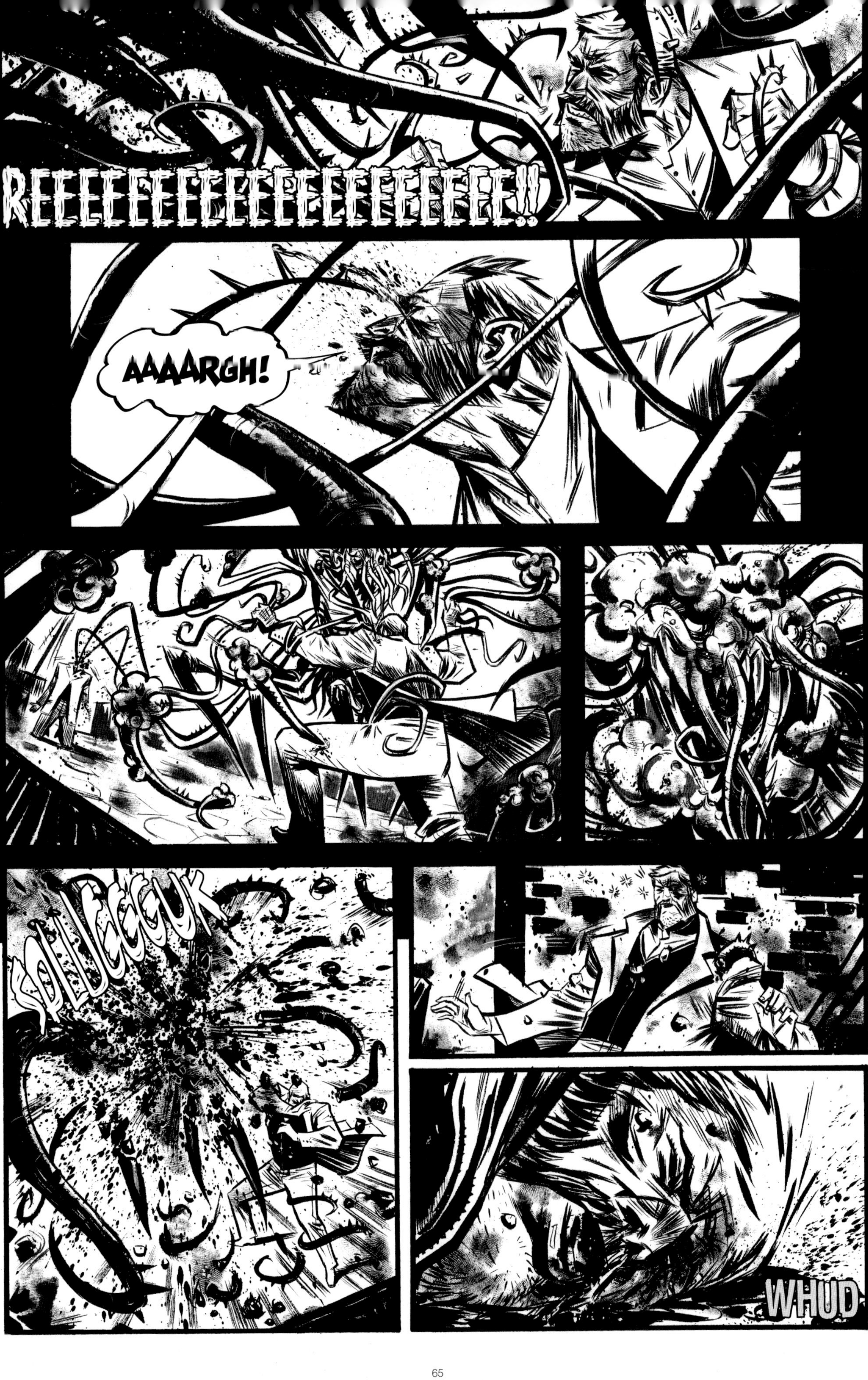
REEEEEEEEEEEEEEEEEEEE!!
AAAARGH!
SPLUCCCUK
WHUD

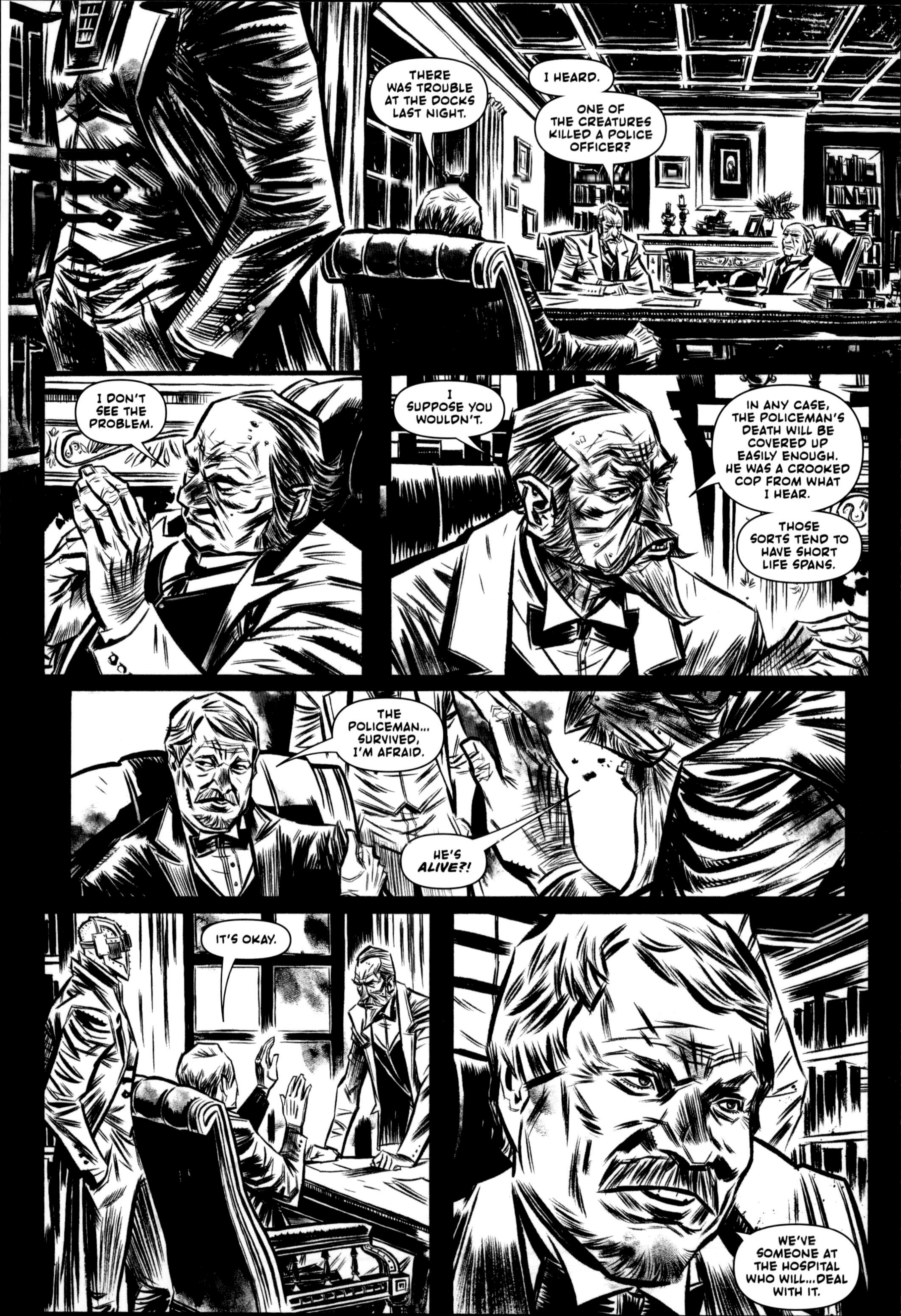
THERE WAS TROUBLE AT THE DOCKS LAST NIGHT.
I HEARD.
ONE OF THE CREATURES KILLED A POLICE OFFICER?
I DON'T SEE THE PROBLEM.
I SUPPOSE YOU WOULDN'T.
IN ANY CASE, THE POLICEMAN'S DEATH WILL BE COVERED UP EASILY ENOUGH. HE WAS A CROOKED COP FROM WHAT I HEAR.
THOSE SORTS TEND TO HAVE SHORT LIFE SPANS.
THE POLICEMAN... SURVIVED, I'M AFRAID.
HE'S *ALIVE?!*
IT'S OKAY.
WE'VE SOMEONE AT THE HOSPITAL WHO WILL...DEAL WITH IT.

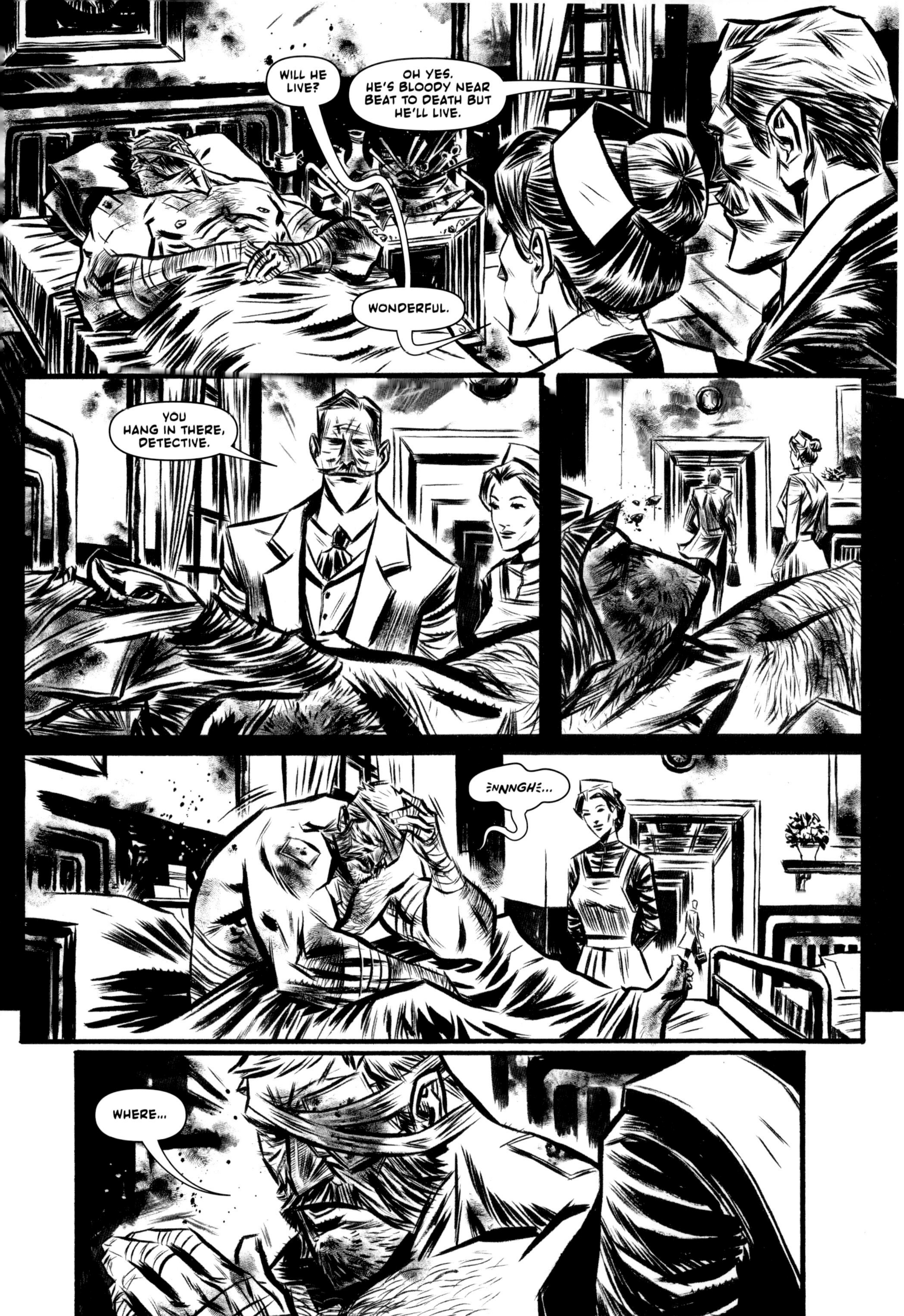
WILL HE LIVE?
OH YES. HE'S BLOODY NEAR BEAT TO DEATH BUT HE'LL LIVE.
WONDERFUL.
YOU HANG IN THERE, DETECTIVE.
NNNGH...
WHERE...

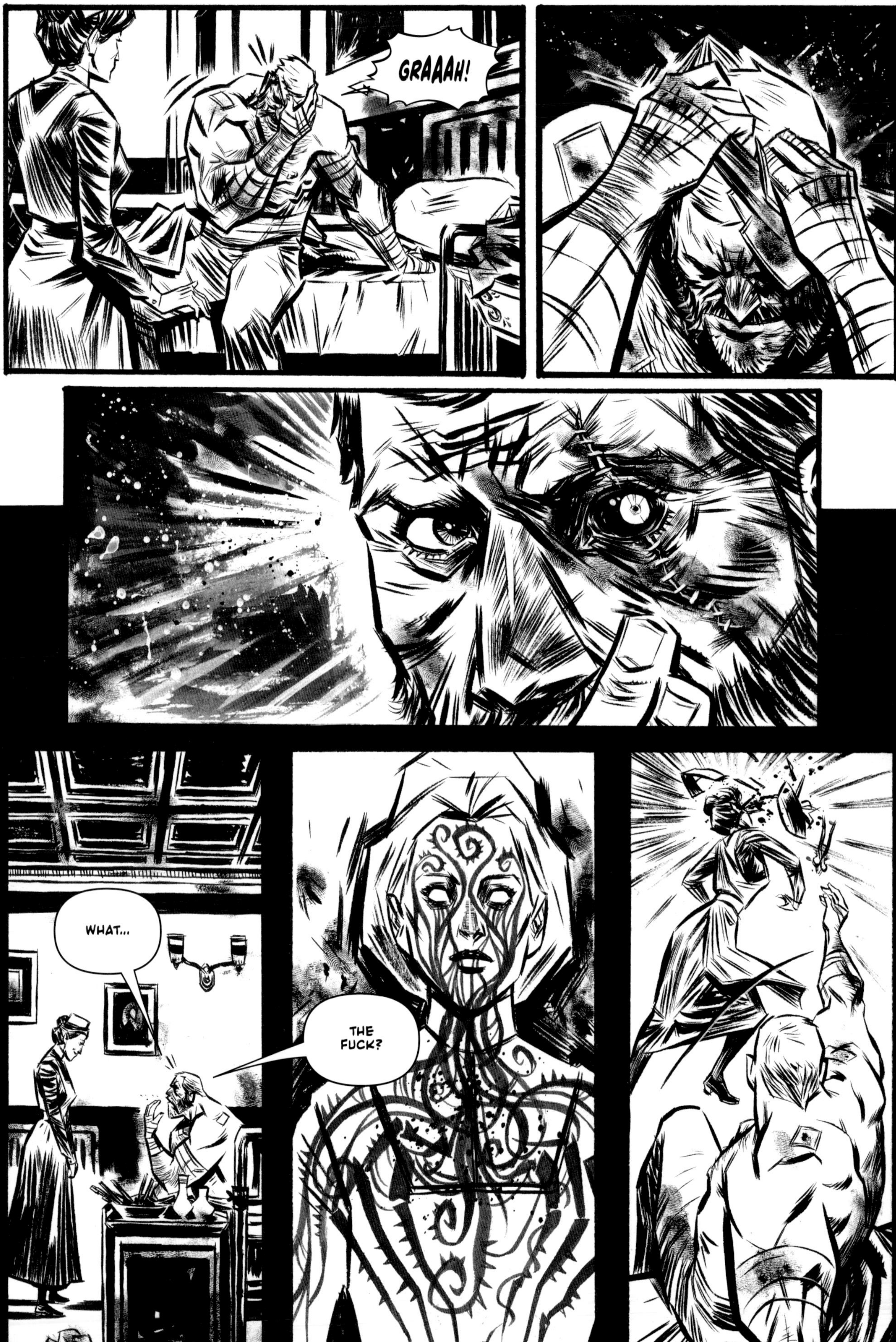
GRAAAH!
WHAT...
THE FUCK?

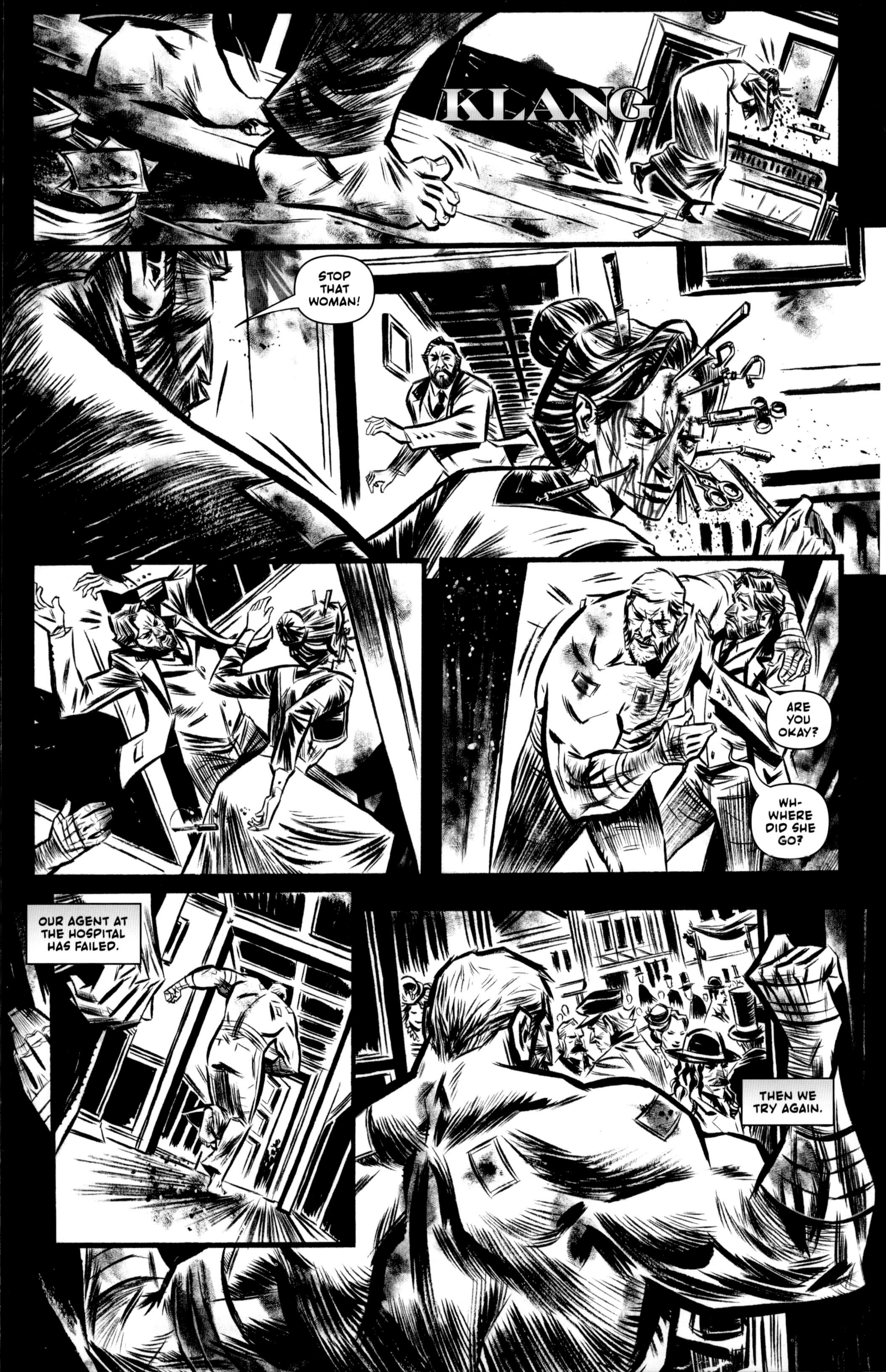
KLANG
STOP THAT WOMAN!
ARE YOU OKAY?
WH- WHERE DID SHE GO?
OUR AGENT AT THE HOSPITAL HAS FAILED.
THEN WE TRY AGAIN.

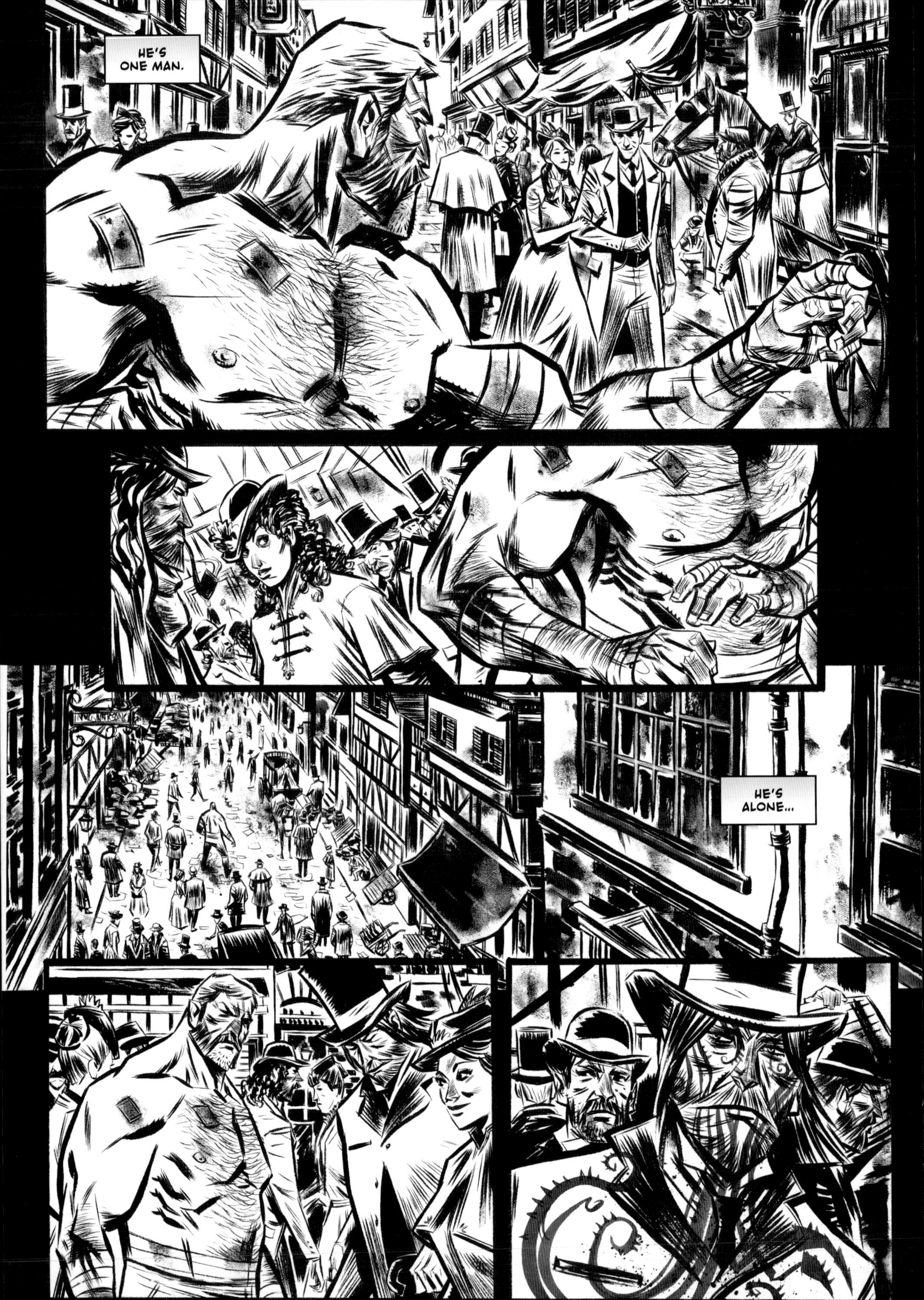
HE'S ONE MAN.
HE'S ALONE...

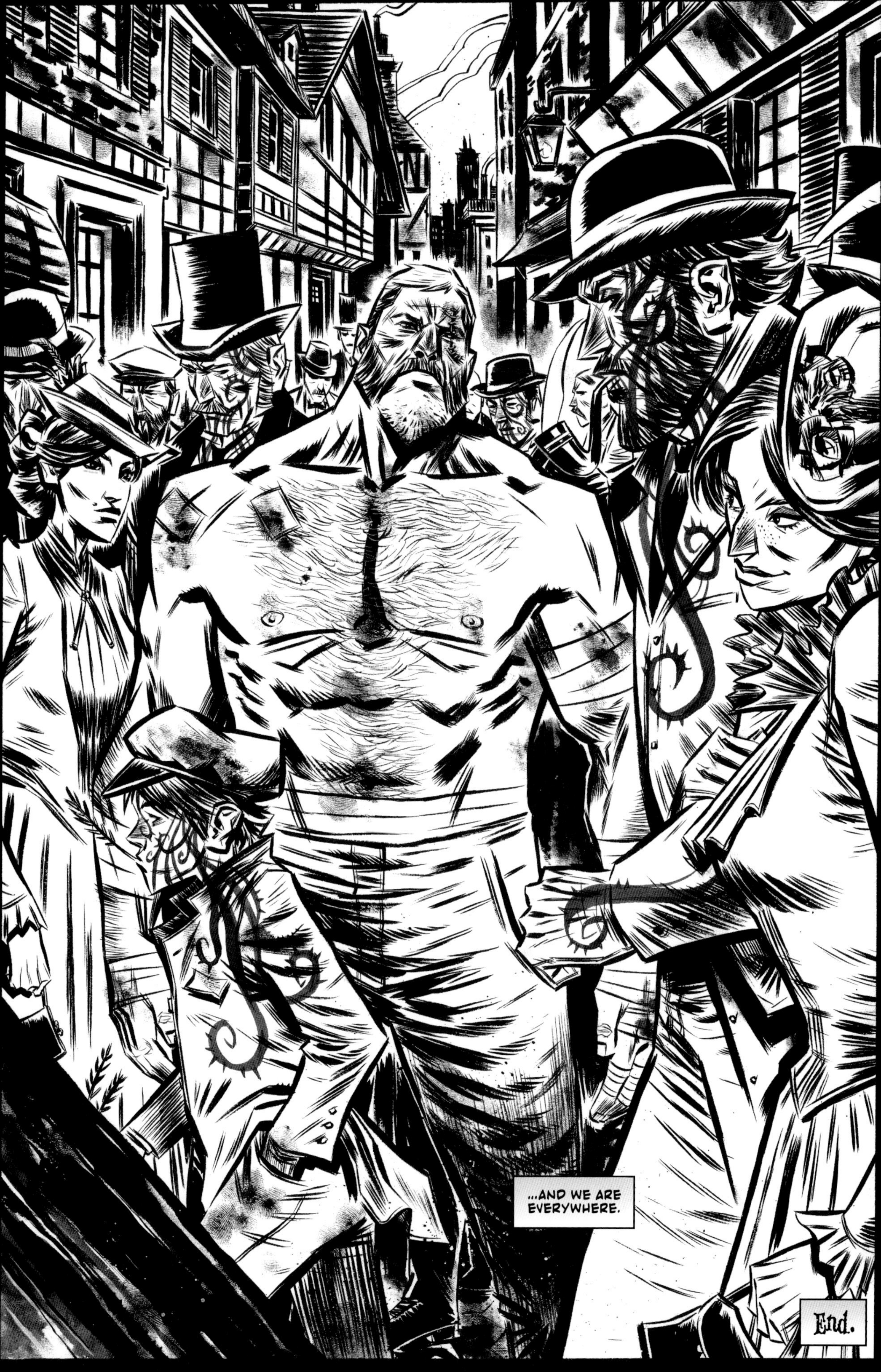
...AND WE ARE EVERYWHERE.
End.

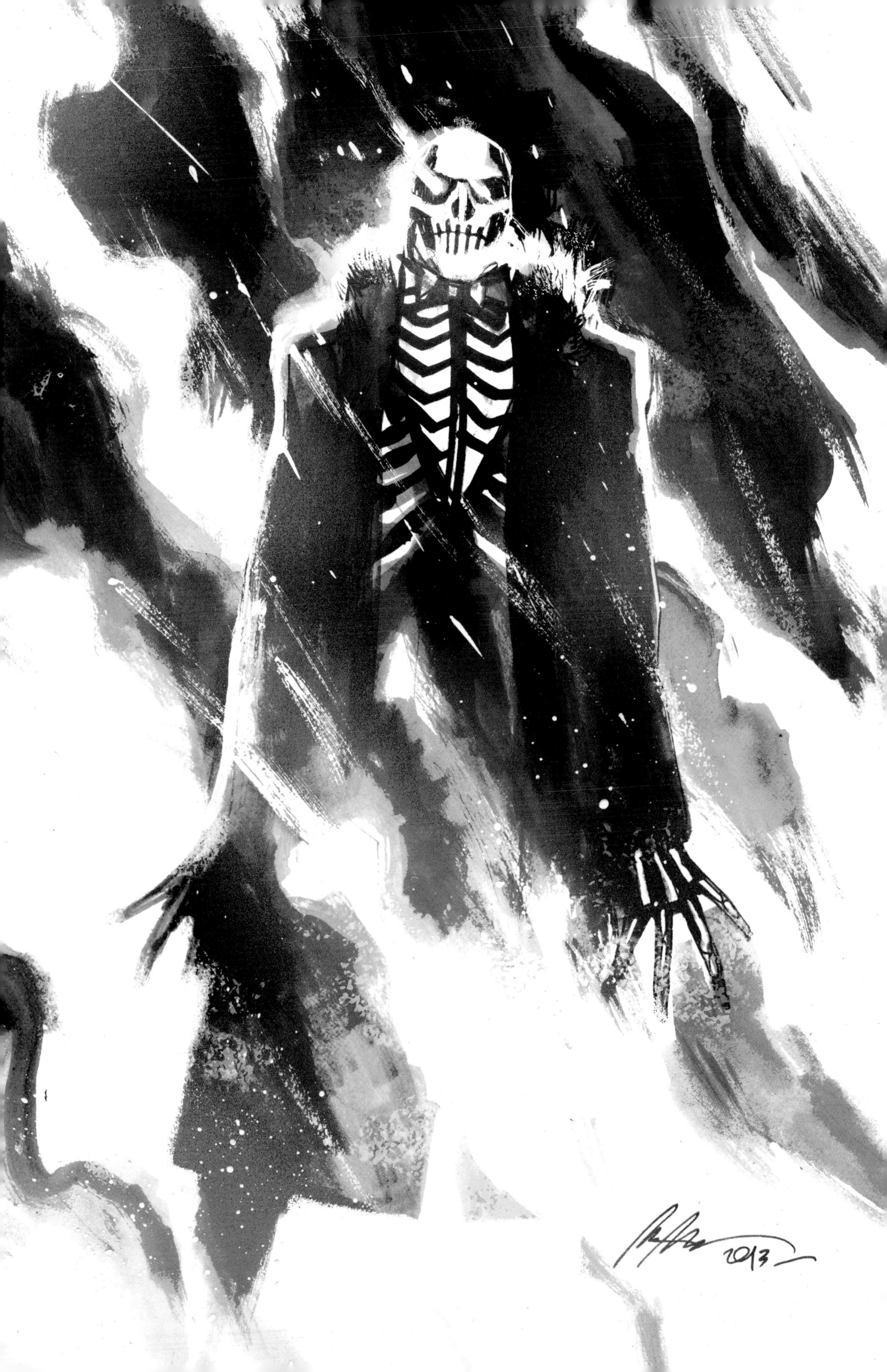

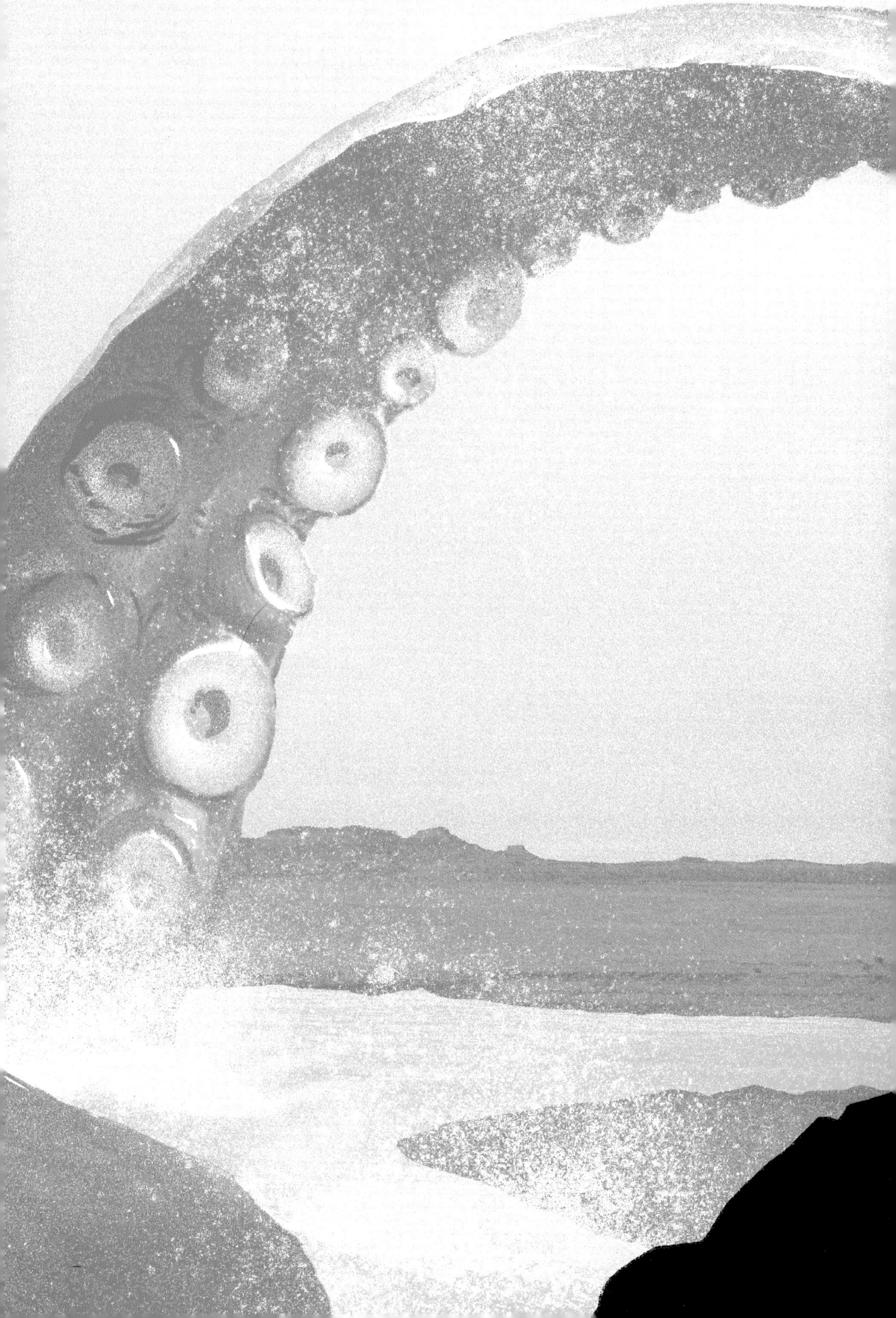

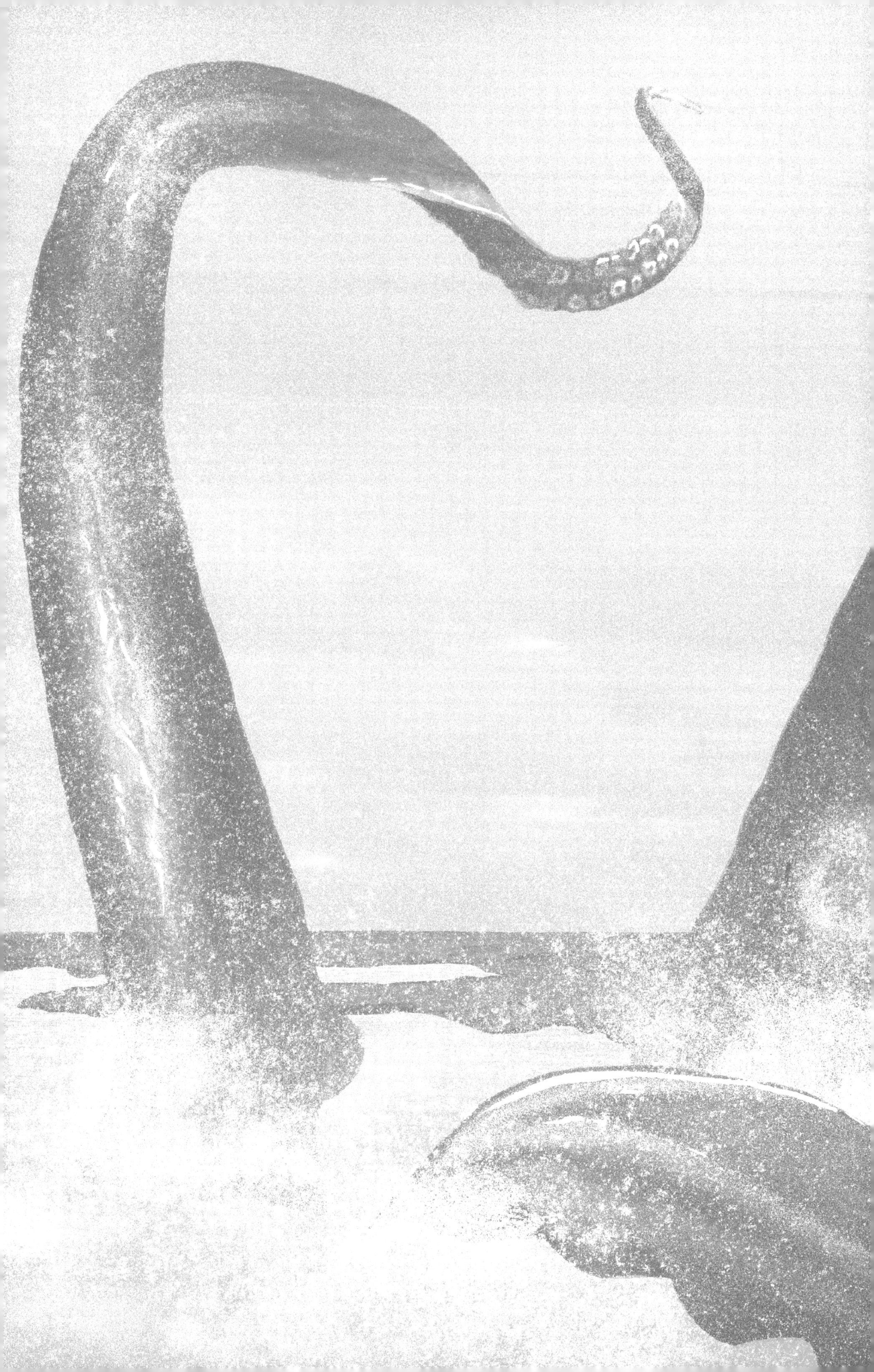

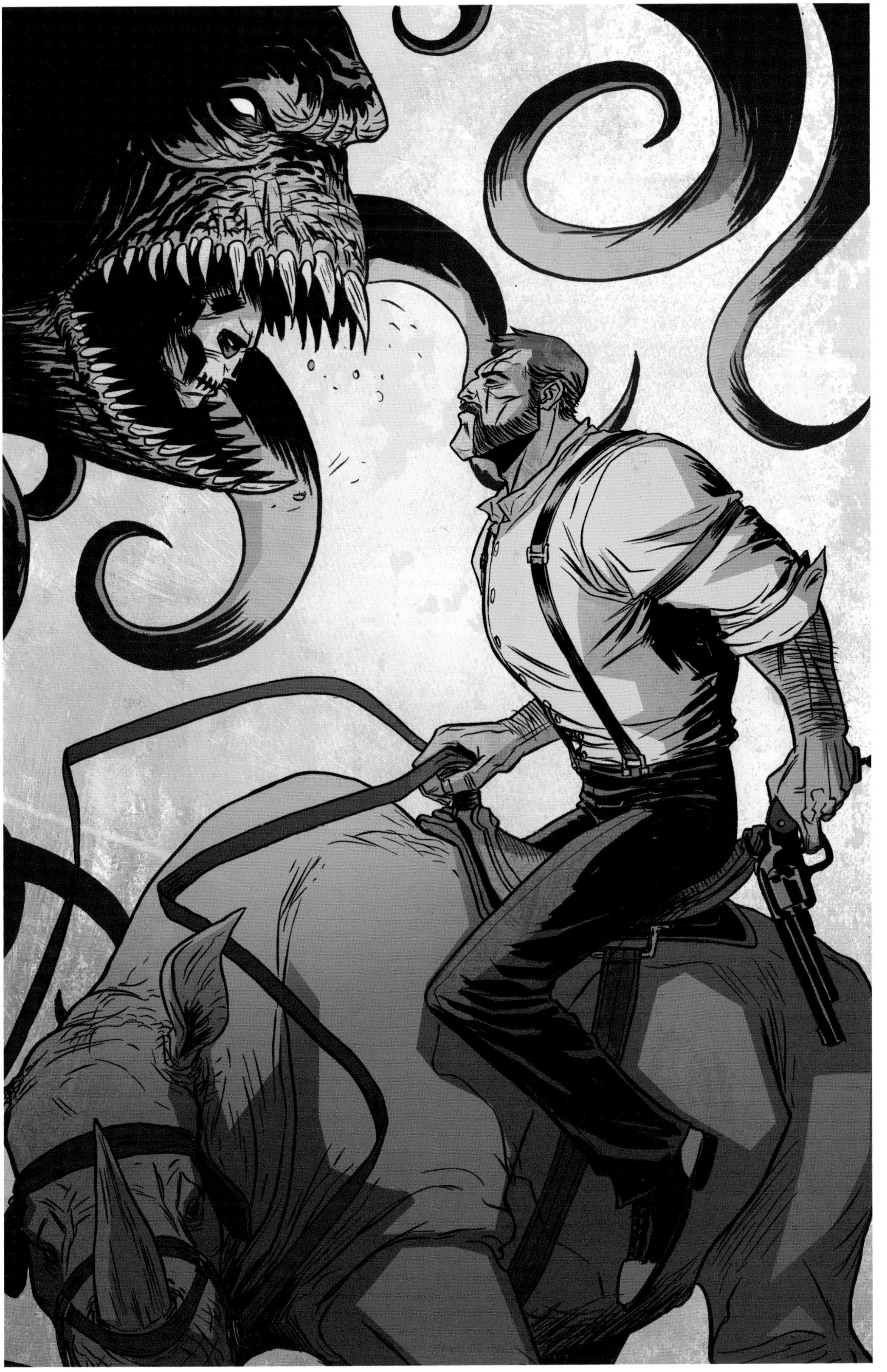

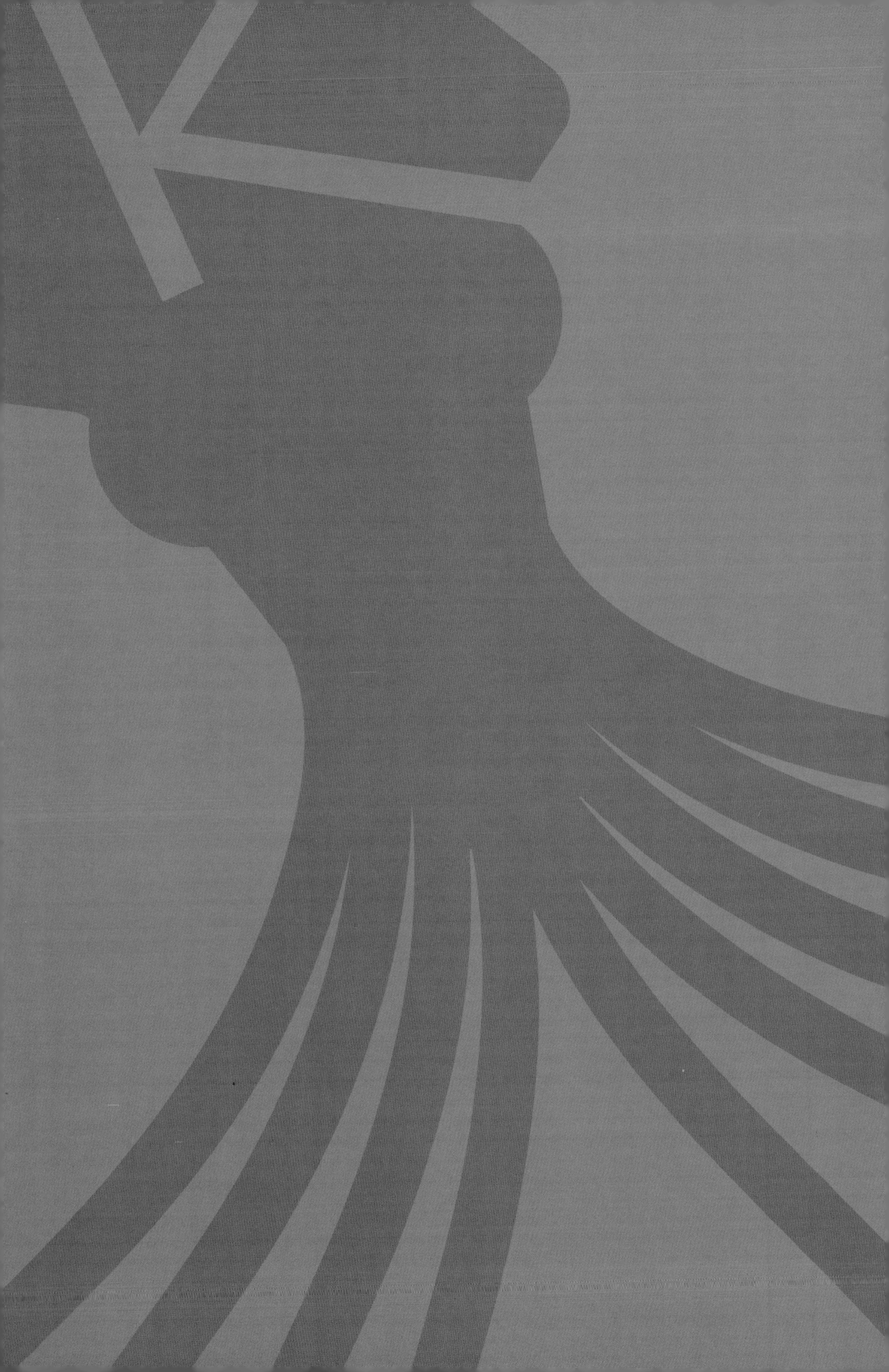

# CHAOS AGENT™

A little chaos never hurt anyone.

Our lives have become so structured. Computer and smartphone technology has changed everything. We have apps that tell us when to take a pill, when to move on to the next task, when that deadline is looming.

Throughout school I was a pretty typical art student slob. Over the past decade, though, something changed. I became… structured. Part of that is working in comics. It's my responsibility to hit deadlines. l have my life structured down to twenty-five minute segments. One day I looked at it all and began to wonder what the world was becoming thanks to all of that structure— without the chaos. Were we tipping some kind of scale?

Out of that, on a drive to an Italian restaurant nestled away in a place called Scammon, Kansas, I told the story of CHAOS AGENT to my captive audience. It came out pretty much fully formed—chaos is the thing that keeps the world going.

A few months later, my frequent collaborator, B. Clay Moore, asked me if I wanted to be a part of this new writing collective he was starting with Seth Peck and Alex Grecian. Out of all of the possible stories I could tell, I went back to CHAOS AGENT. Somehow it just fit.

As an artist who writes, it can be tricky finding an artist to work with on a project. Finding Mike Tisserand, though, was serendipity. Not a lot of guys knock it out of the park on their first book. Mike certainly did.

Along with Mike, I had the amazing fortune to work with Zac Atkinson on colors and Troy Peteri on letters. They took things to a whole new level.

My life is still pretty structured. One of the things on my 'to do' list today was "WRITE INTRO". Every once in a while, though, I throw things for a loop. I try and add a bit of chaos to my life.

Because, you know, a little chaos never hurt anyone.

Jeremy Haun
March 2013


story    Jeremy Haun
art      Mike Tisserand
colors   Zac Atkinson
letters  Troy Peteri

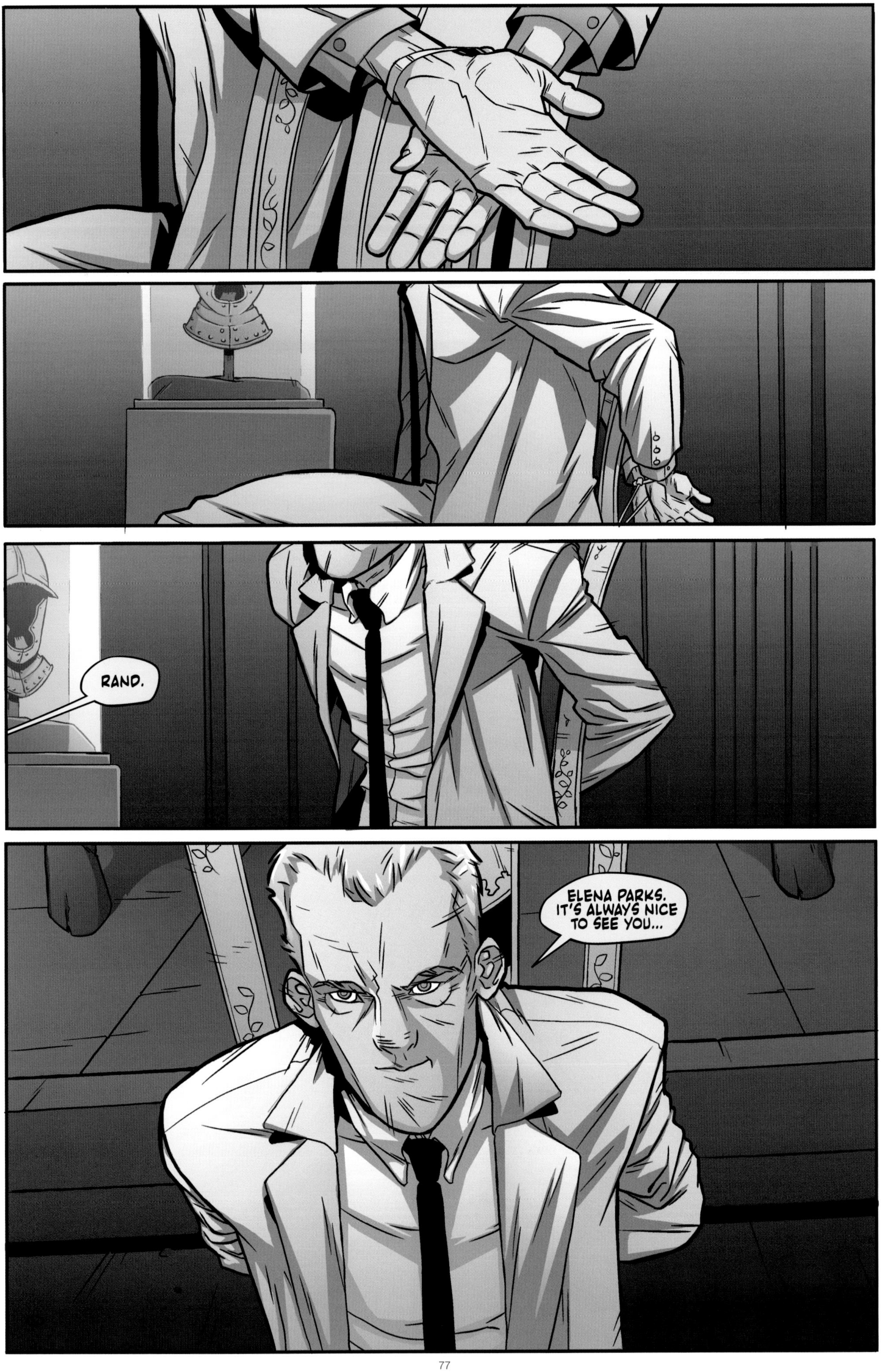
RAND.
ELENA PARKS. IT'S ALWAYS NICE TO SEE YOU...

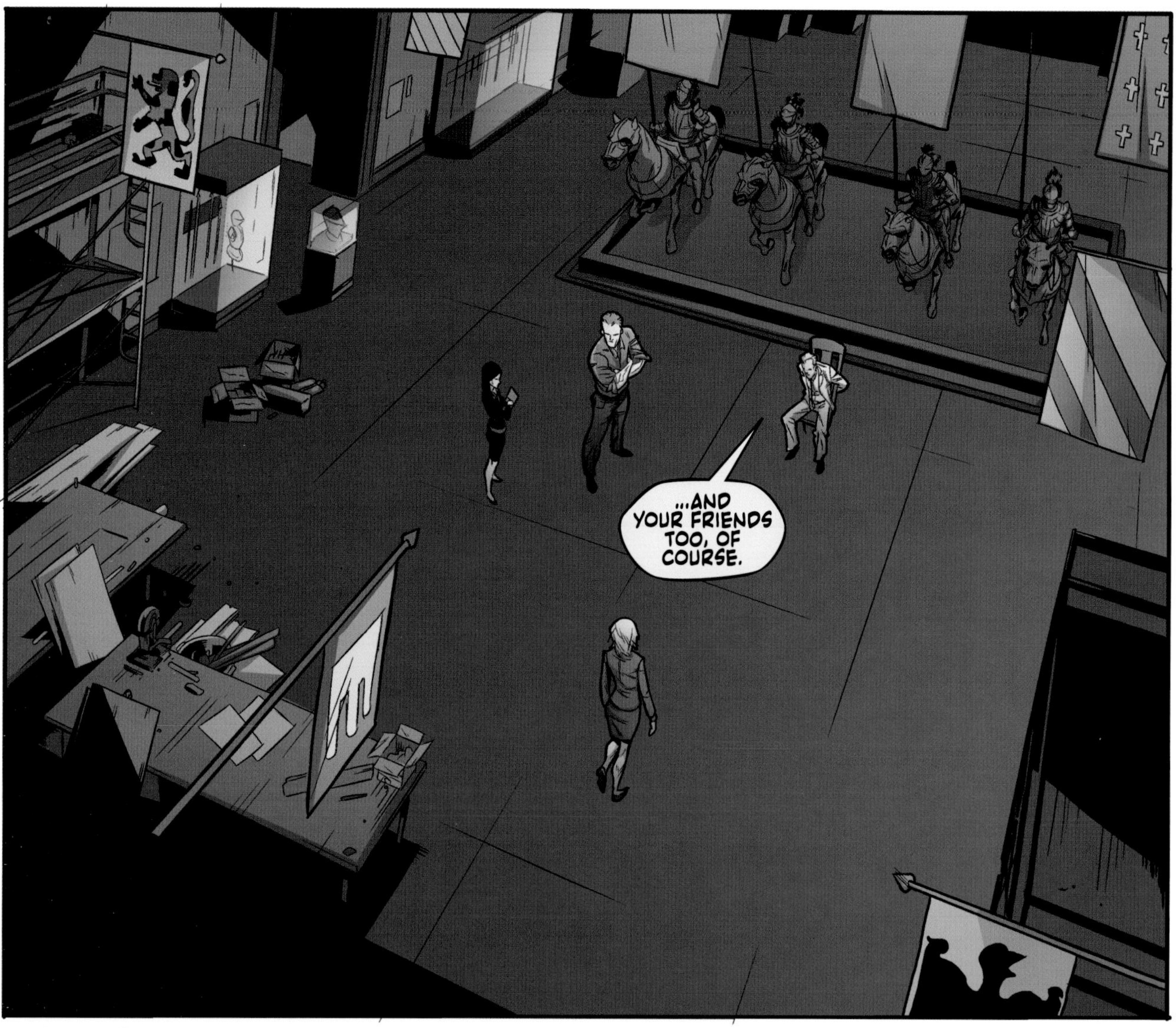
...AND YOUR FRIENDS TOO, OF COURSE.

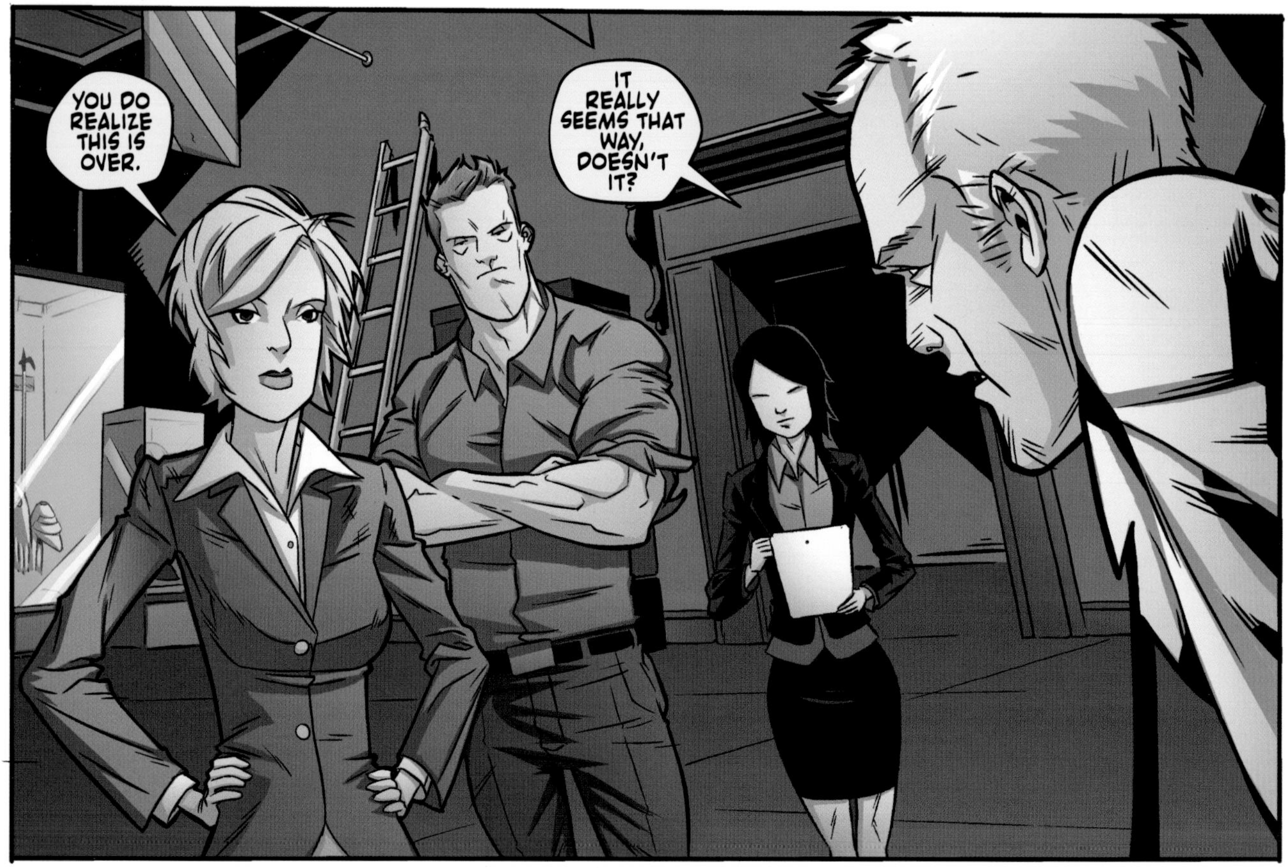
YOU DO REALIZE THIS IS OVER.
IT REALLY SEEMS THAT WAY, DOESN'T IT?

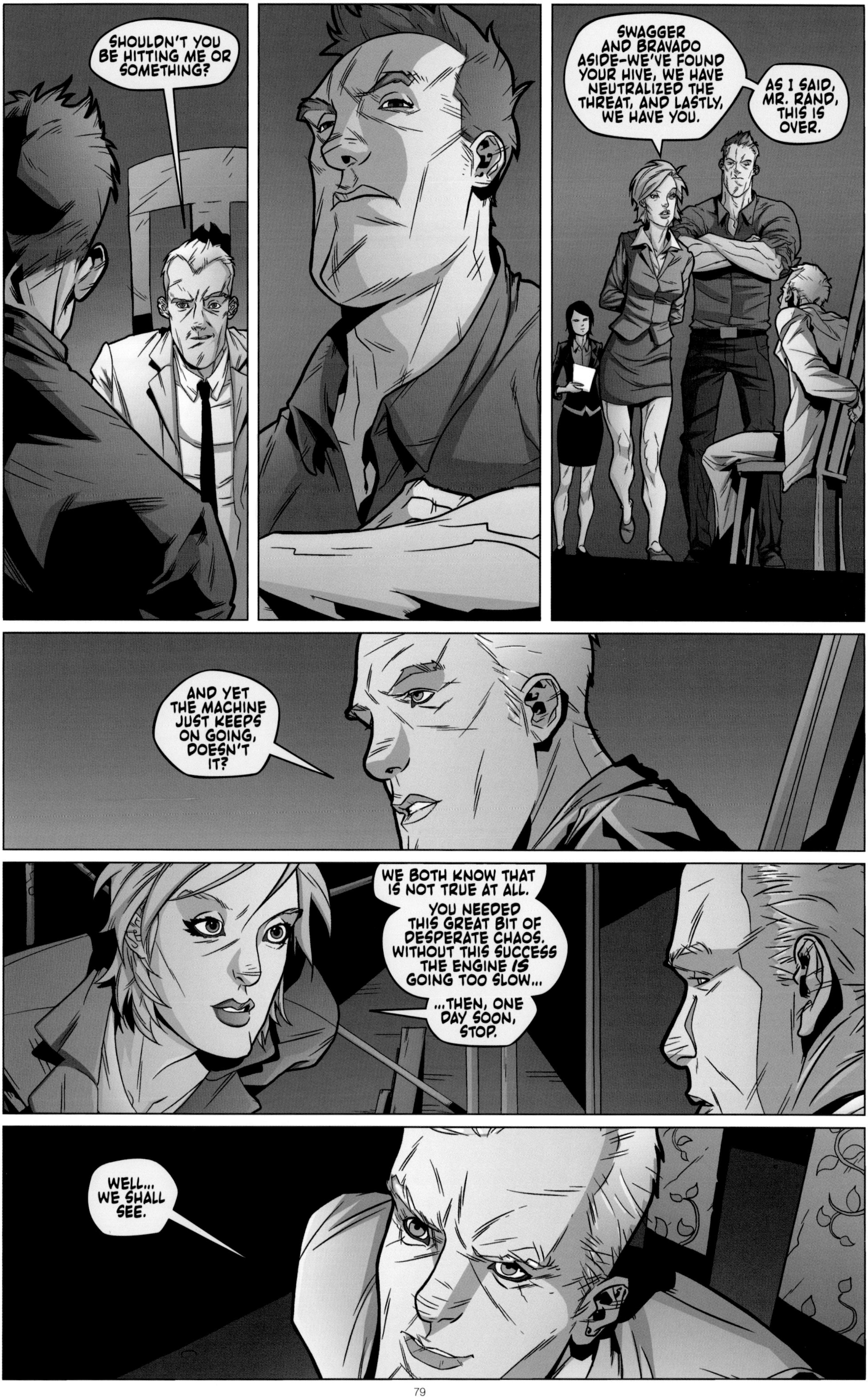
SHOULDN'T YOU BE HITTING ME OR SOMETHING?
SWAGGER AND BRAVADO ASIDE--WE'VE FOUND YOUR HIVE, WE HAVE NEUTRALIZED THE THREAT, AND LASTLY, WE HAVE YOU.
AS I SAID, MR. RAND, THIS IS OVER.
AND YET THE MACHINE JUST KEEPS ON GOING, DOESN'T IT?
WE BOTH KNOW THAT IS NOT TRUE AT ALL.
YOU NEEDED THIS GREAT BIT OF DESPERATE CHAOS. WITHOUT THIS SUCCESS THE ENGINE *IS* GOING TOO SLOW...
...THEN, ONE DAY SOON, STOP.
WELL... WE SHALL SEE.

MS. WING, WHAT IS THE ETA ON THE RETRIEVAL TEAM?
THEY ARE FOUR MINUTES OUT, MA'AM.
ENJOY THE VIEW. YOU HAVE FOUR MINUTES AND THEN WE ARE GOING TO THROW YOU INTO A HOLE SO DEEP, YOU WILL NEVER SEE SUNLIGHT AGAIN.
TELL THE RETRIEVAL TEAM WE WILL MEET THEM AT THE SOUTH ENTRANCE.
YES, MA'AM.
I'M GOING TO HIT YOU... IN THE FACE... UNTIL YOU DIE.
CUNDIFF!

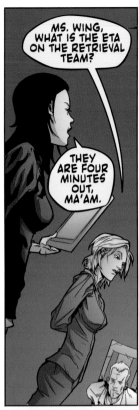

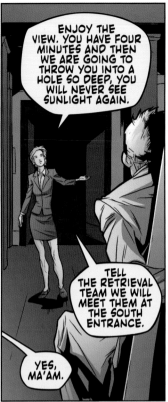

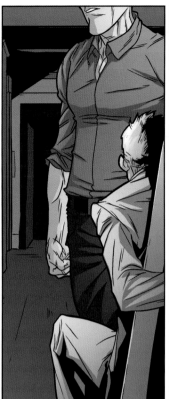

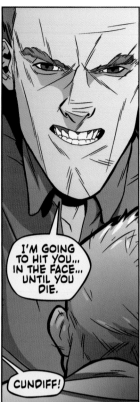

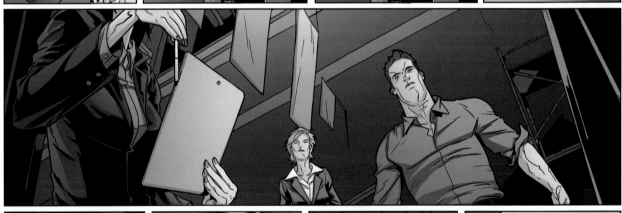

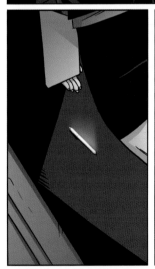

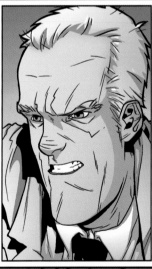

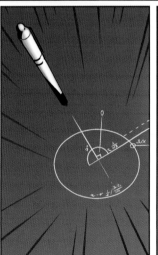

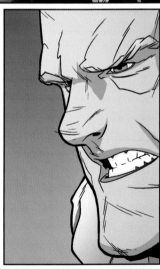

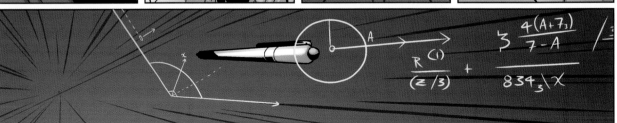

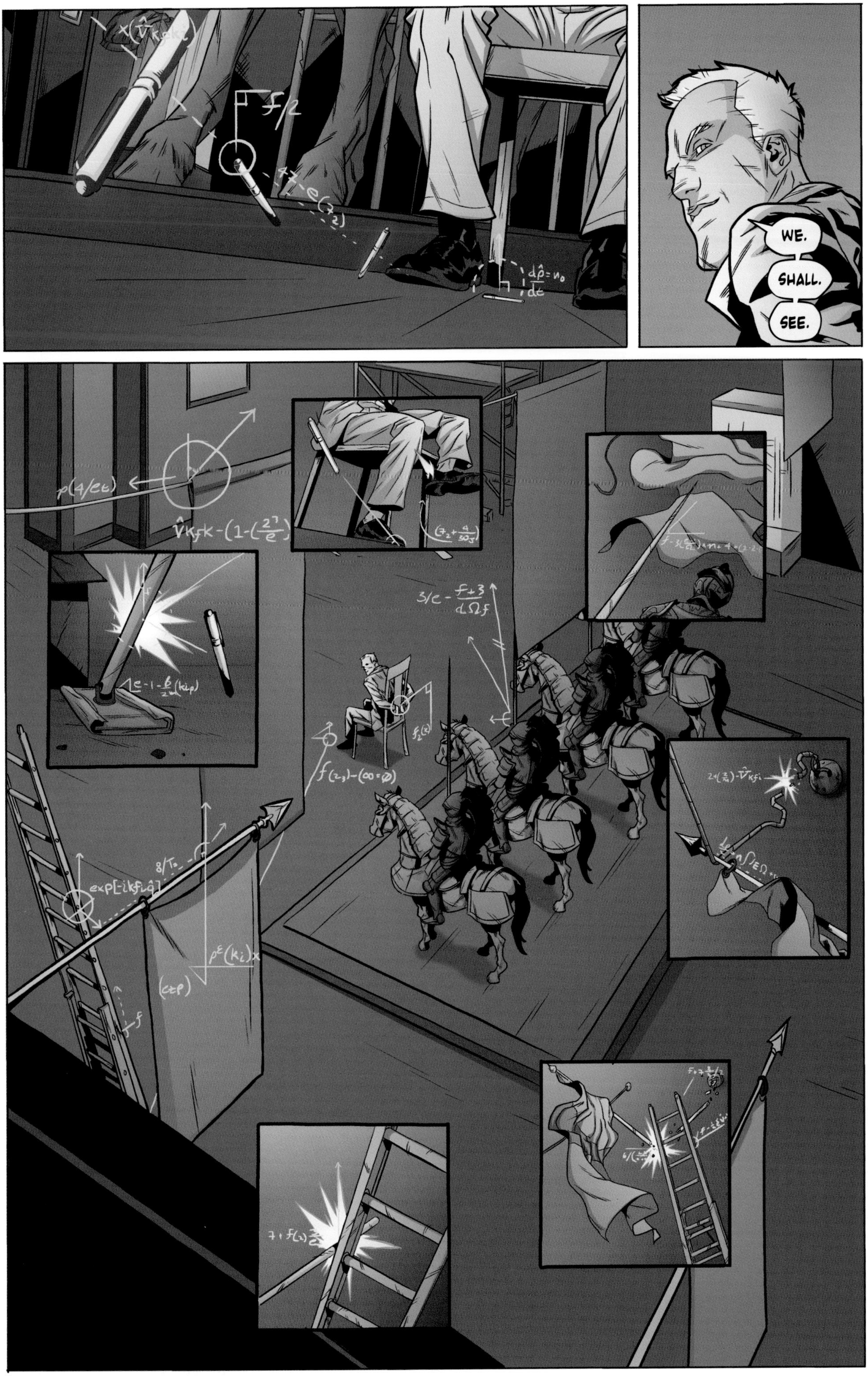
WE.
SHALL.
SEE.

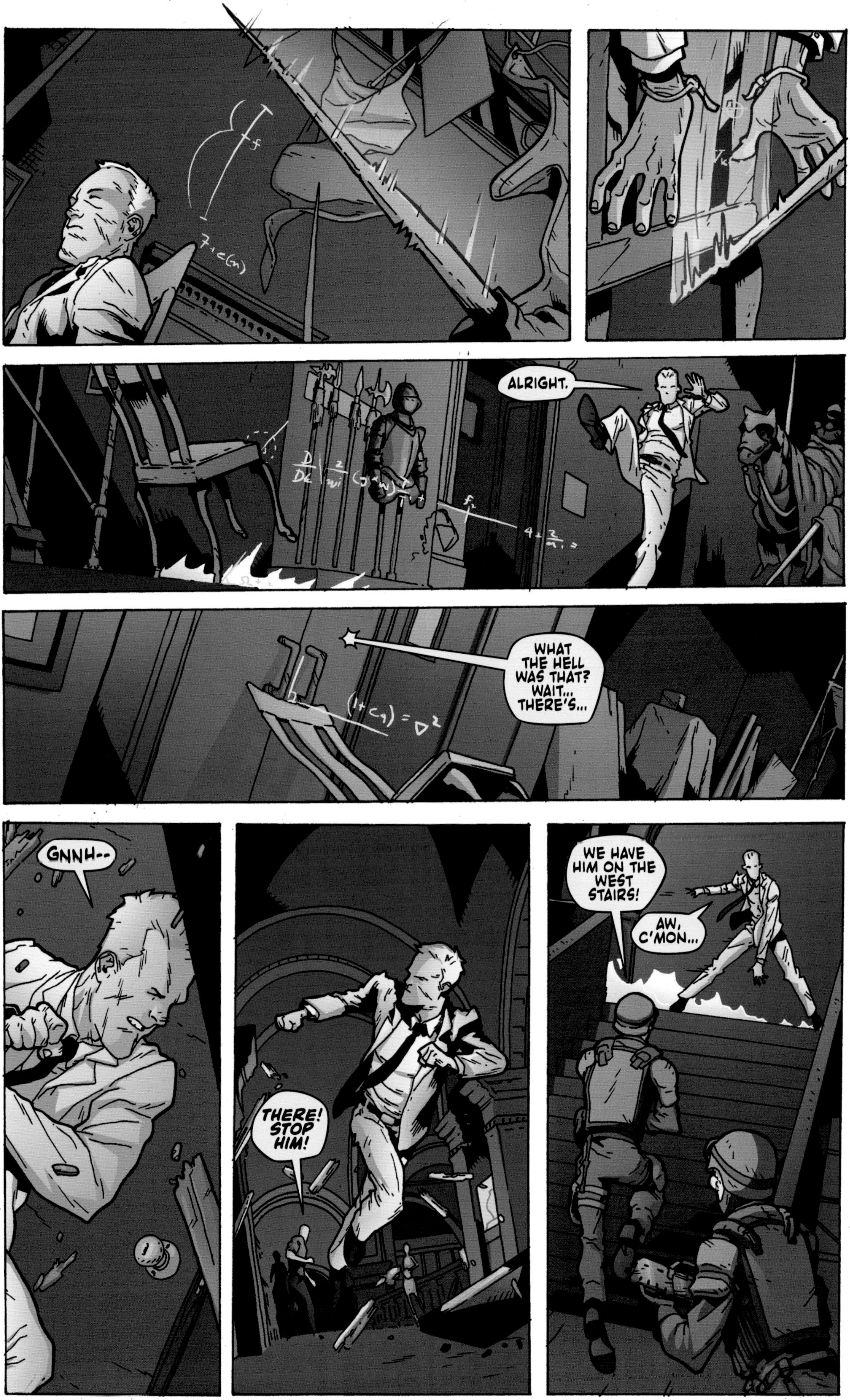
ALRIGHT.
WHAT THE HELL WAS THAT? WAIT... THERE'S...
GNNH--
THERE! STOP HIM!
WE HAVE HIM ON THE WEST STAIRS!
AW, C'MON...

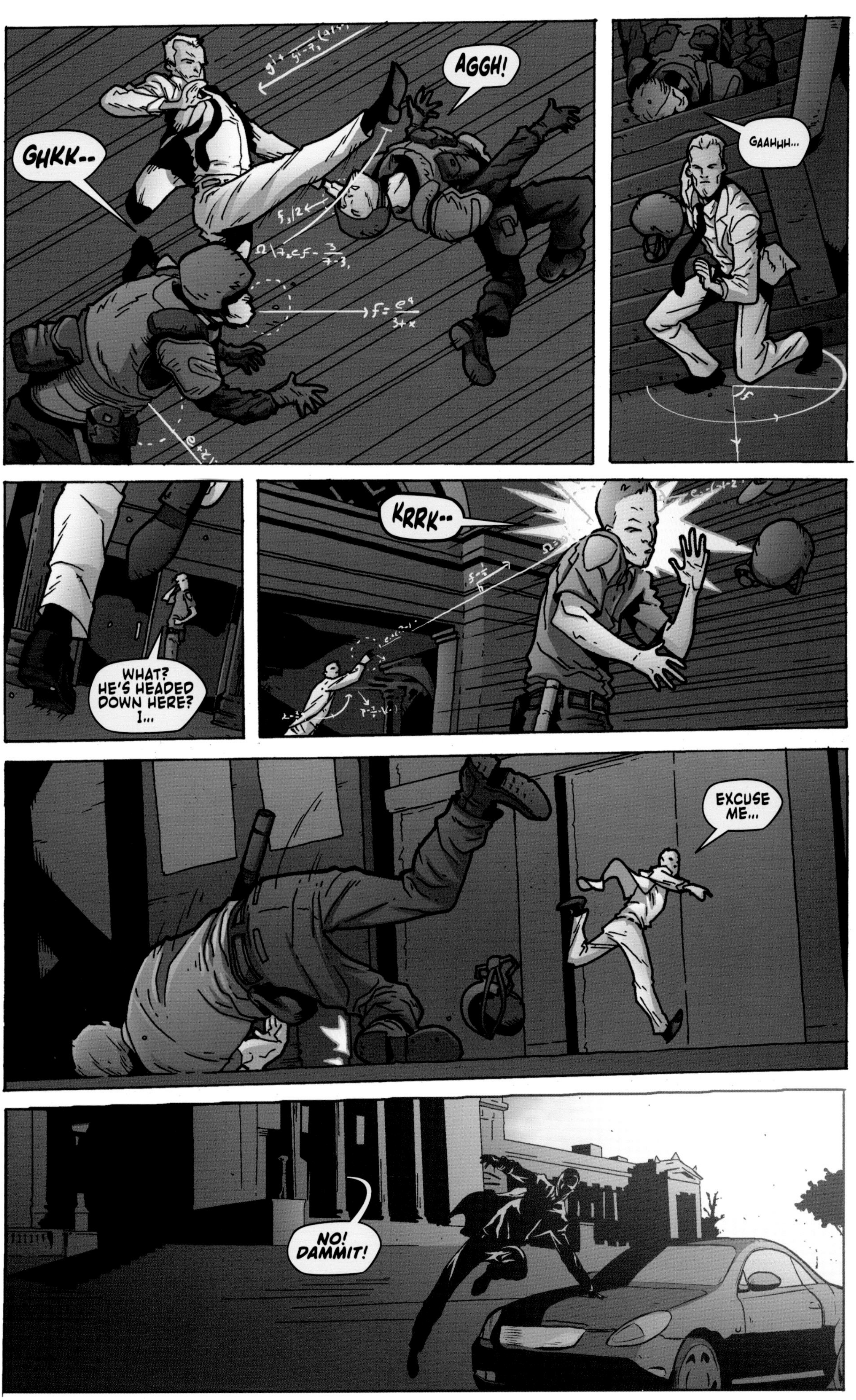
AGGH!
GHKK--
GAAHHH...
WHAT? HE'S HEADED DOWN HERE? I...
KRRK--
EXCUSE ME...
NO! DAMMIT!

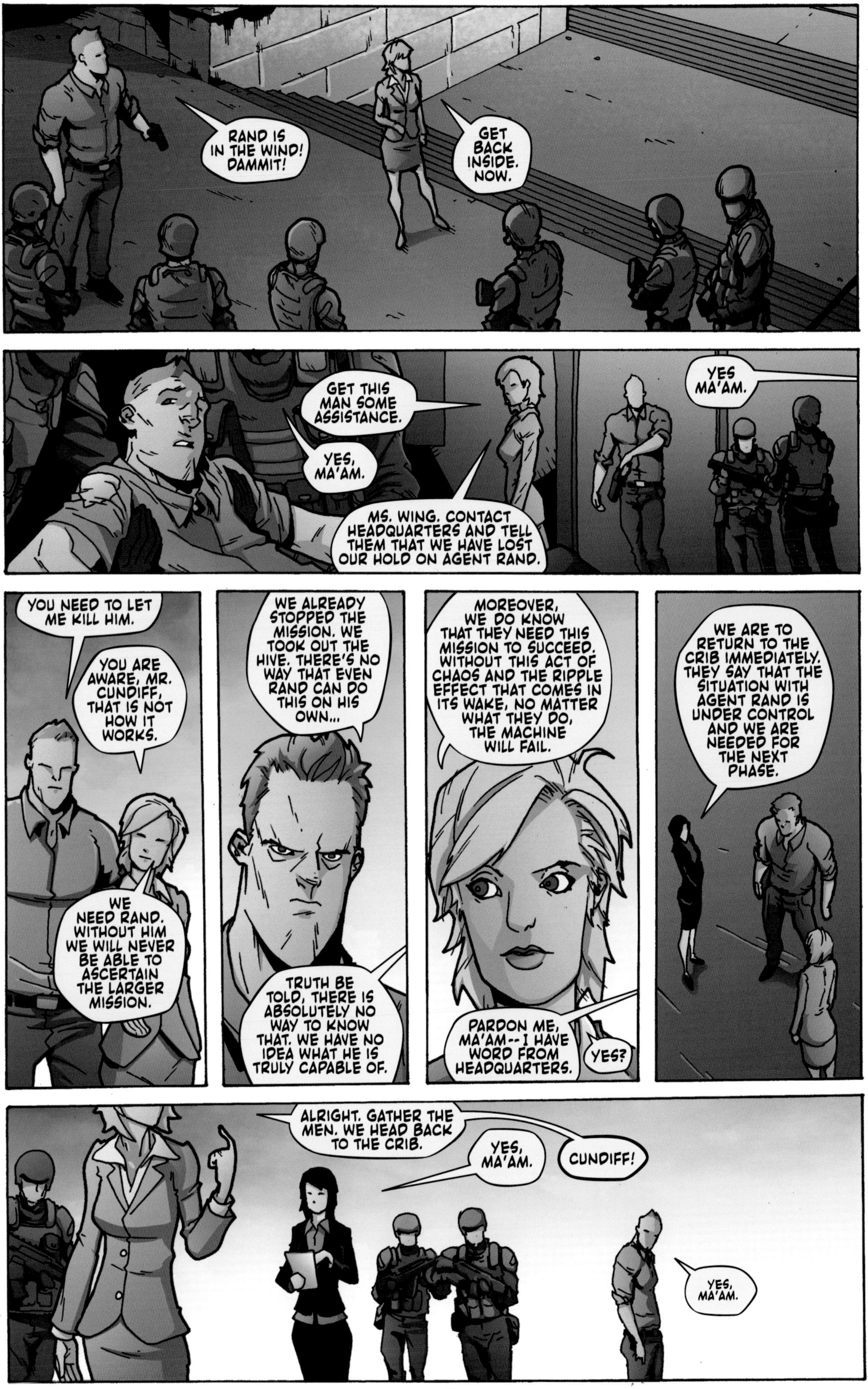
RAND IS IN THE WIND! DAMMIT!
GET BACK INSIDE. NOW.
GET THIS MAN SOME ASSISTANCE.
YES, MA'AM.
MS. WING. CONTACT HEADQUARTERS AND TELL THEM THAT WE HAVE LOST OUR HOLD ON AGENT RAND.
YES MA'AM.
YOU NEED TO LET ME KILL HIM.
YOU ARE AWARE, MR. CUNDIFF, THAT IS NOT HOW IT WORKS.
WE NEED RAND. WITHOUT HIM WE WILL NEVER BE ABLE TO ASCERTAIN THE LARGER MISSION.
WE ALREADY STOPPED THE MISSION. WE TOOK OUT THE HIVE. THERE'S NO WAY THAT EVEN RAND CAN DO THIS ON HIS OWN...
TRUTH BE TOLD, THERE IS ABSOLUTELY NO WAY TO KNOW THAT. WE HAVE NO IDEA WHAT HE IS TRULY CAPABLE OF.
MOREOVER, WE DO KNOW THAT THEY NEED THIS MISSION TO SUCCEED. WITHOUT THIS ACT OF CHAOS AND THE RIPPLE EFFECT THAT COMES IN ITS WAKE, NO MATTER WHAT THEY DO, THE MACHINE WILL FAIL.
PARDON ME, MA'AM-- I HAVE WORD FROM HEADQUARTERS.
YES?
WE ARE TO RETURN TO THE CRIB IMMEDIATELY. THEY SAY THAT THE SITUATION WITH AGENT RAND IS UNDER CONTROL AND WE ARE NEEDED FOR THE NEXT PHASE.
ALRIGHT. GATHER THE MEN. WE HEAD BACK TO THE CRIB.
YES, MA'AM.
CUNDIFF!
YES, MA'AM.

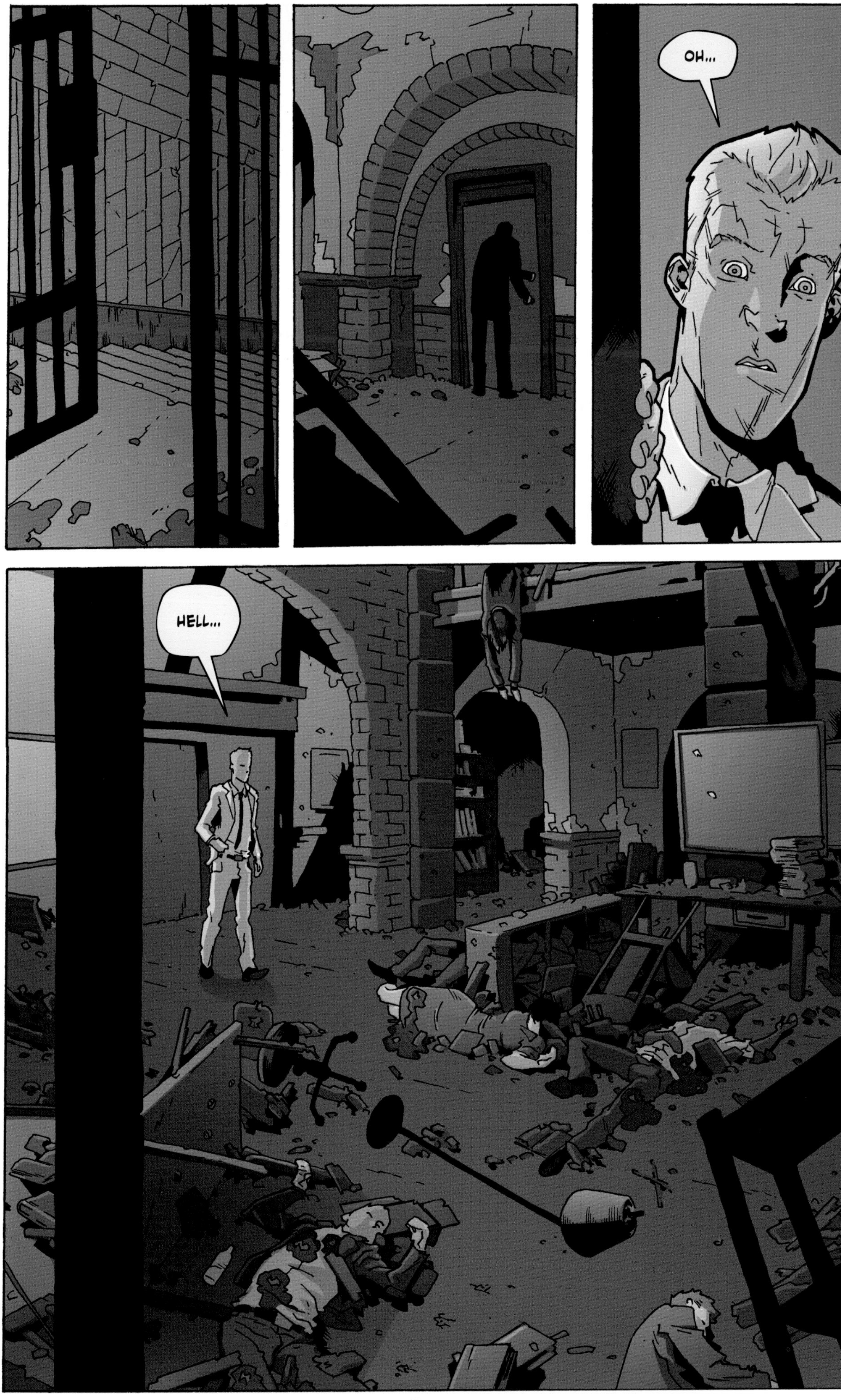
OH...
HELL...

...HEY... BUDDY...

DANTE--!

DON'T EVEN KNOW WHERE THEY CAME FROM, MAN...

ONE MINUTE WE'RE GEARING UP TO HEAD OUT... THEN...

KOF-KOF-

AW HELL... I'VE GOTTA PUT PRESSURE ON THIS...

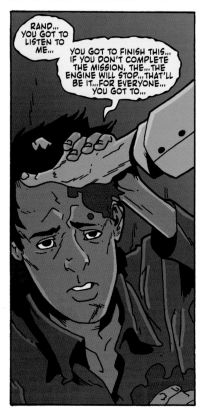

RAND... YOU GOT TO LISTEN TO ME...

YOU GOT TO FINISH THIS... IF YOU DON'T COMPLETE THE MISSION, THE...THE ENGINE WILL STOP...THAT'LL BE IT...FOR EVERYONE... YOU GOT TO...

YOU CAN DO THIS... YOU...

OKAY, BUDDY. OKAY...

I--

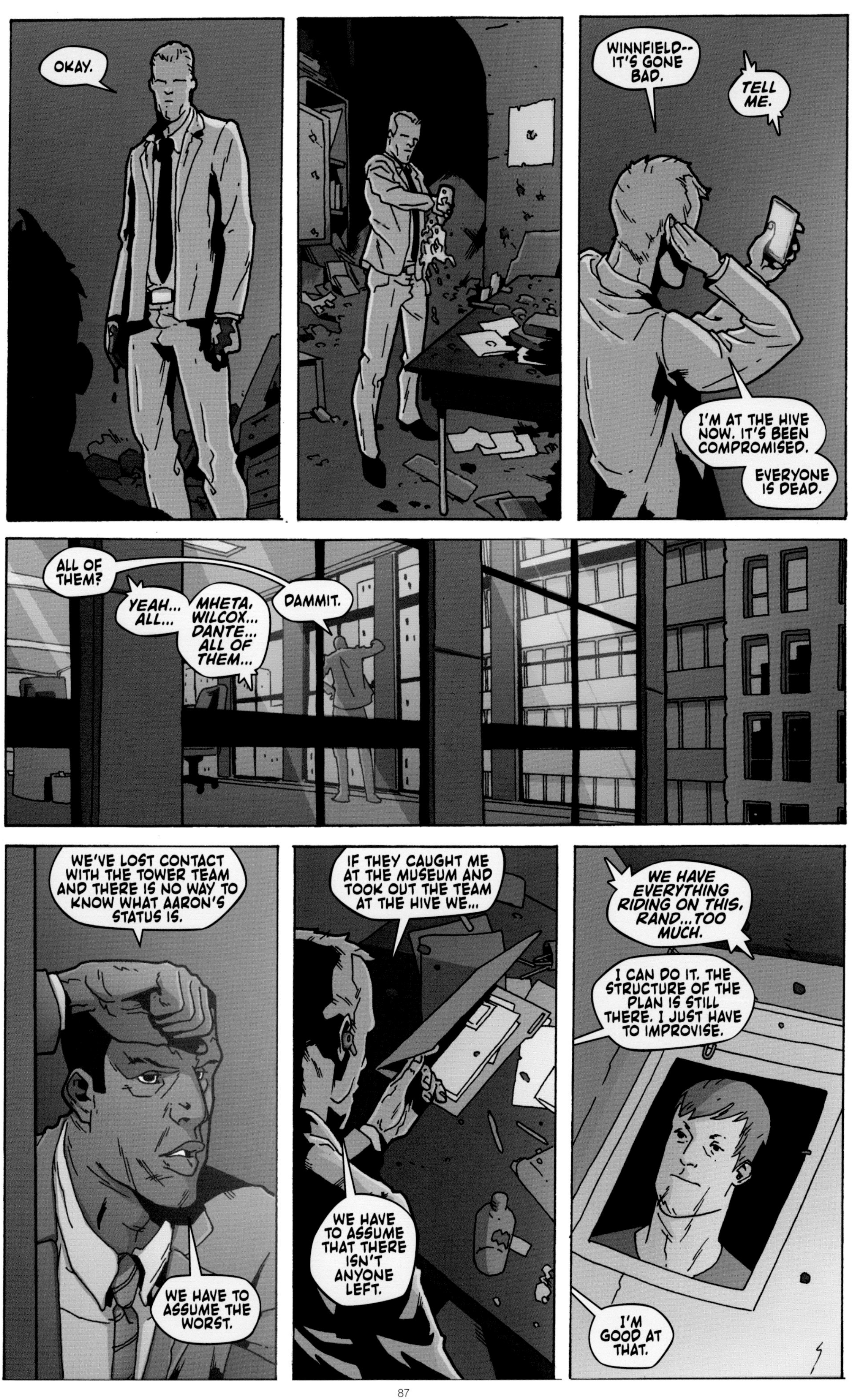
OKAY.
WINNFIELD-- IT'S GONE BAD.
TELL ME.
I'M AT THE HIVE NOW. IT'S BEEN COMPROMISED.
EVERYONE IS DEAD.
ALL OF THEM?
YEAH... ALL...
MHETA, WILCOX... DANTE... ALL OF THEM...
DAMMIT.
WE'VE LOST CONTACT WITH THE TOWER TEAM AND THERE IS NO WAY TO KNOW WHAT AARON'S STATUS IS.
WE HAVE TO ASSUME THE WORST.
IF THEY CAUGHT ME AT THE MUSEUM AND TOOK OUT THE TEAM AT THE HIVE WE...
WE HAVE TO ASSUME THAT THERE ISN'T ANYONE LEFT.
WE HAVE EVERYTHING RIDING ON THIS, RAND...TOO MUCH.
I CAN DO IT. THE STRUCTURE OF THE PLAN IS STILL THERE. I JUST HAVE TO IMPROVISE.
I'M GOOD AT THAT.

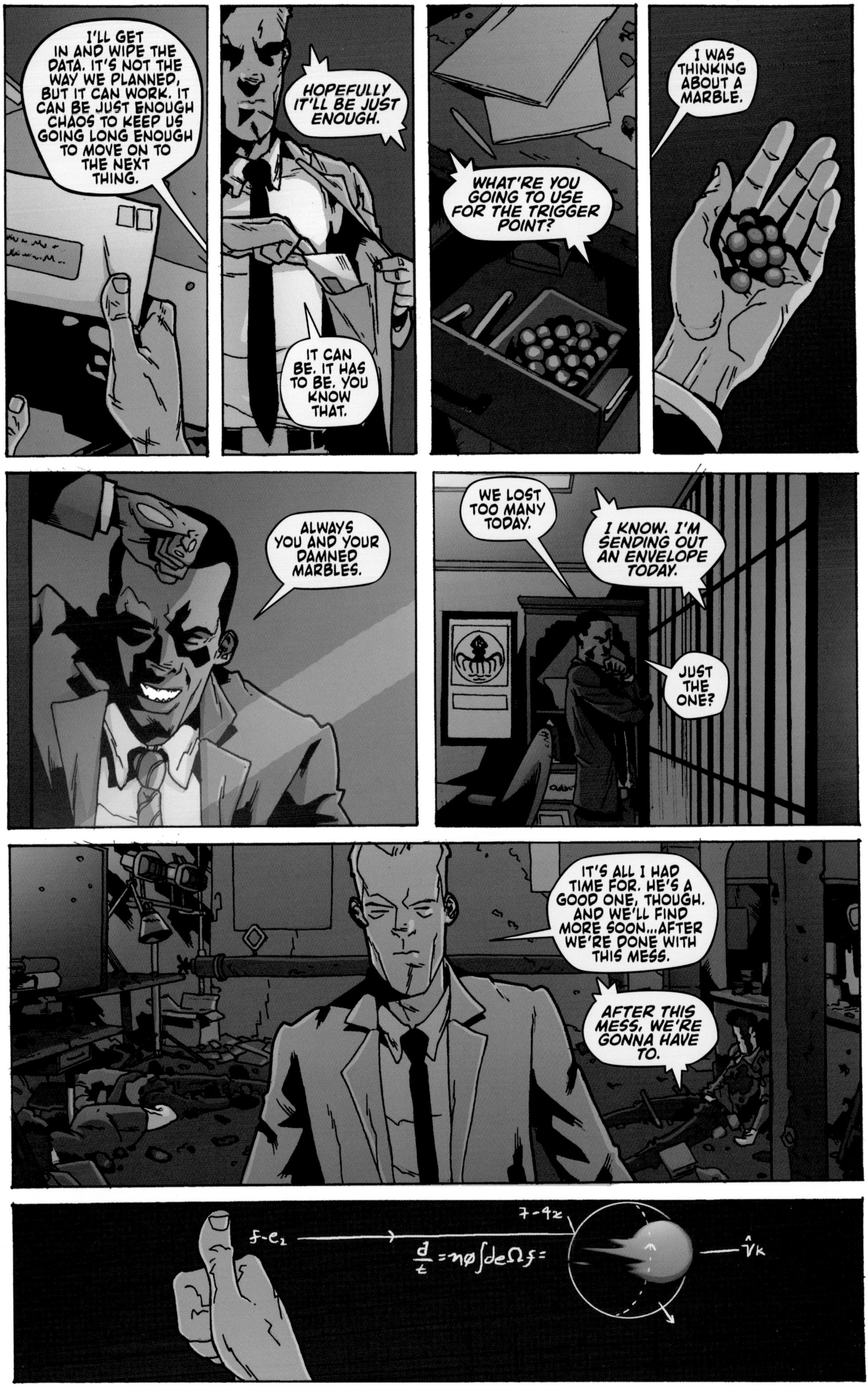
I'LL GET IN AND WIPE THE DATA. IT'S NOT THE WAY WE PLANNED, BUT IT CAN WORK. IT CAN BE JUST ENOUGH CHAOS TO KEEP US GOING LONG ENOUGH TO MOVE ON TO THE NEXT THING.
HOPEFULLY IT'LL BE JUST ENOUGH.
IT CAN BE. IT HAS TO BE. YOU KNOW THAT.
WHAT'RE YOU GOING TO USE FOR THE TRIGGER POINT?
I WAS THINKING ABOUT A MARBLE.
ALWAYS YOU AND YOUR DAMNED MARBLES.
WE LOST TOO MANY TODAY.
I KNOW. I'M SENDING OUT AN ENVELOPE TODAY.
JUST THE ONE?
IT'S ALL I HAD TIME FOR. HE'S A GOOD ONE, THOUGH. AND WE'LL FIND MORE SOON...AFTER WE'RE DONE WITH THIS MESS.
AFTER THIS MESS, WE'RE GONNA HAVE TO.

CRASH

FWOOSH

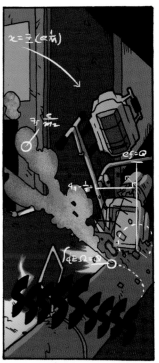

THE HIVE IS CLEAR.

GOOD...

RAND, I'M SORRY IT WENT DOWN LIKE THIS. I--

YEAH...

I'LL SEE YOU WHEN IT'S DONE.

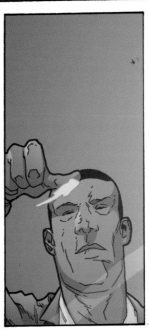

WELL, HERE WE GO.

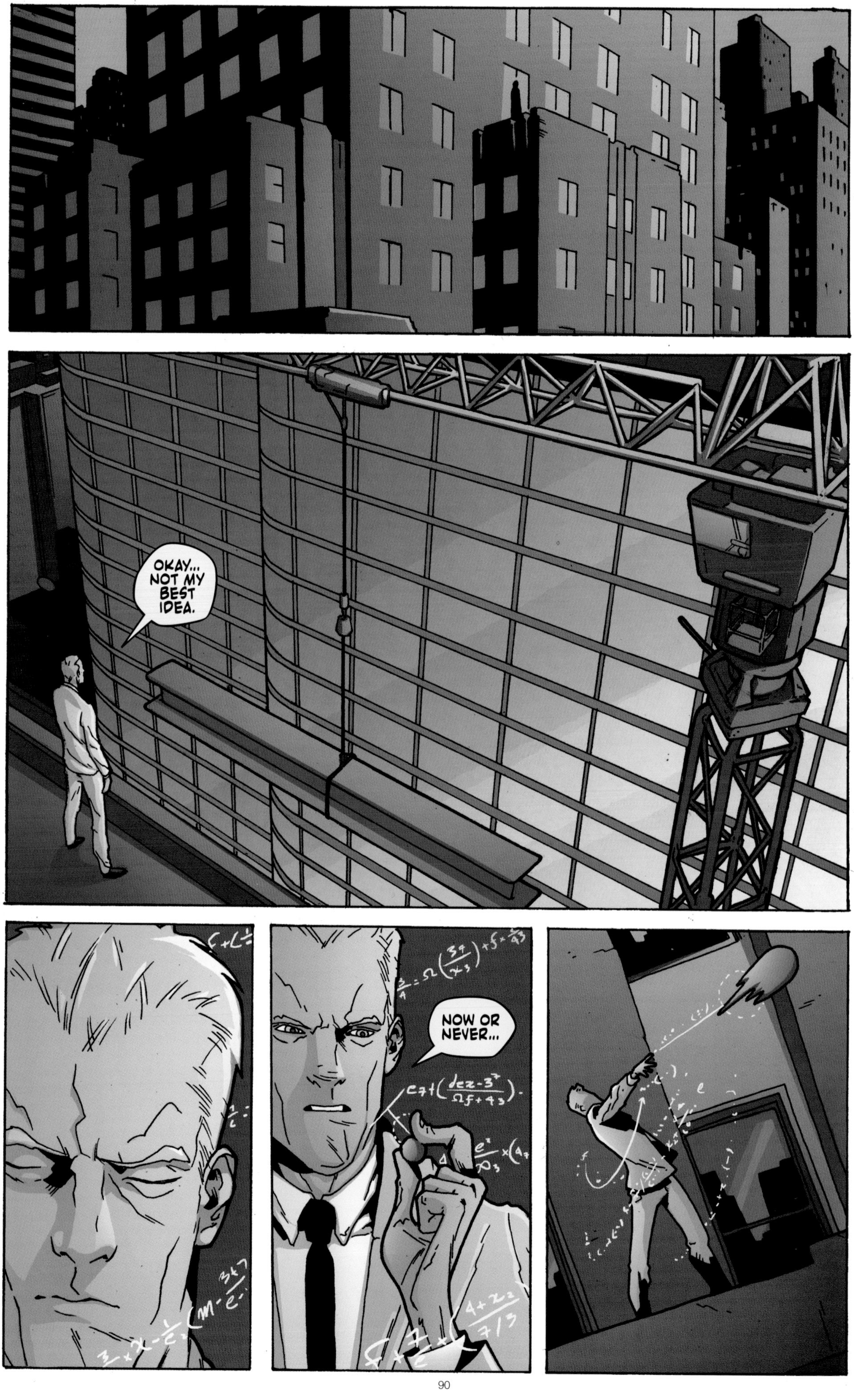
OKAY... NOT MY BEST IDEA.
NOW OR NEVER...

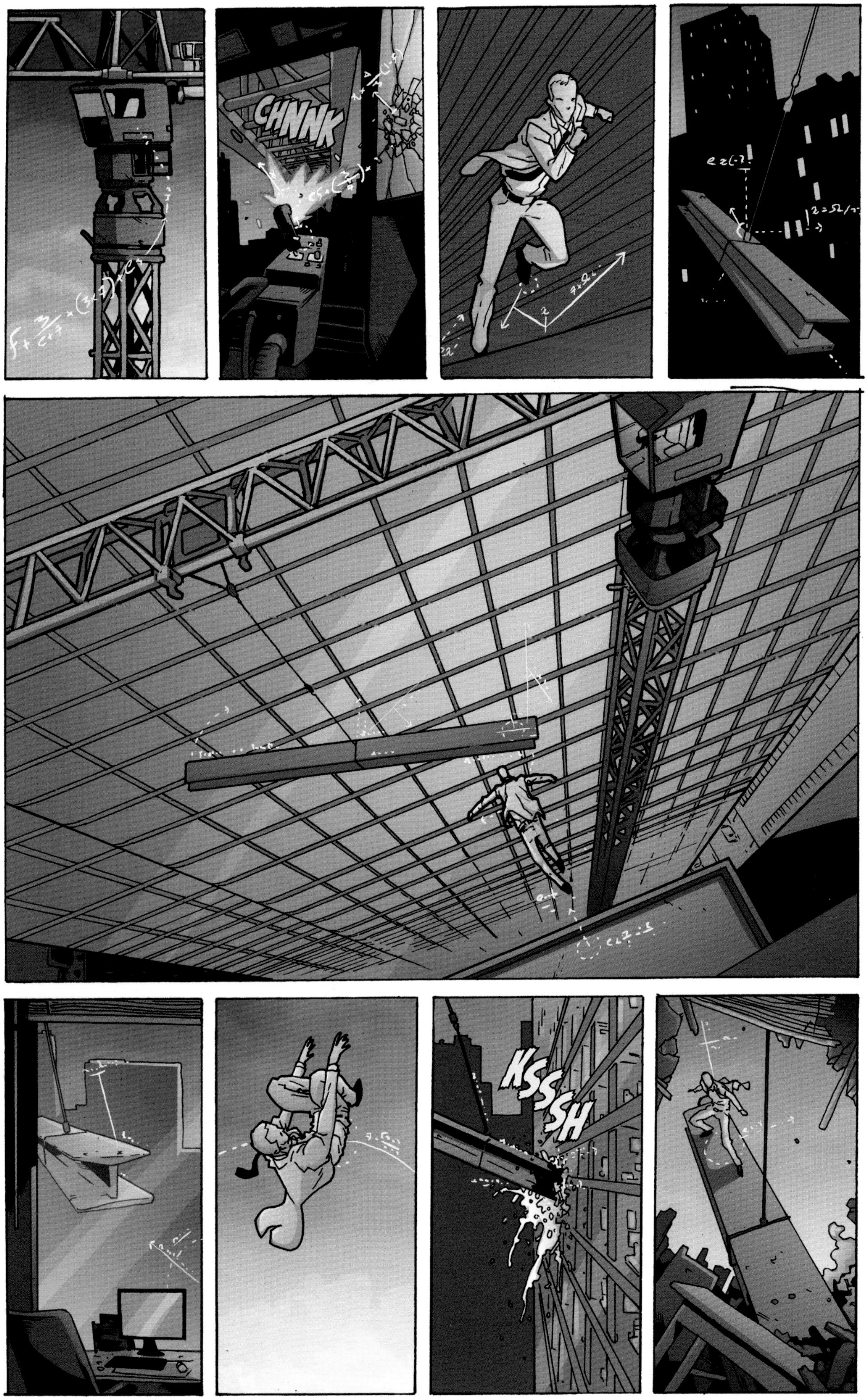
CHNNK
KSSSH

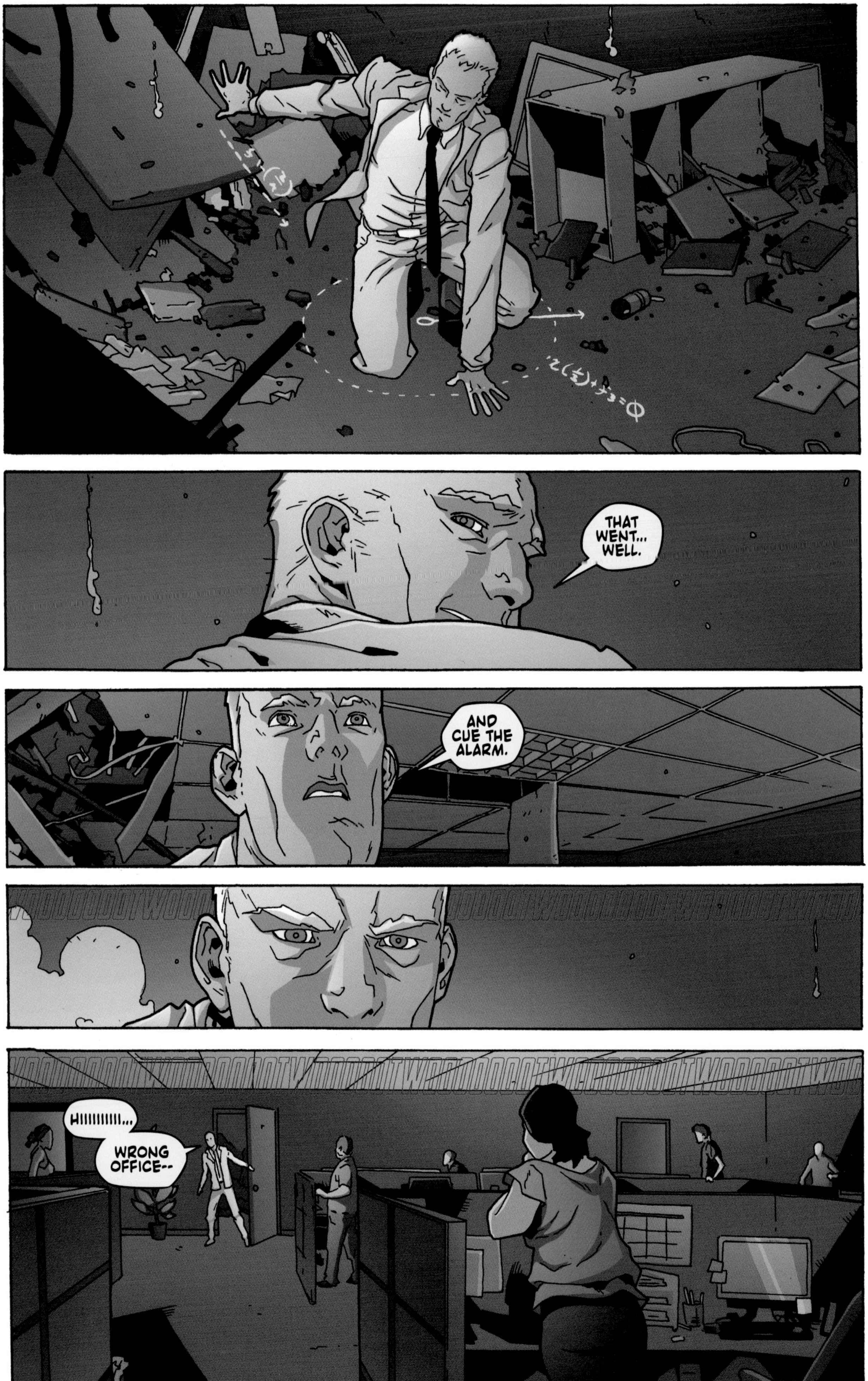
THAT WENT... WELL.
AND CUE THE ALARM.
HIIIIIIIII...
WRONG OFFICE--

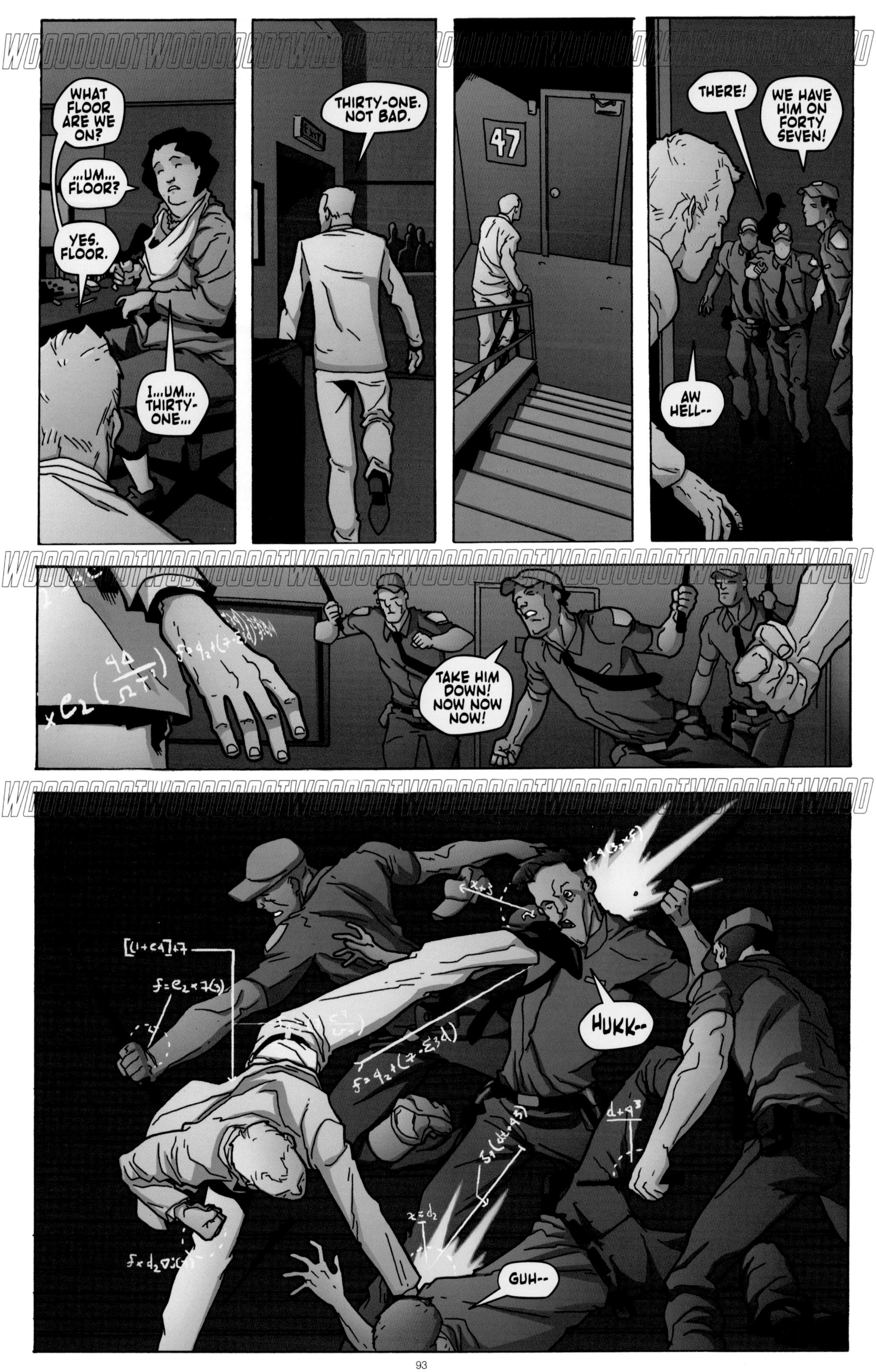
WHAT FLOOR ARE WE ON?
...UM... FLOOR?
YES. FLOOR.
I...UM... THIRTY-ONE...
THIRTY-ONE. NOT BAD.
47
THERE!
WE HAVE HIM ON FORTY SEVEN!
AW HELL--
TAKE HIM DOWN! NOW NOW NOW!
HUKK--
GUH--

AAAGH!

RRAAH!

HHUH--

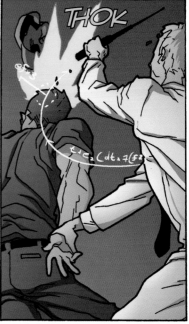

THOK

HUKK-HUKK--

SORRY, GUYS.

DING

↑47

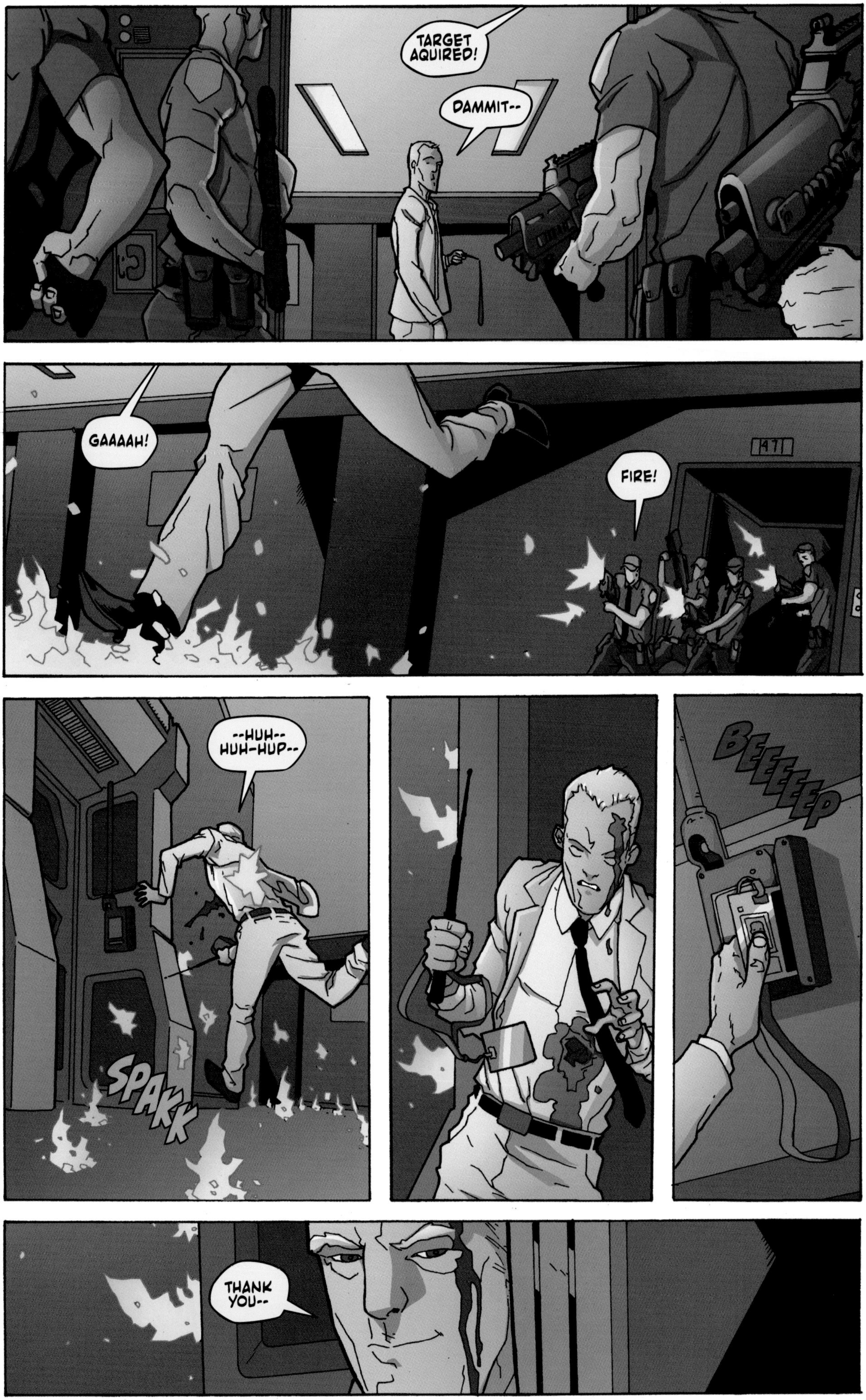
TARGET AQUIRED!
DAMMIT--
GAAAAH!
FIRE!
--HUH-- HUH-HUP--
SPAKK
BEEEEEP
THANK YOU--

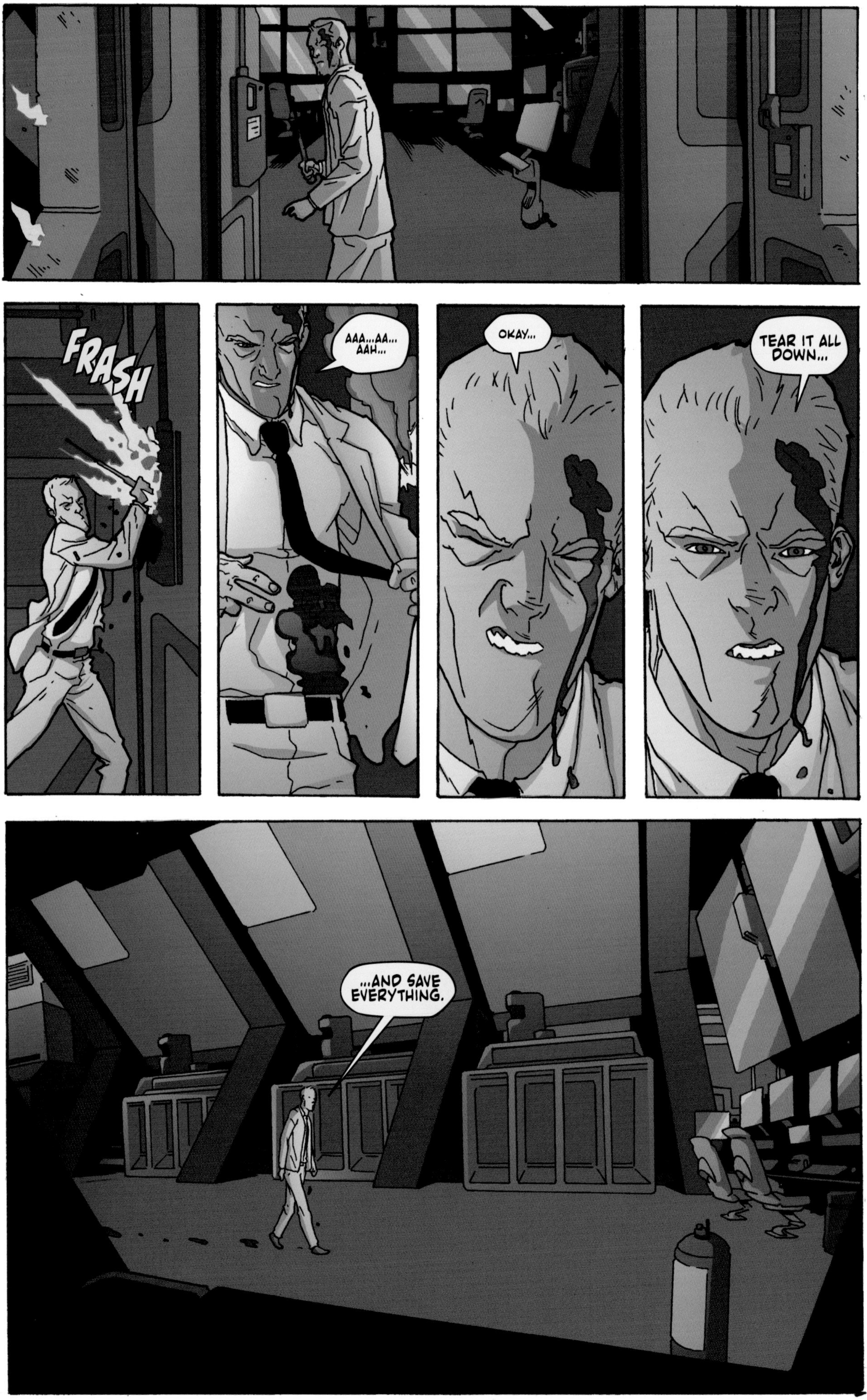
FRASH
AAA...AA... AAH...
OKAY...
TEAR IT ALL DOWN...
...AND SAVE EVERYTHING.

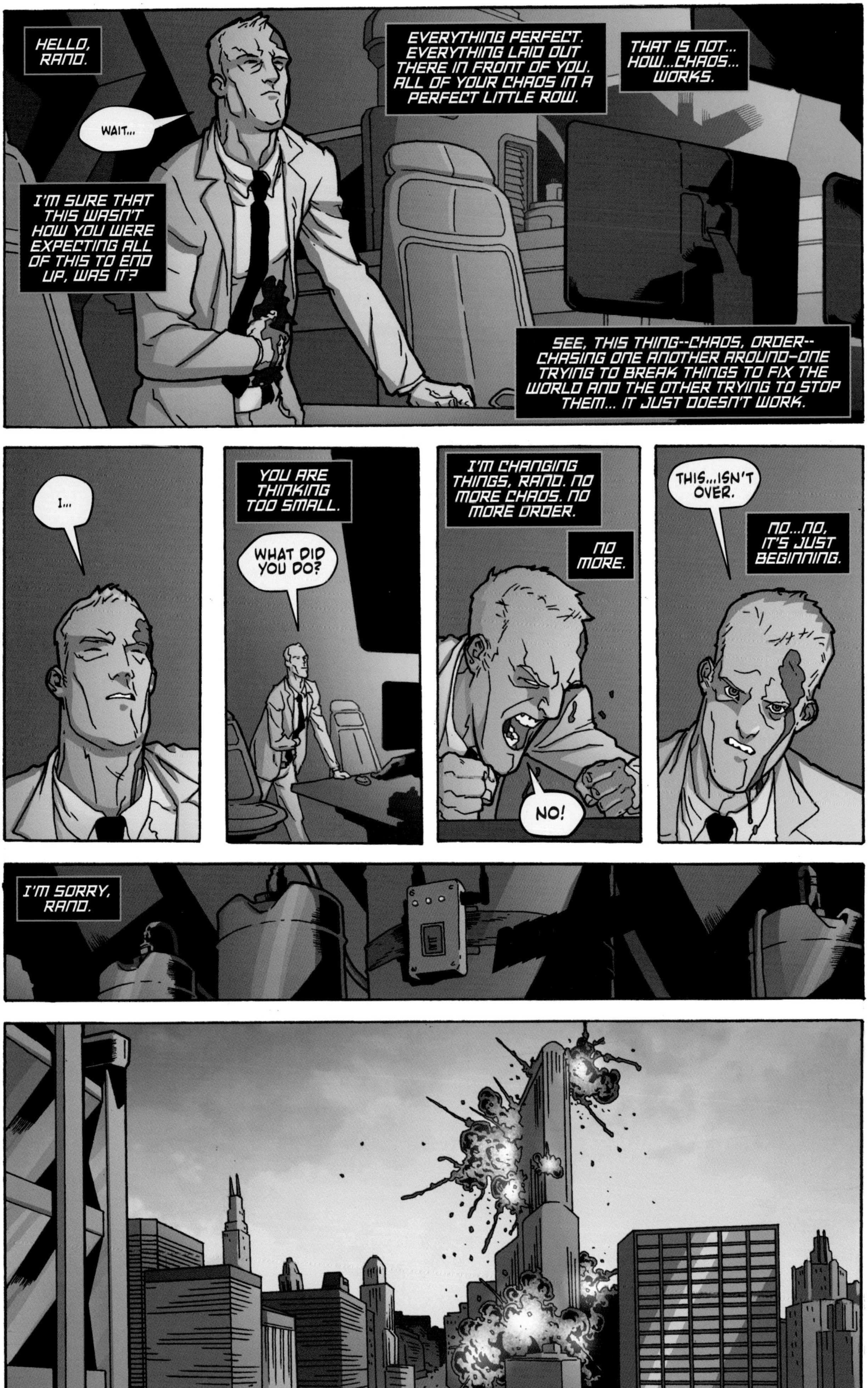
HELLO, RAND.
WAIT...
I'M SURE THAT THIS WASN'T HOW YOU WERE EXPECTING ALL OF THIS TO END UP, WAS IT?
EVERYTHING PERFECT. EVERYTHING LAID OUT THERE IN FRONT OF YOU. ALL OF YOUR CHAOS IN A PERFECT LITTLE ROW.
THAT IS NOT... HOW...CHAOS... WORKS.
SEE, THIS THING--CHAOS, ORDER--CHASING ONE ANOTHER AROUND--ONE TRYING TO BREAK THINGS TO FIX THE WORLD AND THE OTHER TRYING TO STOP THEM... IT JUST DOESN'T WORK.
I...
YOU ARE THINKING TOO SMALL.
WHAT DID YOU DO?
I'M CHANGING THINGS, RAND. NO MORE CHAOS. NO MORE ORDER.
NO MORE.
NO!
THIS...ISN'T OVER.
NO...NO, IT'S JUST BEGINNING.
I'M SORRY, RAND.

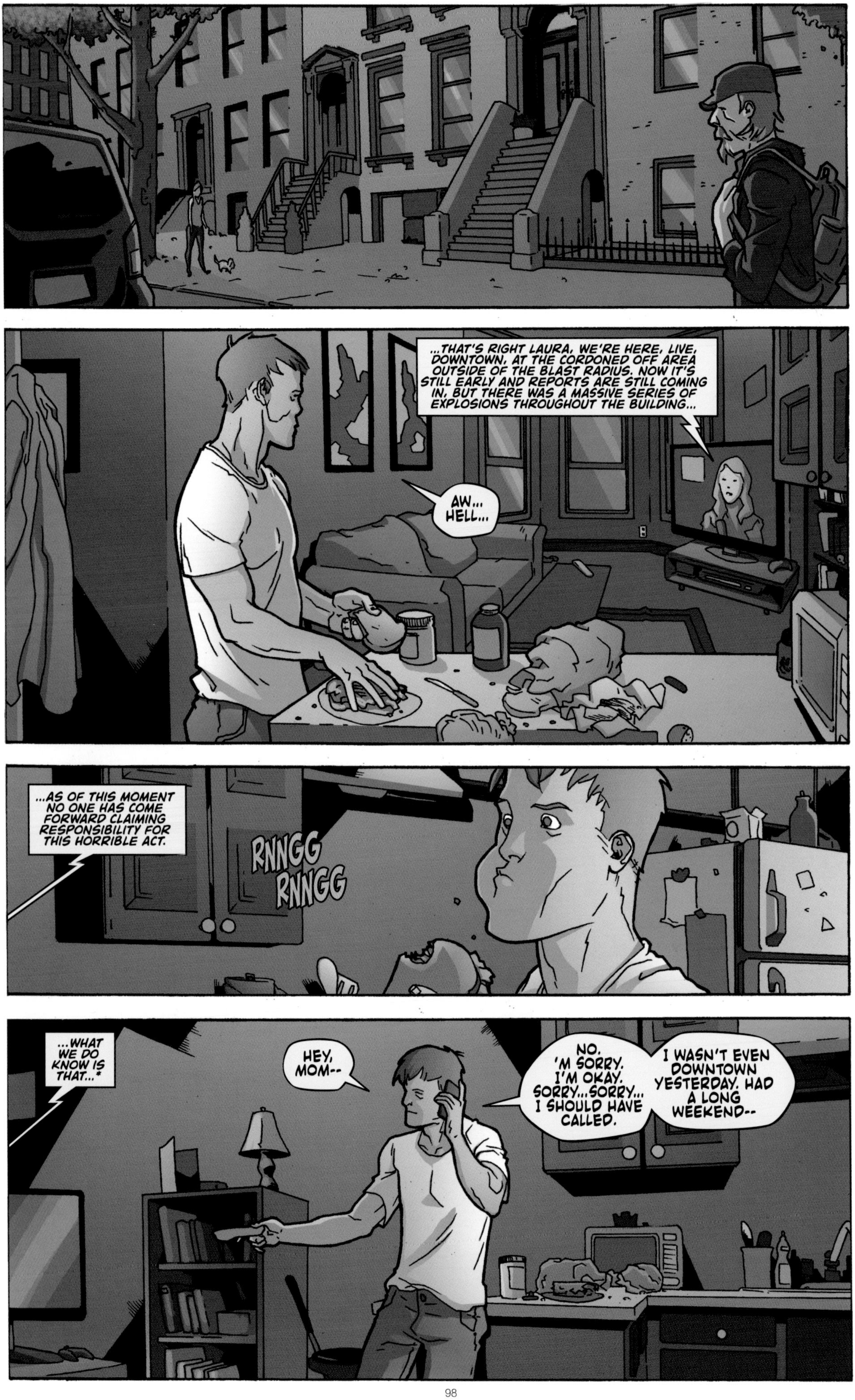
...THAT'S RIGHT LAURA, WE'RE HERE, LIVE, DOWNTOWN, AT THE CORDONED OFF AREA OUTSIDE OF THE BLAST RADIUS. NOW IT'S STILL EARLY AND REPORTS ARE STILL COMING IN, BUT THERE WAS A MASSIVE SERIES OF EXPLOSIONS THROUGHOUT THE BUILDING...
AW... HELL...
...AS OF THIS MOMENT NO ONE HAS COME FORWARD CLAIMING RESPONSIBILITY FOR THIS HORRIBLE ACT.
RNNGG RNNGG
...WHAT WE DO KNOW IS THAT...*
HEY, MOM--
NO. 'M SORRY. I'M OKAY. SORRY...SORRY... I SHOULD HAVE CALLED.
I WASN'T EVEN DOWNTOWN YESTERDAY. HAD A LONG WEEKEND--

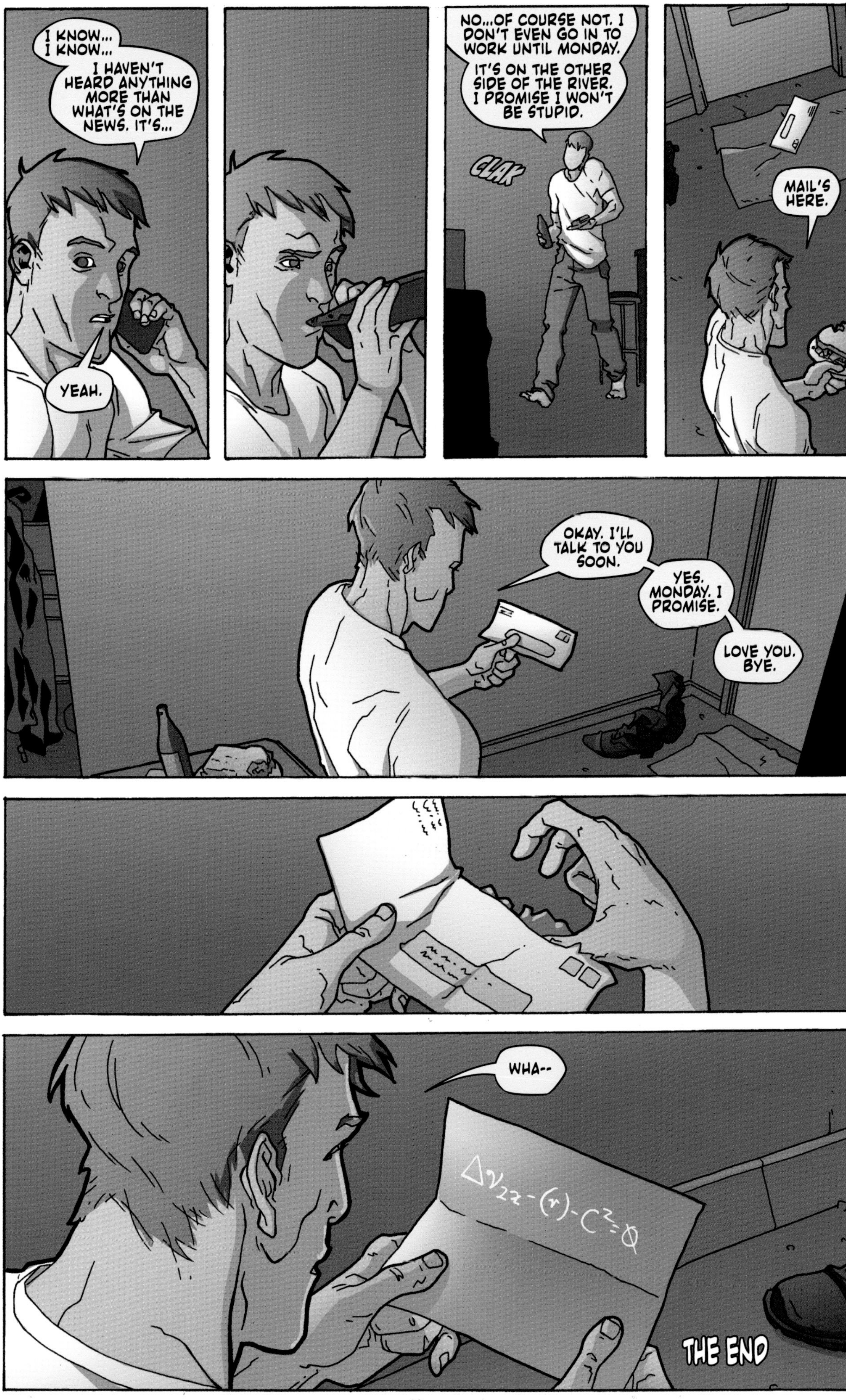
I KNOW... I KNOW... I HAVEN'T HEARD ANYTHING MORE THAN WHAT'S ON THE NEWS. IT'S...
YEAH.
NO...OF COURSE NOT. I DON'T EVEN GO IN TO WORK UNTIL MONDAY.
IT'S ON THE OTHER SIDE OF THE RIVER. I PROMISE I WON'T BE STUPID.
CLAK
MAIL'S HERE.
OKAY. I'LL TALK TO YOU SOON.
YES. MONDAY. I PROMISE.
LOVE YOU. BYE.
WHA--
THE END

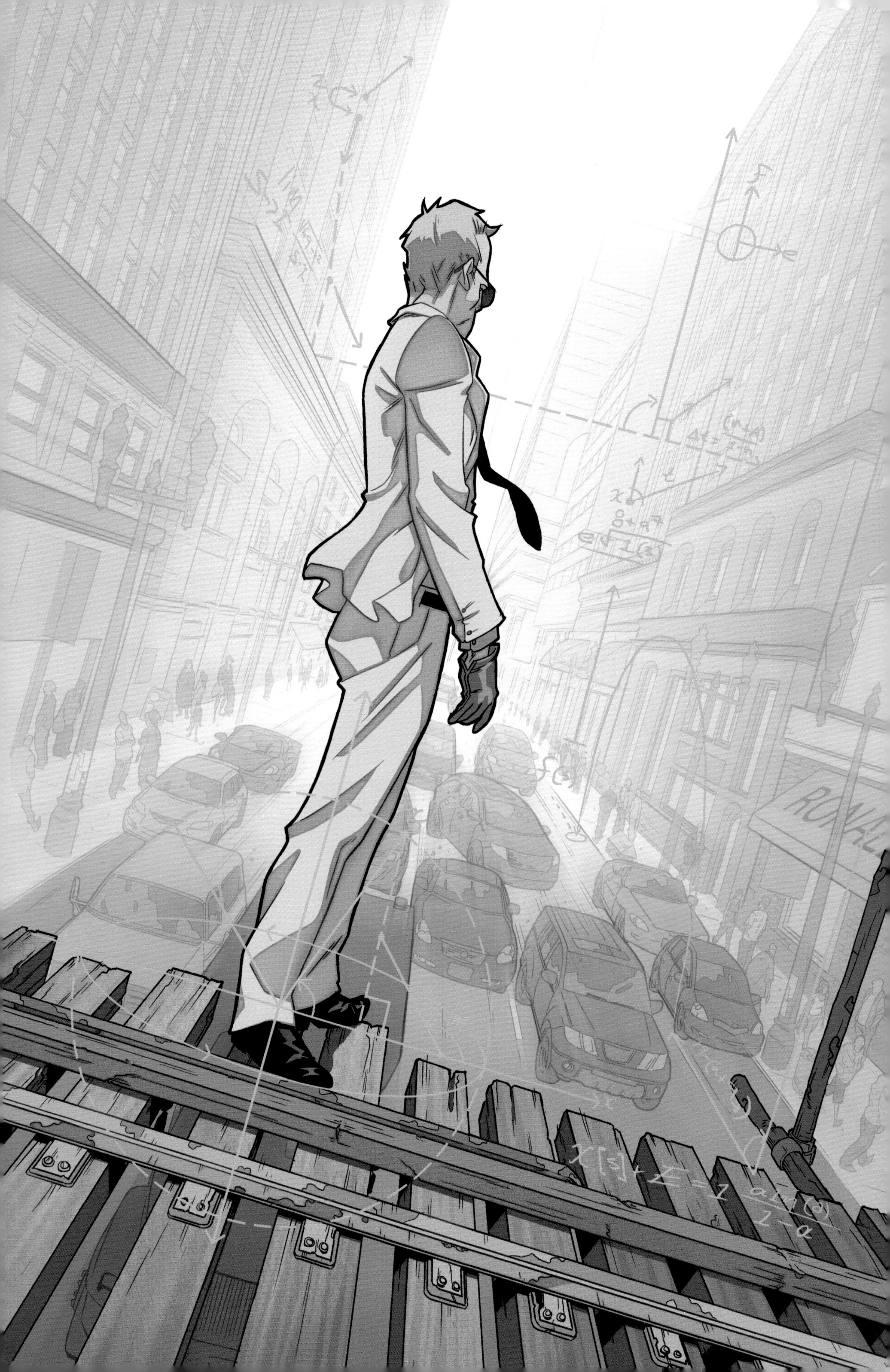

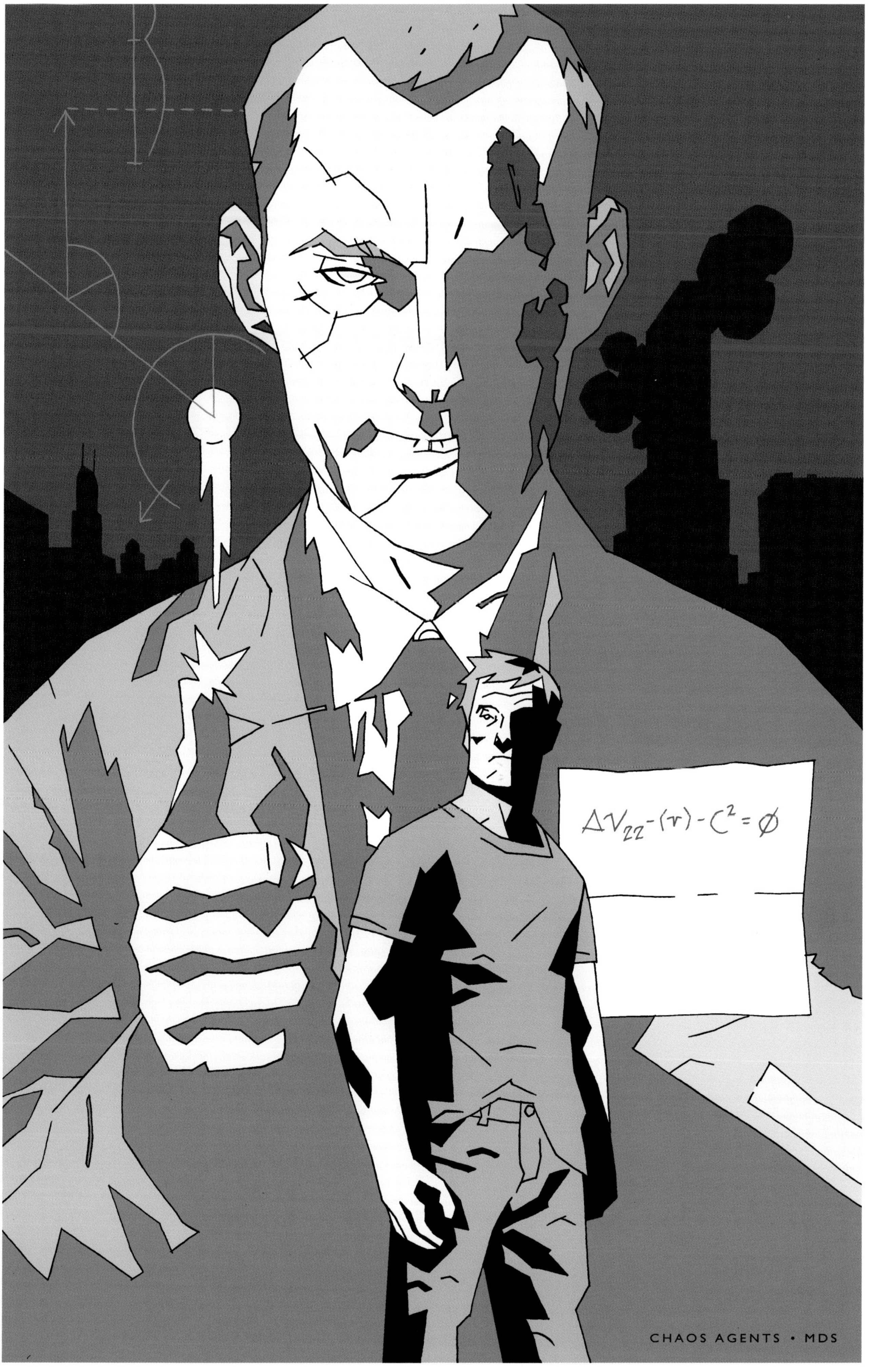
ΔV22-(r)-C² = ∅
CHAOS AGENTS • MDS

# HELLBENT
## A Stone's Throw From Hell

story   B. Clay Moore
art     Andrew R. MacLean
colors  Frank Zigarelli
letters Andrew R. MacLean

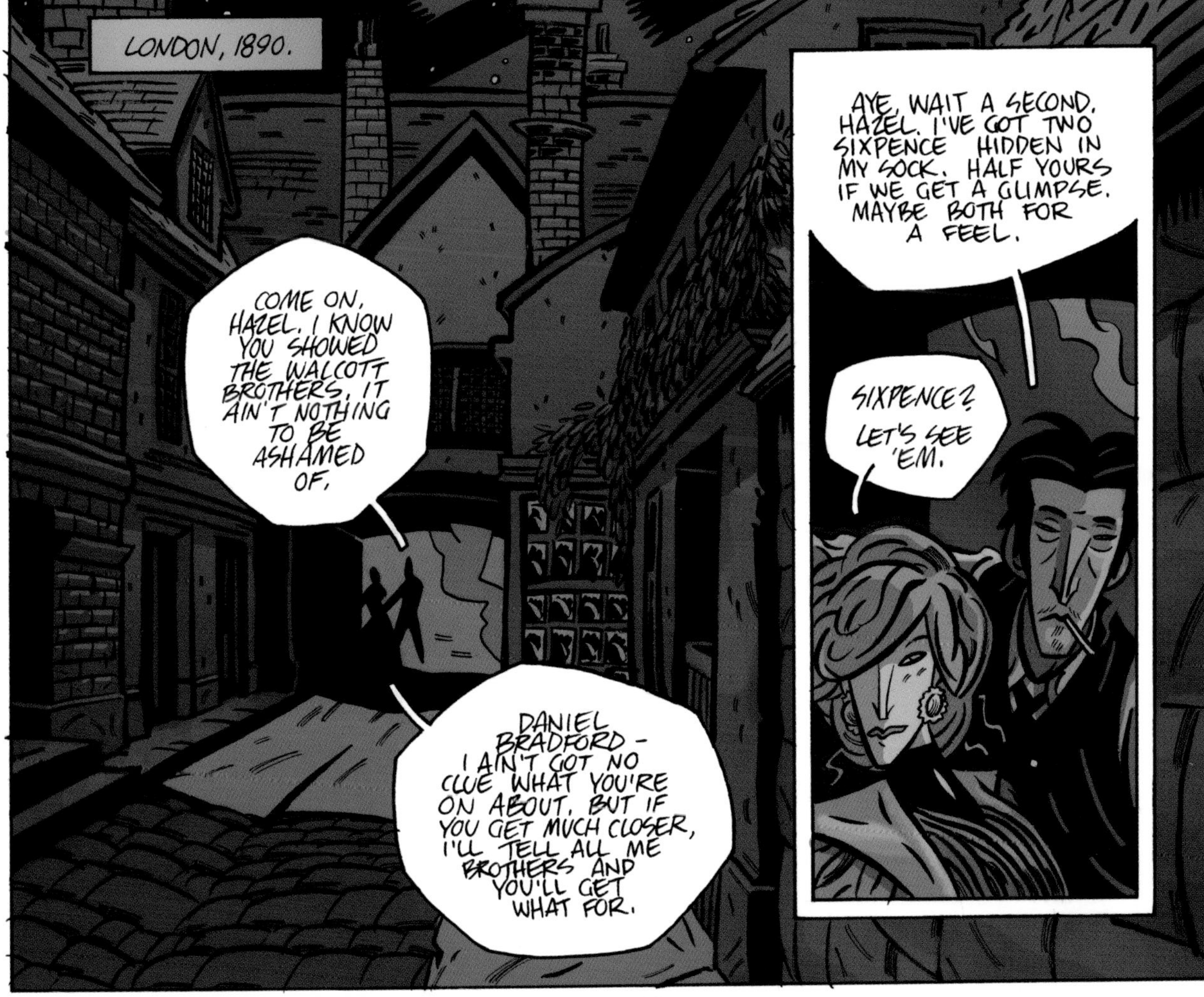
LONDON, 1890.
COME ON, HAZEL. I KNOW YOU SHOWED THE WALCOTT BROTHERS, IT AIN'T NOTHING TO BE ASHAMED OF.
DANIEL BRADFORD - I AIN'T GOT NO CLUE WHAT YOU'RE ON ABOUT, BUT IF YOU GET MUCH CLOSER, I'LL TELL ALL ME BROTHERS AND YOU'LL GET WHAT FOR.
AYE, WAIT A SECOND, HAZEL. I'VE GOT TWO SIXPENCE HIDDEN IN MY SOCK. HALF YOURS IF WE GET A GLIMPSE. MAYBE BOTH FOR A FEEL.
SIXPENCE? LET'S SEE 'EM.

# HELLBENT

"A STONE'S THROW FROM HELL"

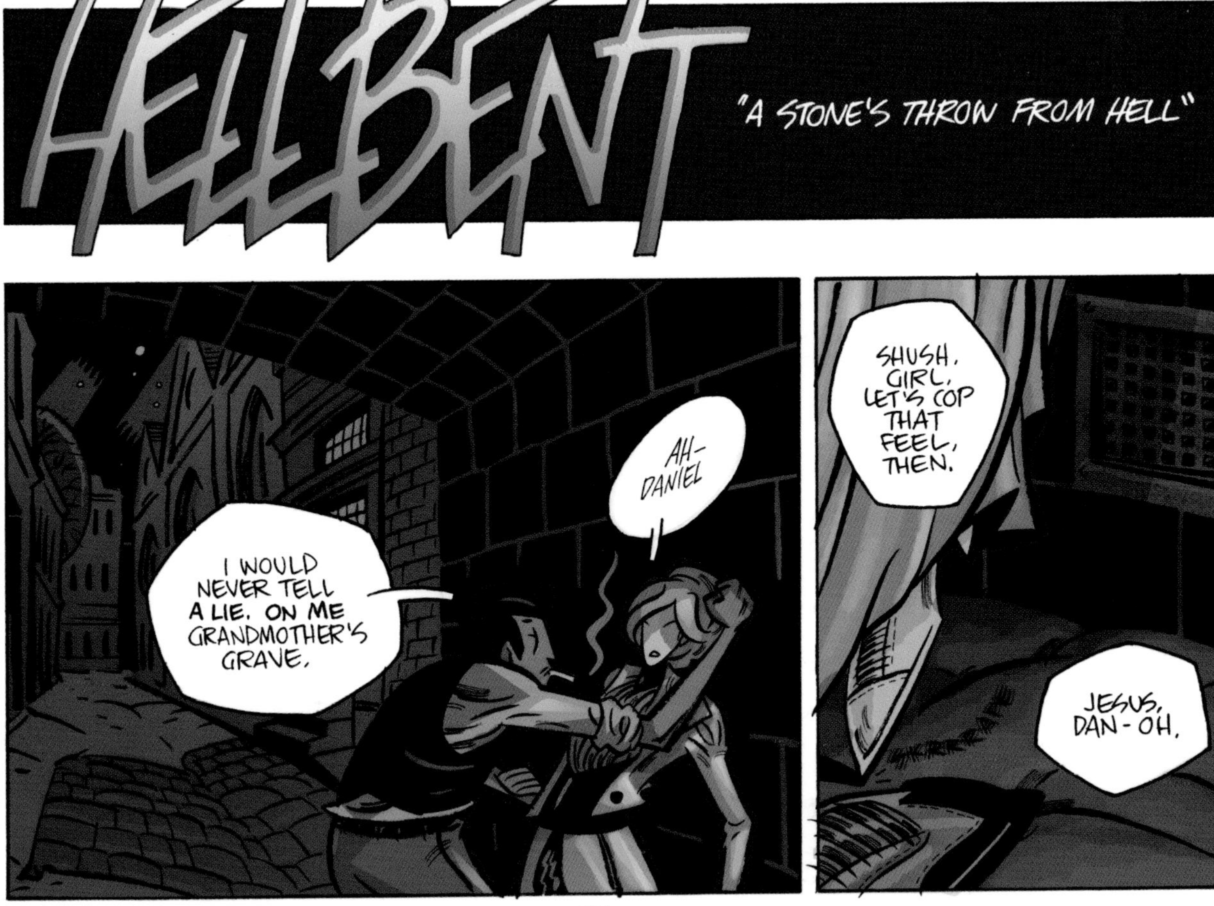
I WOULD NEVER TELL A LIE. ON ME GRANDMOTHER'S GRAVE.
AH-DANIEL
SHUSH, GIRL, LET'S COP THAT FEEL, THEN.
JESUS, DAN-OH.

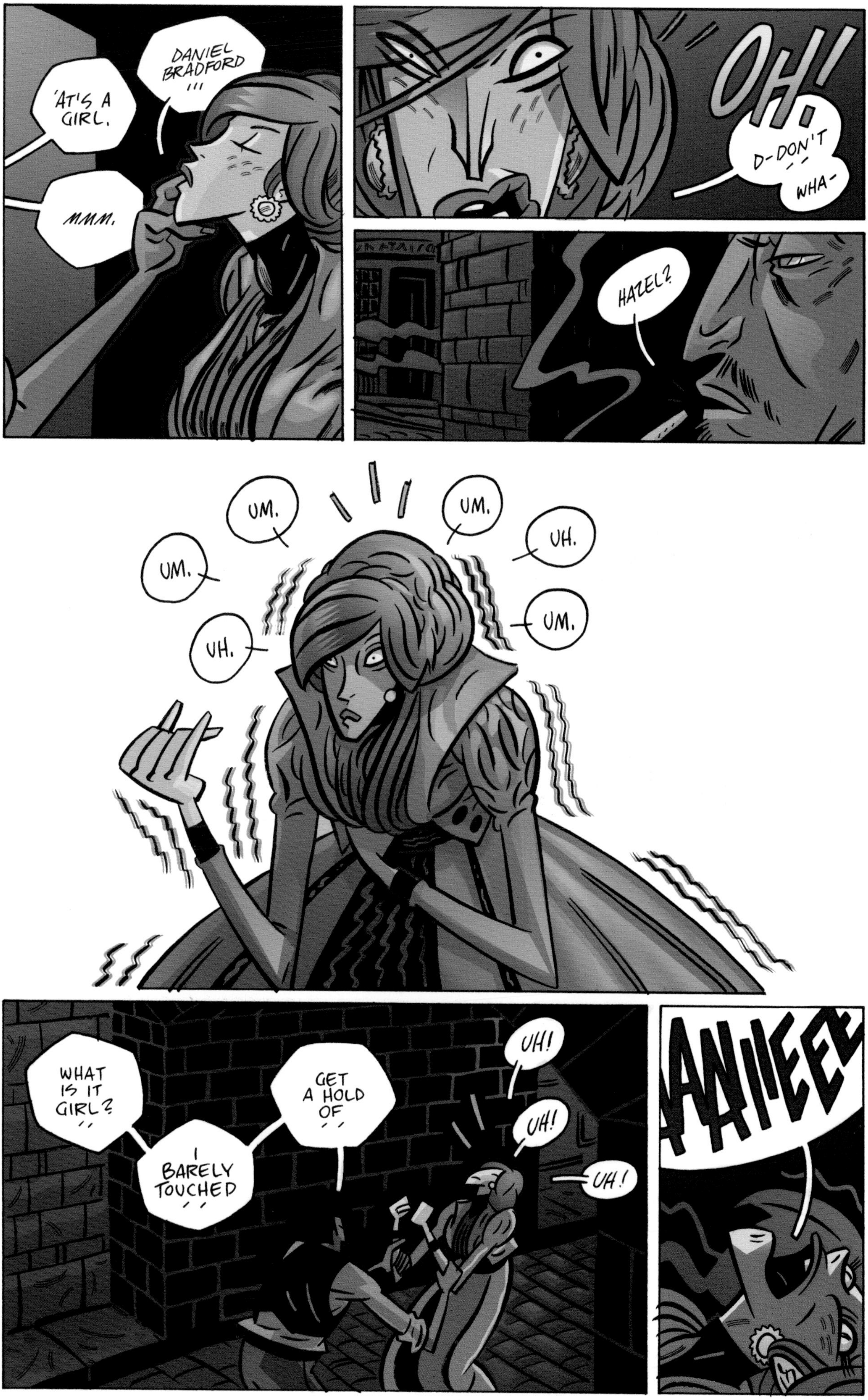
'AT'S A GIRL.
DANIEL BRADFORD ...
MMM.
OH!
D-DON'T --
WHA-
HAZEL?
UM.
UM.
UH.
UM.
UM.
UH.
WHAT IS IT GIRL? --
I BARELY TOUCHED ...
GET A HOLD OF --
UH!
UH!
UH!
AAIIEEE

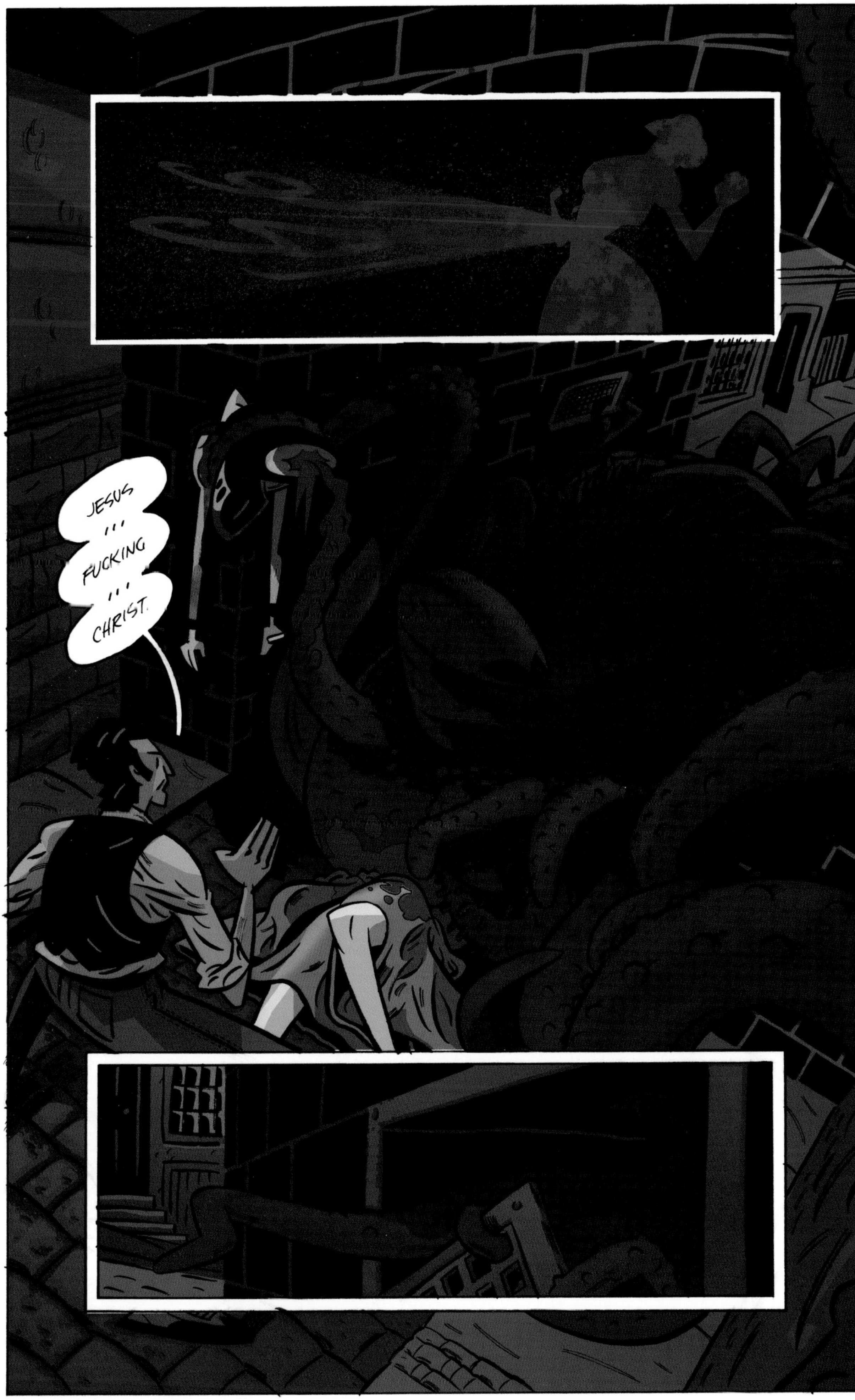
JESUS ... FUCKING ... CHRIST.

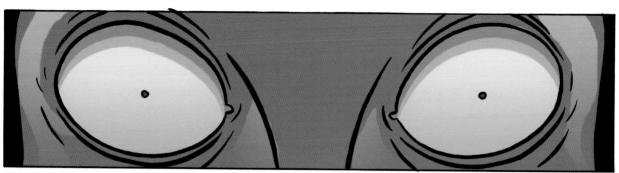

the devil

I ASKED YOU WHAT THE FUCK YOU DID, YOU GRUBBY LITTLE WORM!

GET UP, YA BLOODY SHITE!!! SHE WOULDN'T GIVE IT UP. SO YOU DID **THIS** TO HER? IS THAT WHAT HAPPENS WHEN YOU CAN'T GET YOUR SHABBY LITTLE PECKER INTO A LASS?

WELL, YOU'LL LOVE WHAT THEY'LL BE DOING TO YOU IN NEWGATE

THEY'LL TEAR THE ARSE RIGHT OUT OF YA, BOY.

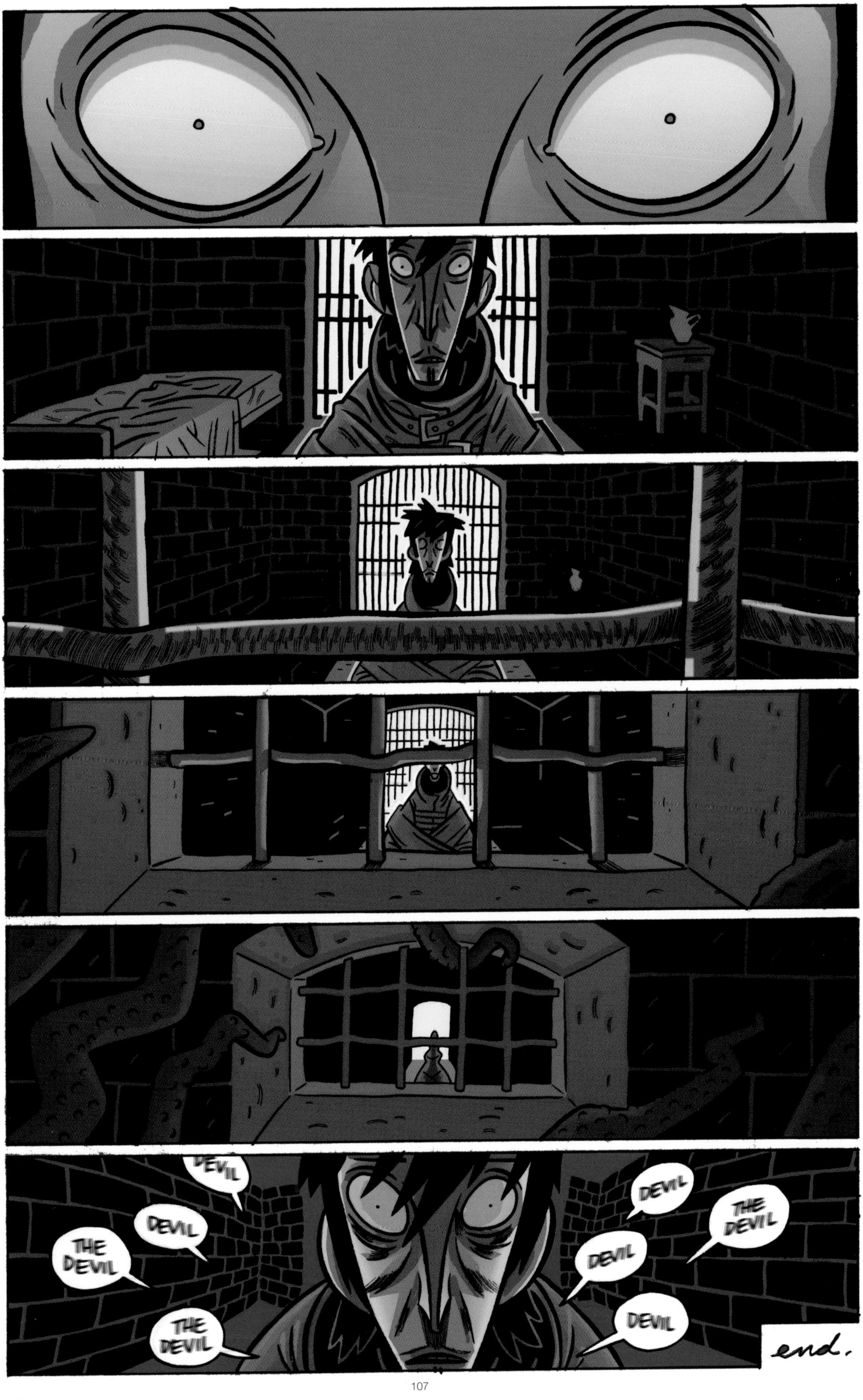
DEVIL
DEVIL
THE DEVIL
THE DEVIL
DEVIL
THE DEVIL
DEVIL
DEVIL
end.

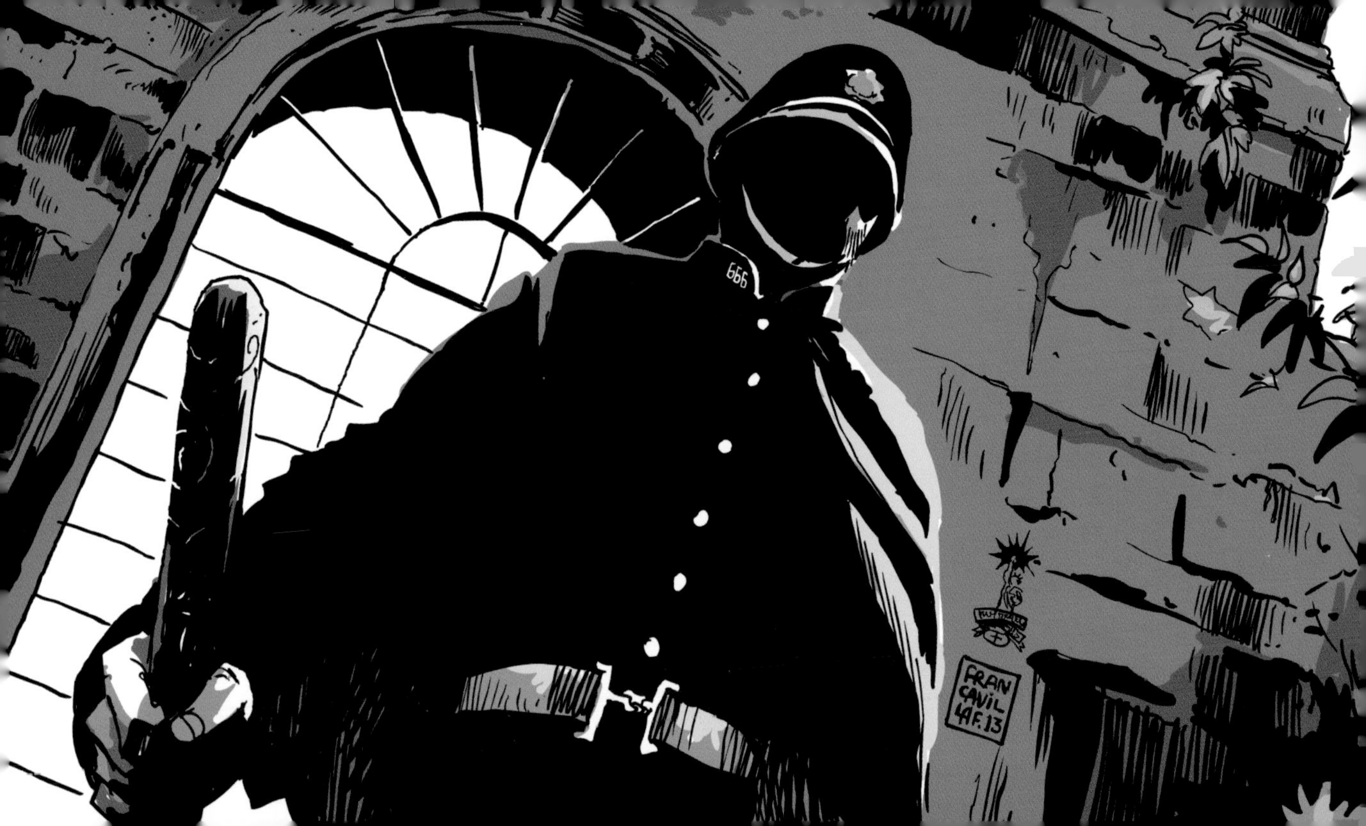
666
FRAN
CAVIL
LAF.13

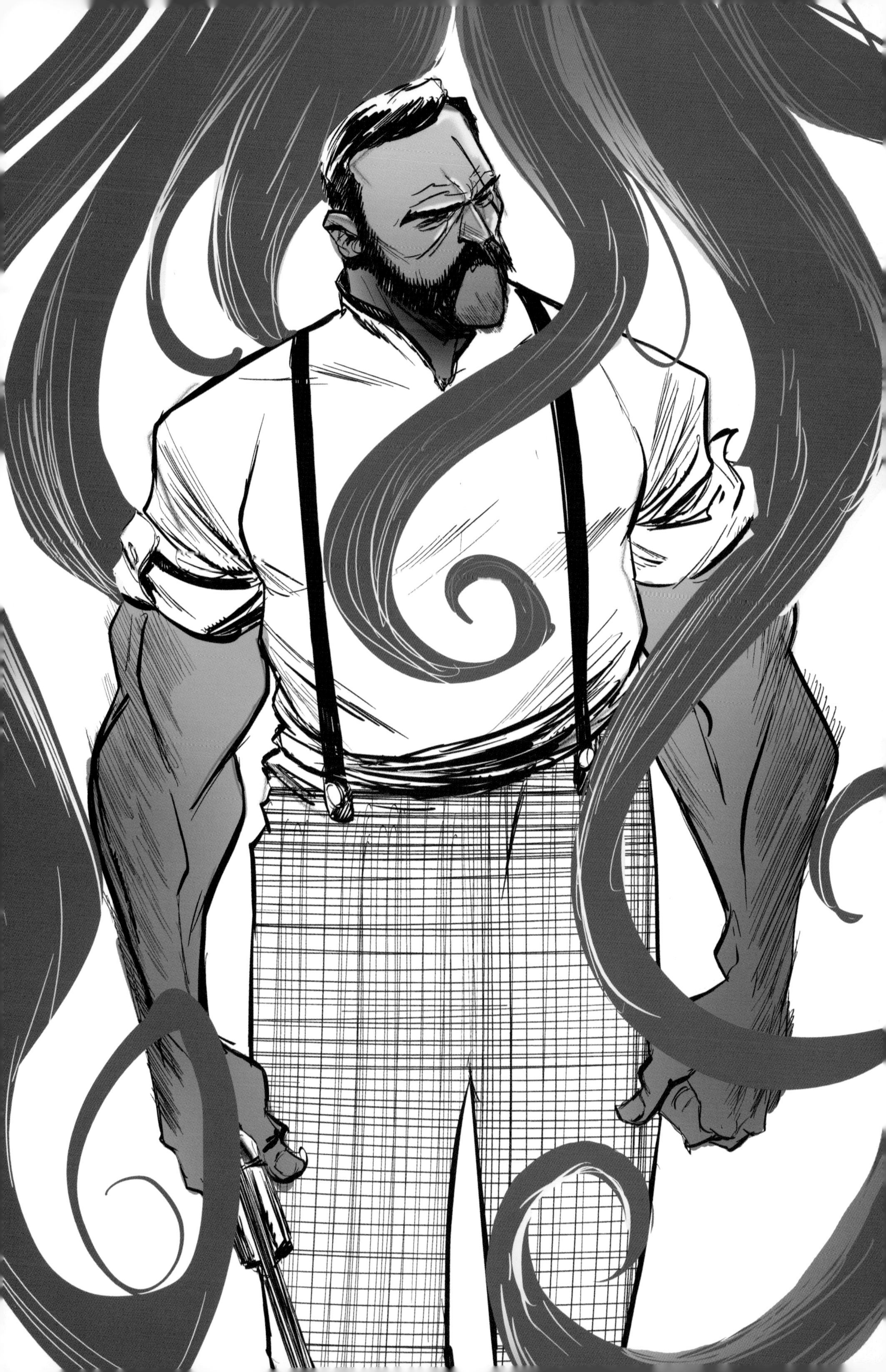

# MIDDLETON ™

When I was a kid I thought Encyclopedia Brown was pretty cool. He was no Thinking Machine, or Sherlock Holmes, or Lord Peter Wimsey. Leroy Brown was kind of a watered down notion. You know, for kids. But he was cool enough.

Then one day I thought "But what if Leroy Brown grew up to become Sherlock Holmes?"

That, I thought, might make a good story.

Then: "What if Leroy Brown teamed up with Sherlock Holmes to solve mysteries?" A good idea, different from the first, but still not an especially great idea. But wait! What if, through the dubious magic of time travel, both those ideas were contained within the same story?

That might be a great idea. It was, at least, pretty cool.

Still, I put that idea away somewhere in the back of my head and forgot about it and, instead, entertained other ideas for two or three decades.

But when the opportunity to work with Phil Hester and Shaky Kane recently fell into my lap, I knew I needed a story worthy of those amazing artists.

And that old neglected mash-up between Encyclopedia Brown and Sherlock Holmes stepped lightly to the border of my conscious mind and cleared its throat and raised its hand. And I smiled.

Because it was still a pretty cool idea for a story.

Alex Grecian
March 2013

story    Alex Grecian
art      Phil Hester
colors   Nick Filardi
letters  Thomas Mauer

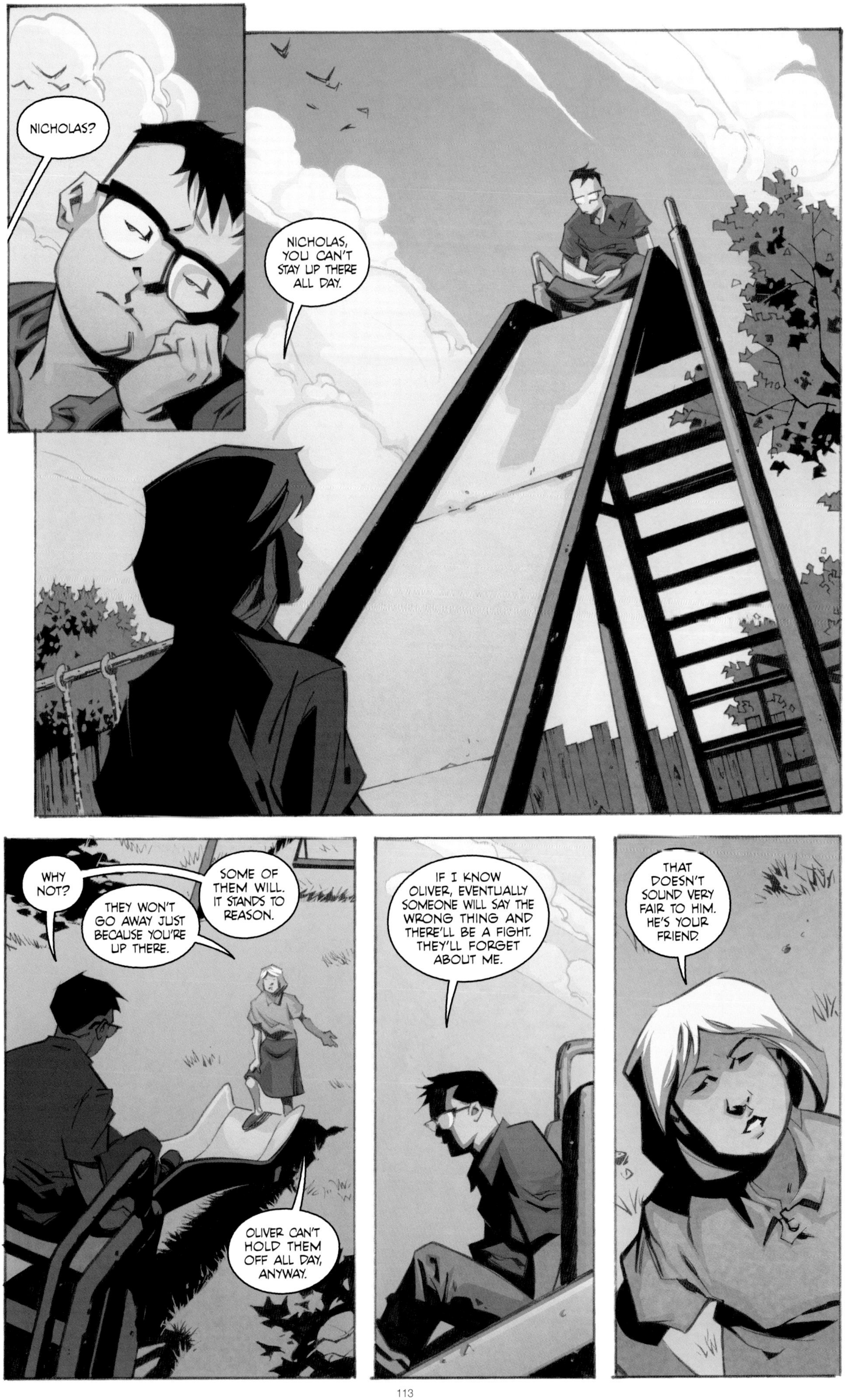
NICHOLAS?
NICHOLAS, YOU CAN'T STAY UP THERE ALL DAY.
WHY NOT?
THEY WON'T GO AWAY JUST BECAUSE YOU'RE UP THERE.
SOME OF THEM WILL. IT STANDS TO REASON.
OLIVER CAN'T HOLD THEM OFF ALL DAY, ANYWAY.
IF I KNOW OLIVER, EVENTUALLY SOMEONE WILL SAY THE WRONG THING AND THERE'LL BE A FIGHT. THEY'LL FORGET ABOUT ME.
THAT DOESN'T SOUND VERY FAIR TO HIM. HE'S YOUR FRIEND.

≈SIGH≈ NO, I SUPPOSE NOT.

IT USED TO BE FUN, YOU KNOW?

BACK WHEN IT WAS MY DAD AND ME, AND I WAS JUST SOLVING PUZZLES AT THE DINNER TABLE...

IN 1945, A TEN-YEAR-OLD AMATEUR DETECTIVE SOLVED THE LOCKED-ROOM MURDER OF A CHICAGO CRIME LORD AND ACCIDENTALLY BECAME AN INTERNATIONAL CELEBRITY. NOW THE WORLD KNOWS HIM AS...

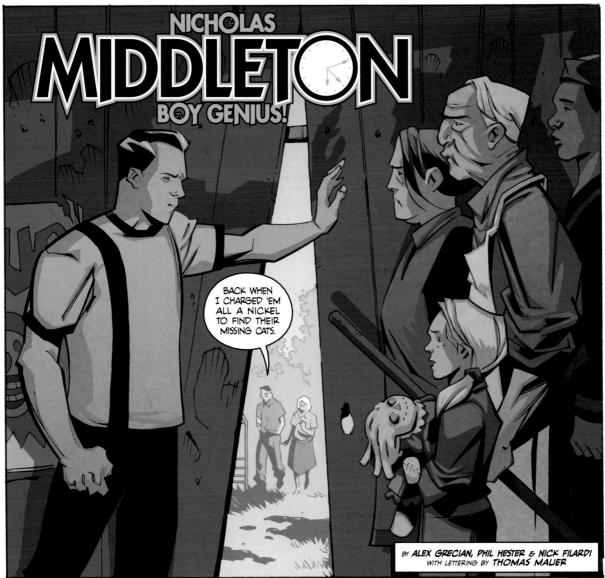

# NICHOLAS MIDDLETON
## BOY GENIUS!

BACK WHEN I CHARGED 'EM ALL A NICKEL TO FIND THEIR MISSING CATS.

BY ALEX GRECIAN, PHIL HESTER & NICK FILARDI
WITH LETTERING BY THOMAS MAUER

114

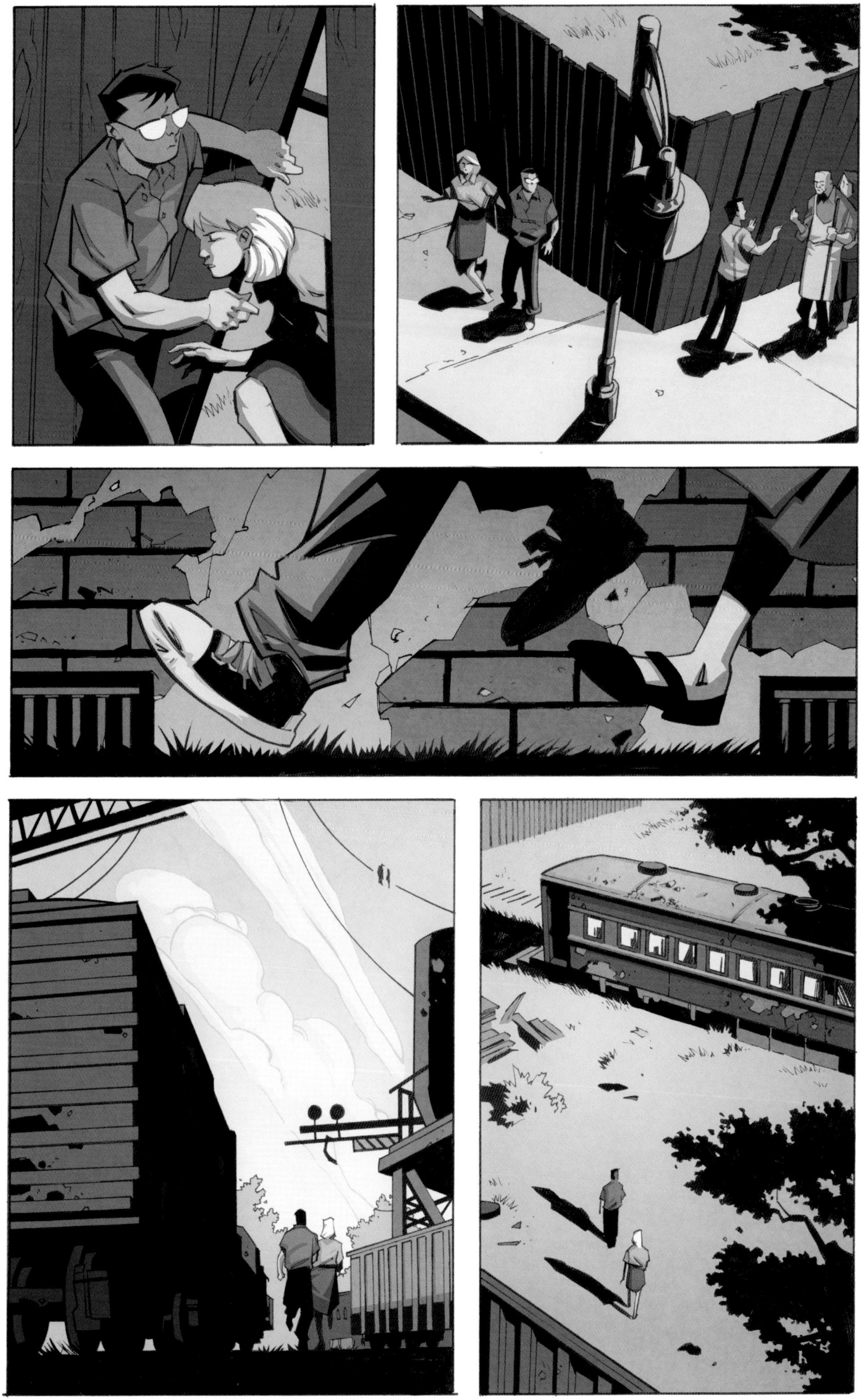

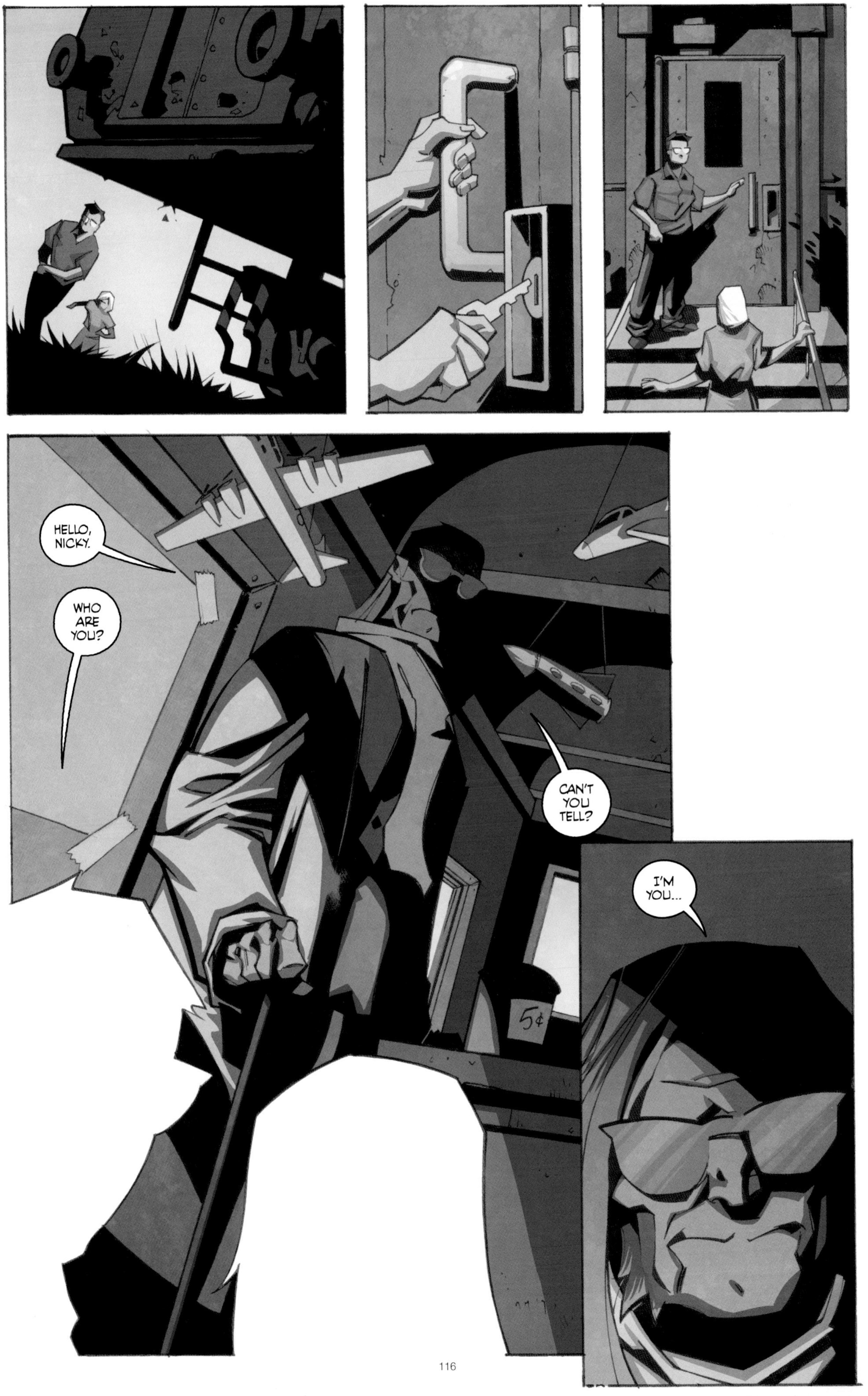
HELLO, NICKY.
WHO ARE YOU?
CAN'T YOU TELL?
I'M YOU...

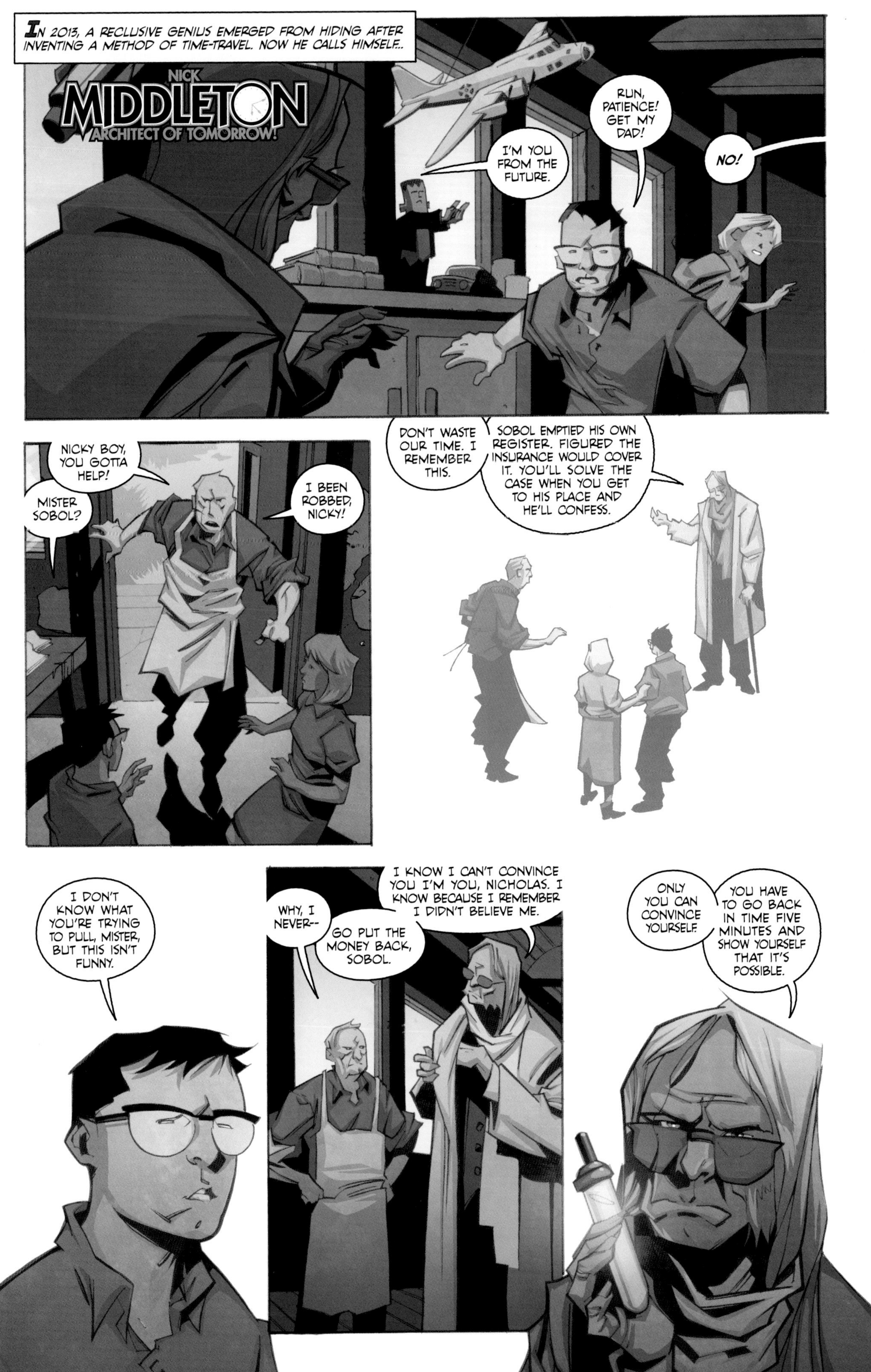

IN 2013, A RECLUSIVE GENIUS EMERGED FROM HIDING AFTER INVENTING A METHOD OF TIME-TRAVEL. NOW HE CALLS HIMSELF...
NICK MIDDLETON ARCHITECT OF TOMORROW!
I'M YOU FROM THE FUTURE.
RUN, PATIENCE! GET MY DAD!
NO!
NICKY BOY, YOU GOTTA HELP!
MISTER SOBOL?
I BEEN ROBBED, NICKY!
DON'T WASTE OUR TIME. I REMEMBER THIS.
SOBOL EMPTIED HIS OWN REGISTER. FIGURED THE INSURANCE WOULD COVER IT. YOU'LL SOLVE THE CASE WHEN YOU GET TO HIS PLACE AND HE'LL CONFESS.
I DON'T KNOW WHAT YOU'RE TRYING TO PULL, MISTER, BUT THIS ISN'T FUNNY.
WHY, I NEVER--
I KNOW I CAN'T CONVINCE YOU I'M YOU, NICHOLAS. I KNOW BECAUSE I REMEMBER I DIDN'T BELIEVE ME.
GO PUT THE MONEY BACK, SOBOL.
ONLY YOU CAN CONVINCE YOURSELF.
YOU HAVE TO GO BACK IN TIME FIVE MINUTES AND SHOW YOURSELF THAT IT'S POSSIBLE.

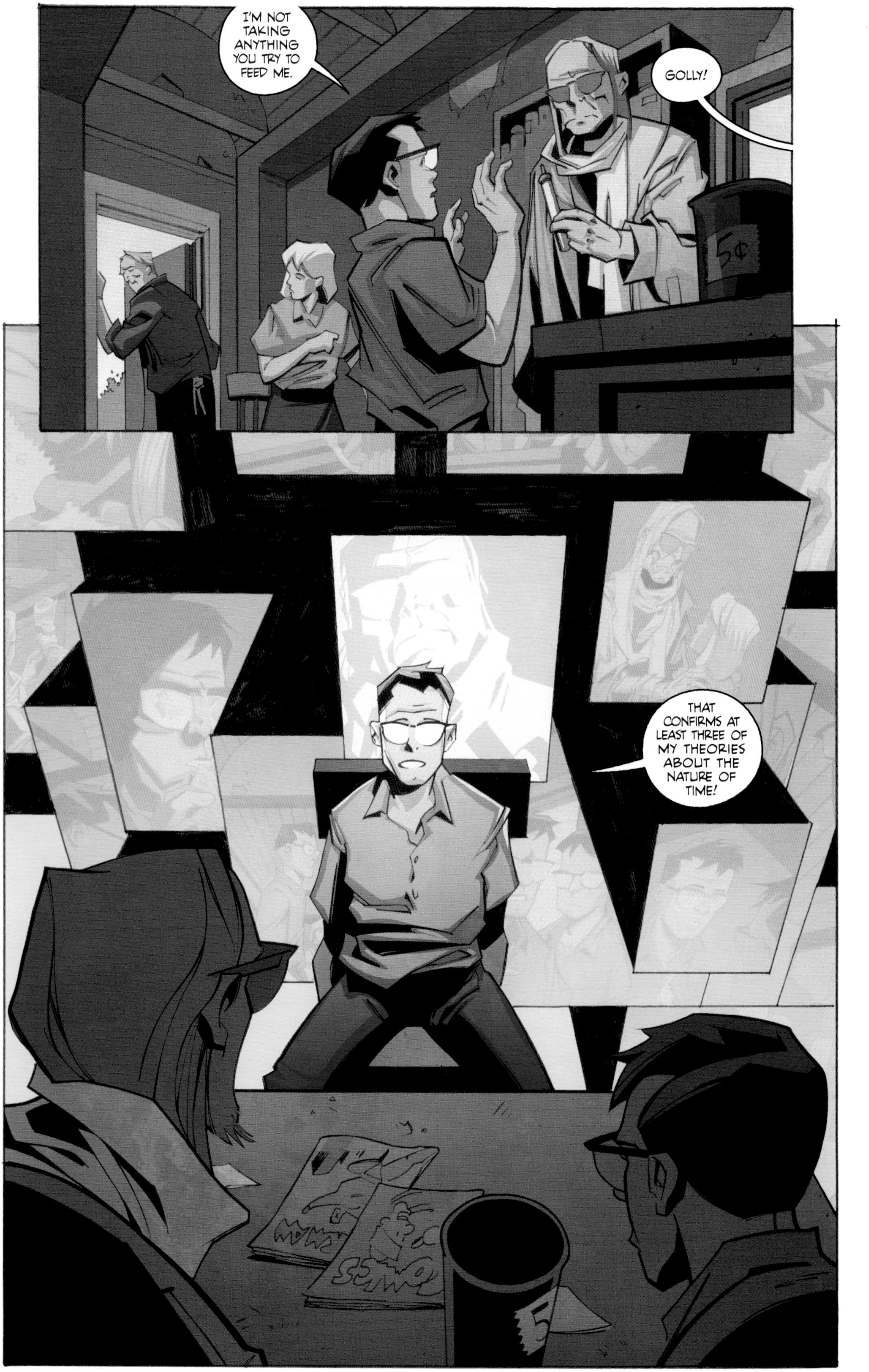
I'M NOT TAKING ANYTHING YOU TRY TO FEED ME.
GOLLY!
5¢
THAT CONFIRMS AT LEAST THREE OF MY THEORIES ABOUT THE NATURE OF TIME!

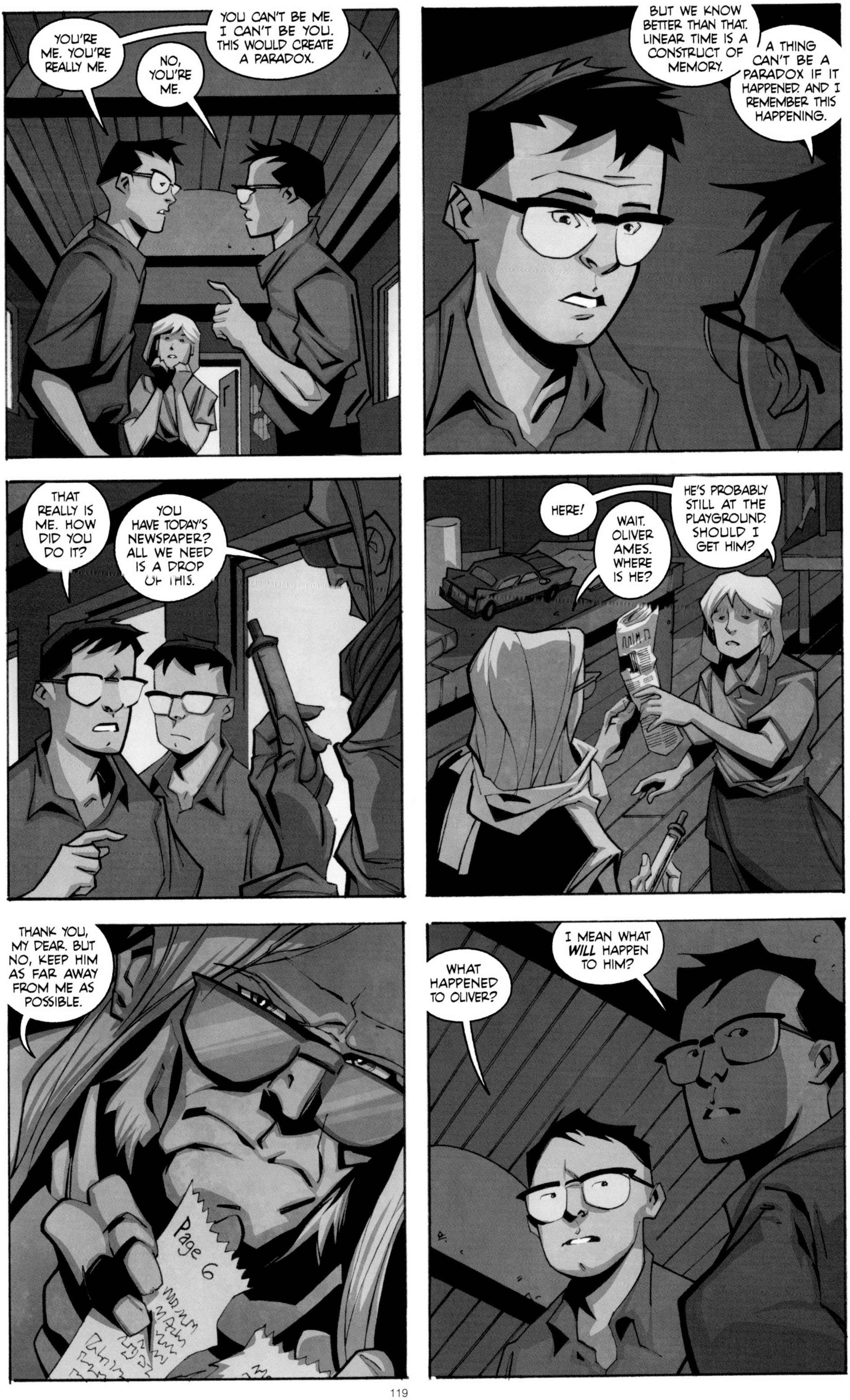
YOU'RE ME. YOU'RE REALLY ME.
YOU CAN'T BE ME. I CAN'T BE YOU. THIS WOULD CREATE A PARADOX.
NO, YOU'RE ME.
BUT WE KNOW BETTER THAN THAT. LINEAR TIME IS A CONSTRUCT OF MEMORY.
A THING CAN'T BE A PARADOX IF IT HAPPENED. AND I REMEMBER THIS HAPPENING.
THAT REALLY IS ME. HOW DID YOU DO IT?
YOU HAVE TODAY'S NEWSPAPER? ALL WE NEED IS A DROP OF THIS.
HERE!
HE'S PROBABLY STILL AT THE PLAYGROUND. SHOULD I GET HIM?
WAIT. OLIVER AMES. WHERE IS HE?
THANK YOU, MY DEAR. BUT NO, KEEP HIM AS FAR AWAY FROM ME AS POSSIBLE.
Page 6
WHAT HAPPENED TO OLIVER?
I MEAN WHAT WILL HAPPEN TO HIM?

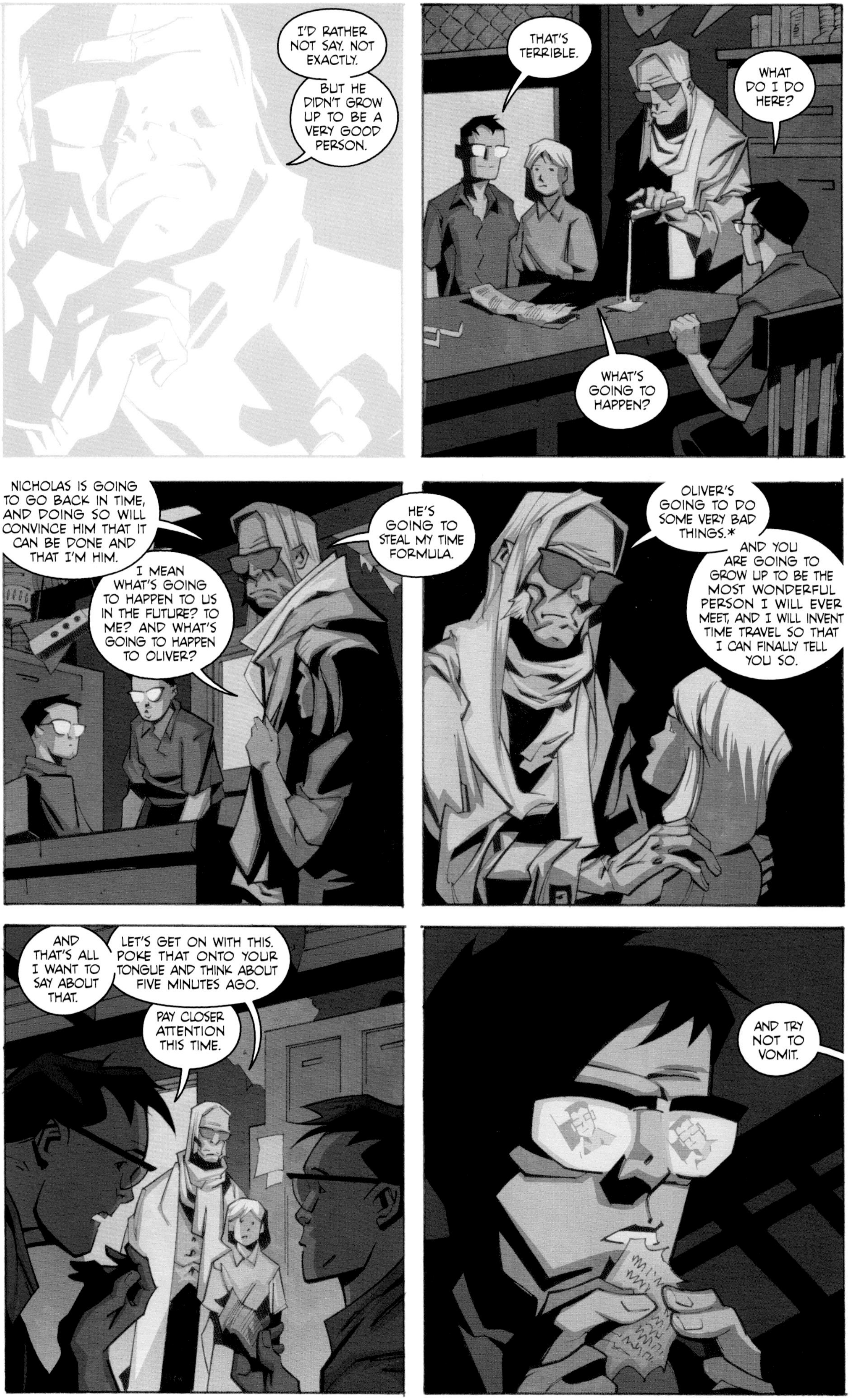
I'D RATHER NOT SAY. NOT EXACTLY.
BUT HE DIDN'T GROW UP TO BE A VERY GOOD PERSON.
THAT'S TERRIBLE.
WHAT DO I DO HERE?
WHAT'S GOING TO HAPPEN?
NICHOLAS IS GOING TO GO BACK IN TIME, AND DOING SO WILL CONVINCE HIM THAT IT CAN BE DONE AND THAT I'M HIM.
I MEAN WHAT'S GOING TO HAPPEN TO US IN THE FUTURE? TO ME? AND WHAT'S GOING TO HAPPEN TO OLIVER?
HE'S GOING TO STEAL MY TIME FORMULA.
OLIVER'S GOING TO DO SOME VERY BAD THINGS.*
AND YOU ARE GOING TO GROW UP TO BE THE MOST WONDERFUL PERSON I WILL EVER MEET, AND I WILL INVENT TIME TRAVEL SO THAT I CAN FINALLY TELL YOU SO.
AND THAT'S ALL I WANT TO SAY ABOUT THAT.
LET'S GET ON WITH THIS. POKE THAT ONTO YOUR TONGUE AND THINK ABOUT FIVE MINUTES AGO.
PAY CLOSER ATTENTION THIS TIME.
AND TRY NOT TO VOMIT.

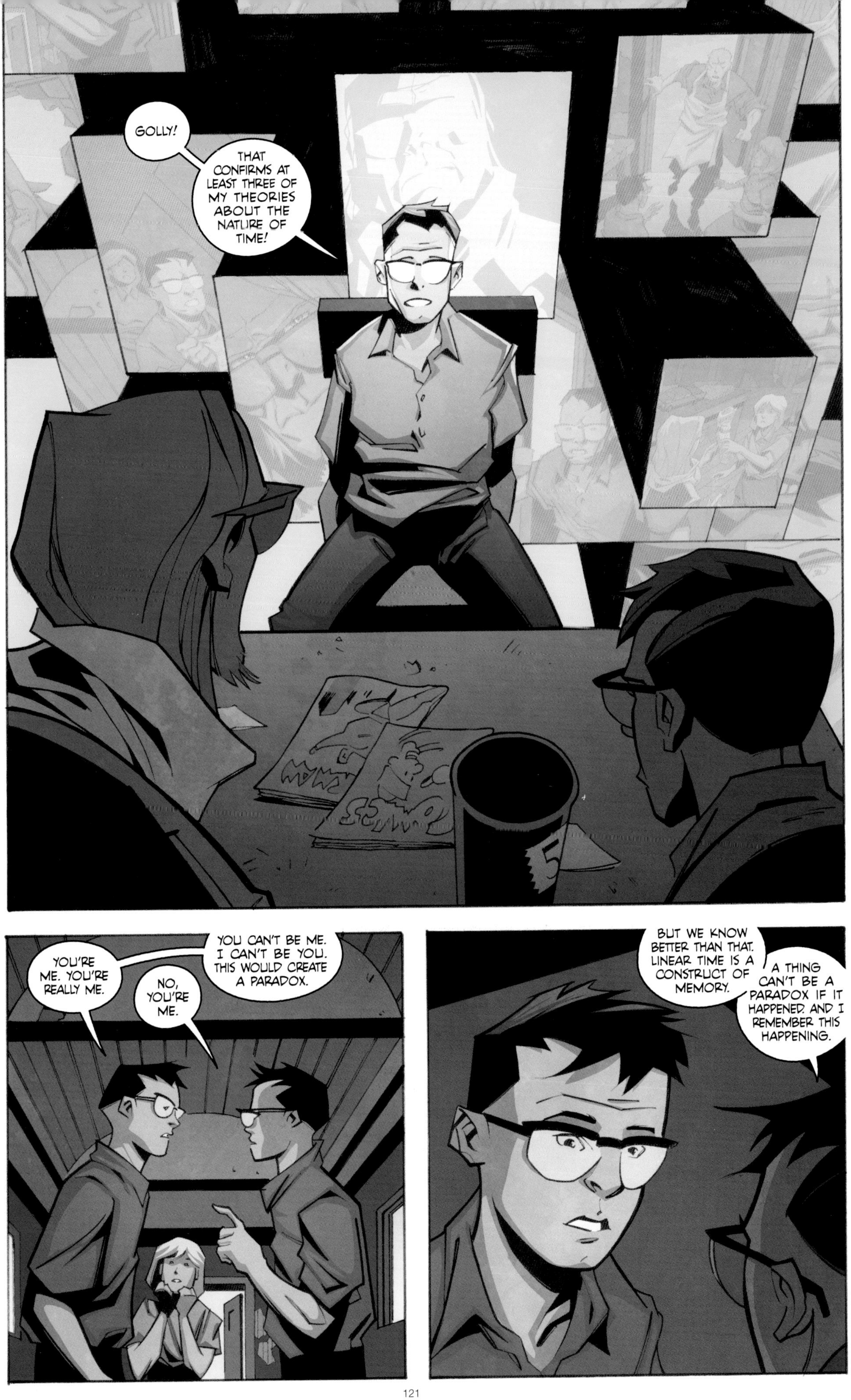
GOLLY!
THAT CONFIRMS AT LEAST THREE OF MY THEORIES ABOUT THE NATURE OF TIME!
YOU'RE ME. YOU'RE REALLY ME.
NO, YOU'RE ME.
YOU CAN'T BE ME. I CAN'T BE YOU. THIS WOULD CREATE A PARADOX.
BUT WE KNOW BETTER THAN THAT. LINEAR TIME IS A CONSTRUCT OF MEMORY.
A THING CAN'T BE A PARADOX IF IT HAPPENED. AND I REMEMBER THIS HAPPENING.

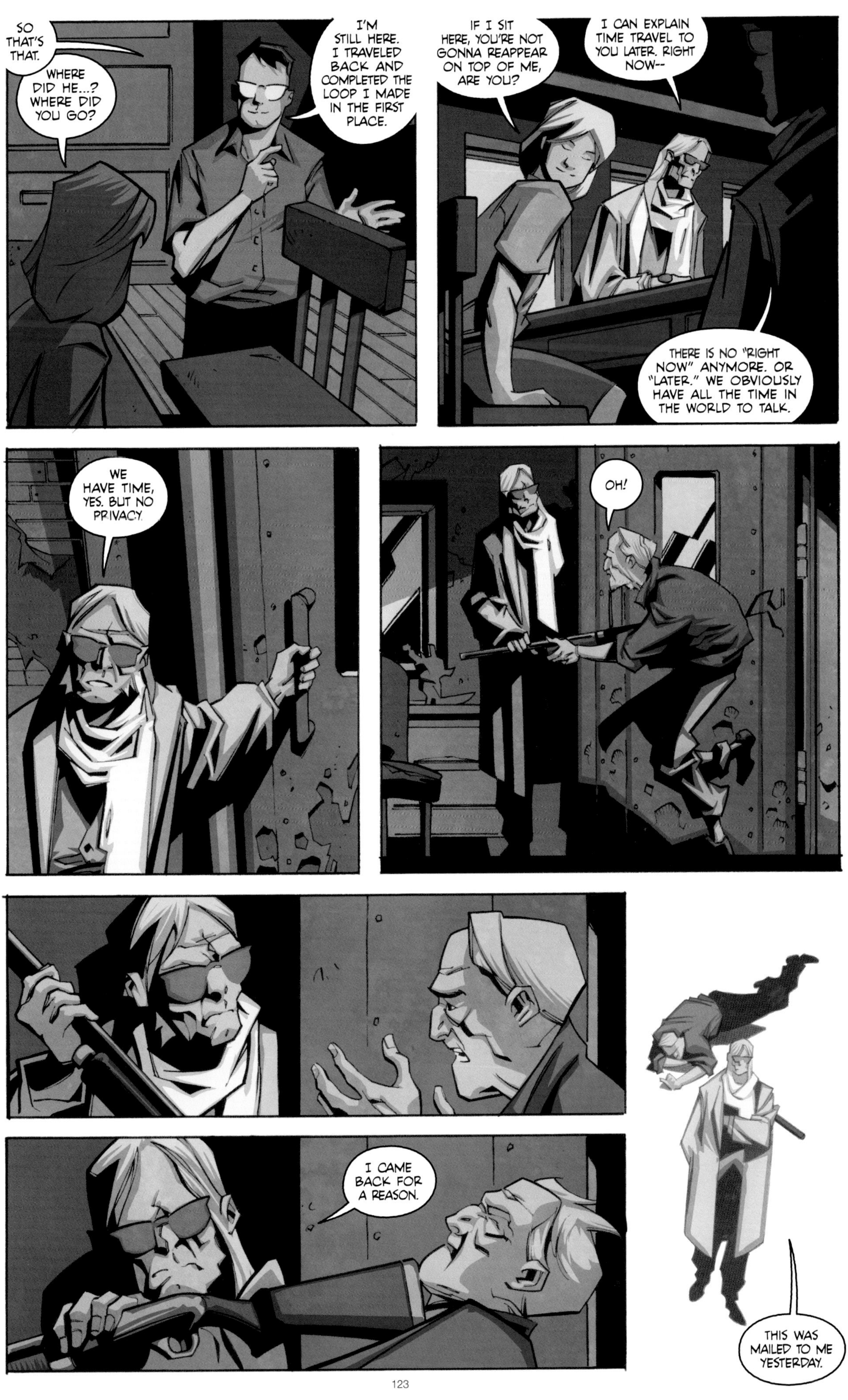
SO THAT'S THAT.
WHERE DID HE...? WHERE DID YOU GO?
I'M STILL HERE. I TRAVELED BACK AND COMPLETED THE LOOP I MADE IN THE FIRST PLACE.
IF I SIT HERE, YOU'RE NOT GONNA REAPPEAR ON TOP OF ME, ARE YOU?
I CAN EXPLAIN TIME TRAVEL TO YOU LATER. RIGHT NOW--
THERE IS NO "RIGHT NOW" ANYMORE. OR "LATER." WE OBVIOUSLY HAVE ALL THE TIME IN THE WORLD TO TALK.
WE HAVE TIME, YES. BUT NO PRIVACY.
OH!
I CAME BACK FOR A REASON.
THIS WAS MAILED TO ME YESTERDAY.

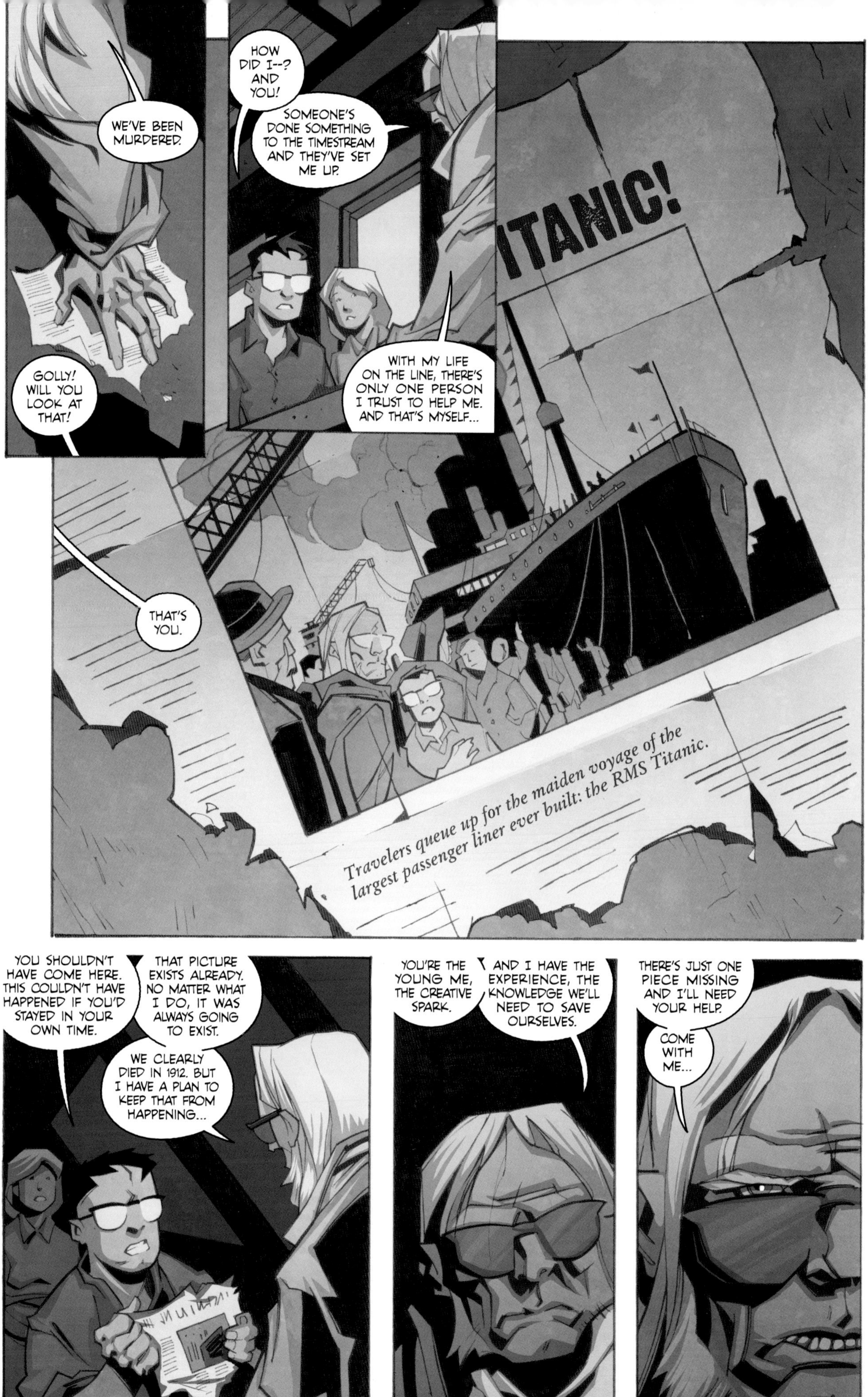
WE'VE BEEN MURDERED.
HOW DID I--? AND YOU!
SOMEONE'S DONE SOMETHING TO THE TIMESTREAM AND THEY'VE SET ME UP.
GOLLY! WILL YOU LOOK AT THAT!
WITH MY LIFE ON THE LINE, THERE'S ONLY ONE PERSON I TRUST TO HELP ME. AND THAT'S MYSELF...
TITANIC!
THAT'S YOU.
Travelers queue up for the maiden voyage of the largest passenger liner ever built: the RMS Titanic.
YOU SHOULDN'T HAVE COME HERE. THIS COULDN'T HAVE HAPPENED IF YOU'D STAYED IN YOUR OWN TIME.
THAT PICTURE EXISTS ALREADY. NO MATTER WHAT I DO, IT WAS ALWAYS GOING TO EXIST.
WE CLEARLY DIED IN 1912. BUT I HAVE A PLAN TO KEEP THAT FROM HAPPENING...
YOU'RE THE YOUNG ME, THE CREATIVE SPARK.
AND I HAVE THE EXPERIENCE, THE KNOWLEDGE WE'LL NEED TO SAVE OURSELVES.
THERE'S JUST ONE PIECE MISSING AND I'LL NEED YOUR HELP.
COME WITH ME...

...I CAN'T FACE MYSELF ALONE.
IN 1969, A WORLD-WEARY CELEBRITY ABANDONED HIS WIFE AND FAMILY. HE FLED THE PUBLIC SPOTLIGHT AND SPIRALED OUT OF SIGHT. BUT THERE'S NO ESCAPING HIS REPUTATION AS...
NICKY MIDDLETON
WORLD'S GREATEST DETECTIVE!
A BEGINNING...

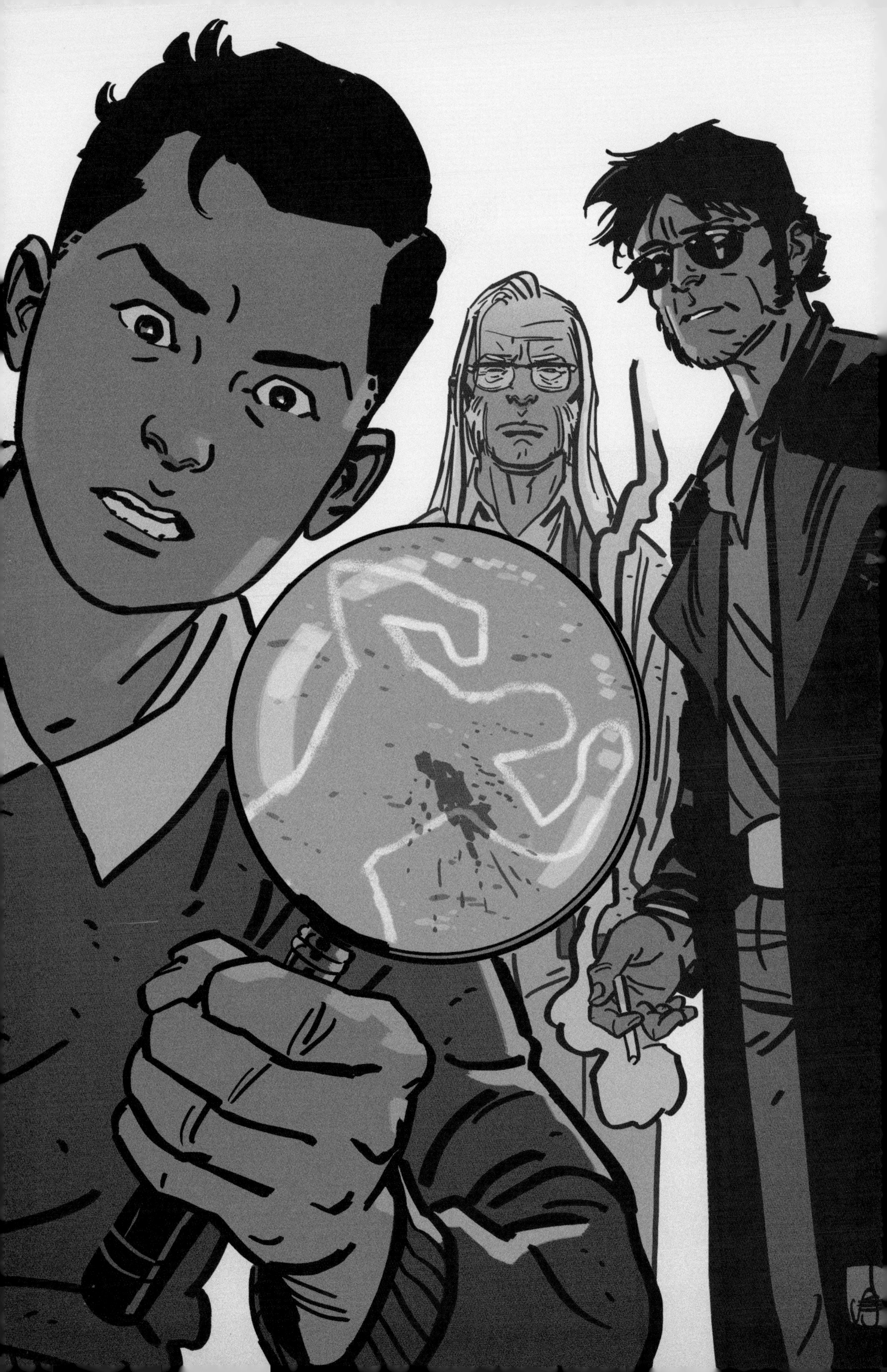

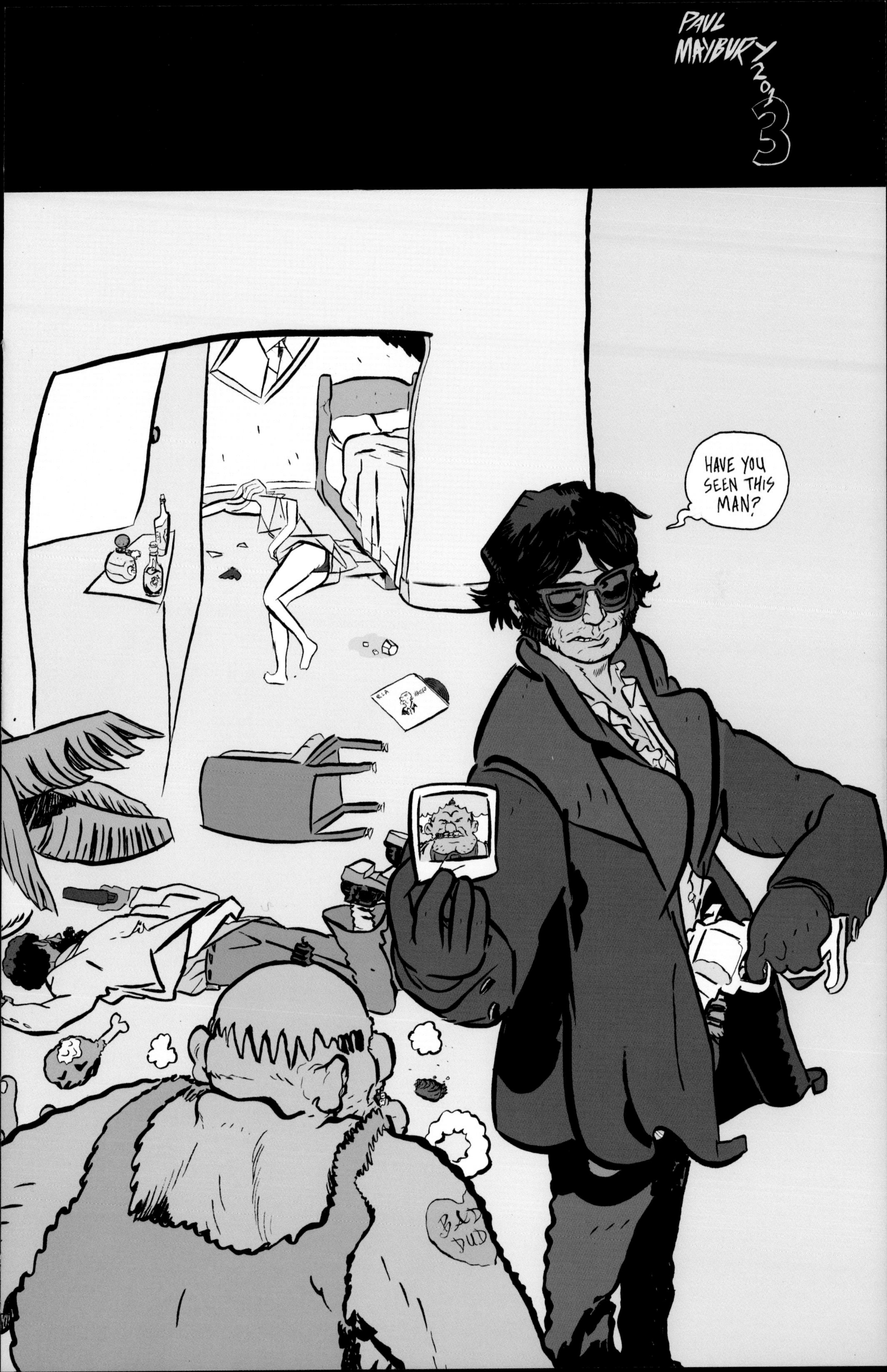
PAUL MAYBURY 2013
HAVE YOU SEEN THIS MAN?
BAD DUD

# OLD DOG™

OLD DOG is intended as a rumination on aging, and of coming to grips with personal history, appropriately or not.

This initial, self-contained story introduces the two major players in what will someday be a much longer work. On the one hand, we have Jack Boxer, whose roots stretch back to prohibition and Chicago in the Roaring Twenties. A man whose past has beaten him into submission, or, as it happens, into temporary submission.

On the other hand we have Cassandra Falcon, a once aspiring starlet with history of her own to carry as a burden. Unlike Jack, Cassandra wears her history on her sleeve, and makes no effort to hide behind the hand she's been dealt.

Although the first project of mine that attracted much notice was *Hawaiian Dick*, a book set in the early Fifties, this is the first time I've really tackled noir in a hard-boiled sense. And OLD DOG is noir in the truest sense, seeking to examine the darkness that lies within two broken people.

For years, Chris Mitten and I have casually kicked around the notion of doing something together, so it was only natural that I would approach him about OLD DOG, especially understanding how perfectly his style would work in the world I was setting out to establish. And, to my relief, he graciously agreed to collaborate with me on the concept.

As always, that's when things really began to take shape. Chris immediately gave Jack Boxer definition, and once we knew exactly who he was, and what he looked like, Jack pretty much led us through his own story. From there, Chris exceeded every expectation, deciding, on top of penciling and inking the story, to add his own color as well. As a writer of comics, the only way to be truly satisfied with your work is if your collaborator is fully engaged, and pushing himself to do his best work in service to the story.

So, yeah. I'm truly satisfied with this one.

B. Clay Moore
March 2013

story    B. Clay Moore
art      Christopher Mitten
letters  Thomas Mauer

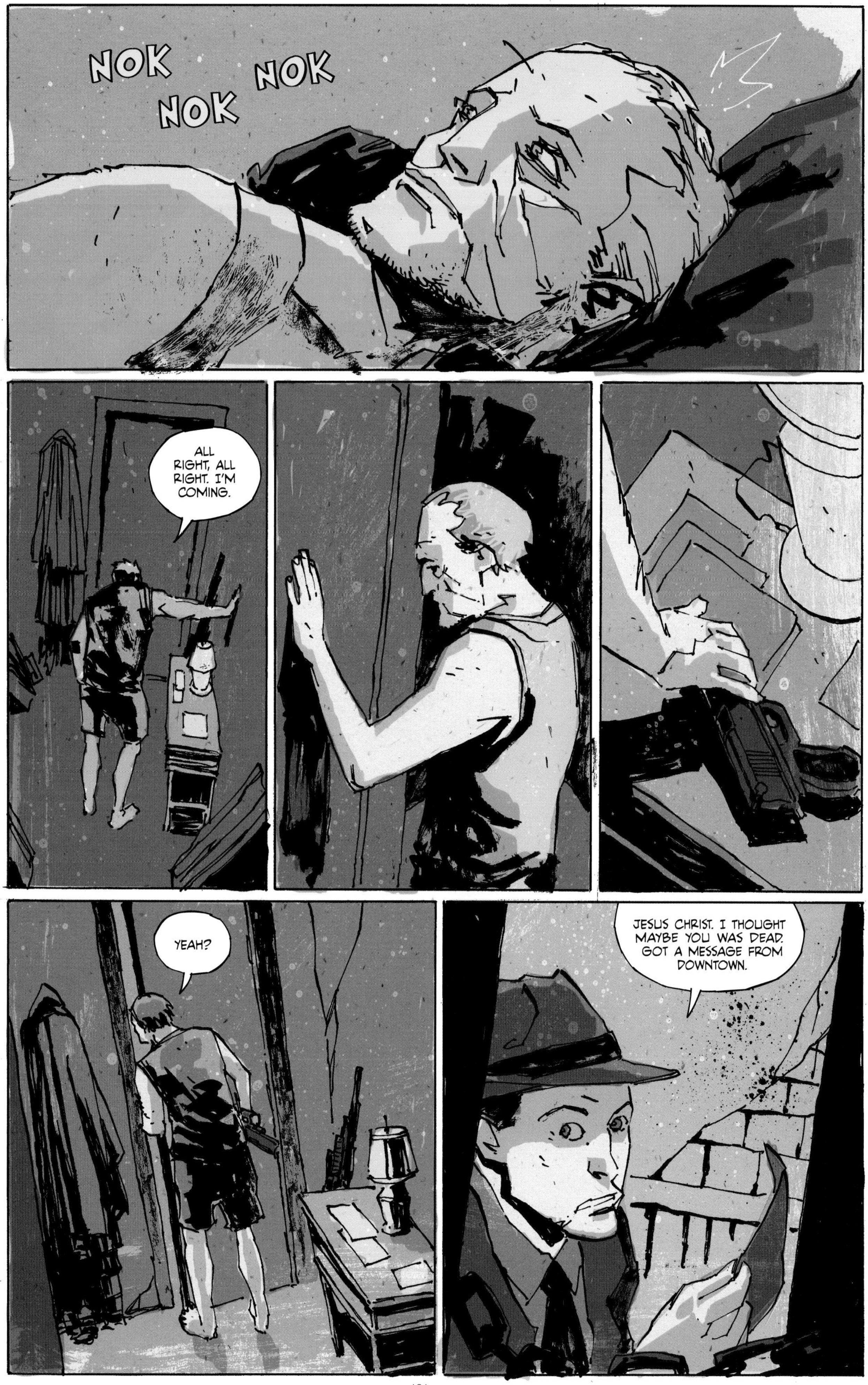
NOK
NOK
NOK
ALL RIGHT, ALL RIGHT. I'M COMING.
YEAH?
JESUS CHRIST. I THOUGHT MAYBE YOU WAS DEAD. GOT A MESSAGE FROM DOWNTOWN.

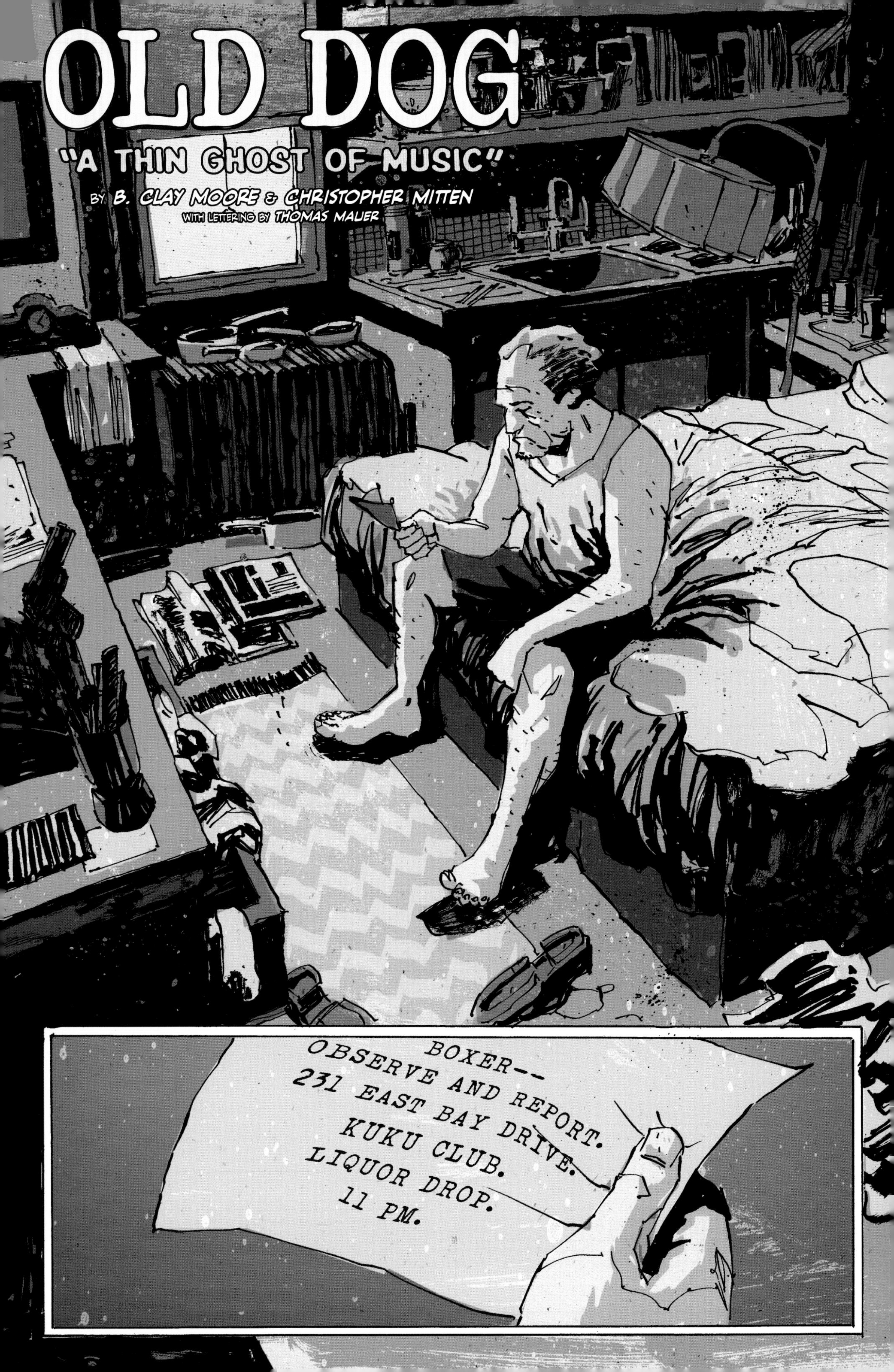
OLD DOG
"A THIN GHOST OF MUSIC"
BY B. CLAY MOORE & CHRISTOPHER MITTEN
WITH LETTERING BY THOMAS MAUER
BOXER--
OBSERVE AND REPORT.
231 EAST BAY DRIVE.
KUKU CLUB.
LIQUOR DROP.
11 PM.

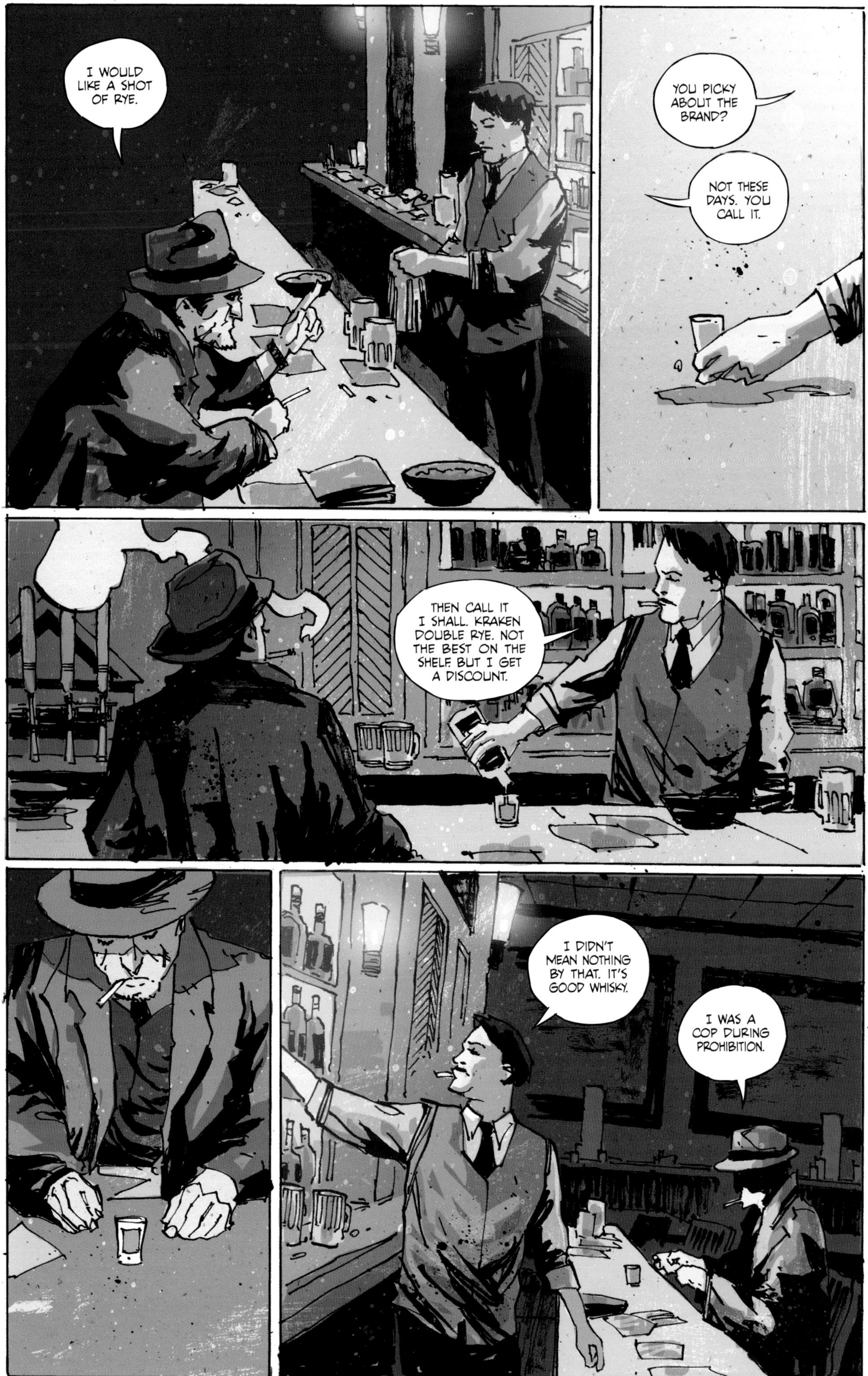
I WOULD LIKE A SHOT OF RYE.
YOU PICKY ABOUT THE BRAND?
NOT THESE DAYS. YOU CALL IT.
THEN CALL IT I SHALL. KRAKEN DOUBLE RYE. NOT THE BEST ON THE SHELF. BUT I GET A DISCOUNT.
I DIDN'T MEAN NOTHING BY THAT. IT'S GOOD WHISKY.
I WAS A COP DURING PROHIBITION.

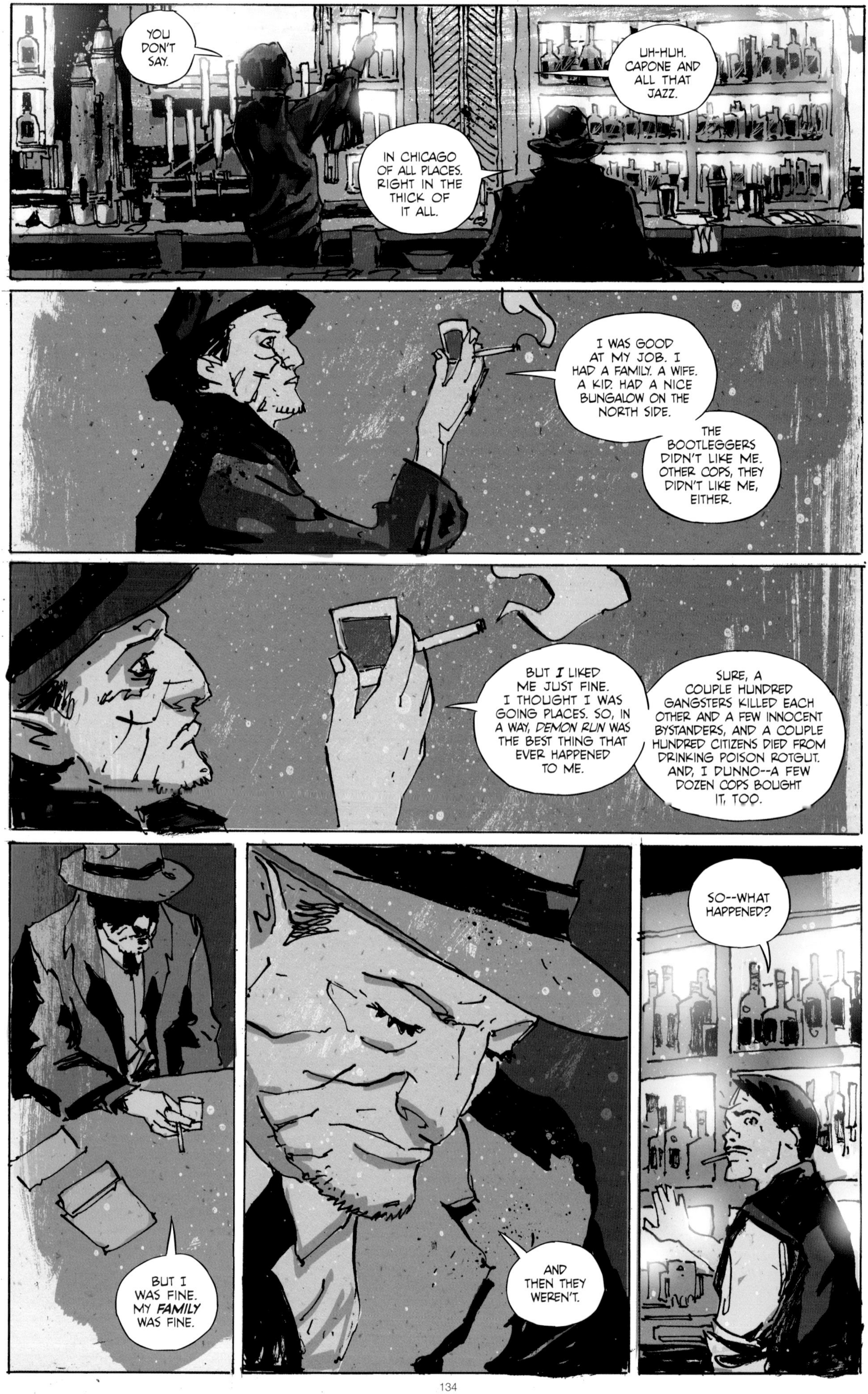
YOU DON'T SAY.
UH-HUH. CAPONE AND ALL THAT JAZZ.
IN CHICAGO OF ALL PLACES. RIGHT IN THE THICK OF IT ALL.
I WAS GOOD AT MY JOB. I HAD A FAMILY. A WIFE. A KID. HAD A NICE BUNGALOW ON THE NORTH SIDE.
THE BOOTLEGGERS DIDN'T LIKE ME. OTHER COPS, THEY DIDN'T LIKE ME, EITHER.
SURE, A COUPLE HUNDRED GANGSTERS KILLED EACH OTHER AND A FEW INNOCENT BYSTANDERS, AND A COUPLE HUNDRED CITIZENS DIED FROM DRINKING POISON ROTGUT. AND, I DUNNO--A FEW DOZEN COPS BOUGHT IT, TOO.
BUT *I* LIKED ME JUST FINE. I THOUGHT I WAS GOING PLACES. SO, IN A WAY, *DEMON RUN* WAS THE BEST THING THAT EVER HAPPENED TO ME.
BUT I WAS FINE. MY ***FAMILY*** WAS FINE.
AND THEN THEY WEREN'T.
SO--WHAT HAPPENED?

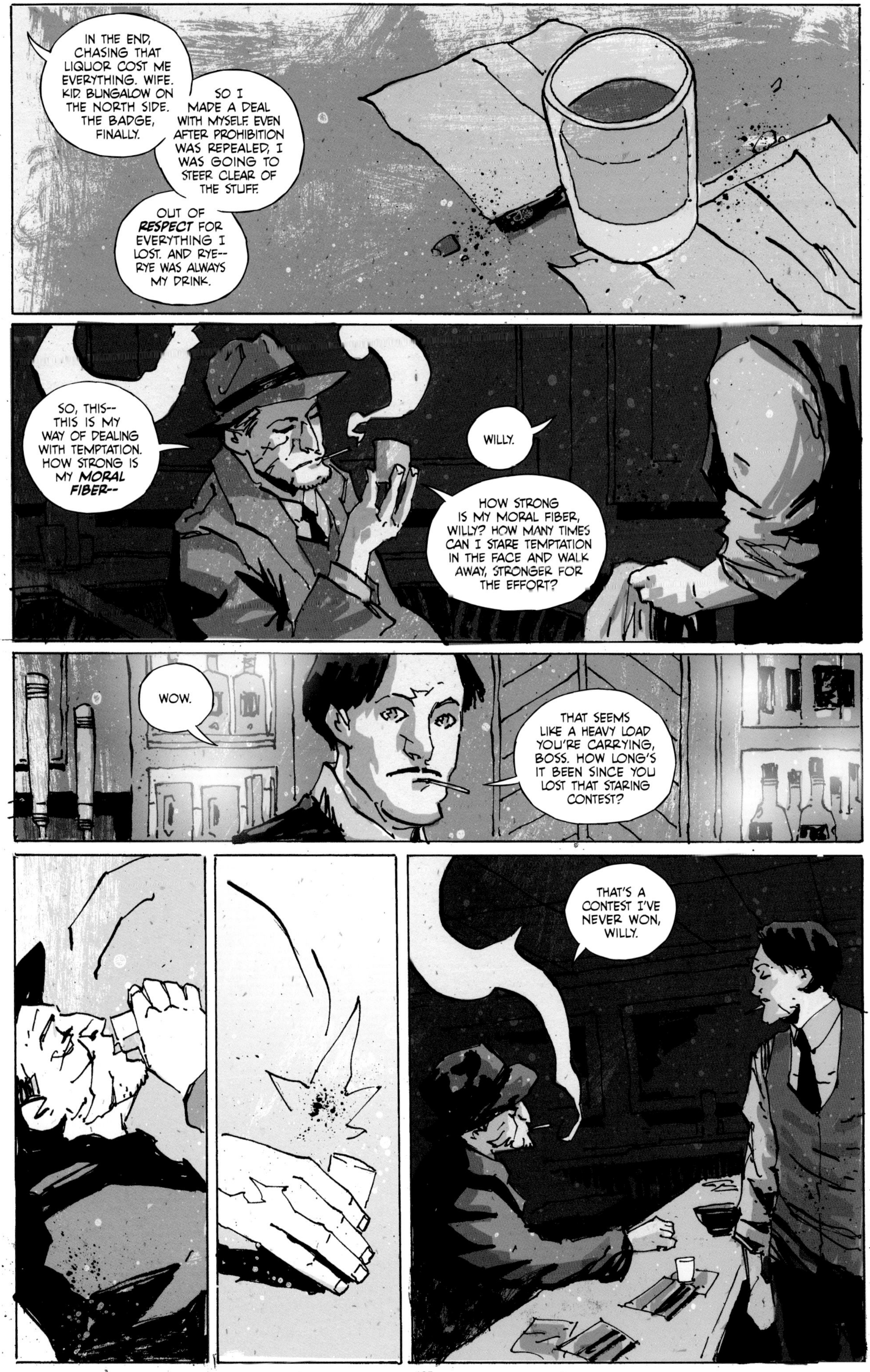
IN THE END, CHASING THAT LIQUOR COST ME EVERYTHING. WIFE. KID. BUNGALOW ON THE NORTH SIDE. THE BADGE, FINALLY.
SO I MADE A DEAL WITH MYSELF. EVEN AFTER PROHIBITION WAS REPEALED, I WAS GOING TO STEER CLEAR OF THE STUFF.
OUT OF RESPECT FOR EVERYTHING I LOST. AND RYE-- RYE WAS ALWAYS MY DRINK.
SO, THIS-- THIS IS MY WAY OF DEALING WITH TEMPTATION. HOW STRONG IS MY MORAL FIBER--
WILLY.
HOW STRONG IS MY MORAL FIBER, WILLY? HOW MANY TIMES CAN I STARE TEMPTATION IN THE FACE AND WALK AWAY, STRONGER FOR THE EFFORT?
WOW.
THAT SEEMS LIKE A HEAVY LOAD YOU'RE CARRYING, BOSS. HOW LONG'S IT BEEN SINCE YOU LOST THAT STARING CONTEST?
THAT'S A CONTEST I'VE NEVER WON, WILLY.

HOPE YOU DON'T MIND. THE MAID LET ME IN.

JESUS.

WHAT THE FUCK ARE YOU DOING HERE, BOXER? WHAT DO YOU NOT UNDERSTAND ABOUT DISCRETION?

YOU GAVE ME A BADGE, CAPTAIN. THAT MAKES THIS MY HOME OFFICE, SO TO SPEAK.

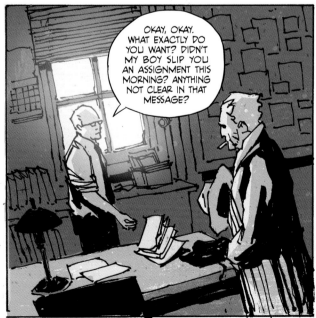

OKAY, OKAY. WHAT EXACTLY DO YOU WANT? DIDN'T MY BOY SLIP YOU AN ASSIGNMENT THIS MORNING? ANYTHING NOT CLEAR IN THAT MESSAGE?

NO, I GOT IT. OBSERVE AND REPORT. EASY AS PIE. BUT I WANT TO POKE AROUND A LITTLE FIRST. AND FOR THAT I NEED TO COVER EXPENSES.

SO YOU NEED MONEY? CASH?

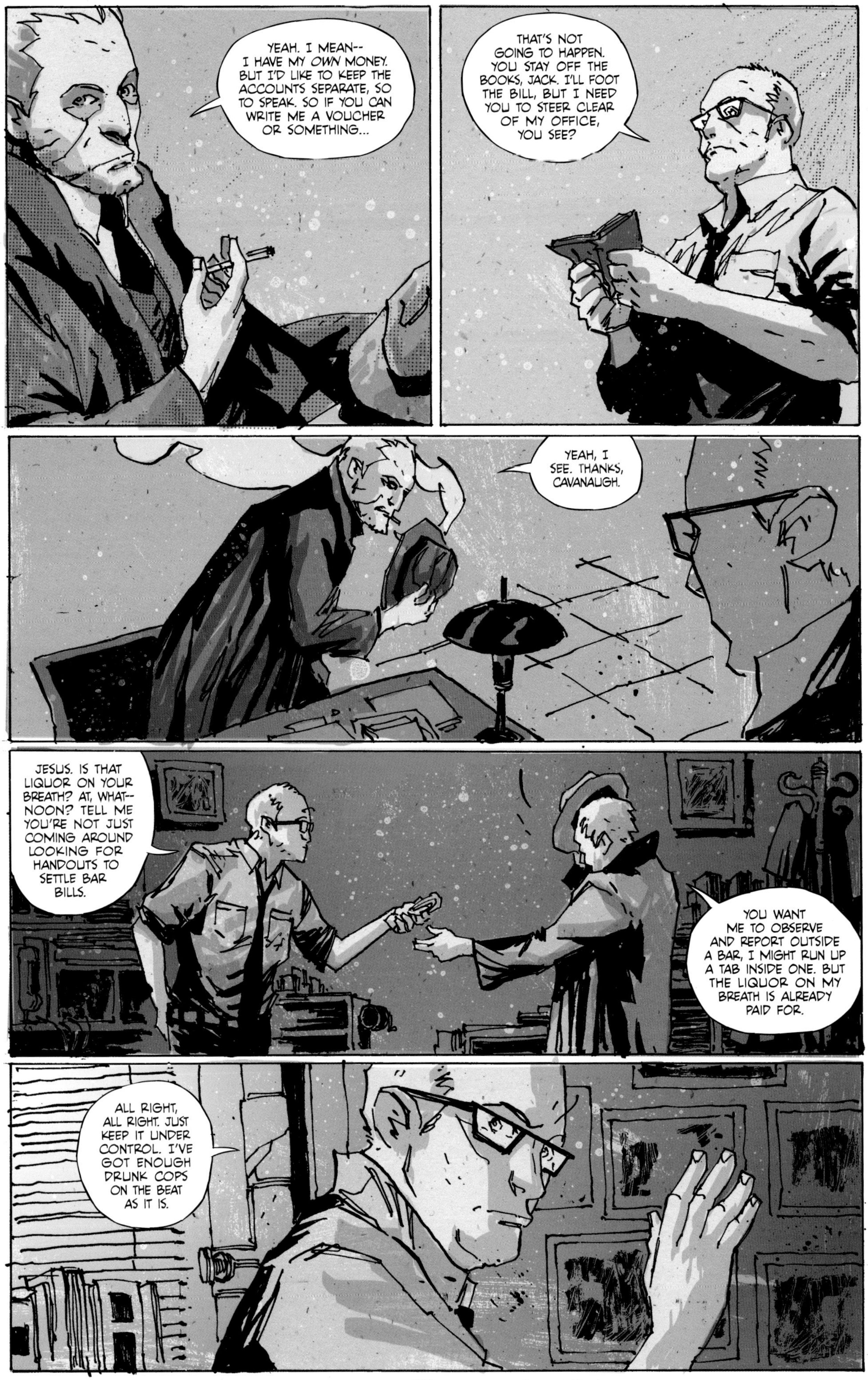
YEAH. I MEAN-- I HAVE MY *OWN* MONEY. BUT I'D LIKE TO KEEP THE ACCOUNTS SEPARATE, SO TO SPEAK. SO IF YOU CAN WRITE ME A VOUCHER OR SOMETHING...
THAT'S NOT GOING TO HAPPEN. YOU STAY OFF THE BOOKS, JACK. I'LL FOOT THE BILL, BUT I NEED YOU TO STEER CLEAR OF MY OFFICE, YOU SEE?
YEAH, I SEE. THANKS, CAVANAUGH.
JESUS. IS THAT LIQUOR ON YOUR BREATH? AT, WHAT-- NOON? TELL ME YOU'RE NOT JUST COMING AROUND LOOKING FOR HANDOUTS TO SETTLE BAR BILLS.
YOU WANT ME TO OBSERVE AND REPORT OUTSIDE A BAR, I MIGHT RUN UP A TAB INSIDE ONE. BUT THE LIQUOR ON MY BREATH IS ALREADY PAID FOR.
ALL RIGHT, ALL RIGHT. JUST KEEP IT UNDER CONTROL. I'VE GOT ENOUGH DRUNK COPS ON THE BEAT AS IT IS.

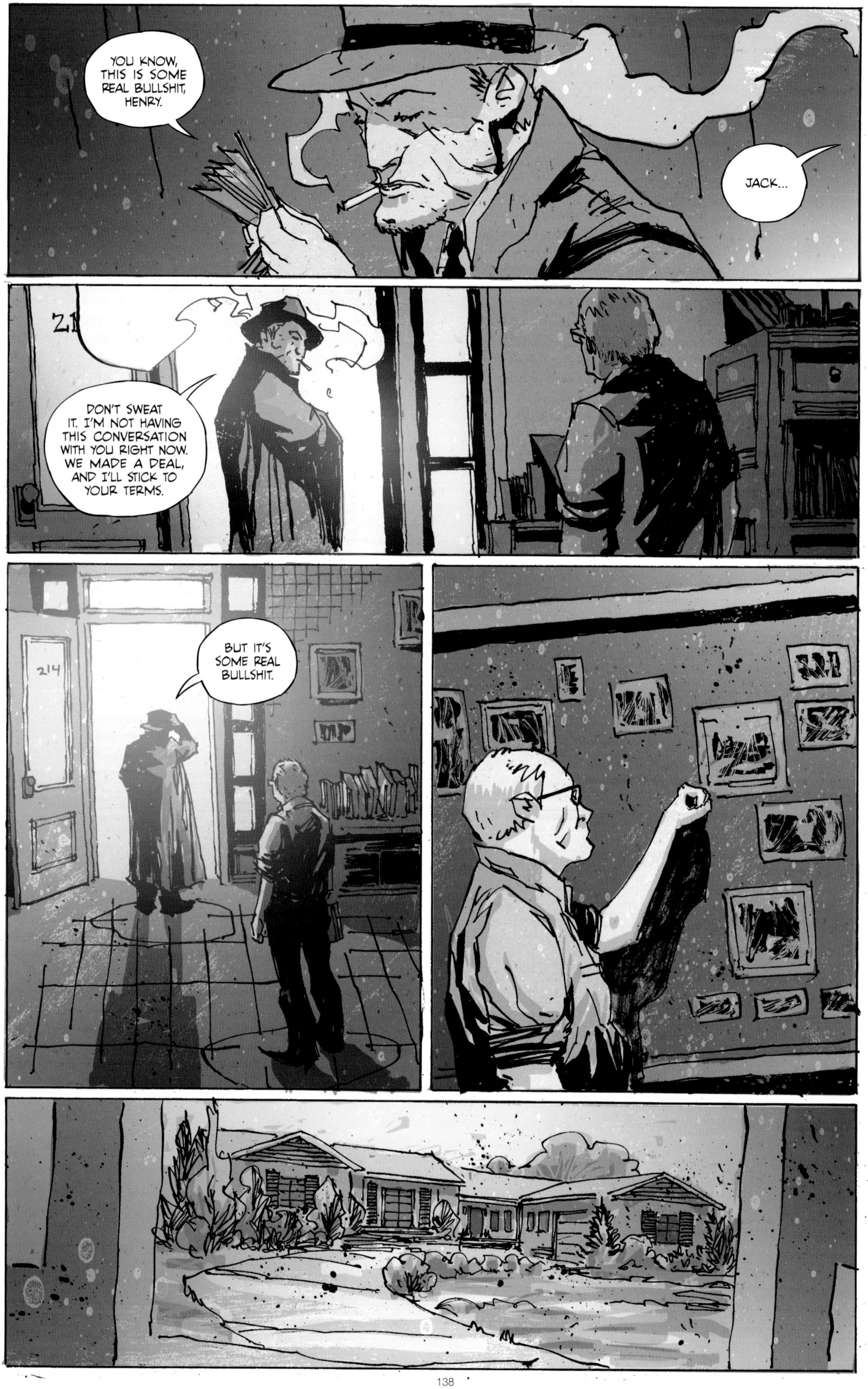
YOU KNOW, THIS IS SOME REAL BULLSHIT, HENRY.
JACK...
DON'T SWEAT IT. I'M NOT HAVING THIS CONVERSATION WITH YOU RIGHT NOW. WE MADE A DEAL, AND I'LL STICK TO YOUR TERMS.
BUT IT'S SOME REAL BULLSHIT.

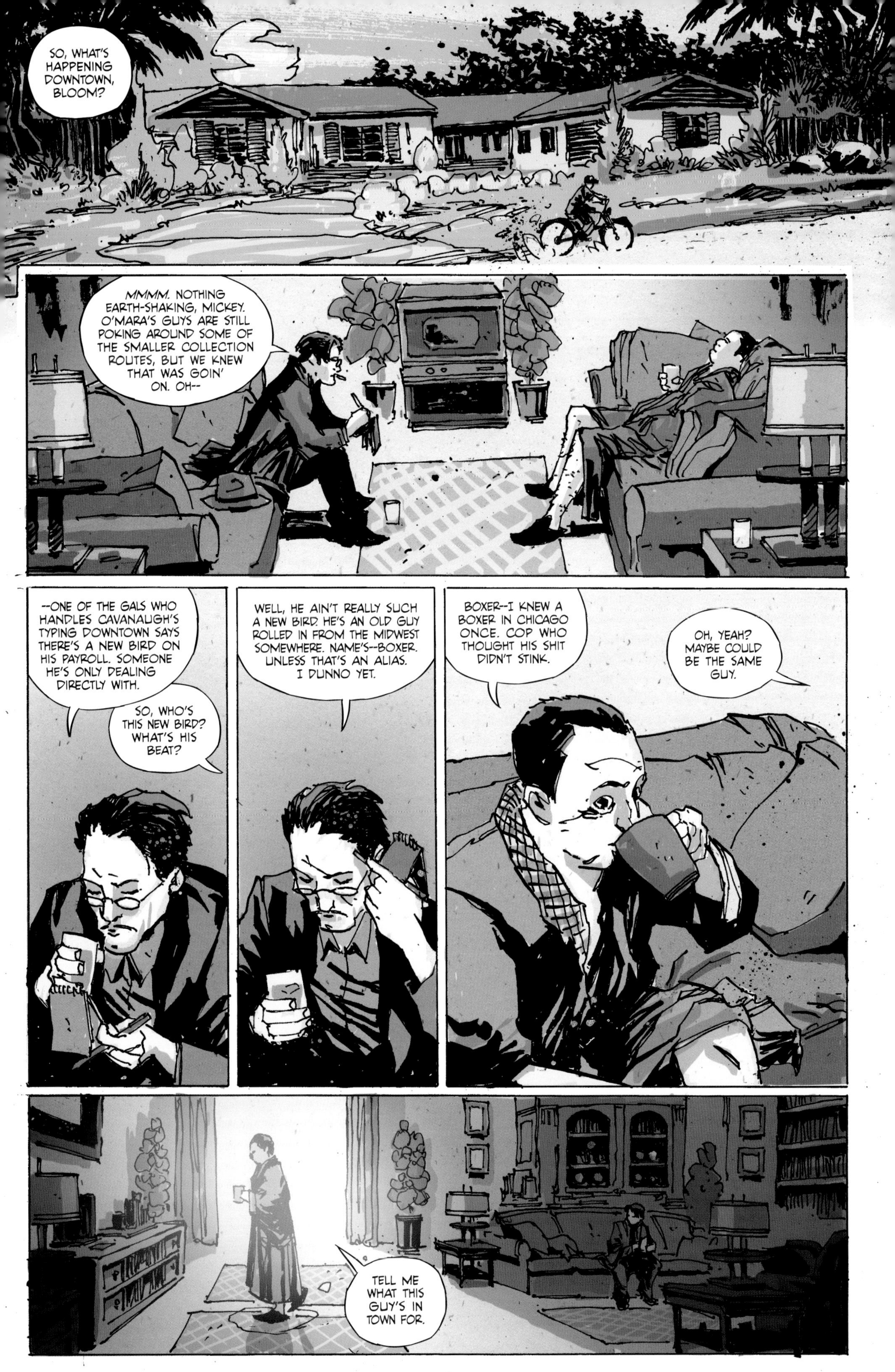
SO, WHAT'S HAPPENING DOWNTOWN, BLOOM?
MMMM. NOTHING EARTH-SHAKING, MICKEY. O'MARA'S GUYS ARE STILL POKING AROUND SOME OF THE SMALLER COLLECTION ROUTES, BUT WE KNEW THAT WAS GOIN' ON. OH--
--ONE OF THE GALS WHO HANDLES CAVANAUGH'S TYPING DOWNTOWN SAYS THERE'S A NEW BIRD ON HIS PAYROLL. SOMEONE HE'S ONLY DEALING DIRECTLY WITH.
SO, WHO'S THIS NEW BIRD? WHAT'S HIS BEAT?
WELL, HE AIN'T REALLY SUCH A NEW BIRD. HE'S AN OLD GUY ROLLED IN FROM THE MIDWEST SOMEWHERE. NAME'S--BOXER. UNLESS THAT'S AN ALIAS. I DUNNO YET.
BOXER--I KNEW A BOXER IN CHICAGO ONCE. COP WHO THOUGHT HIS SHIT DIDN'T STINK.
OH, YEAH? MAYBE COULD BE THE SAME GUY.
TELL ME WHAT THIS GUY'S IN TOWN FOR.

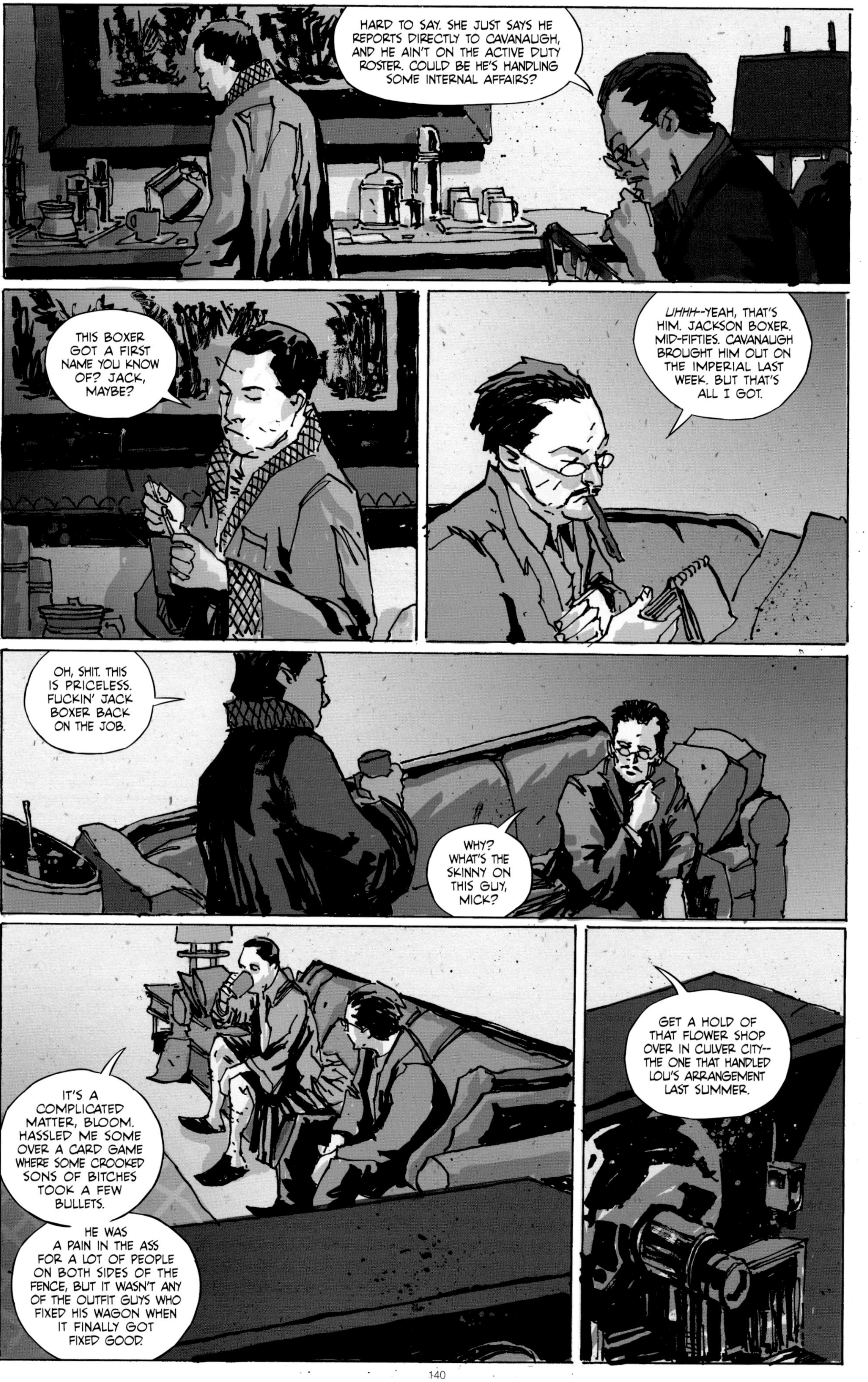

HARD TO SAY. SHE JUST SAYS HE REPORTS DIRECTLY TO CAVANAUGH, AND HE AIN'T ON THE ACTIVE DUTY ROSTER. COULD BE HE'S HANDLING SOME INTERNAL AFFAIRS?
THIS BOXER GOT A FIRST NAME YOU KNOW OF? JACK, MAYBE?
*UHHH*--YEAH, THAT'S HIM. JACKSON BOXER. MID-FIFTIES. CAVANAUGH BROUGHT HIM OUT ON THE IMPERIAL LAST WEEK. BUT THAT'S ALL I GOT.
OH, SHIT. THIS IS PRICELESS. FUCKIN' JACK BOXER BACK ON THE JOB.
WHY? WHAT'S THE SKINNY ON THIS GUY, MICK?
IT'S A COMPLICATED MATTER, BLOOM. HASSLED ME SOME OVER A CARD GAME WHERE SOME CROOKED SONS OF BITCHES TOOK A FEW BULLETS.
HE WAS A PAIN IN THE ASS FOR A LOT OF PEOPLE ON BOTH SIDES OF THE FENCE, BUT IT WASN'T ANY OF THE OUTFIT GUYS WHO FIXED HIS WAGON WHEN IT FINALLY GOT FIXED GOOD.
GET A HOLD OF THAT FLOWER SHOP OVER IN CULVER CITY-- THE ONE THAT HANDLED LOU'S ARRANGEMENT LAST SUMMER.

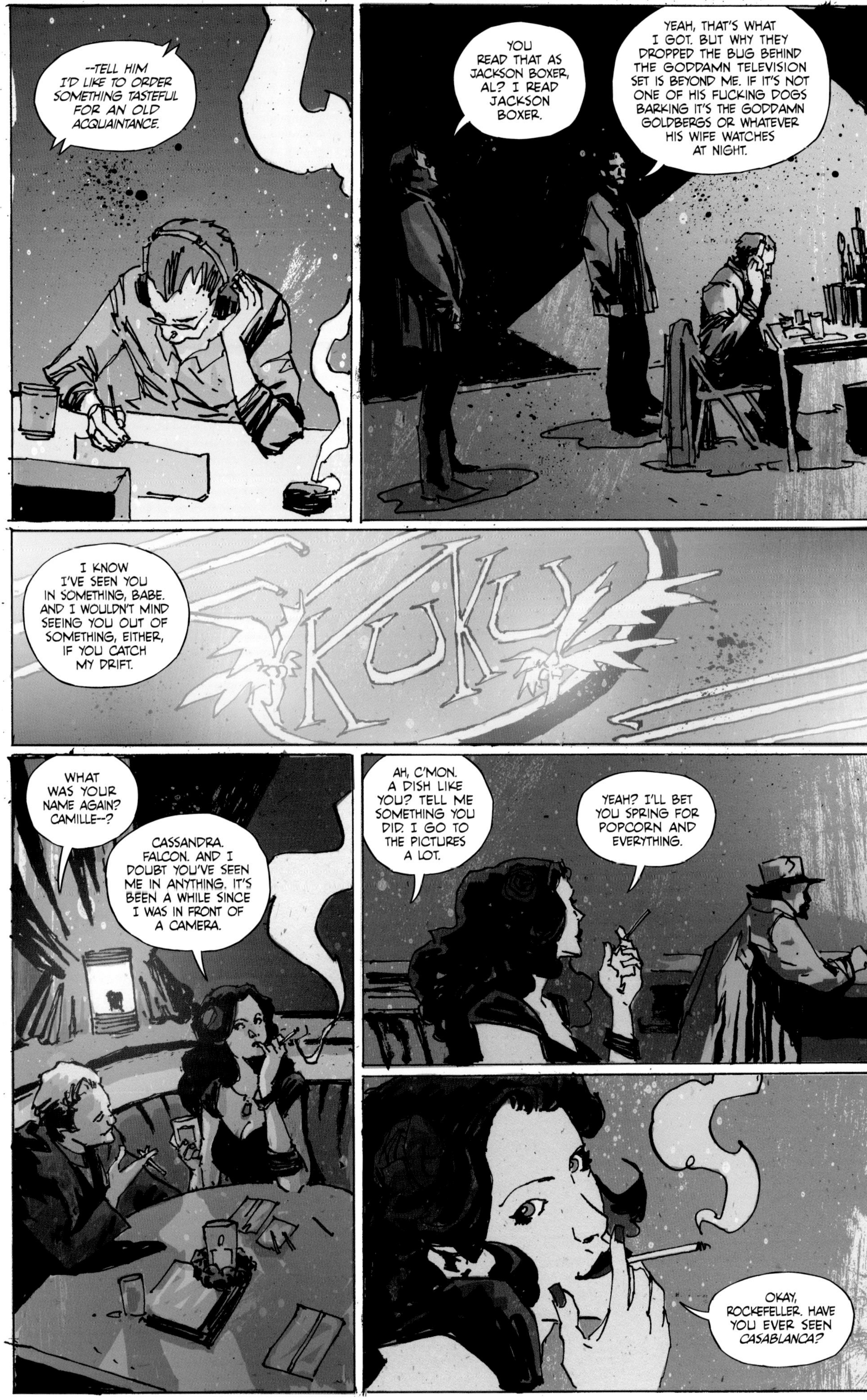
--TELL HIM I'D LIKE TO ORDER SOMETHING TASTEFUL FOR AN OLD ACQUAINTANCE.
YOU READ THAT AS JACKSON BOXER, AL? I READ JACKSON BOXER.
YEAH, THAT'S WHAT I GOT. BUT WHY THEY DROPPED THE BUG BEHIND THE GODDAMN TELEVISION SET IS BEYOND ME. IF IT'S NOT ONE OF HIS FUCKING DOGS BARKING IT'S THE GODDAMN GOLDBERGS OR WHATEVER HIS WIFE WATCHES AT NIGHT.
I KNOW I'VE SEEN YOU IN SOMETHING, BABE. AND I WOULDN'T MIND SEEING YOU OUT OF SOMETHING, EITHER, IF YOU CATCH MY DRIFT.
KUKU
WHAT WAS YOUR NAME AGAIN? CAMILLE--?
CASSANDRA. FALCON. AND I DOUBT YOU'VE SEEN ME IN ANYTHING. IT'S BEEN A WHILE SINCE I WAS IN FRONT OF A CAMERA.
AH, C'MON. A DISH LIKE YOU? TELL ME SOMETHING YOU DID. I GO TO THE PICTURES A LOT.
YEAH? I'LL BET YOU SPRING FOR POPCORN AND EVERYTHING.
OKAY, ROCKEFELLER. HAVE YOU EVER SEEN *CASABLANCA?*

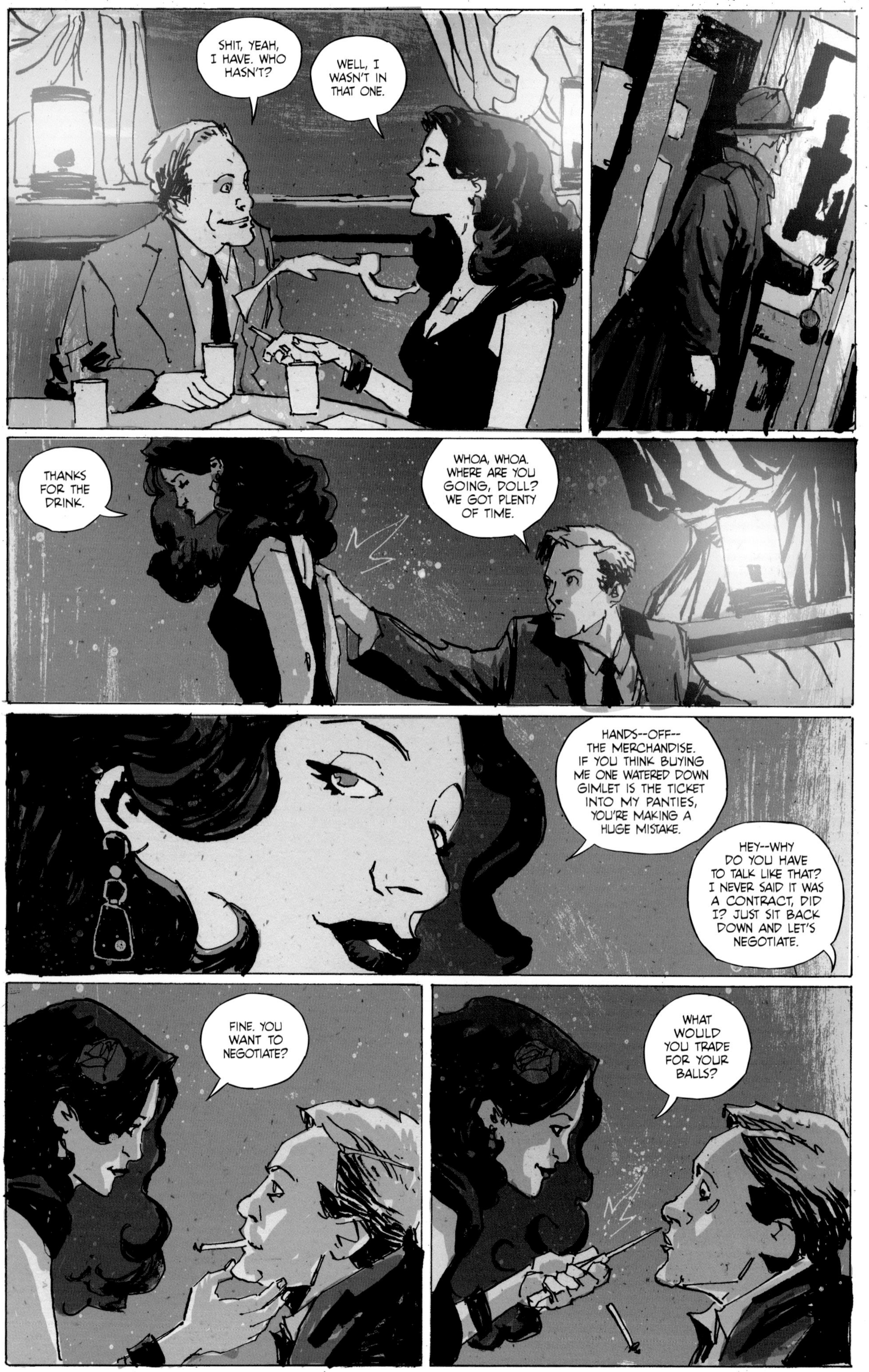
SHIT, YEAH, I HAVE. WHO HASN'T?
WELL, I WASN'T IN THAT ONE.
THANKS FOR THE DRINK.
WHOA, WHOA. WHERE ARE YOU GOING, DOLL? WE GOT PLENTY OF TIME.
HANDS--OFF--THE MERCHANDISE. IF YOU THINK BUYING ME ONE WATERED DOWN GIMLET IS THE TICKET INTO MY PANTIES, YOU'RE MAKING A HUGE MISTAKE.
HEY--WHY DO YOU HAVE TO TALK LIKE THAT? I NEVER SAID IT WAS A CONTRACT, DID I? JUST SIT BACK DOWN AND LET'S NEGOTIATE.
FINE. YOU WANT TO NEGOTIATE?
WHAT WOULD YOU TRADE FOR YOUR BALLS?

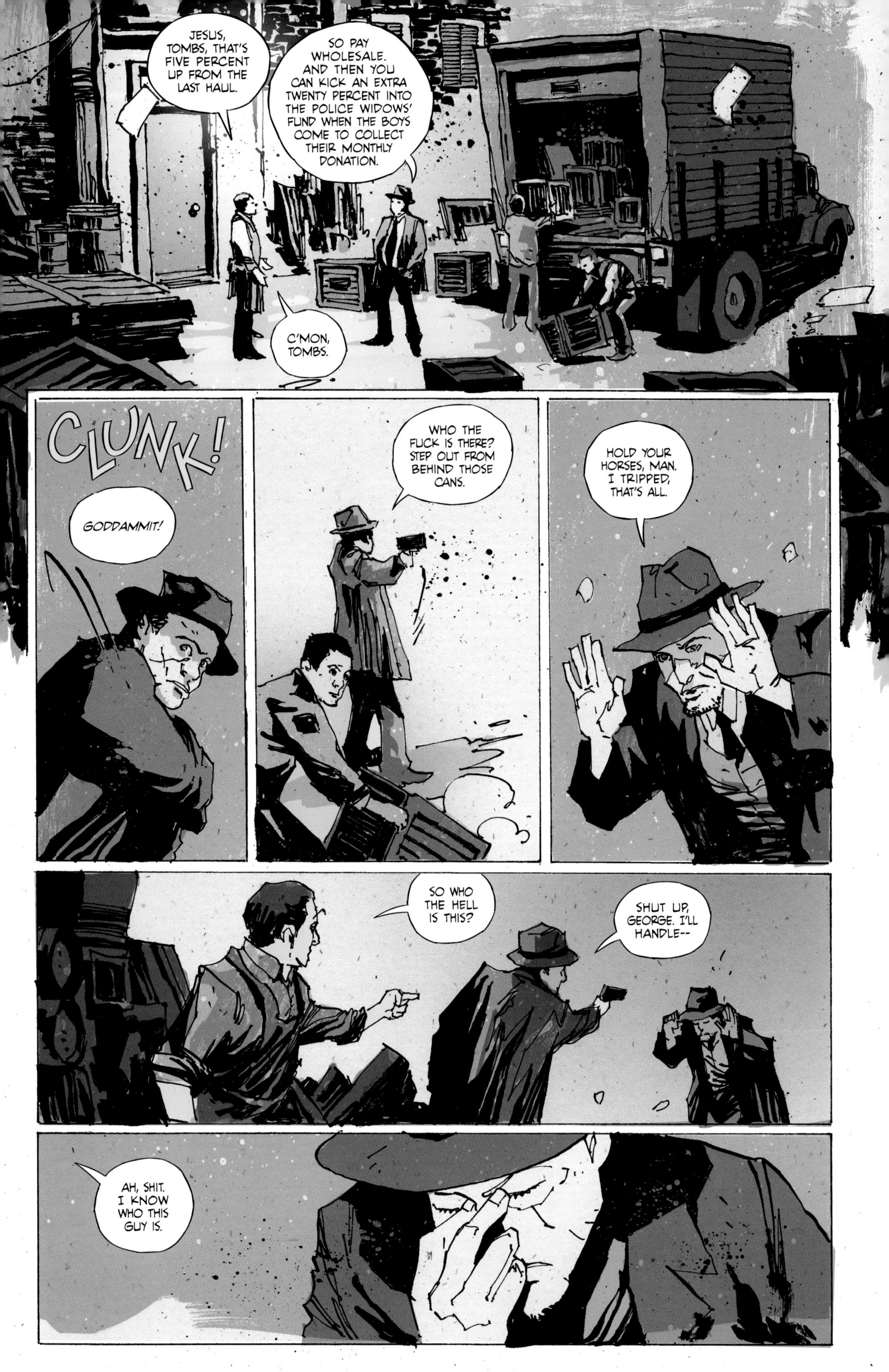
JESUS, TOMBS, THAT'S FIVE PERCENT UP FROM THE LAST HAUL.
SO PAY WHOLESALE. AND THEN YOU CAN KICK AN EXTRA TWENTY PERCENT INTO THE POLICE WIDOWS' FUND WHEN THE BOYS COME TO COLLECT THEIR MONTHLY DONATION.
C'MON, TOMBS.
CLUNK!
GODDAMMIT!
WHO THE FUCK IS THERE? STEP OUT FROM BEHIND THOSE CANS.
HOLD YOUR HORSES, MAN. I TRIPPED, THAT'S ALL.
SO WHO THE HELL IS THIS?
SHUT UP, GEORGE. I'LL HANDLE--
AH, SHIT. I KNOW WHO THIS GUY IS.

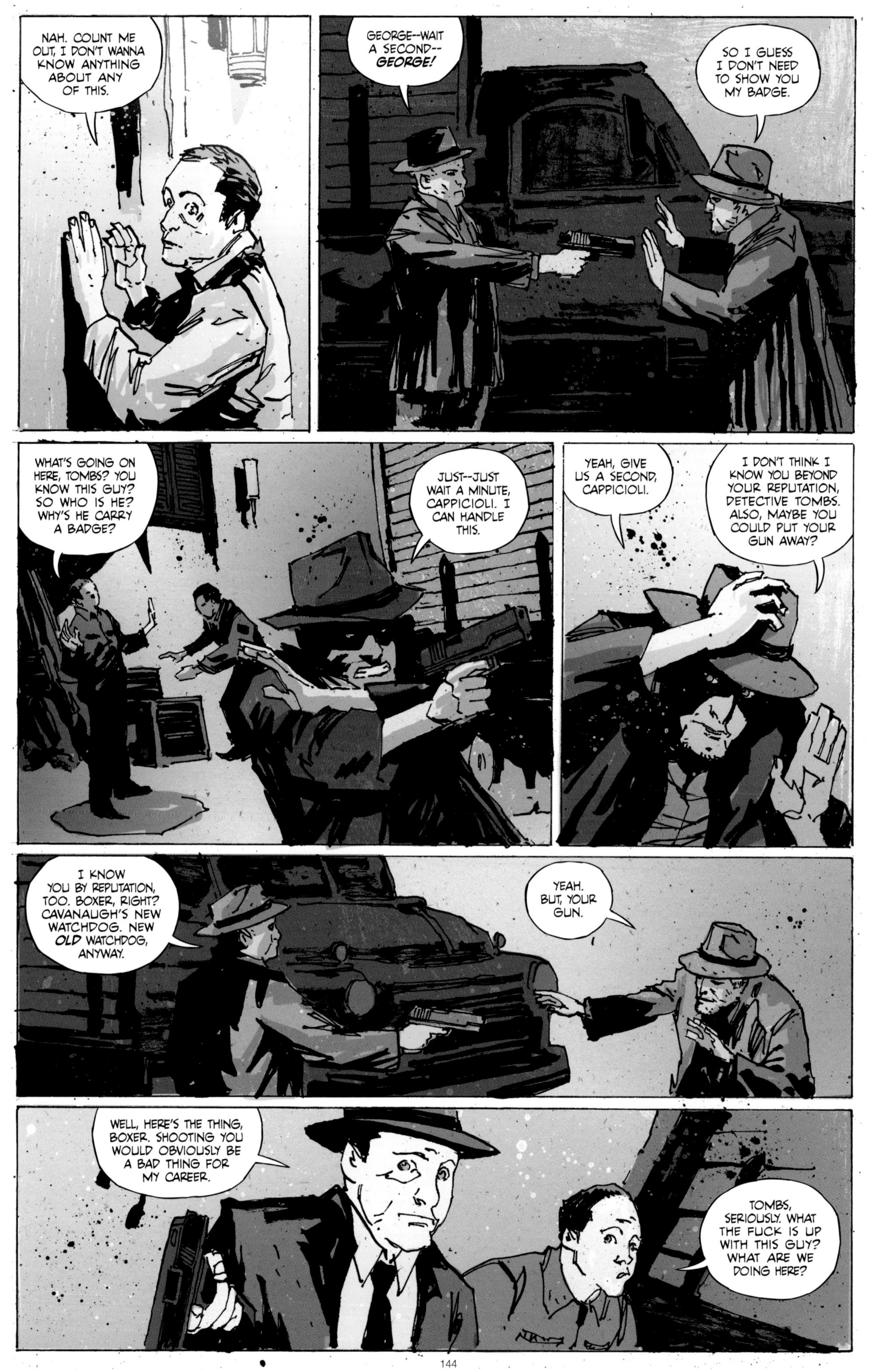

NAH. COUNT ME OUT, I DON'T WANNA KNOW ANYTHING ABOUT ANY OF THIS.
GEORGE--WAIT A SECOND-- **GEORGE!**
SO I GUESS I DON'T NEED TO SHOW YOU MY BADGE.
WHAT'S GOING ON HERE, TOMBS? YOU KNOW THIS GUY? SO WHO IS HE? WHY'S HE CARRY A BADGE?
JUST--JUST WAIT A MINUTE, CAPPICIOLI. I CAN HANDLE THIS.
YEAH, GIVE US A SECOND, CAPPICIOLI.
I DON'T THINK I KNOW YOU BEYOND YOUR REPUTATION, DETECTIVE TOMBS. ALSO, MAYBE YOU COULD PUT YOUR GUN AWAY?
I KNOW YOU BY REPUTATION, TOO. BOXER, RIGHT? CAVANAUGH'S NEW WATCHDOG. NEW ***OLD*** WATCHDOG, ANYWAY.
YEAH. BUT, YOUR GUN.
WELL, HERE'S THE THING, BOXER. SHOOTING YOU WOULD OBVIOUSLY BE A BAD THING FOR MY CAREER.
TOMBS, SERIOUSLY. WHAT THE FUCK IS UP WITH THIS GUY? WHAT ARE WE DOING HERE?

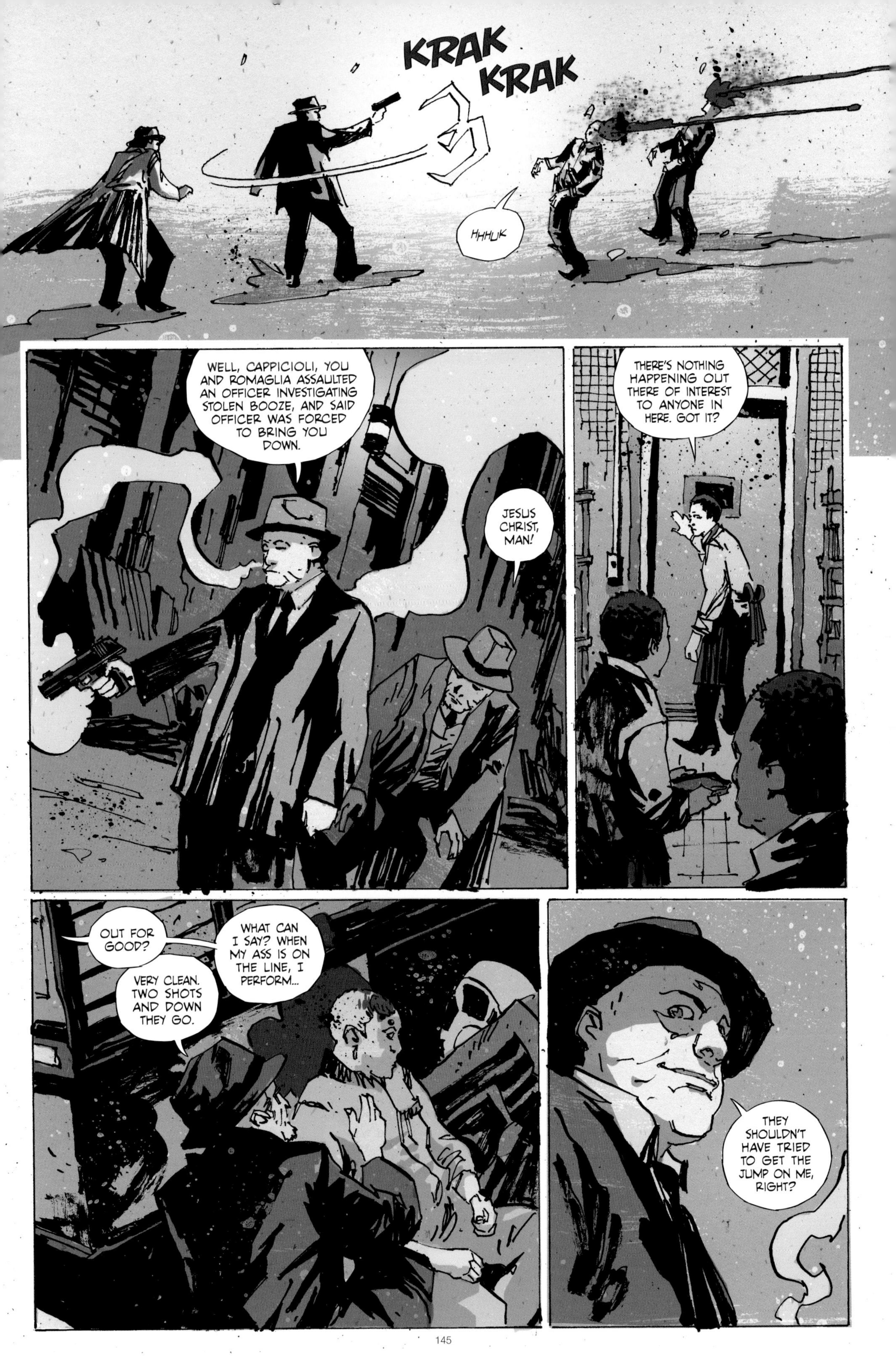
KRAK KRAK
HHHUK
WELL, CAPPICIOLI, YOU AND ROMAGLIA ASSAULTED AN OFFICER INVESTIGATING STOLEN BOOZE, AND SAID OFFICER WAS FORCED TO BRING YOU DOWN.
JESUS CHRIST, MAN!
THERE'S NOTHING HAPPENING OUT THERE OF INTEREST TO ANYONE IN HERE. GOT IT?
OUT FOR GOOD?
VERY CLEAN. TWO SHOTS AND DOWN THEY GO.
WHAT CAN I SAY? WHEN MY ASS IS ON THE LINE, I PERFORM...
THEY SHOULDN'T HAVE TRIED TO GET THE JUMP ON ME, RIGHT?

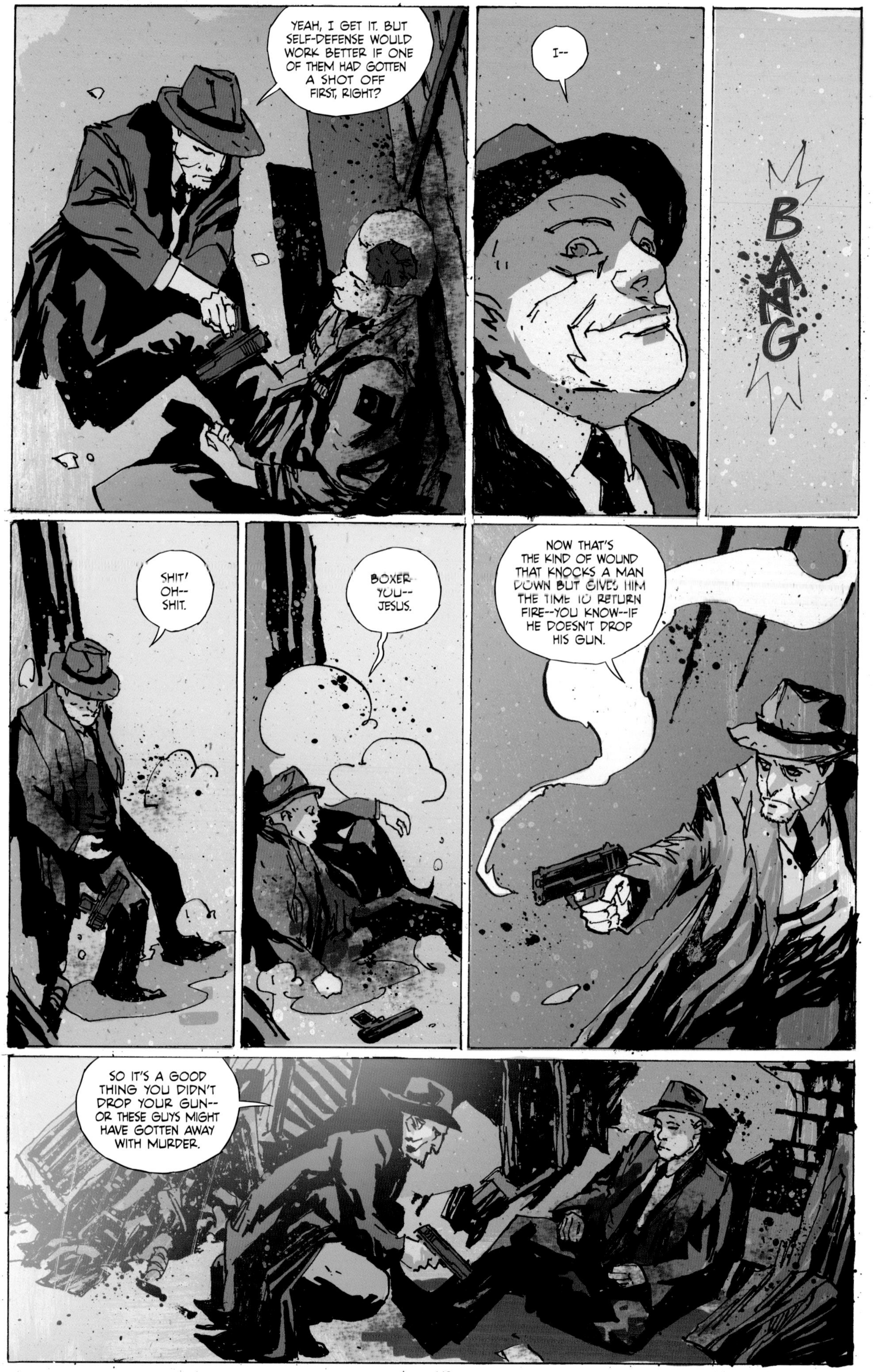
YEAH, I GET IT. BUT SELF-DEFENSE WOULD WORK BETTER IF ONE OF THEM HAD GOTTEN A SHOT OFF FIRST, RIGHT?
I--
BANG
SHIT! OH-- SHIT.
BOXER YOU-- JESUS.
NOW THAT'S THE KIND OF WOUND THAT KNOCKS A MAN DOWN BUT GIVES HIM THE TIME TO RETURN FIRE--YOU KNOW--IF HE DOESN'T DROP HIS GUN.
SO IT'S A GOOD THING YOU DIDN'T DROP YOUR GUN-- OR THESE GUYS MIGHT HAVE GOTTEN AWAY WITH MURDER.

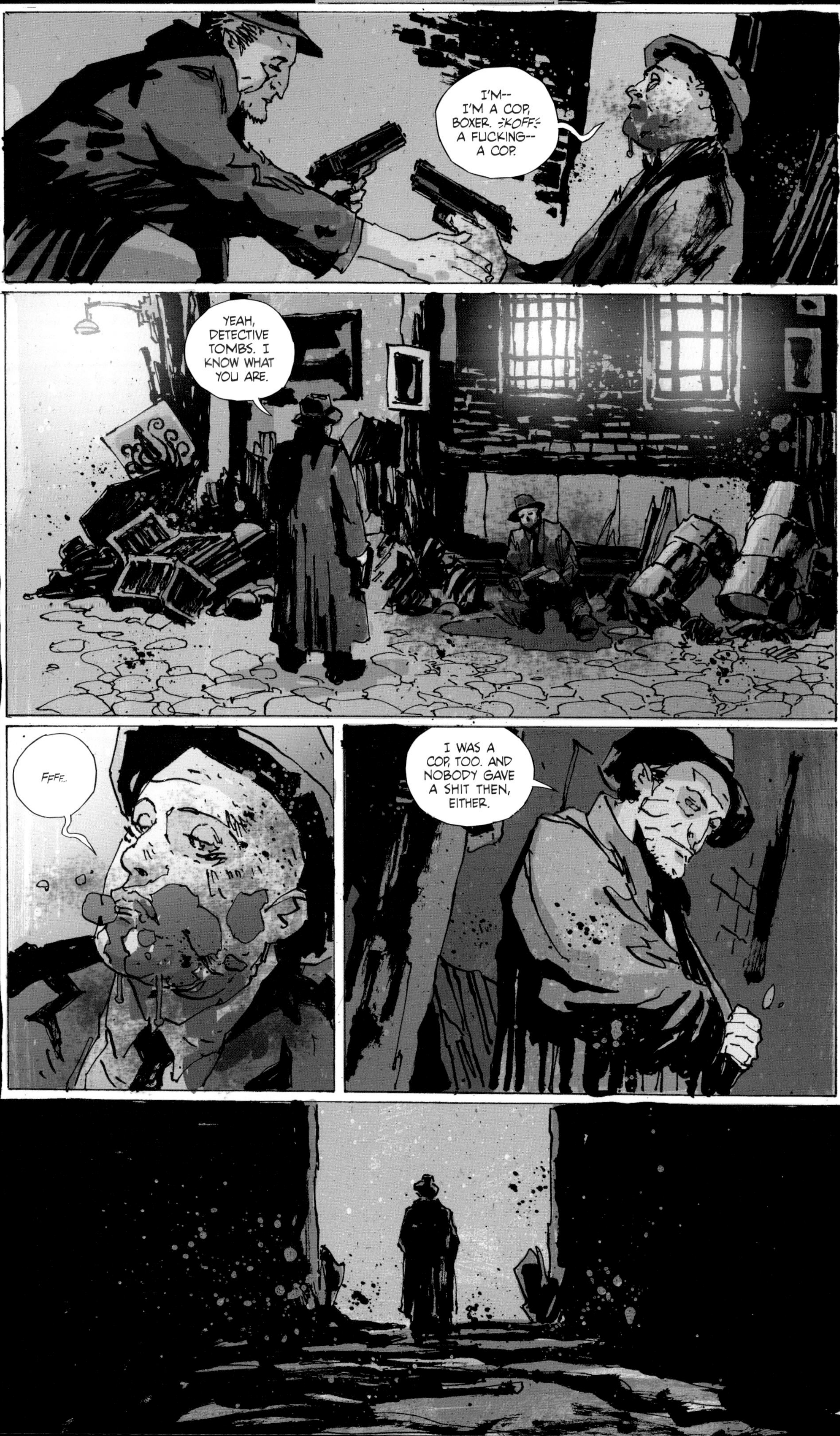
I'M--
I'M A COP, BOXER. -KOFF- A FUCKING-- A COP.
YEAH, DETECTIVE TOMBS. I KNOW WHAT YOU ARE.
FFFF..
I WAS A COP, TOO. AND NOBODY GAVE A SHIT THEN, EITHER.

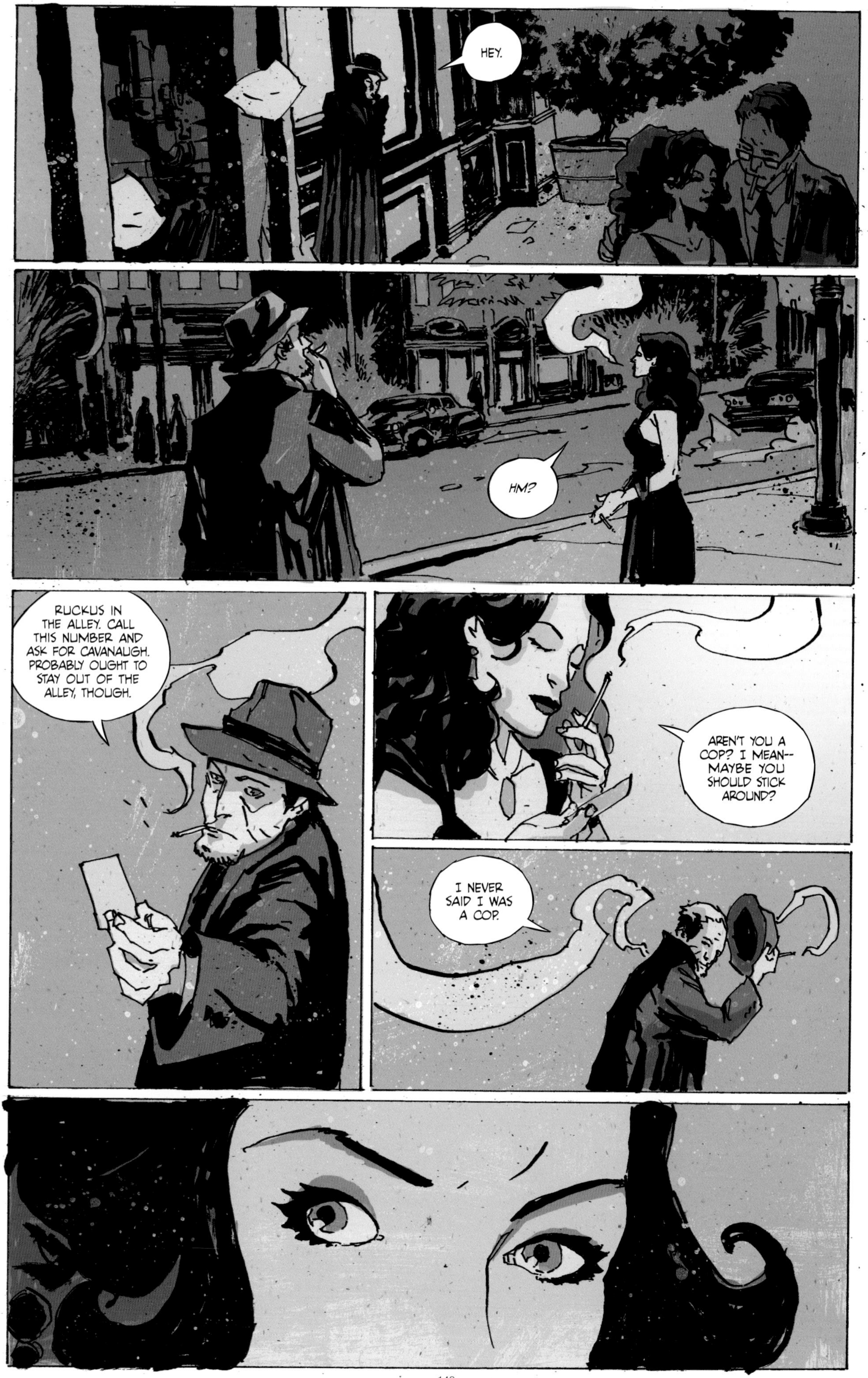
HEY.
HM?
RUCKUS IN THE ALLEY. CALL THIS NUMBER AND ASK FOR CAVANAUGH. PROBABLY OUGHT TO STAY OUT OF THE ALLEY, THOUGH.
AREN'T YOU A COP? I MEAN-- MAYBE YOU SHOULD STICK AROUND?
I NEVER SAID I WAS A COP.

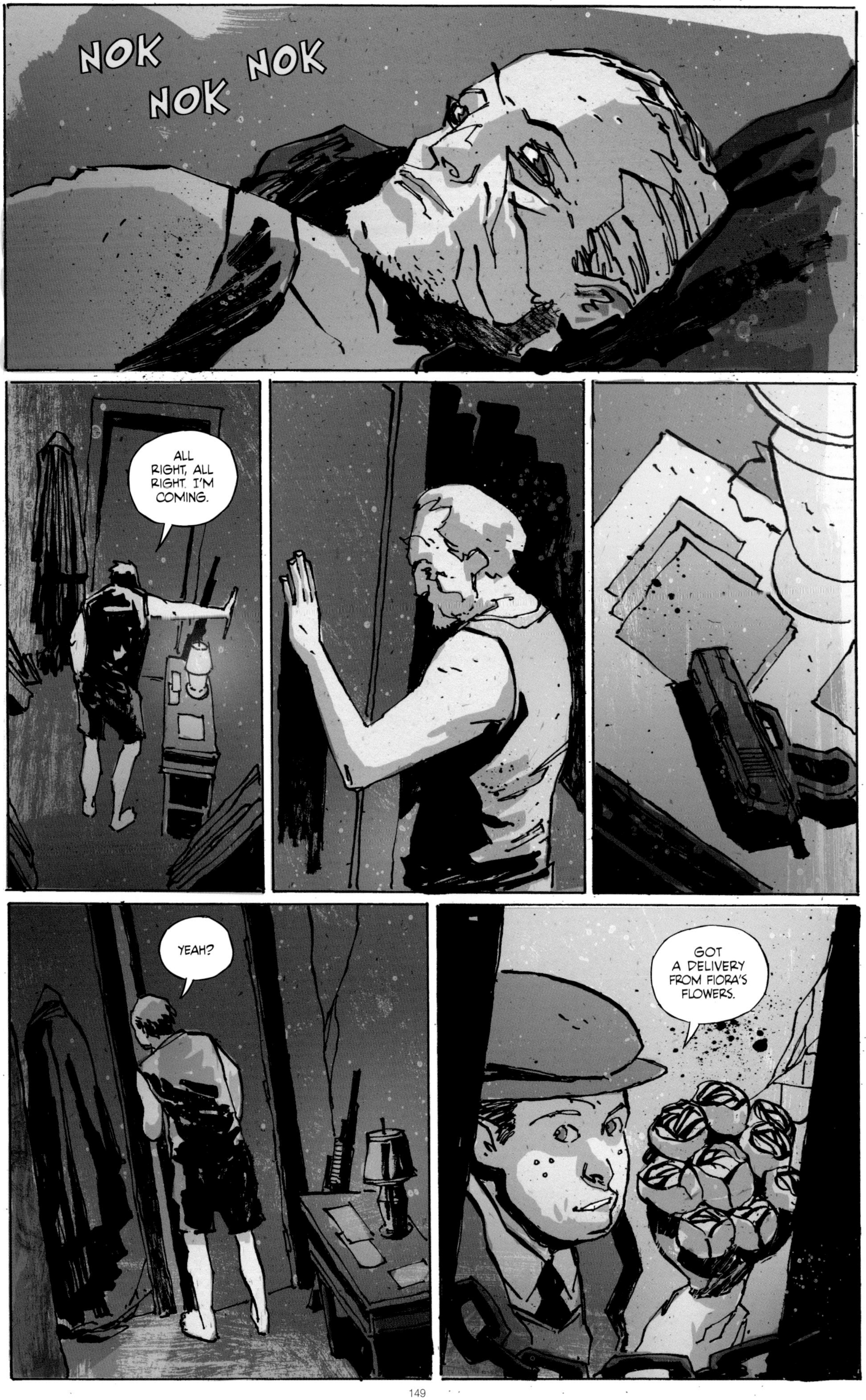
NOK
NOK
NOK
ALL RIGHT, ALL RIGHT. I'M COMING.
YEAH?
GOT A DELIVERY FROM FIORA'S FLOWERS.

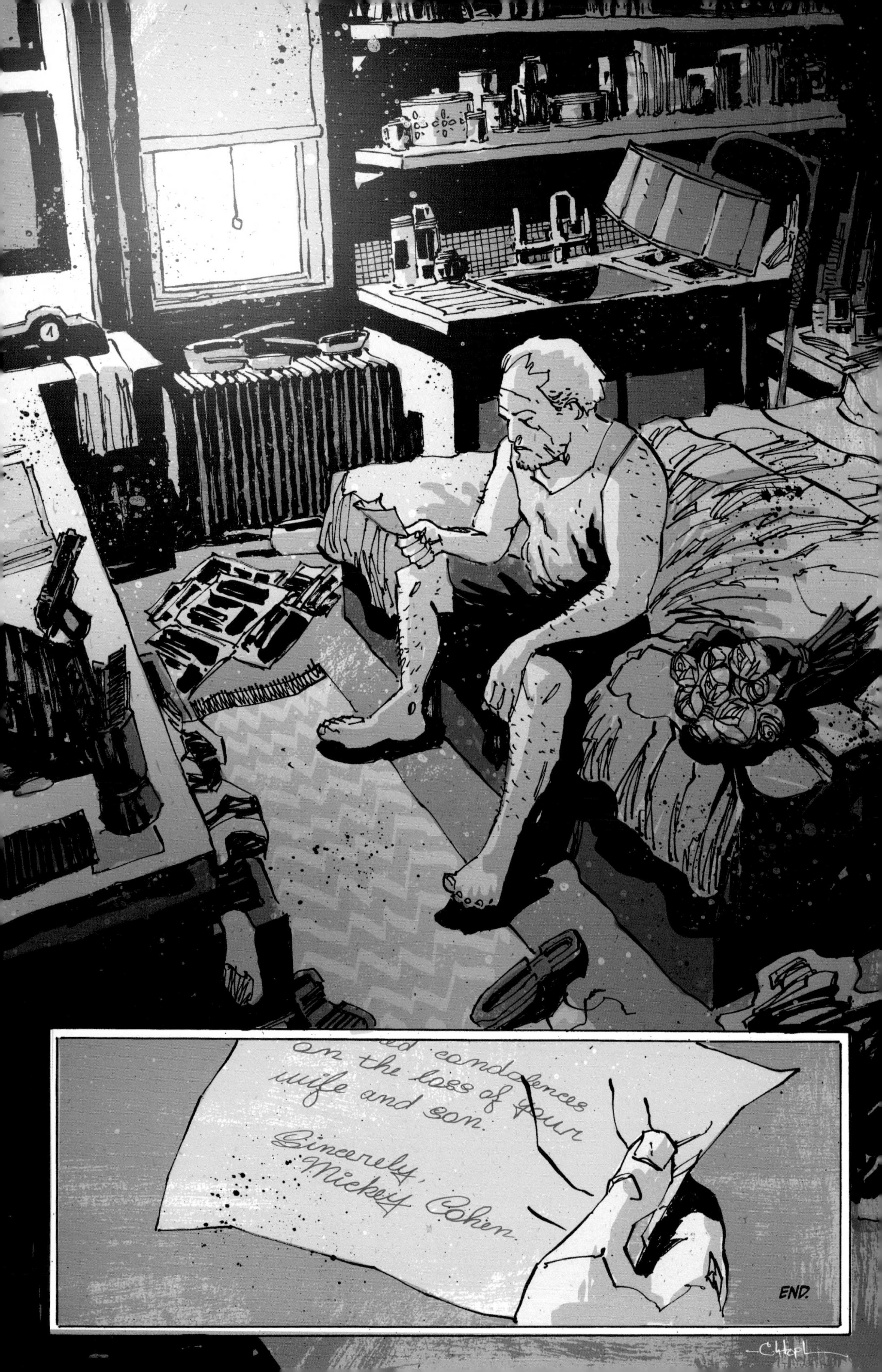
condolences
on the loss of your
wife and son.
Sincerely,
Mickey Cohen.
END.

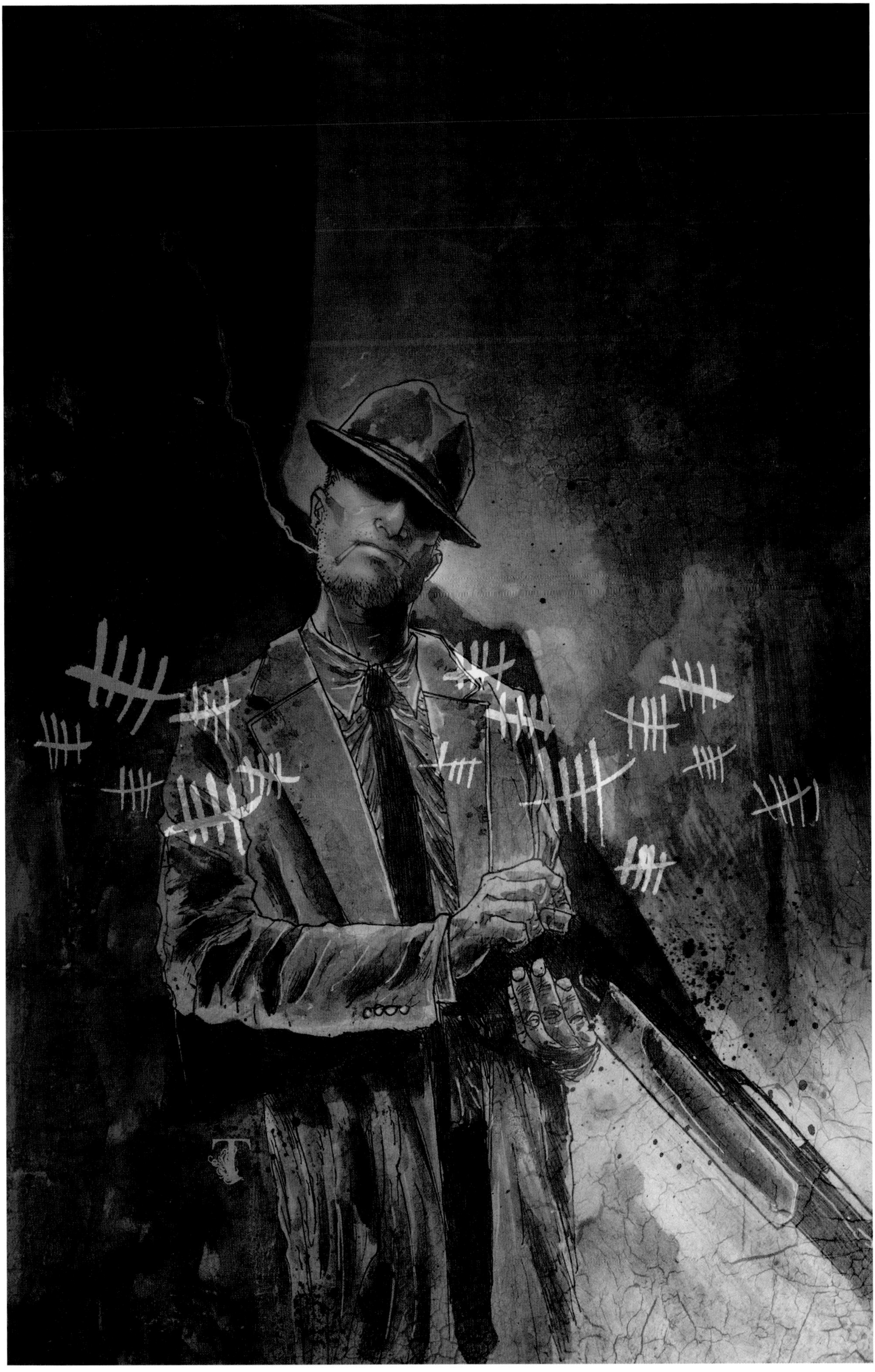

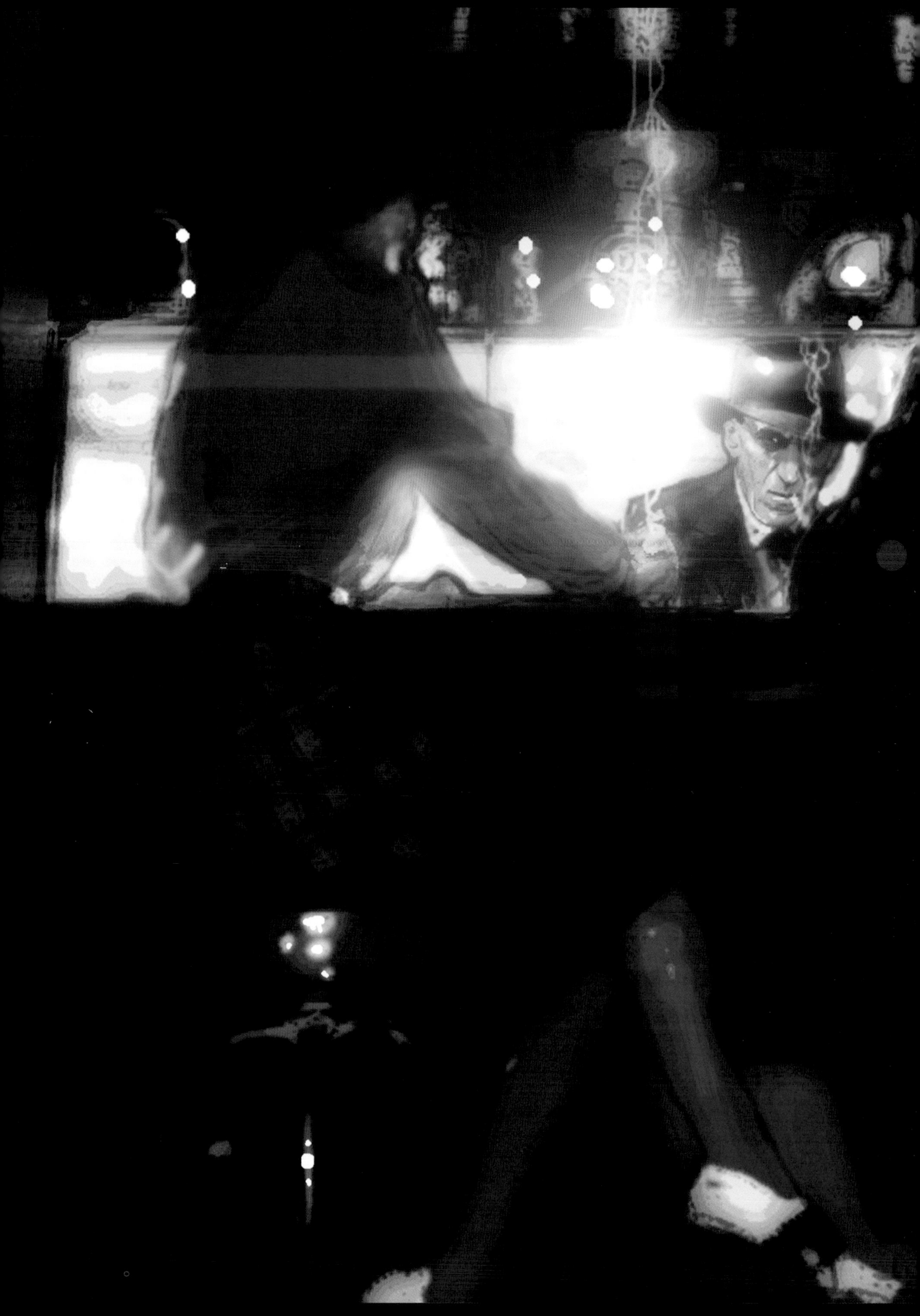

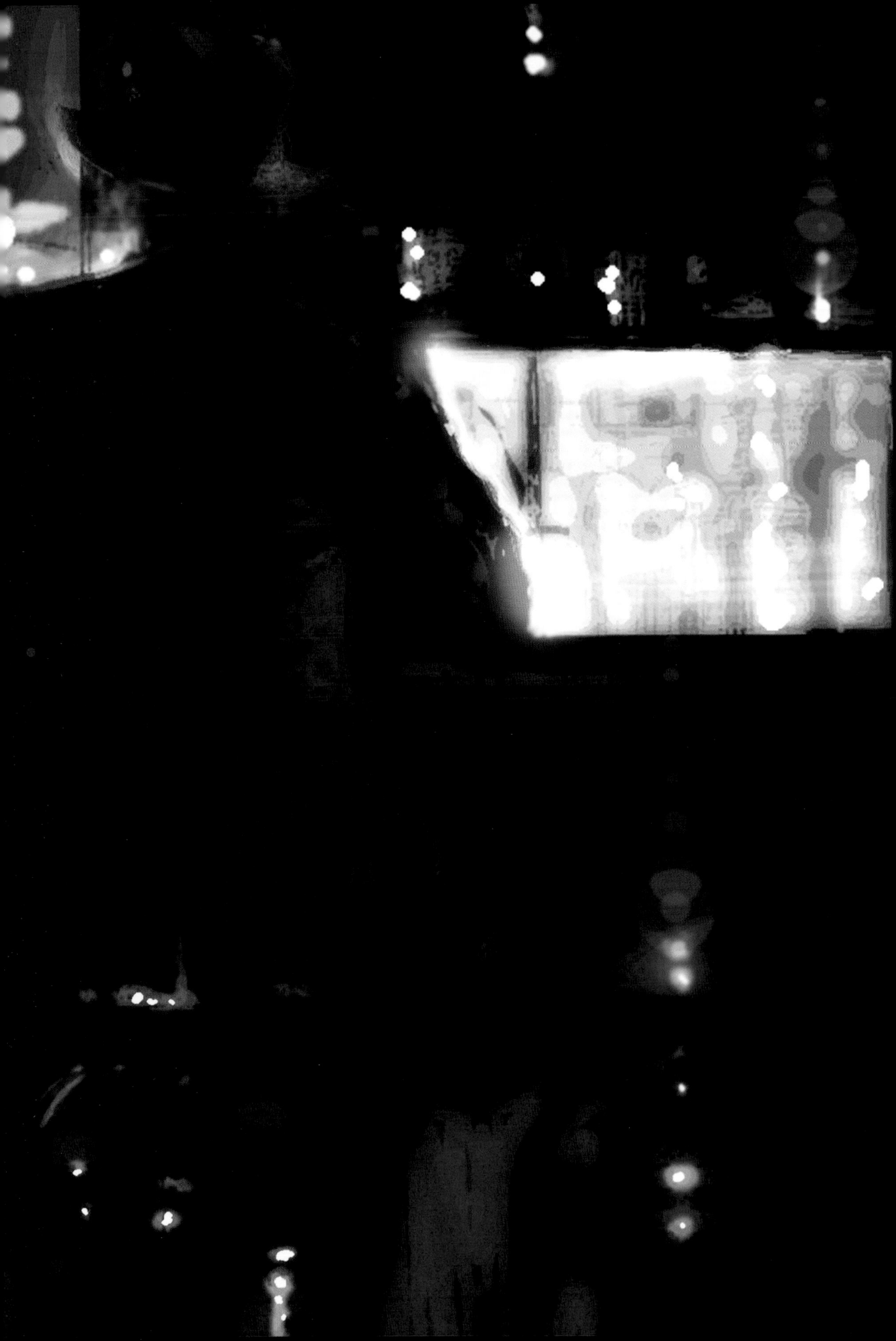

# MIDDLETON
## The Strange Case of Ethan Frost

story    B. Clay Moore
art      Alejandro Aragón
letters  Thomas Mauer
font     Steven Griffin

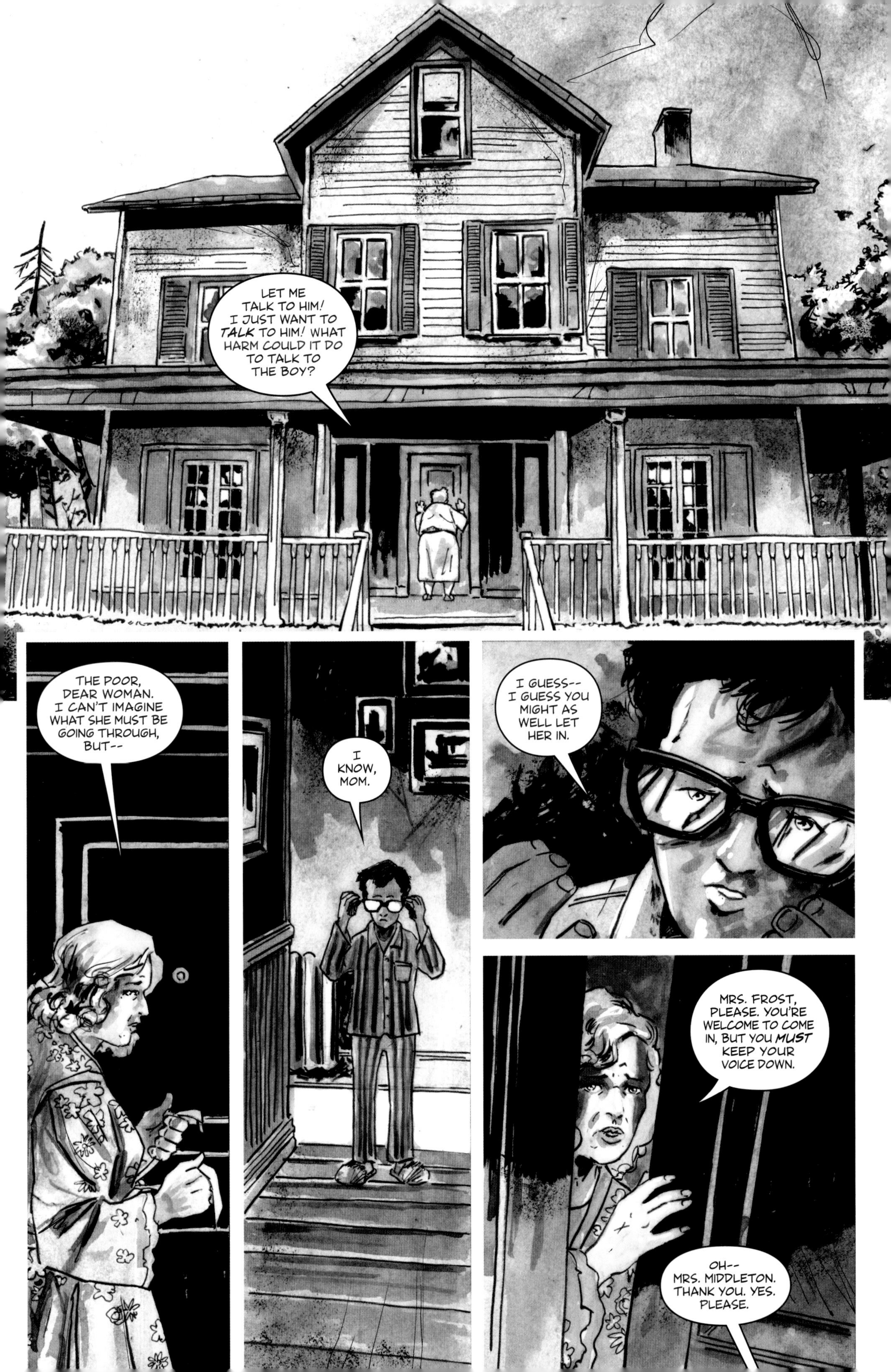
LET ME TALK TO HIM! I JUST WANT TO *TALK* TO HIM! WHAT HARM COULD IT DO TO TALK TO THE BOY?
THE POOR, DEAR WOMAN. I CAN'T IMAGINE WHAT SHE MUST BE GOING THROUGH, BUT--
I KNOW, MOM.
I GUESS-- I GUESS YOU MIGHT AS WELL LET HER IN.
MRS. FROST, PLEASE. YOU'RE WELCOME TO COME IN, BUT YOU *MUST* KEEP YOUR VOICE DOWN.
OH-- MRS. MIDDLETON. THANK YOU. YES. PLEASE.

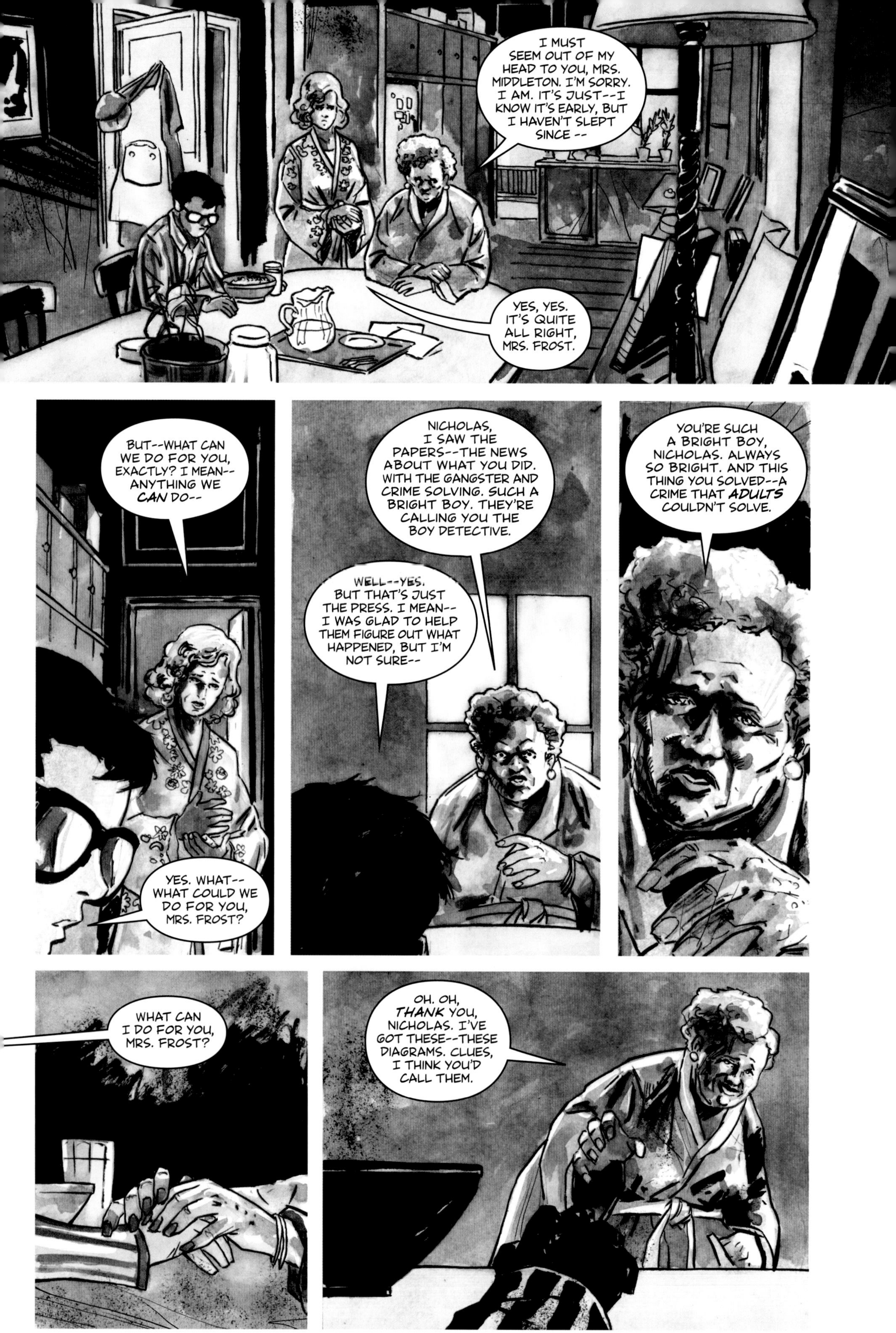
I MUST SEEM OUT OF MY HEAD TO YOU, MRS. MIDDLETON. I'M SORRY. I AM. IT'S JUST--I KNOW IT'S EARLY, BUT I HAVEN'T SLEPT SINCE --
YES, YES. IT'S QUITE ALL RIGHT, MRS. FROST.
BUT--WHAT CAN WE DO FOR YOU, EXACTLY? I MEAN--ANYTHING WE CAN DO--
YES. WHAT--WHAT COULD WE DO FOR YOU, MRS. FROST?
NICHOLAS, I SAW THE PAPERS--THE NEWS ABOUT WHAT YOU DID. WITH THE GANGSTER AND CRIME SOLVING. SUCH A BRIGHT BOY. THEY'RE CALLING YOU THE BOY DETECTIVE.
WELL--YES. BUT THAT'S JUST THE PRESS. I MEAN--I WAS GLAD TO HELP THEM FIGURE OUT WHAT HAPPENED, BUT I'M NOT SURE--
YOU'RE SUCH A BRIGHT BOY, NICHOLAS. ALWAYS SO BRIGHT. AND THIS THING YOU SOLVED--A CRIME THAT ADULTS COULDN'T SOLVE.
WHAT CAN I DO FOR YOU, MRS. FROST?
OH. OH, THANK YOU, NICHOLAS. I'VE GOT THESE--THESE DIAGRAMS. CLUES, I THINK YOU'D CALL THEM.

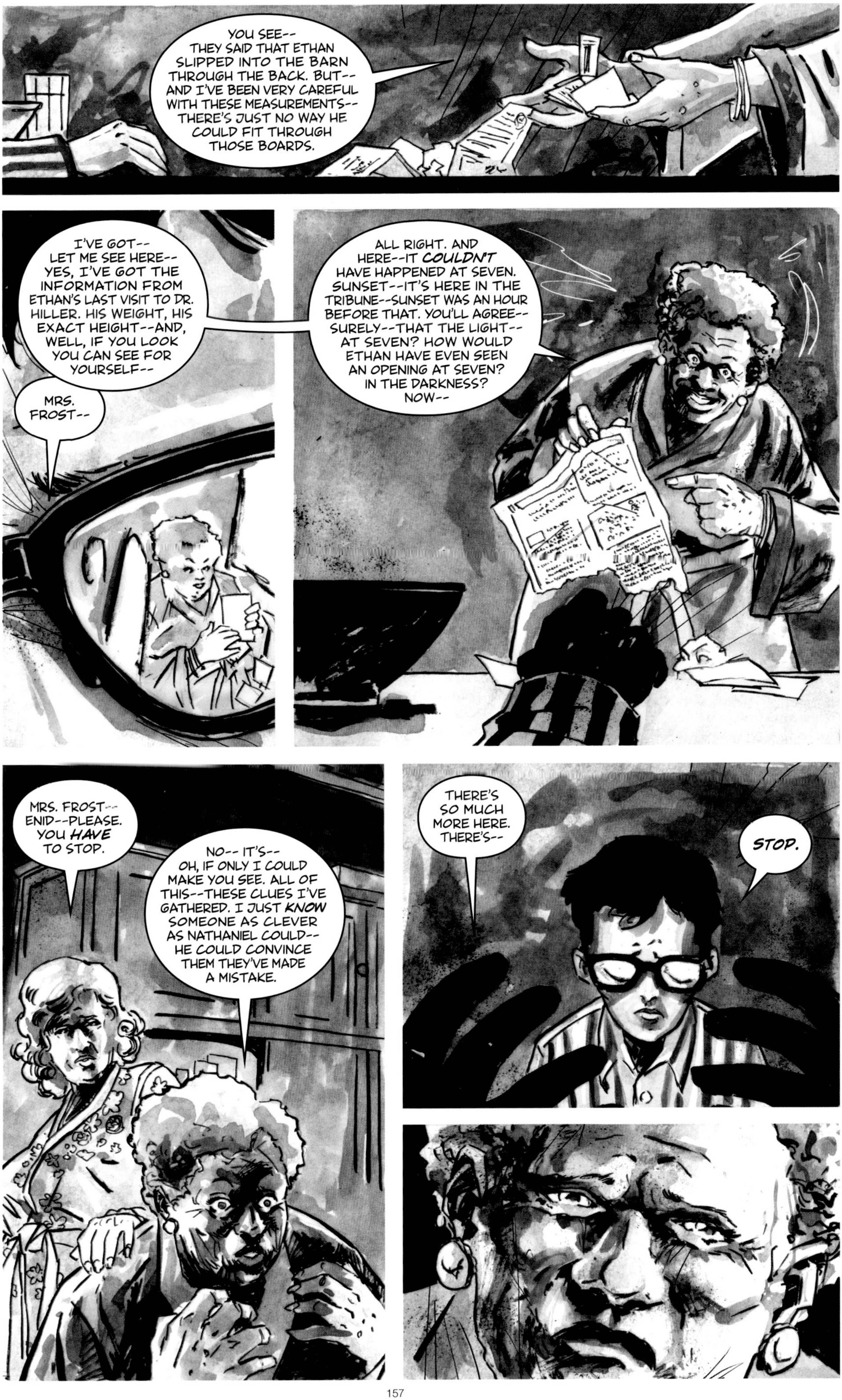
YOU SEE-- THEY SAID THAT ETHAN SLIPPED INTO THE BARN THROUGH THE BACK. BUT-- AND I'VE BEEN VERY CAREFUL WITH THESE MEASUREMENTS-- THERE'S JUST NO WAY HE COULD FIT THROUGH THOSE BOARDS.
I'VE GOT-- LET ME SEE HERE-- YES, I'VE GOT THE INFORMATION FROM ETHAN'S LAST VISIT TO DR. HILLER. HIS WEIGHT, HIS EXACT HEIGHT--AND, WELL, IF YOU LOOK YOU CAN SEE FOR YOURSELF--
MRS. FROST--
ALL RIGHT. AND HERE--IT COULDN'T HAVE HAPPENED AT SEVEN. SUNSET--IT'S HERE IN THE TRIBUNE--SUNSET WAS AN HOUR BEFORE THAT. YOU'LL AGREE-- SURELY--THAT THE LIGHT-- AT SEVEN? HOW WOULD ETHAN HAVE EVEN SEEN AN OPENING AT SEVEN? IN THE DARKNESS? NOW--
MRS. FROST-- ENID--PLEASE. YOU HAVE TO STOP.
NO-- IT'S-- OH, IF ONLY I COULD MAKE YOU SEE. ALL OF THIS--THESE CLUES I'VE GATHERED. I JUST KNOW SOMEONE AS CLEVER AS NATHANIEL COULD-- HE COULD CONVINCE THEM THEY'VE MADE A MISTAKE.
THERE'S SO MUCH MORE HERE. THERE'S--
STOP.

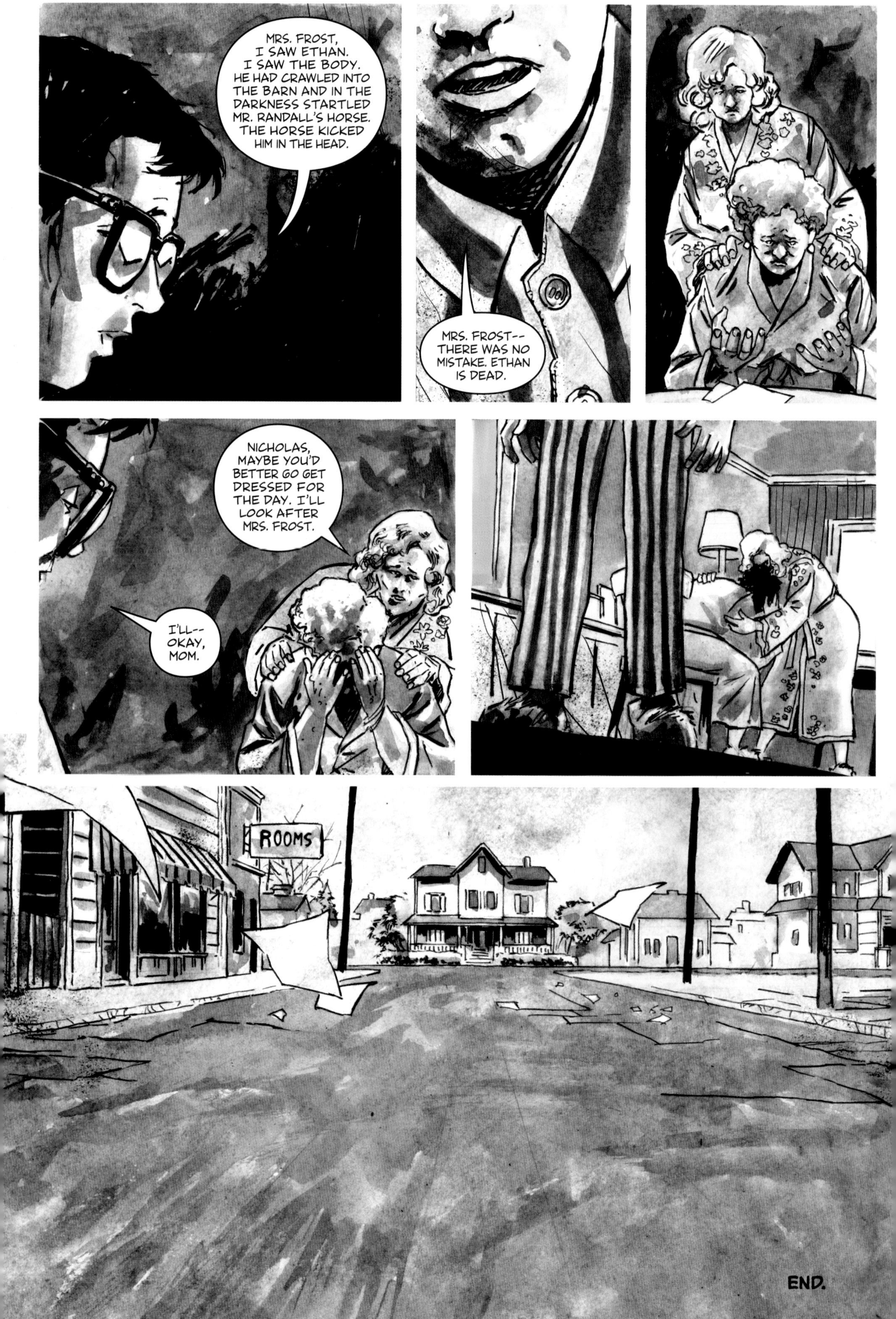
MRS. FROST, I SAW ETHAN. I SAW THE BODY. HE HAD CRAWLED INTO THE BARN AND IN THE DARKNESS STARTLED MR. RANDALL'S HORSE. THE HORSE KICKED HIM IN THE HEAD.
MRS. FROST-- THERE WAS NO MISTAKE. ETHAN IS DEAD.
NICHOLAS, MAYBE YOU'D BETTER GO GET DRESSED FOR THE DAY. I'LL LOOK AFTER MRS. FROST.
I'LL-- OKAY, MOM.
ROOMS
END.

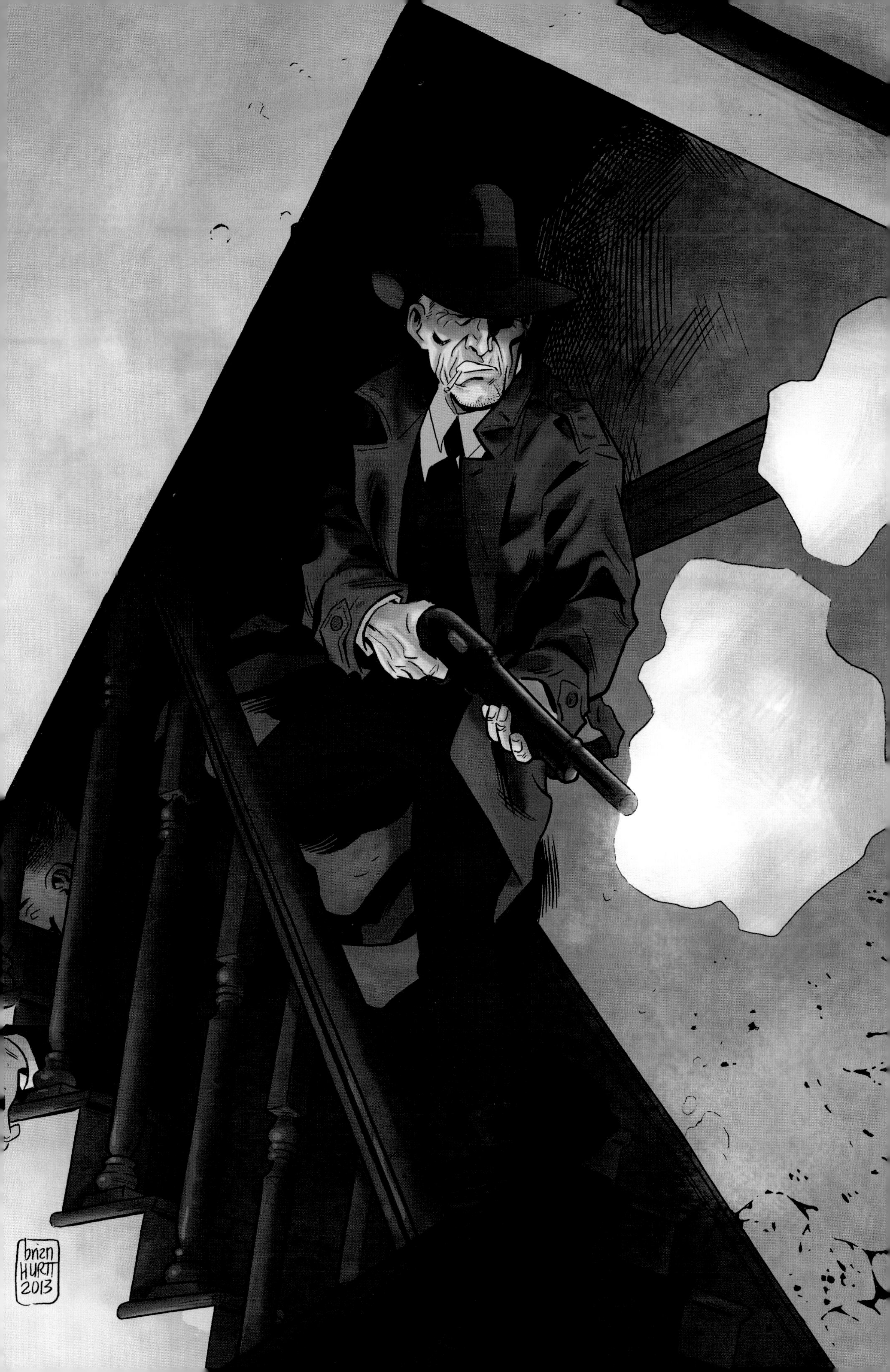
brian
HURTT
2013

# OLD DOG

story    Seth Peck
art    Brian Koschak
colors    Amber Stone
letters    Dave Lanphear

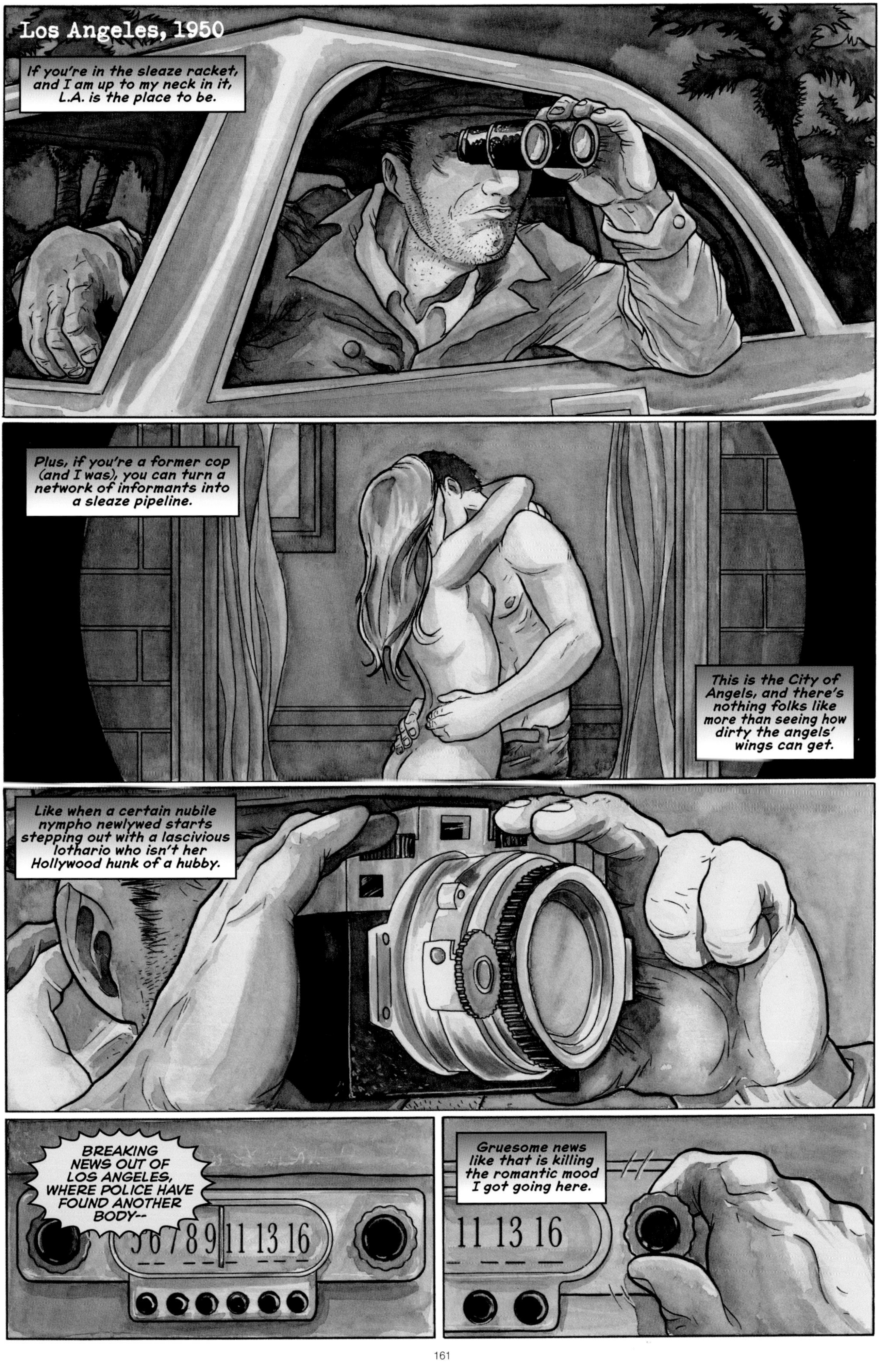
Los Angeles, 1950
If you're in the sleaze racket, and I am up to my neck in it, L.A. is the place to be.
Plus, if you're a former cop (and I was), you can turn a network of informants into a sleaze pipeline.
This is the City of Angels, and there's nothing folks like more than seeing how dirty the angels' wings can get.
Like when a certain nubile nympho newlywed starts stepping out with a lascivious lothario who isn't her Hollywood hunk of a hubby.
BREAKING NEWS OUT OF LOS ANGELES, WHERE POLICE HAVE FOUND ANOTHER BODY--
6 7 8 9 11 13 16
Gruesome news like that is killing the romantic mood I got going here.
11 13 16

*I guess if I keep working out of a toilet like this, I should expect pieces of crap to keep showing up.*

*Pierce is one of my more trustworthy informants, but if he were any bigger of a rat, I'd have to put out a trap.*

I'M TELLING YOU, SAM, THIS IS LEGIT. A FULL-FLEDGED ORGY UP IN THE HILLS, FULL OF A-LISTERS. THEY EVEN BRING IN COLORED PEOPLE, COSTUMES, PROPS, FOR LIKE, WEIRDO SEX SHIT.

Uh-huh.

I'M SERIOUS. HALF OF MGM'S STABLE IS UP THERE, GETTING DOWN AND DIRTY WHILE THEY GUZZLE BOOZE AND SMOKE REEFER!

YOU GET SOME PICS OF A BROAD LIKE GARBO OR HEPBURN WITH A COLORED FELLA? *SHUSH* WOULD PAY GOOD MONEY FOR THAT, RIGHT?

MAYBE.

*They'd pay a fortune, but no need to get Pierce all worked up.*

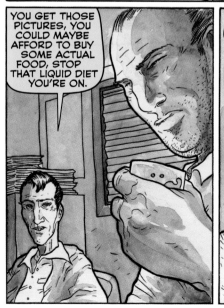

YOU GET THOSE PICTURES, YOU COULD MAYBE AFFORD TO BUY SOME ACTUAL FOOD, STOP THAT LIQUID DIET YOU'RE ON.

OKAY, I'LL LOOK INTO IT. NOW GET OUT.

YOU'RE SPOILING MY LUNCH.

SURE THING. JUST MAKE SURE I GET A LOOK AT THEM PICTURES TOO, SAMMY.

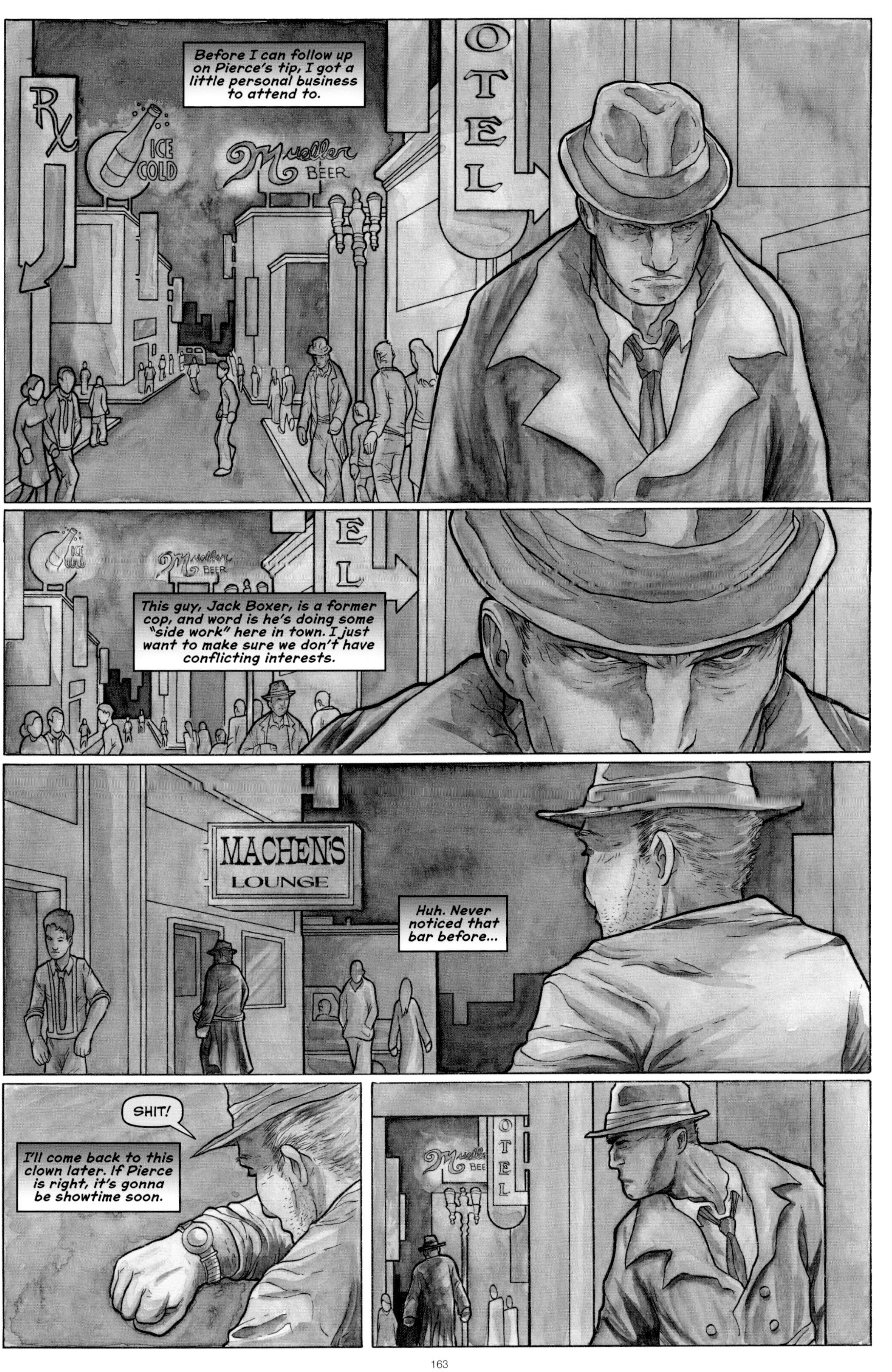
Before I can follow up on Pierce's tip, I got a little personal business to attend to.
OTEL
ICE COLD
Mueller BEER
This guy, Jack Boxer, is a former cop, and word is he's doing some "side work" here in town. I just want to make sure we don't have conflicting interests.
MACHEN'S LOUNGE
Huh. Never noticed that bar before...
SHIT!
I'll come back to this clown later. If Pierce is right, it's gonna be showtime soon.

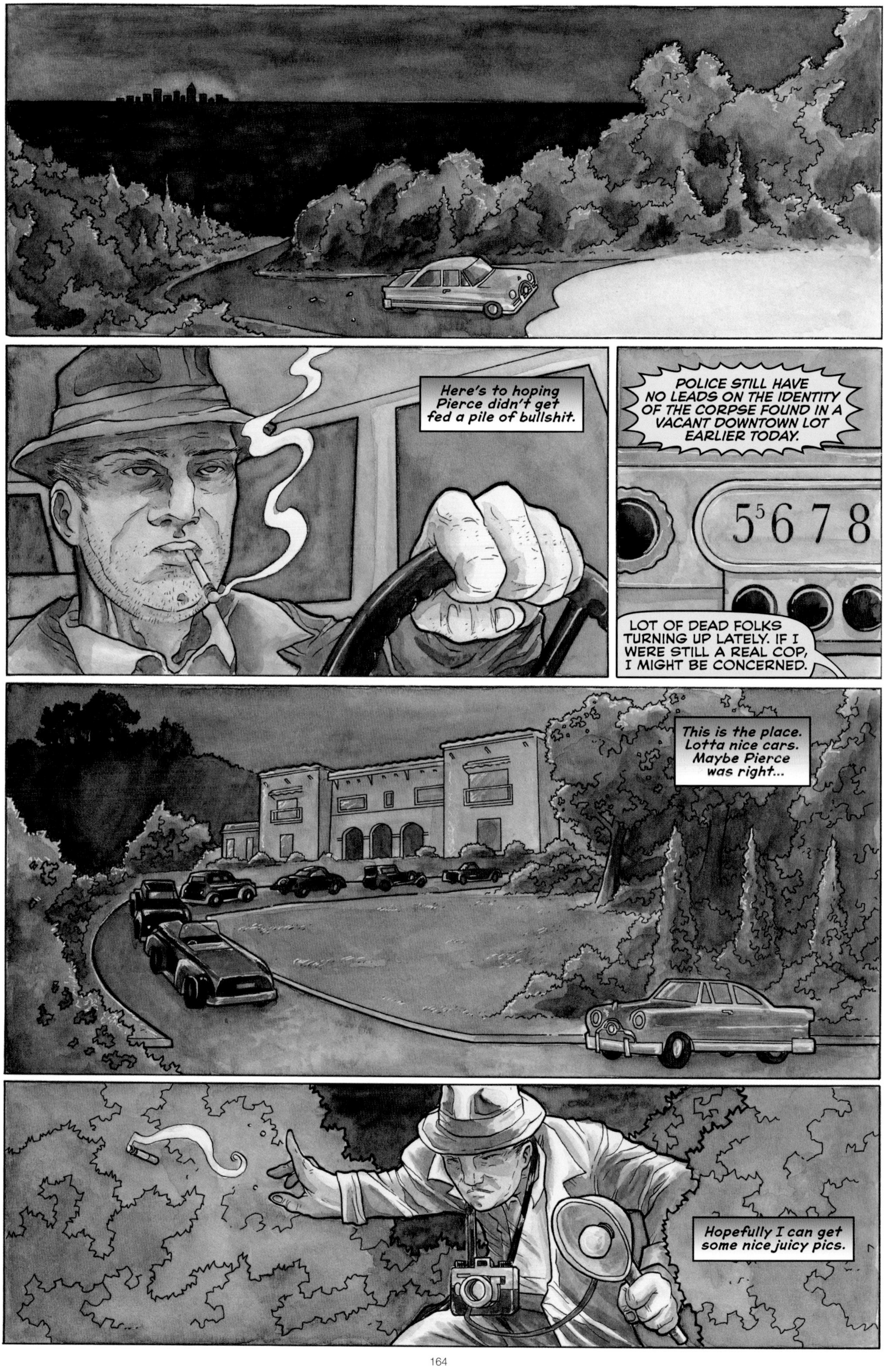
Here's to hoping Pierce didn't get fed a pile of bullshit.
POLICE STILL HAVE NO LEADS ON THE IDENTITY OF THE CORPSE FOUND IN A VACANT DOWNTOWN LOT EARLIER TODAY.
5⁵678
LOT OF DEAD FOLKS TURNING UP LATELY. IF I WERE STILL A REAL COP, I MIGHT BE CONCERNED.
This is the place. Lotta nice cars. Maybe Pierce was right...
Hopefully I can get some nice juicy pics.

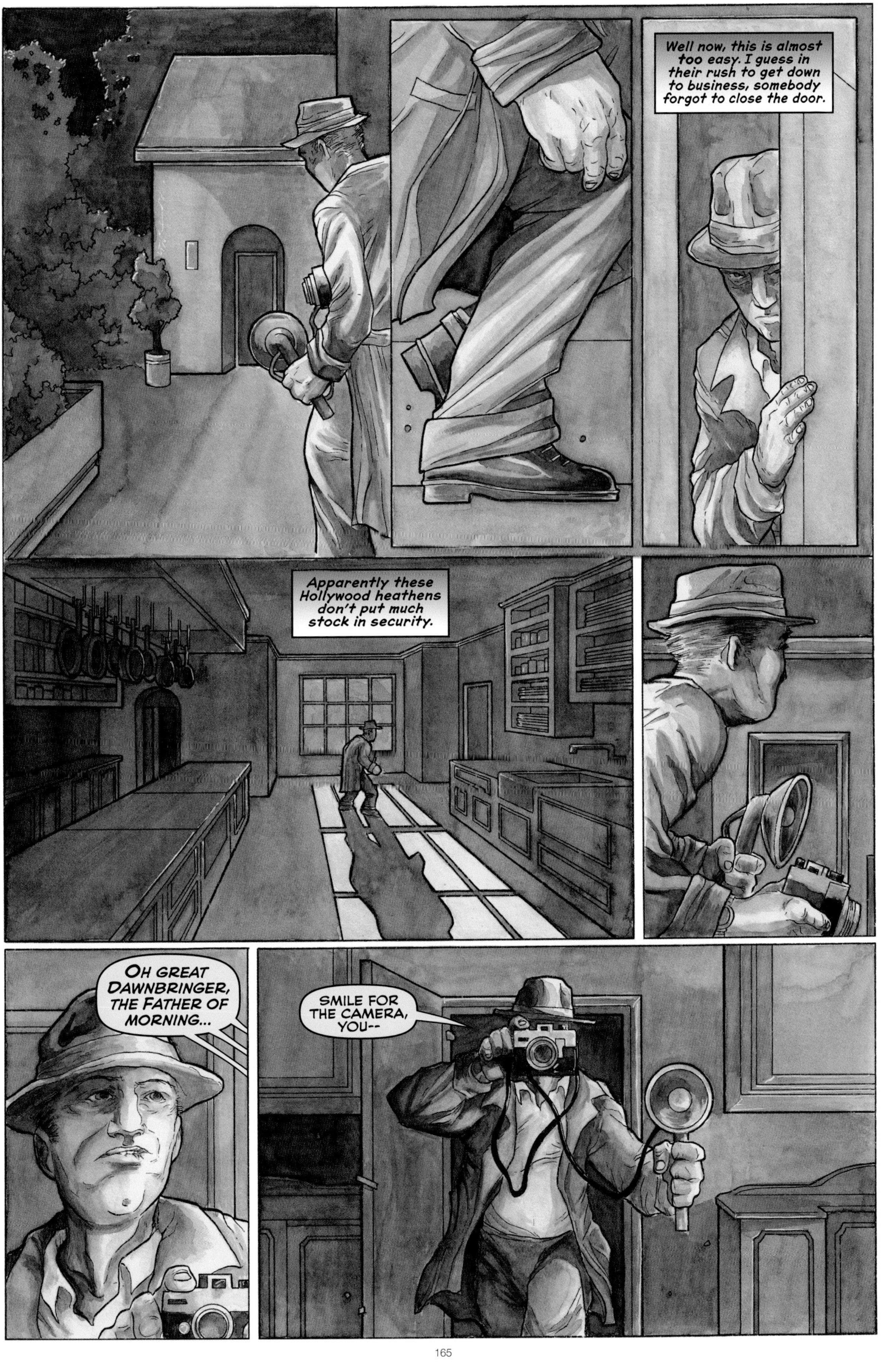
Well now, this is almost too easy. I guess in their rush to get down to business, somebody forgot to close the door.
Apparently these Hollywood heathens don't put much stock in security.
OH GREAT DAWNBRINGER, THE FATHER OF MORNING...
SMILE FOR THE CAMERA, YOU--

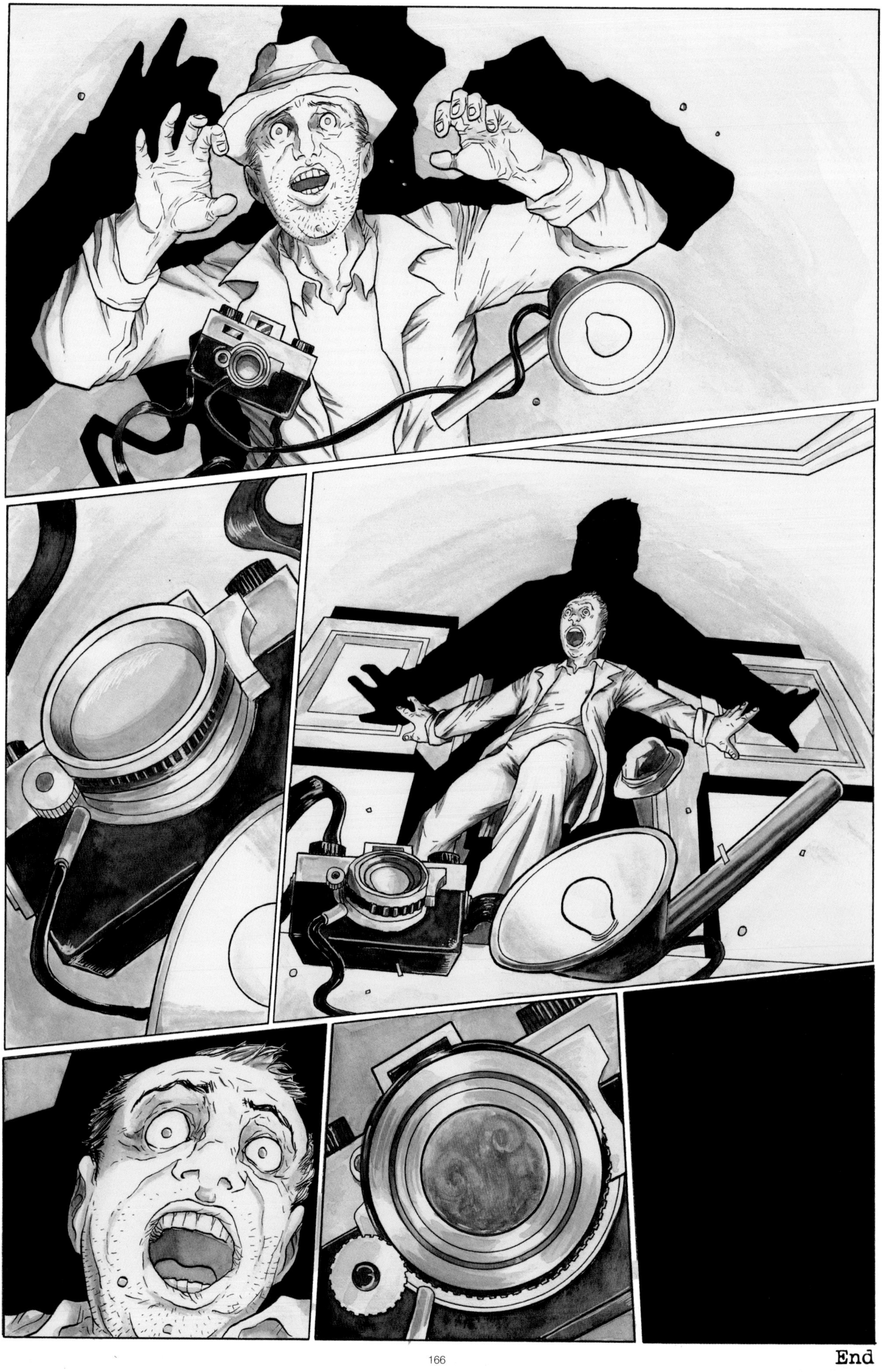

End

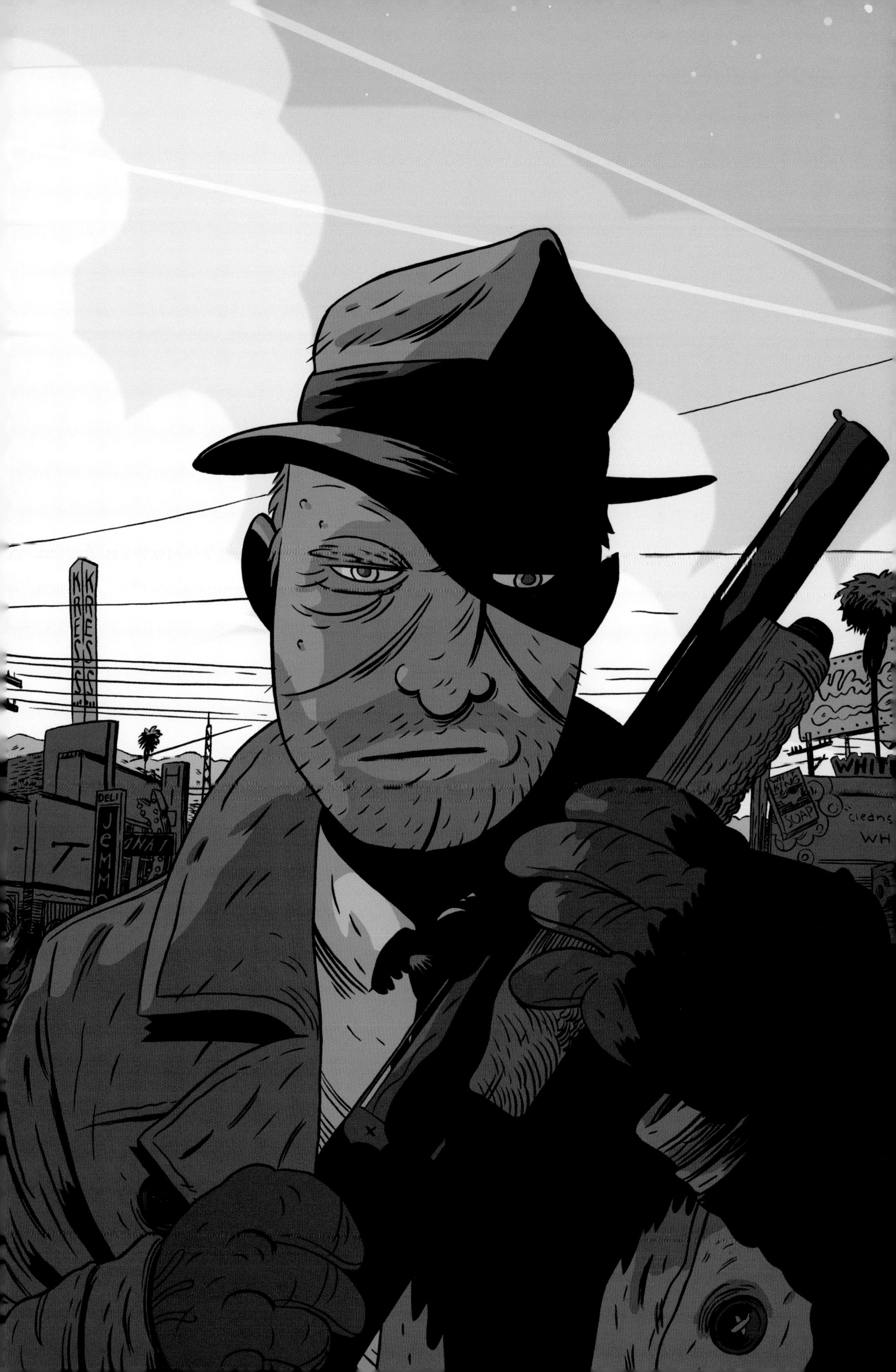
KRESS
KRESS
DELI
SOAP
cleans

# HELLBENT

story    Jeremy Haun
layouts  Kevin Mellon
pencils  Cory Smith
inks     Jeremy Haun
colors   Frank Zigarelli
letters  Troy Peteri

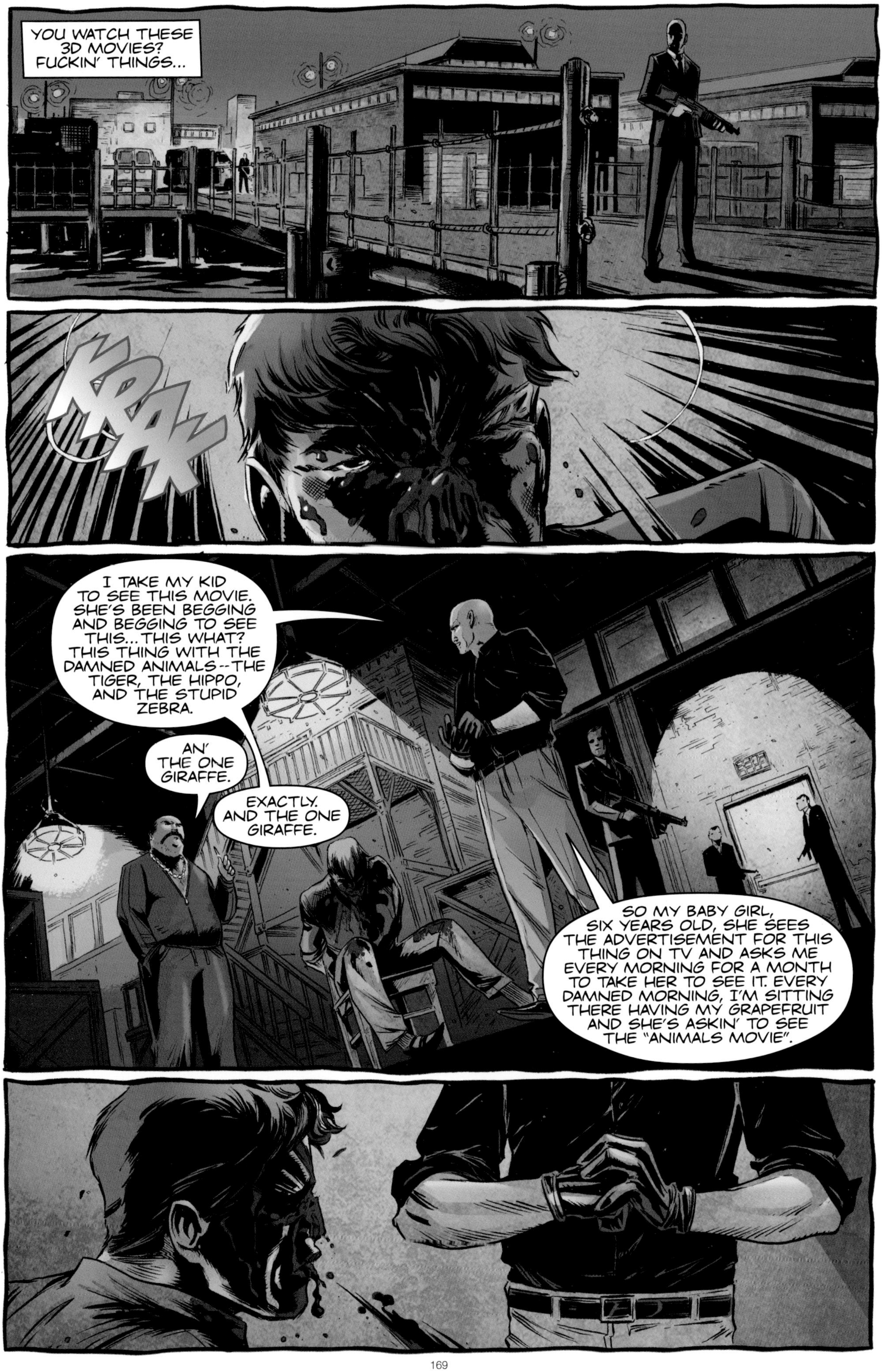

YOU WATCH THESE 3D MOVIES? FUCKIN' THINGS...
KRAK
I TAKE MY KID TO SEE THIS MOVIE. SHE'S BEEN BEGGING AND BEGGING TO SEE THIS...THIS WHAT? THIS THING WITH THE DAMNED ANIMALS--THE TIGER, THE HIPPO, AND THE STUPID ZEBRA.
AN' THE ONE GIRAFFE.
EXACTLY. AND THE ONE GIRAFFE.
SO MY BABY GIRL, SIX YEARS OLD, SHE SEES THE ADVERTISEMENT FOR THIS THING ON TV AND ASKS ME EVERY MORNING FOR A MONTH TO TAKE HER TO SEE IT. EVERY DAMNED MORNING, I'M SITTING THERE HAVING MY GRAPEFRUIT AND SHE'S ASKIN' TO SEE THE "ANIMALS MOVIE".

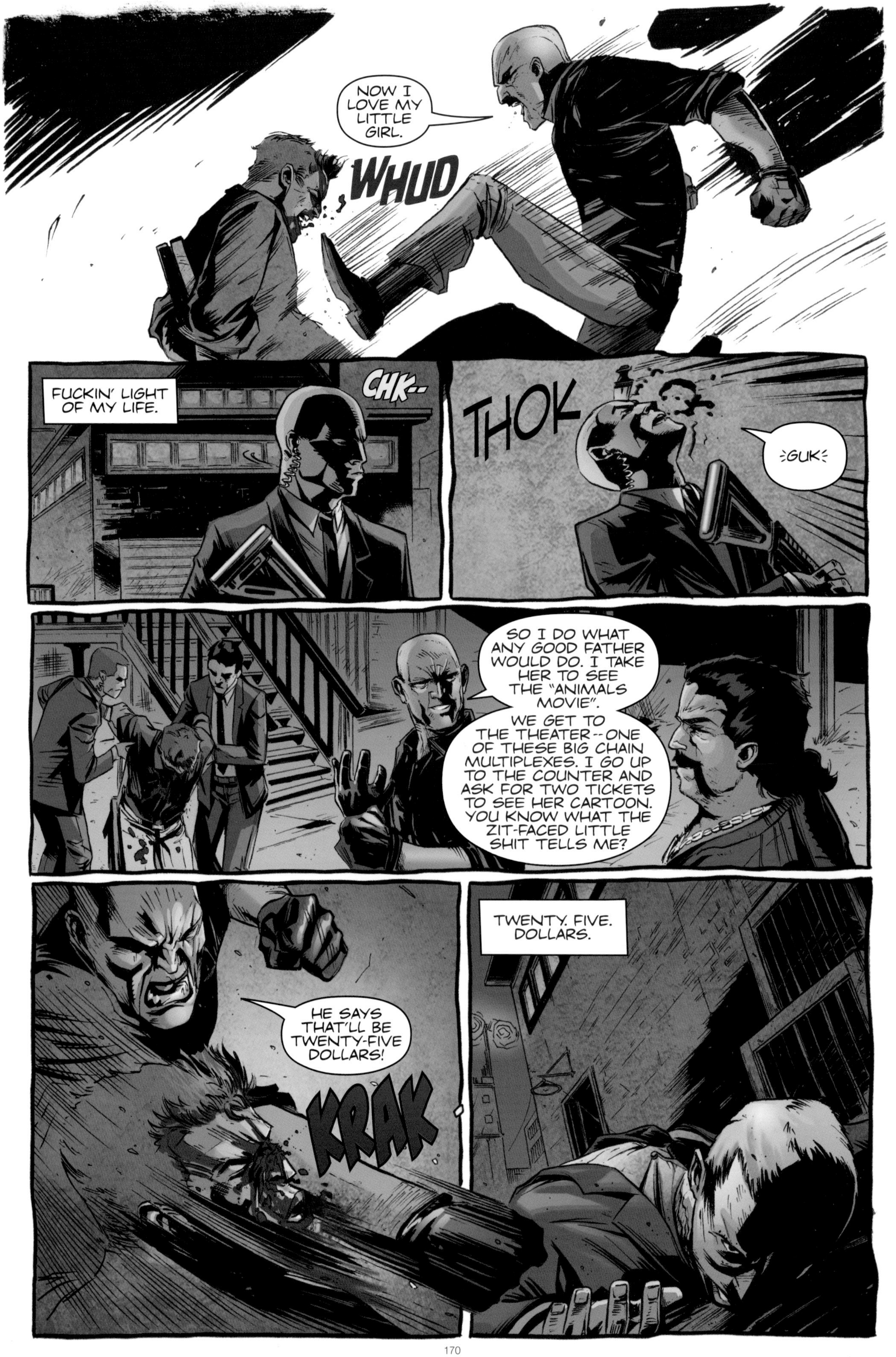
NOW I LOVE MY LITTLE GIRL.
WHUD
FUCKIN' LIGHT OF MY LIFE.
CHK--
THOK
GUK
SO I DO WHAT ANY GOOD FATHER WOULD DO. I TAKE HER TO SEE THE "ANIMALS MOVIE".
WE GET TO THE THEATER--ONE OF THESE BIG CHAIN MULTIPLEXES. I GO UP TO THE COUNTER AND ASK FOR TWO TICKETS TO SEE HER CARTOON. YOU KNOW WHAT THE ZIT-FACED LITTLE SHIT TELLS ME?
HE SAYS THAT'LL BE TWENTY-FIVE DOLLARS!
KRAK
TWENTY. FIVE. DOLLARS.

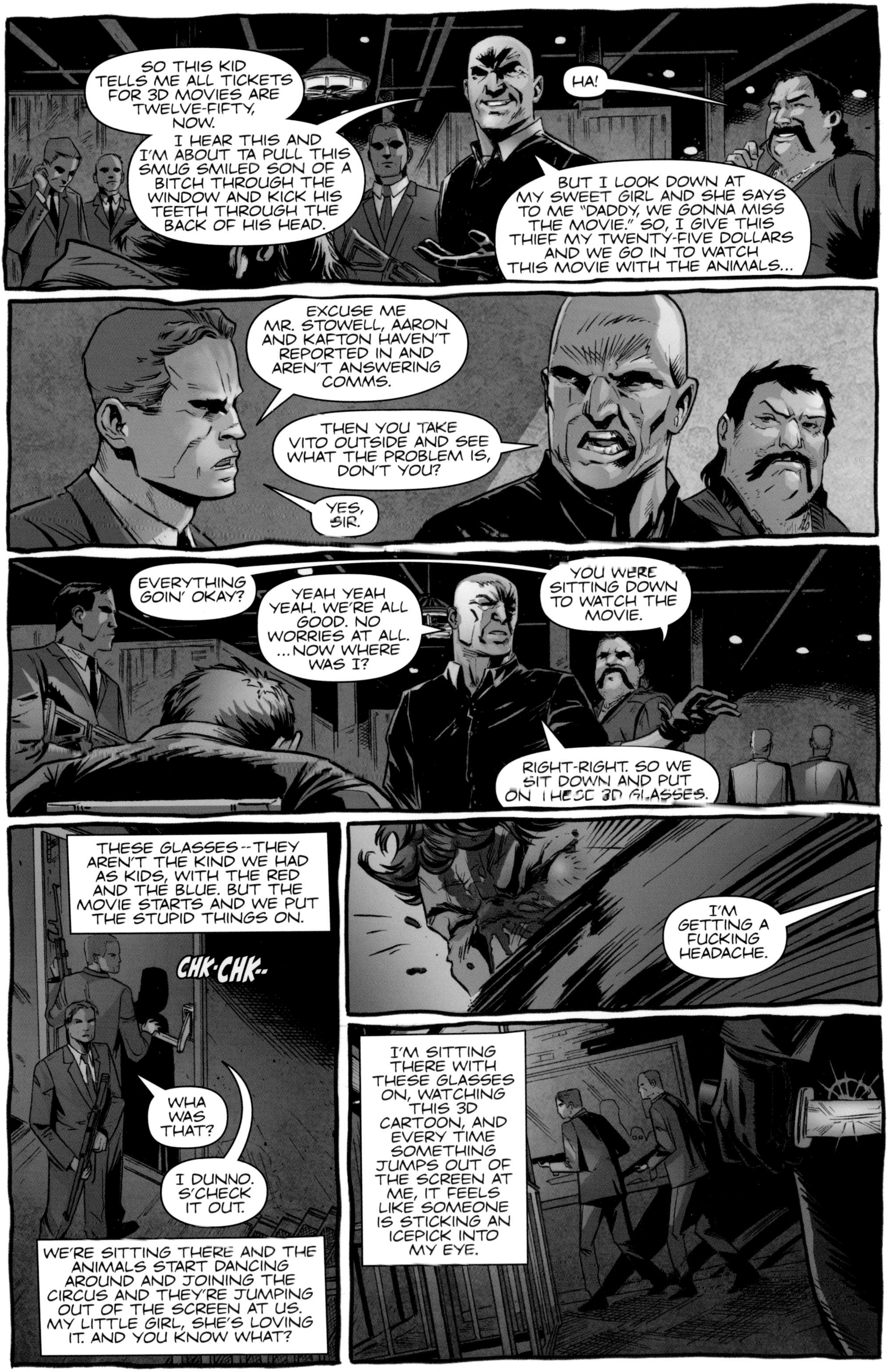
SO THIS KID TELLS ME ALL TICKETS FOR 3D MOVIES ARE TWELVE-FIFTY, NOW.
I HEAR THIS AND I'M ABOUT TA PULL THIS SMUG SMILED SON OF A BITCH THROUGH THE WINDOW AND KICK HIS TEETH THROUGH THE BACK OF HIS HEAD.
HA!
BUT I LOOK DOWN AT MY SWEET GIRL AND SHE SAYS TO ME "DADDY, WE GONNA MISS THE MOVIE." SO, I GIVE THIS THIEF MY TWENTY-FIVE DOLLARS AND WE GO IN TO WATCH THIS MOVIE WITH THE ANIMALS...
EXCUSE ME MR. STOWELL, AARON AND KAFTON HAVEN'T REPORTED IN AND AREN'T ANSWERING COMMS.
THEN YOU TAKE VITO OUTSIDE AND SEE WHAT THE PROBLEM IS, DON'T YOU?
YES, SIR.
EVERYTHING GOIN' OKAY?
YEAH YEAH YEAH. WE'RE ALL GOOD. NO WORRIES AT ALL. ...NOW WHERE WAS I?
YOU WERE SITTING DOWN TO WATCH THE MOVIE.
RIGHT-RIGHT. SO WE SIT DOWN AND PUT ON THESE 3D GLASSES.
THESE GLASSES--THEY AREN'T THE KIND WE HAD AS KIDS, WITH THE RED AND THE BLUE. BUT THE MOVIE STARTS AND WE PUT THE STUPID THINGS ON.
CHK-CHK--
WHA WAS THAT?
I DUNNO. S'CHECK IT OUT.
WE'RE SITTING THERE AND THE ANIMALS START DANCING AROUND AND JOINING THE CIRCUS AND THEY'RE JUMPING OUT OF THE SCREEN AT US. MY LITTLE GIRL, SHE'S LOVING IT. AND YOU KNOW WHAT?
I'M GETTING A FUCKING HEADACHE.
I'M SITTING THERE WITH THESE GLASSES ON, WATCHING THIS 3D CARTOON, AND EVERY TIME SOMETHING JUMPS OUT OF THE SCREEN AT ME, IT FEELS LIKE SOMEONE IS STICKING AN ICEPICK INTO MY EYE.

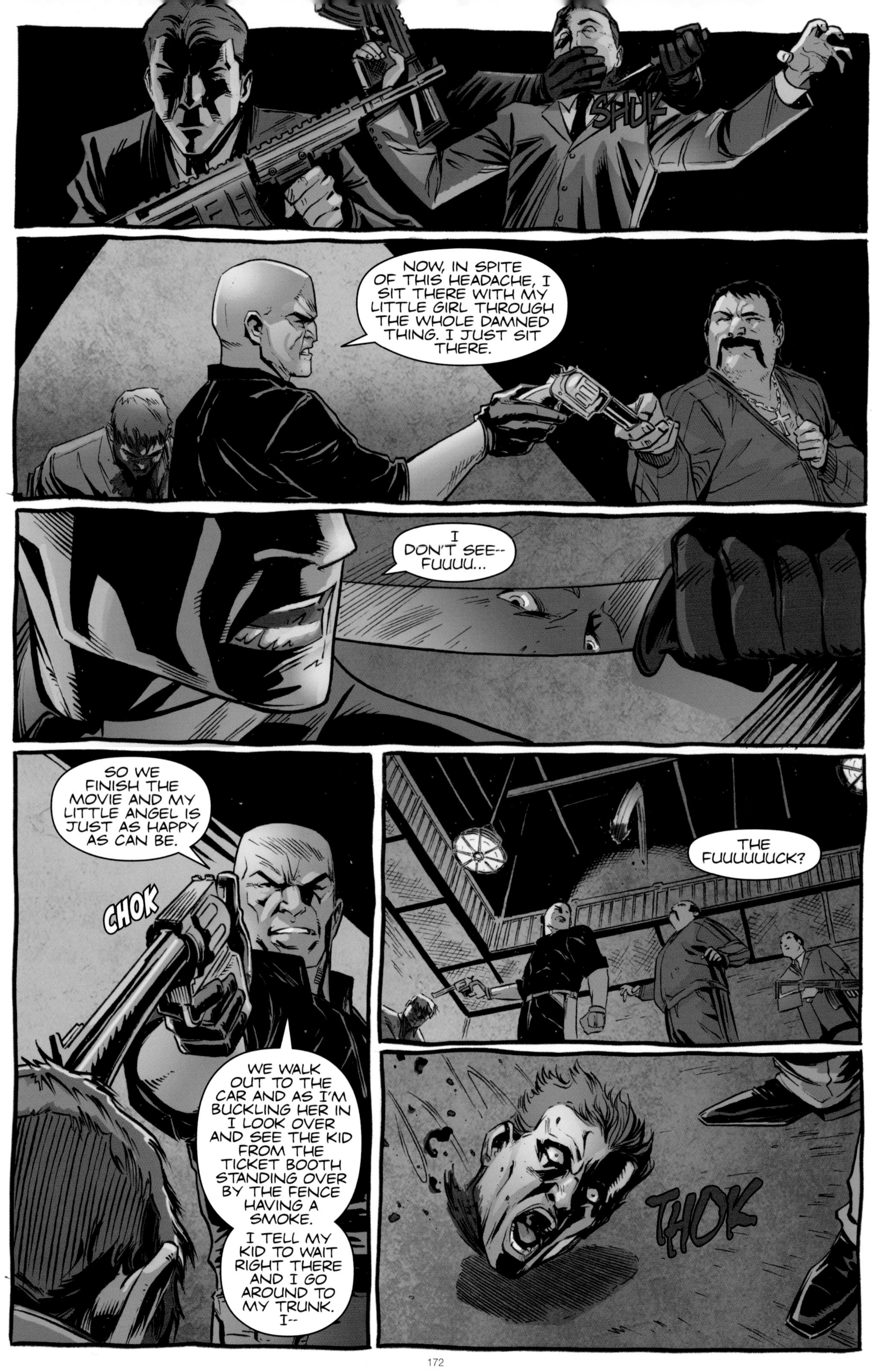
SHUK
NOW, IN SPITE OF THIS HEADACHE, I SIT THERE WITH MY LITTLE GIRL THROUGH THE WHOLE DAMNED THING. I JUST SIT THERE.
I DON'T SEE-- FUUUU...
SO WE FINISH THE MOVIE AND MY LITTLE ANGEL IS JUST AS HAPPY AS CAN BE.
CHOK
WE WALK OUT TO THE CAR AND AS I'M BUCKLING HER IN I LOOK OVER AND SEE THE KID FROM THE TICKET BOOTH STANDING OVER BY THE FENCE HAVING A SMOKE.
I TELL MY KID TO WAIT RIGHT THERE AND I GO AROUND TO MY TRUNK. I--
THE FUUUUUUCK?
THOK

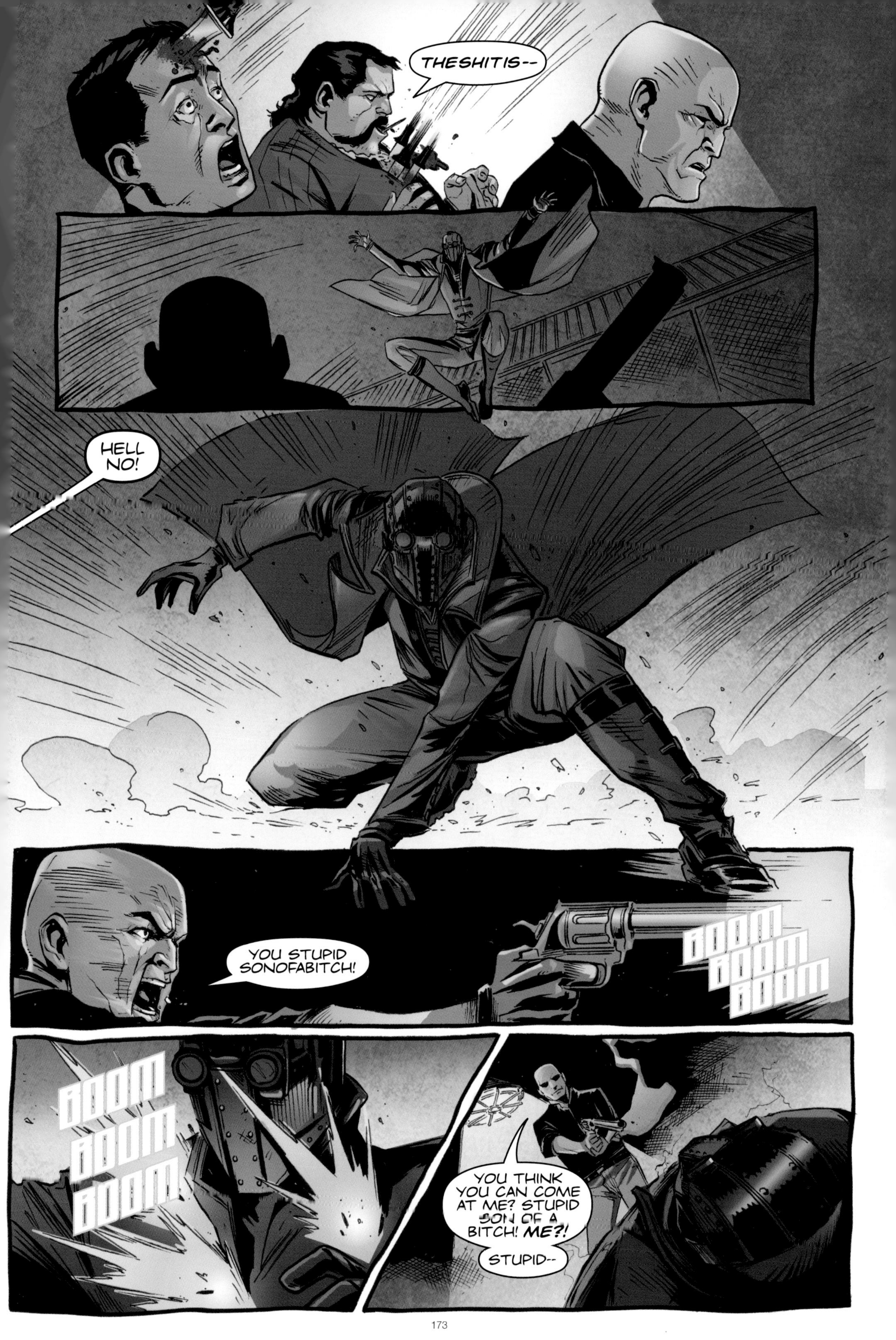
THESHITIS--
HELL NO!
YOU STUPID SONOFABITCH!
BOOM BOOM BOOM
BOOM BOOM BOOM
YOU THINK YOU CAN COME AT ME? STUPID SON OF A BITCH! ME?!
STUPID--

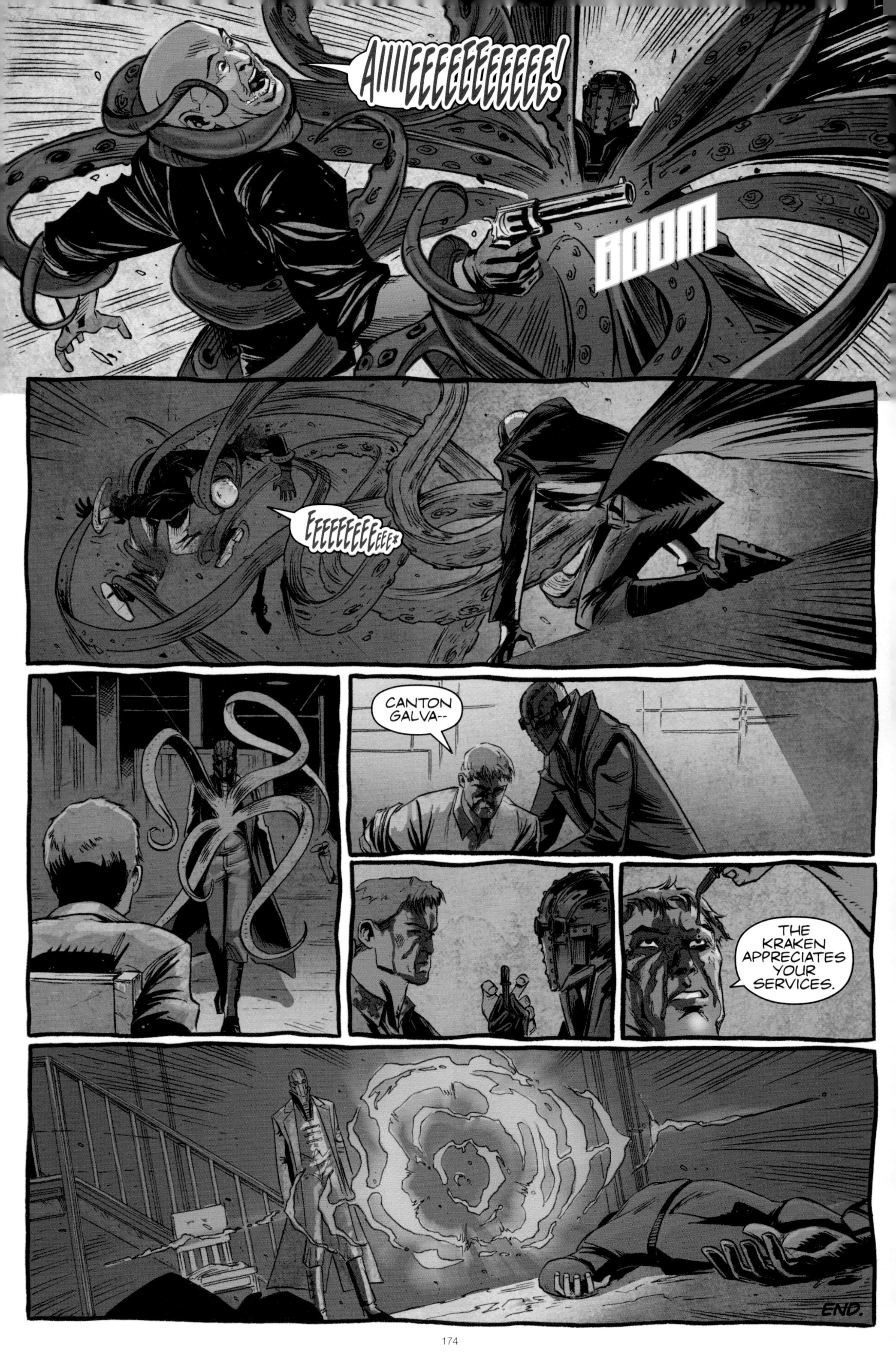
AIIIIEEEEEEEEEEEE!
BOOM
EEEEEEEEEeee*
CANTON GALVA--
THE KRAKEN APPRECIATES YOUR SERVICES.
END.

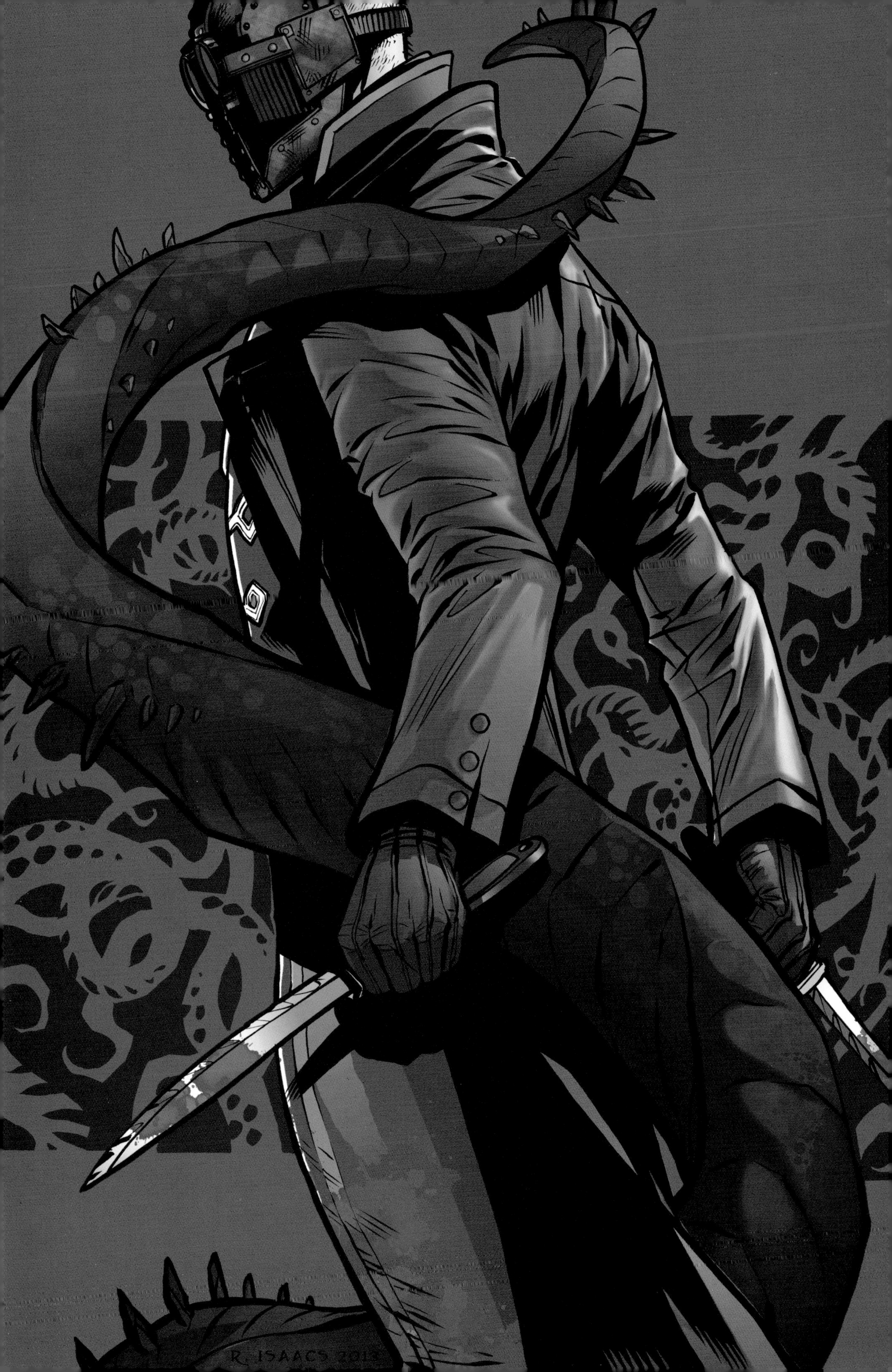
R. ISAACS 2013

# MIDDLETON
## *Oliver's Going To Do Some Very Bad Things

story    Alex Grecian
art      Shaky Kane
letters  Thomas Mauer

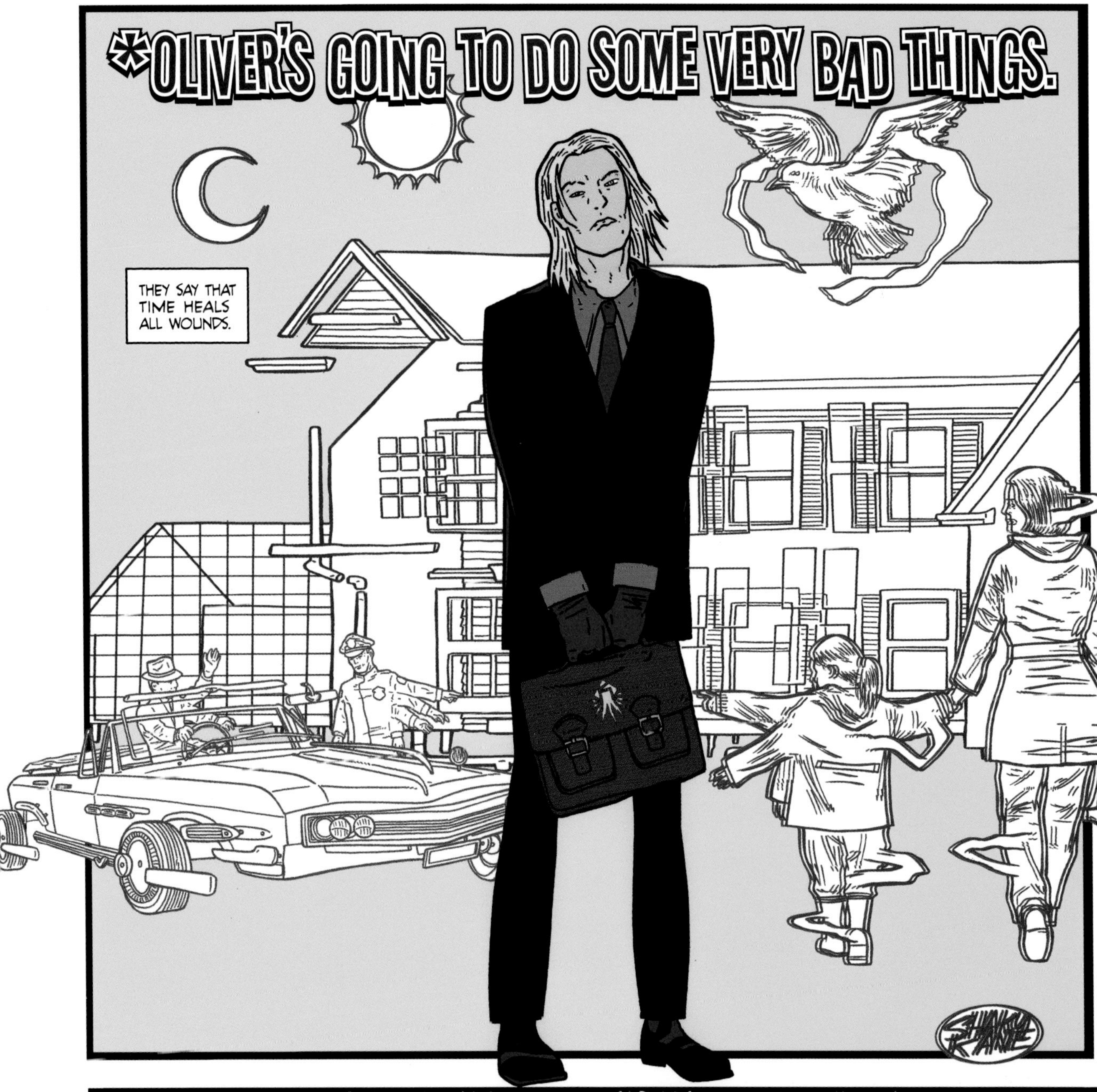
*OLIVER'S GOING TO DO SOME VERY BAD THINGS.
THEY SAY THAT TIME HEALS ALL WOUNDS.

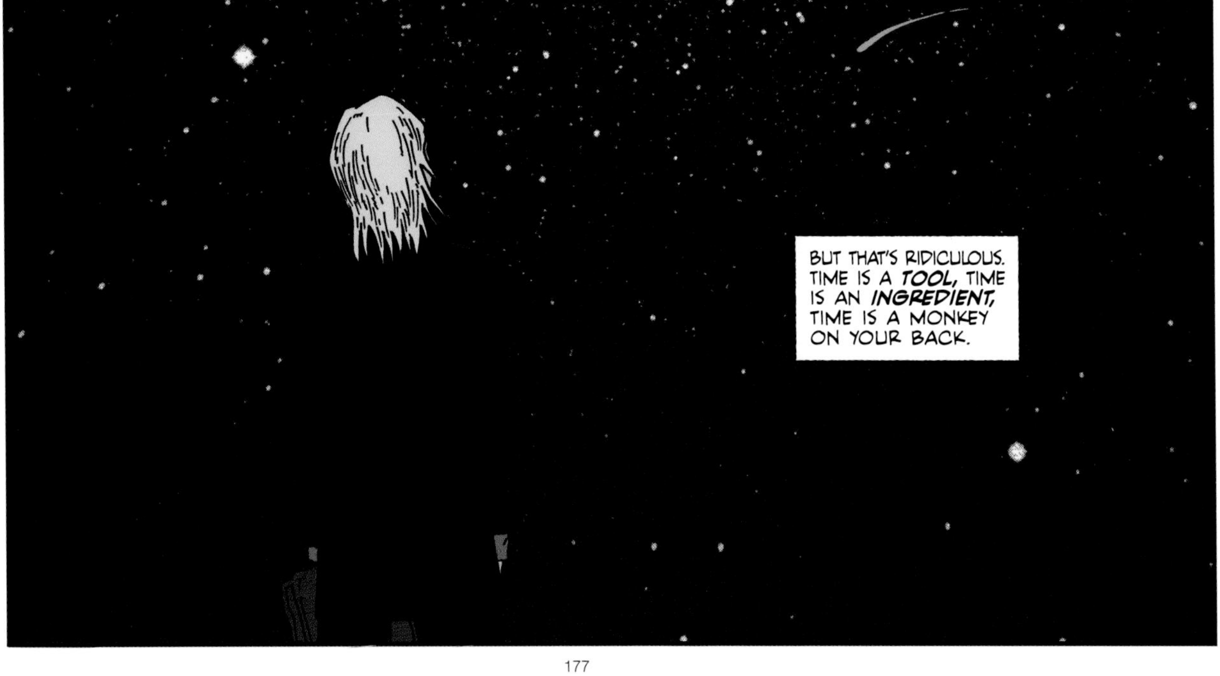
BUT THAT'S RIDICULOUS. TIME IS A *TOOL,* TIME IS AN *INGREDIENT,* TIME IS A MONKEY ON YOUR BACK.

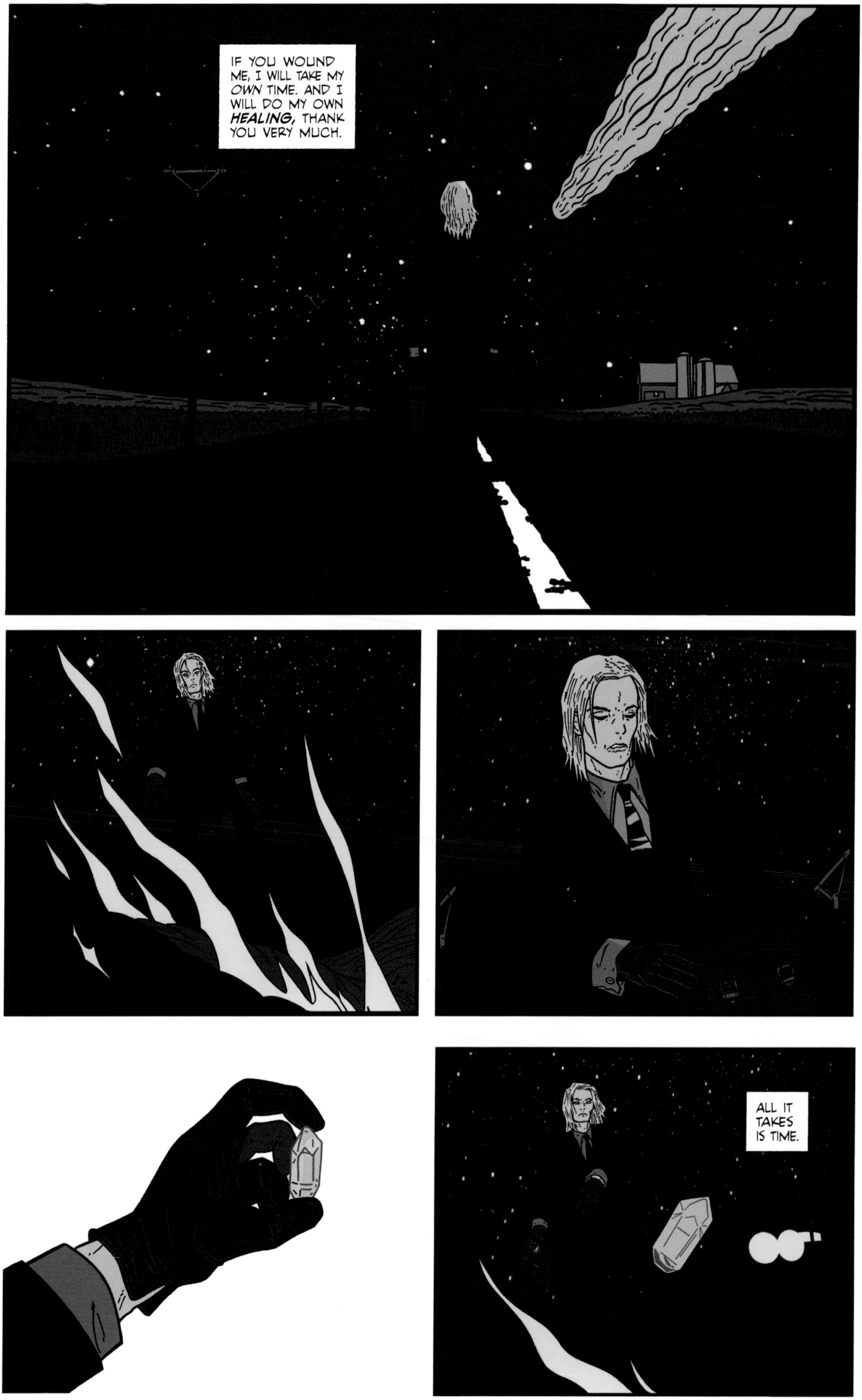
IF YOU WOUND ME, I WILL TAKE MY OWN TIME. AND I WILL DO MY OWN HEALING, THANK YOU VERY MUCH.
ALL IT TAKES IS TIME.

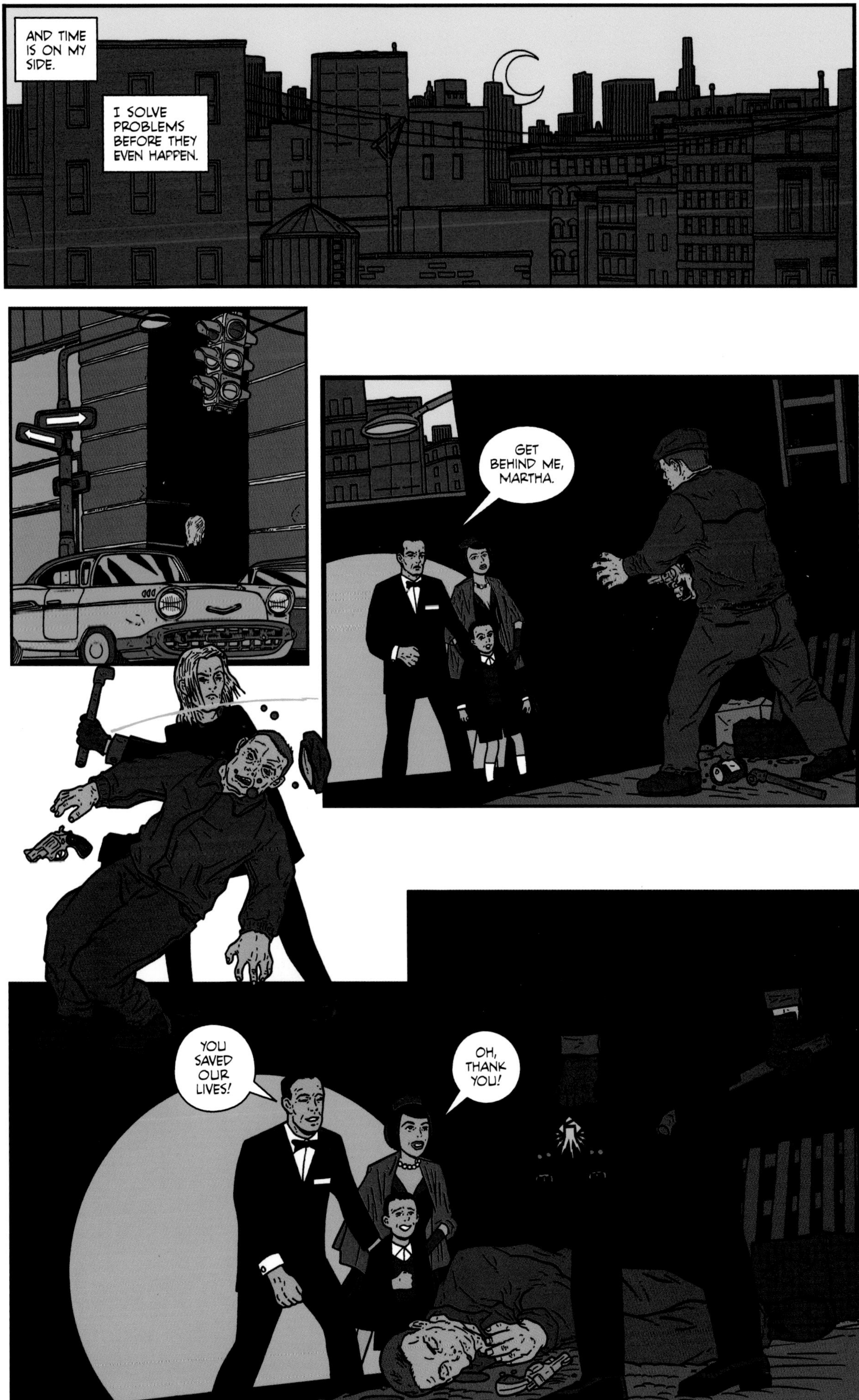
AND TIME IS ON MY SIDE.
I SOLVE PROBLEMS BEFORE THEY EVEN HAPPEN.
GET BEHIND ME, MARTHA.
YOU SAVED OUR LIVES!
OH, THANK YOU!

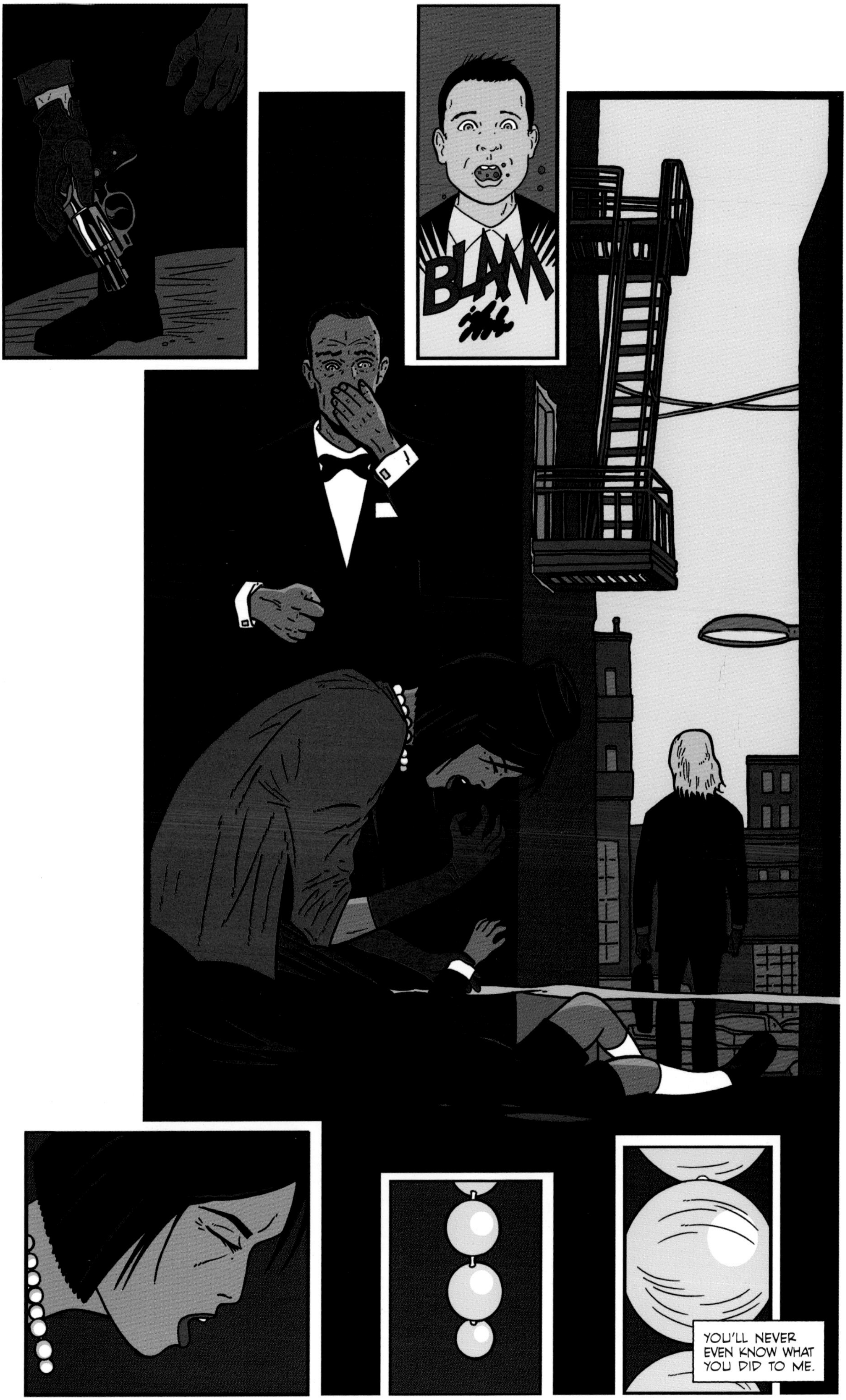
BLAM
YOU'LL NEVER EVEN KNOW WHAT YOU DID TO ME.

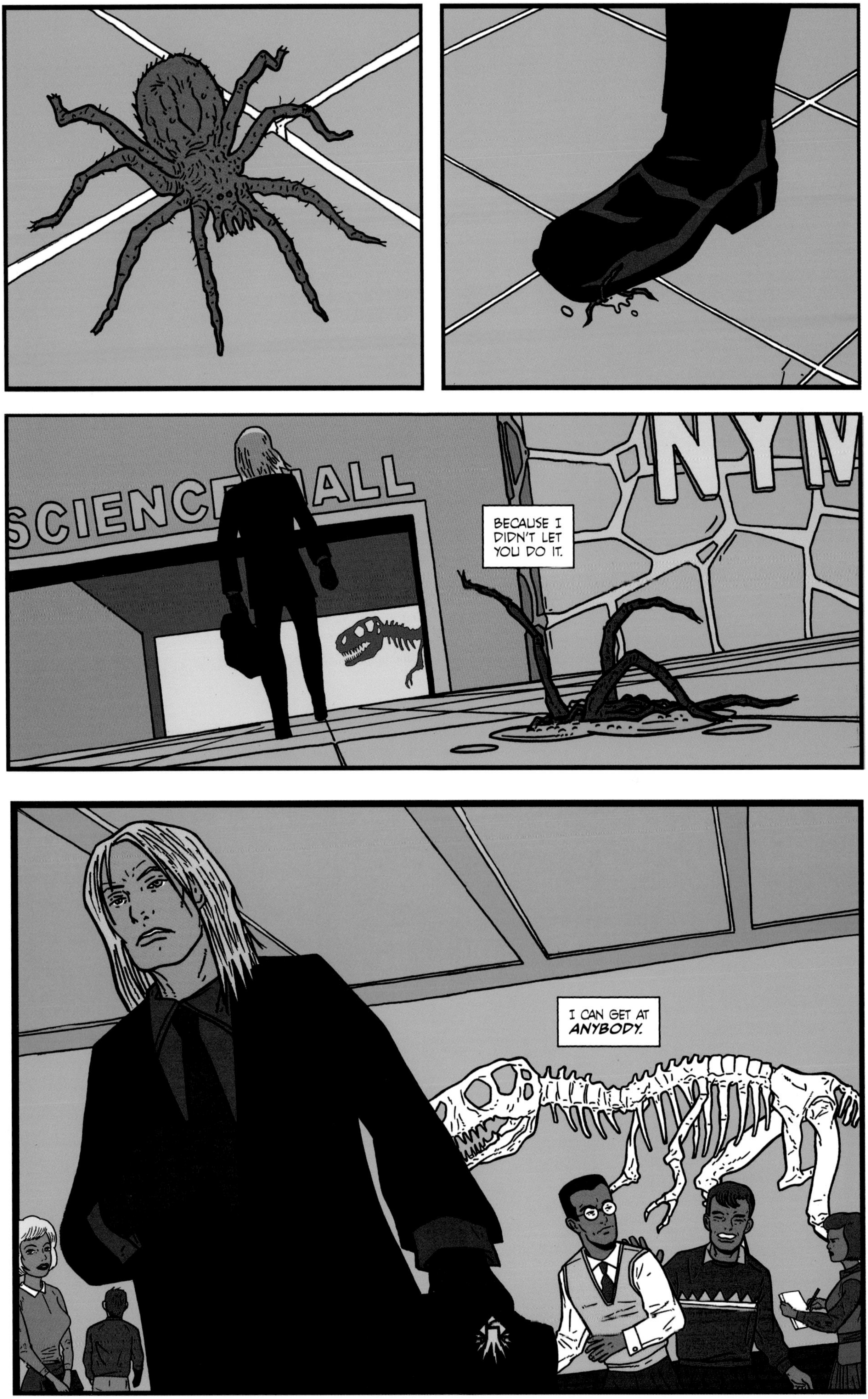
SCIENCE HALL
NYM
BECAUSE I DIDN'T LET YOU DO IT.
I CAN GET AT *ANYBODY.*

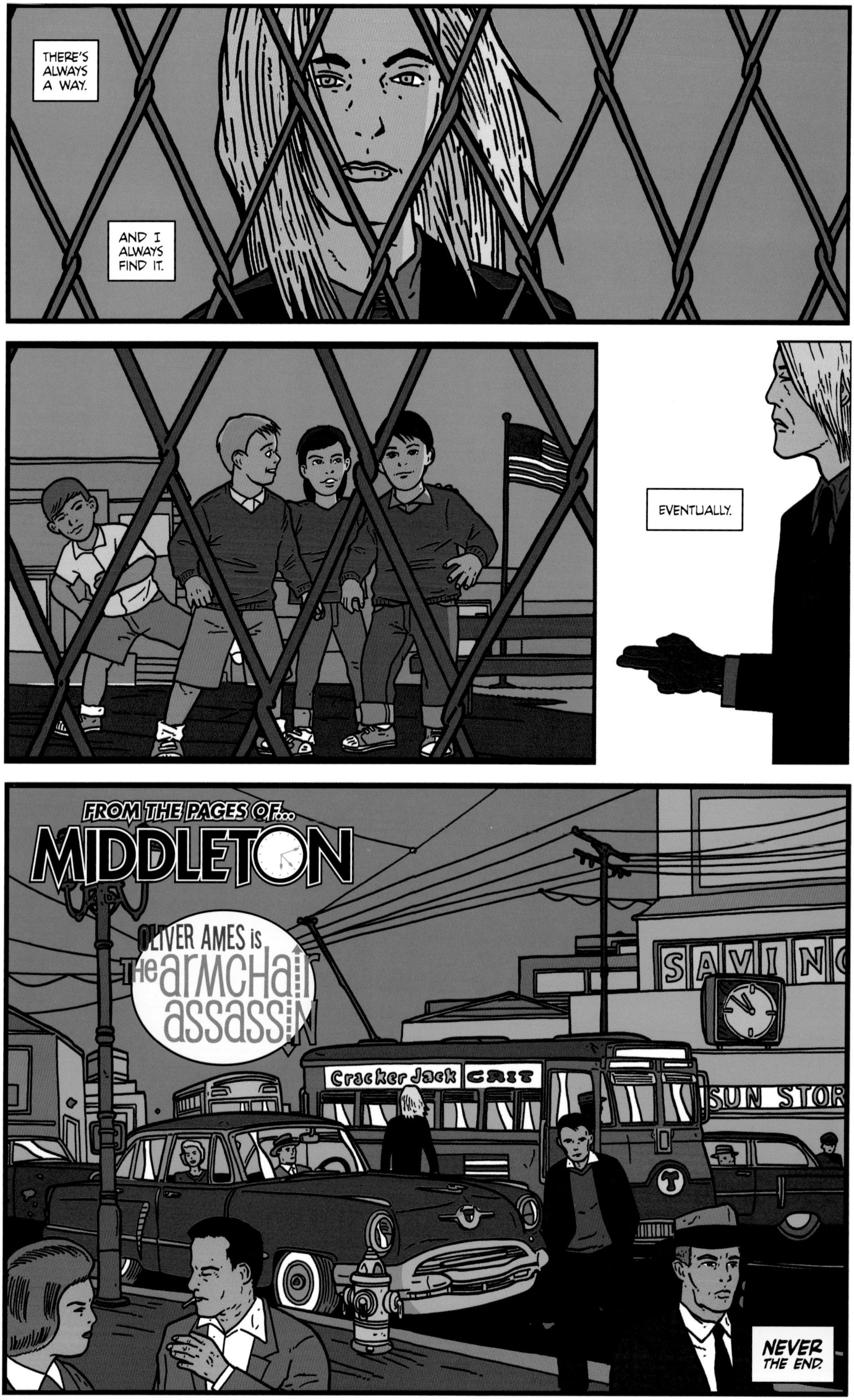
THERE'S ALWAYS A WAY.
AND I ALWAYS FIND IT.
EVENTUALLY.
FROM THE PAGES OF...
MIDDLETON
OLIVER AMES is THE armchair assassin
Cracker Jack
NEVER THE END.

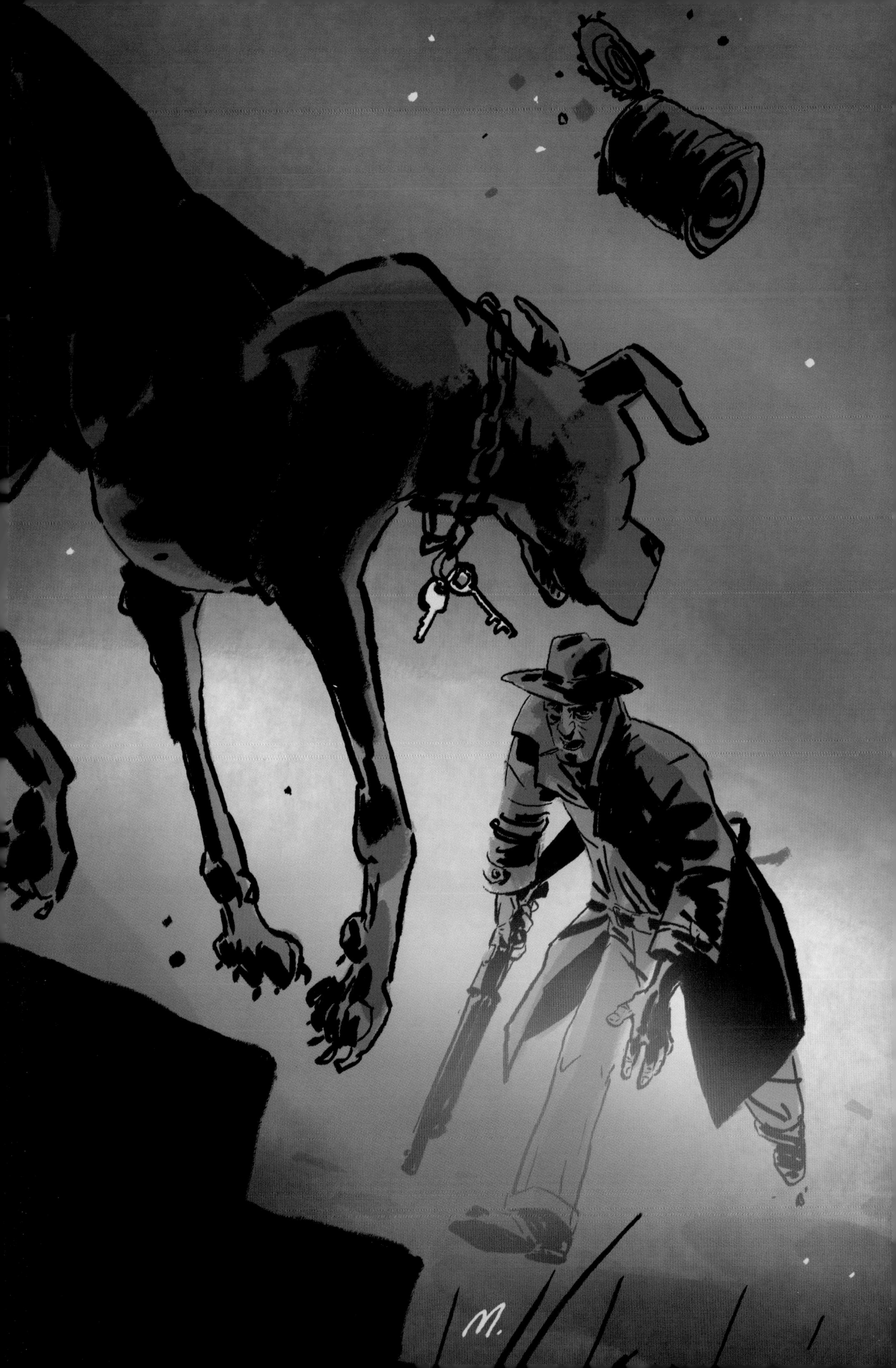

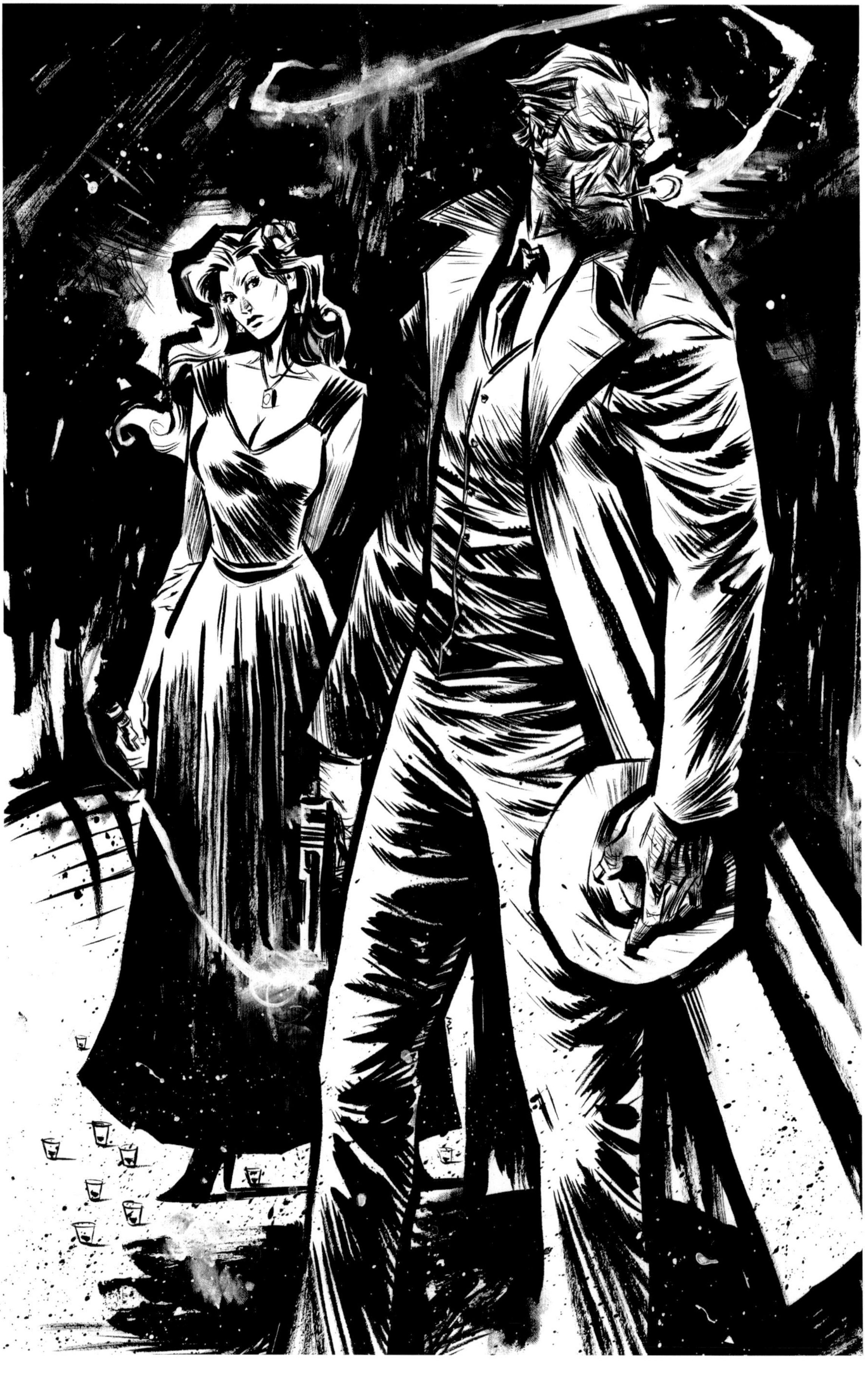

# THE DESCENT BECKONS
## B. Clay Moore

ILLUSTRATION Tigh Walker

*T*he voice he remembered most vividly was Fanny Brice's.
　*Not his wife's voice. Not his son's voice. Fanny Brice's voice.*
　*For some reason, the record on the phonograph was skipping, endlessly, in the middle of "I'd Rather Be Blue Over You," which had been his wife's favorite record. But instead of turning off the record, the cop in the living room had simply adjusted the volume downward. In years to come, he would remember the conversation that followed obliquely. A gathering of static figures serenaded by the barely-above-a-whisper sound of Fanny Brice reaching the bridge and then bumping a second backward and then reaching the bridge and then...*

The Caldwell case was all but settled. While he hadn't been able to prove willful negligence on the part of Hank Caldwell, he had unearthed enough "unusual" circumstances regarding the claim to justify a rate increase in the Caldwell policy above and beyond what would normally have been called for.

So, job well done, right?

Jackson Boxer pulled the form from his Underwood and leaned back in his straining office chair. The chair had been with him since his former life. The office had recently been renovated, which meant huge, ugly green metal desks for everyone, but he had insisted on keeping his chair. Something comfortable about the way the seat fit his ass. Something familiar about the way the stout wooden legs housed the hard rubber wheels. He didn't cling to much from his old life, and he figured there wasn't much that could be called sentimental about a chair, but he felt better with it under his ass.

Deciding to step outside for a smoke before turning his report in to Jenkins, he leaned for his cigarettes, grabbed the crumpled pack, and stood up.

*The grad student he used to fuck. She knew. Of course she knew.*
　*When he was drinking, it didn't take much to get him to tell the story, and he was always half lit when he was with her. She'd push him on it, trying to convince herself that there was some sacred bruising to his soul that would make sleeping with him more palatable. One of the last nights in her bed, she really pushed. Post-coital conversation. "Was she the love of your life?" she asked, dabbing paint on her toenails.*
　*Exhaling smoke from his Chesterfield, he hadn't given any thought to brushing the question aside. He knew this affair was on its last legs, and letting her hear what was in his head wouldn't be something she could use against him down the road. "She was my wife. He was my son. They trusted me to take care of them. But I was so wrapped up in posing for photographs with an axe in my hand that I let my guard down. I let them down. Doesn't matter if she was the love of my life. I was her husband. I was his father. The only job that really mattered was to protect and provide, and I failed at both."*
　*He'd been right about the relationship being on its last legs. Probably his blunt confession didn't help. The grad student had poked around inside his skull and failed to find much to latch onto. So he moved on, a story for her to tell around campfires while smoking reefer with other city girls. The cop from the Roaring Twenties who lost his family and checked out on life.*

The door to Jenkins' office was open, as it usually was. Jenkins had recently relocated to the Chicago office from somewhere back East. He was younger than the previous supervisor by a good twenty years, and he acted like that was supposed to bother Boxer and the other older guys in the office. But it didn't. Boxer didn't aspire to Jenkins' job. Hell, he knew he was overqualified for the job he had. But it was all he needed these days.

"Come on in, Jack. Got something to run past you," said Jenkins, peering over his wire-rimmed glasses at a few stapled pages he held in his small, clean hands. His desk was crowded with neat piles of similarly stapled reports. A small, simply framed photograph of a sober-looking brunette in her early thirties was the only personal artifact to be found between the stacks. Boxer had never asked about the photograph, and Jenkins had never seemed anxious to explain it.

Boxer crossed lazily to the desk and adopted his usual deadpan expression. He'd learned decades ago that a blank expression was like an empty canvas. People felt compelled to fill in the details. So he waited quietly for Jenkins to run something past him.

Jenkins dropped the report onto his desk blotter and looked up, past Boxer. He pointed somewhere beyond Jack and made a motion with his finger, indicating he wanted Jack to close the door.

Jack lingered an instant, and then shuffled over to the door, closing it gently, noting idly that the six men in the larger, open office were all sitting at their ugly green desks with their heads down, lost in their own paperwork.

*When Dave Alexander rolled through town a few months back, Jack agreed to meet him for a drink. Two old prohibition cops sharing a bottle of Jameson in the corner of a bar they'd both raided twenty years earlier. Neither of them commented on the irony. Dwelling on irony was wasted time.*

*Dave had gotten out later than Jack, and for altogether different reasons. He'd collected his pension and left Chicago behind for Milwaukee, where he and his wife ran a hardware store in the suburbs. The two hadn't been the best of friends during their time on the force together, but they had shared experiences. And Dave had been there for Jack afterward. When Jack was obsessing over who, Dave was one of the guys who convinced him the only thing that really mattered was why.*

*And, yeah. He knew why.*

*So it surprised Jack when Dave seemed to bring the conversation back around to who, almost twenty years down the road.*

*Jack had returned from a trip to the John and found Dave staring intently at a twisted cocktail straw wrapped around a forefinger. Rather than ask what was on his mind, Jack sat down and picked up his whisky glass. If Dave had something to say, he'd say it.*

*"Jack – something has been nagging at me lately. And I don't really know why."*

*Jack sipped his drink. Dave turned to look at him. Sincerity in his watery eyes, Jack supposed.*

*"Lately it's been bugging me that I steered you away from poking around after – you know. After the accident."*

*Jack shrugged and held Dave's gaze. "Is that how you think of it? As an accident? Because of all the things it was, that's the one thing it wasn't."*

*Dave turned back to his own glass and swirled the whisky in small circles. He started to speak, and then gulped down a stiff belt. Without turning to look at Jack, he replied in a weary voice. "I know what it was, Jack. I'm not saying I have any answers for you, but I think it would have been..." He stopped, seemingly unable to find the word he was looking for. He stopped looking for the word and waved at the bartender for a last round.*

*The last round nudged the conversation back toward small talk about the here and now, and no more was said about who or why.*

Jenkins' brow creased and he ran a delicate hand across his mouth, as if he wasn't sure how to broach the subject. Whatever the subject was.

"Jack," he began, in a serious voice. "I have to admit I'm not completely up to speed on every little detail of every employee's background." He stopped and picked up a dull pencil, fingering it as he continued. "But I do know that you were a cop once upon a time. I've always assumed that's why you're such an effective investigator."

He looked up, maybe expecting a response from Jack. Jack obliged.

"I guess it doesn't hurt."

Jenkins nodded slowly before continuing. "Well, okay. I guess what I'm trying to say is that I hope nothing in your past gets in the way of the job you're doing now."

Jack was clueless. He nodded back at Jenkins and decided not to probe the issue. "Okay. I don't think it ever would," he said.

Jenkins gave an approving nod and picked up a pink note that was sitting on his desk blotter. He held it out for Jack to take. So Jack took it.

"Whatever this is about? It's your business, Jack. That's all I'm saying," he said, as if he was doing Jack a favor.

Jack glanced down at the note, but decided not to read it until he was back at his desk. "That seems fair, Mr. Jenkins," he said, before turning and heading lazily for the door.

Settled back in the old rolling chair, he unfolded the note. Below the block-printed WHILE YOU WERE OUT was a number, a name, and a request to return a call to Los Angeles, California. The name on the slip of paper was Captain Henry Cavanaugh.

Henry Cavanaugh.

Cavanaugh had been a junior detective during Jack's glory days in Chicago. As with virtually everyone else he had known in his former life, he had lost track of Cavanaugh after Jack left the department. But it didn't surprise him to see that he'd made captain. Even if it was in a place as remote as Los Angeles.

Jack slid open the middle drawer of his desk and dug under a pile of paper clips for a foil-wrapped stick of Black Jack gum. Chewing the licorice-flavored stick deliberately, he stared at the note, weighing whatever options he had.

Jack didn't really believe in fate or destiny. He didn't believe God left signposts along the way, intended to steer you into making the right decisions in life. But he also knew you could never really escape your own life. That was the main reason he'd never left Chicago.

Rather than bolt for the wide open spaces with his tail tucked between his legs, Jack had simply shifted his focus to new directions in life. After all, he wasn't the only one who'd lost at the game. By now, virtually all of the old players were dim reflections in rearview mirrors. Prohibition was fodder for low budget gangster movies and costume parties. Capone had rotted to death from the inside out. Eliot Ness was a civilian, drinking his life away somewhere in Ohio. And too many guys never made it out of prohibition alive. Or with all of their working parts in order.

*He'd walked past the music store a thousand times before, never really giving it much notice. It was just another building he passed between his apartment and his office. Now and then a poster in the window might catch his eye, but he'd never felt compelled to walk in until that day a few weeks ago. The truth is, he'd only stepped inside to get out of the rain, which had been steady all afternoon, but was suddenly dumping buckets of water on the heads of Chicago's rush hour foot traffic.*

*Rather than stand in the doorway watching the skies, he idly browsed the wooden racks full of small vinyl discs, and slowly spun a rotating wire spinner full of sheet music. Despite providing a warm shelter from the storm, the shop was relatively empty. Against one wall was a long, low counter manned by a disinterested looking clerk in his late twenties. He was standing behind the counter, flipping through a music trade. The wall behind him was decorated with posters and photographs of musicians, some of whom Jack recognized, most of whom he didn't. Against the wall opposite the counter were a series of listening booths, all but one unoccupied. In between the two walls were the rows of wooden racks, dotted here and there with the wire spinner racks and cardboard specialty displays. Light classical music drifted through the air.*

*As he made his way to the back of the store, he saw that the rear wall was largely taken up by a series of vertical shelves, with each slot containing a group of records in weathered paper sleeves. A sign marked* Used 78s *was taped to the wall above the shelves.*

*Something compelled him to browse.*

*There were a handful of Fanny Brice records on the shelves, including "I'd Rather Be Blue." He held the disc in his hands. Flipped it over. The song on the other side was called "If You Want the Rainbow (You Must Have the Rain)." The title didn't ring any bells, but he smiled at the sentiment. He studied the drawing on the black label. The little dog staring down the barrel of a phonograph, illustrated in gold, like the text and the scroll that decorated the edge of the label. He felt a brief, stupid compulsion to pull the record from the paper sleeve and examine if for scratches.*

*Instead, he slid the disc back into the shelving and walked to the front of the store to see if the rain had let up.*

Long distance took its time connecting him with the Los Angeles Police Department, which gave him plenty of time to hang up, wad the note into a tiny ball and drop it into the wastebasket under his desk. But he had a feeling Cavanaugh would call again, so he figured he might as well see how things played out sooner than later.

When Cavanaugh's voice finally came on the line, Jack didn't recognize it. But he could picture Henry Cavanaugh's face. He'd seen it at his office door enough back in the old days. Cavanaugh had been one of the younger go-getters in the department, and always seemed to be in awe of the older guys like Jack. Like the other younger guys, he'd hang around Jack's office, looking for tips on how to make a reputation of his own.

Jack batted away the inevitable small talk. Told Cavanaugh he'd been working at Fidelity Insurance since he left the department. Eighteen years and counting. He didn't ask Cavanaugh how he ended up in Los Angeles, or how the family was. He just waited for Cavanaugh to tell him what the call was about.

After a long, silent beat, Cavanaugh shifted gears. "So, Jack. I know you're doing fine where you are. I checked around, and it's pretty obvious that you're the best investigator Fidelity's ever seen."

Another silent beat, Jack still waiting.

Cavanaugh cleared his throat and finally got to the point. "Jack," he said with purpose. "I want to talk to you about coming out here and doing some work for me."

Jack finally spoke up. "Why would I do that, Henry?" He asked evenly, hoping Cavanaugh didn't sense anticipation in his voice.

"The thing is, Jack," Cavanaugh said. "I think I might have some new information on who was responsible for the deaths of your wife and son."

And somewhere deep inside, Jack felt something struggling desperately to climb to the surface.

He closed his eyes and took a quiet, deep breath, refusing to let it happen.

"What exactly do you need me to do for you, Henry?"

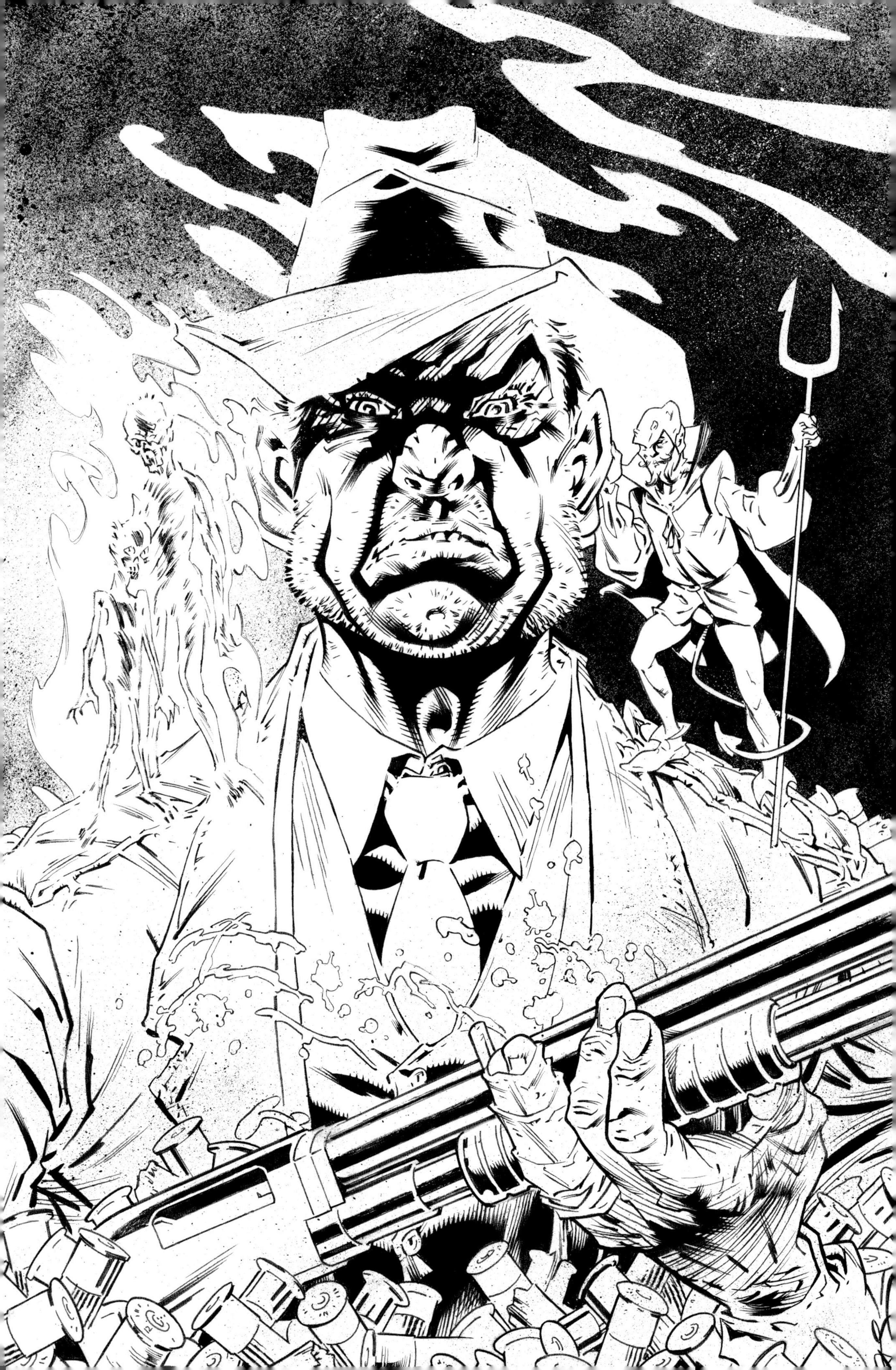

# CREATORS

**Alex Grecian** is the New York Times bestselling author of the 'Scotland Yard Murder Squad' novels, including *THE YARD, THE BLACK COUNTRY*, and the forthcoming *THE DEVIL'S WORKSHOP*. He also co-created the long-running and critically acclaimed comic book series *PROOF*, which NPR named one of the best books of 2009. He has written an original e-book, *THE BLUE GIRL*, and an original graphic novel, *SEVEN SONS*, as well as a multitude of short stories, both comics and prose, for various anthologies.

**Jeremy Haun** has been drawing comics for over a decade. He has worked for nearly every publisher in the medium, including DC Comics, Marvel Comics, Top Cow Produtions, Image Comics, and Oni Press. In that time he has drawn *The Darkness*, *Arkham Reborn*, and *Detective Comics*. He is the co-creator and artist of *THE BEAUTY*, Top Cow's 2011 Pilot Season winner. He created and wrote the Oni Press original graphic novel, *NARCOLEPTIC SUNDAY*. He co-created *BATTLE HYMN* and *THE LEADING MAN* with B. Clay Moore. He lives in a crumbling mansion in Joplin, Missouri with his wife, two kids, and a rather large cat.

**B. Clay Moore** has written comic books for virtually every major publisher, including Image Comics, Marvel Comics, DC Comics, WildStorm, Oni Press and Top Cow Productions. He is the co-creator of a handful of critically acclaimed creator-owned books. *HAWAIIAN DICK* was named by *Wizard Magazine* one of the top 100 graphic novels published during their lifetime, and *BATTLE HYMN* was listed in the book *500 Essential Graphic Novels*. *THE LEADING MAN* is currently under option with Universal Pictures. His most recent creator-owned work includes *JSA THE LIBERTY FILES: THE WHISTLING SKULL* with Tony Harris, from DC Comics, and *ALOHA, HAWAIIAN DICK* with artist Jacob Wyatt, from Image Comics.

**Seth Peck** lives in Kansas City with his wife and five children. He is the writer and co-creator of '76, *SORROW* (with Rick Remender and Francesco Francavilla), and has written both *Wolverine: Fear Itself*, and *X-Men* for Marvel Comics. His work was featured in the Eisner-Award-winning *Comic Book Tattoo* and the anthology *24Seven*.

**Alejandro Aragón** is a newcomer artist who has been working for several companies around the comic market. He was art assistant to Leandro Fernandez for two years, co-creator of *Overlook* (Shadowline, 2009), collaborator on *Deadlands*, and artist over the second year of *28 Days Later* for BOOM! Studios. At the present time, he is working on a graphic novel about a movie project to be announced this year. *alearagon.blogspot.com*

**Zac Atkinson** is an artist and colorist based out of a small town in central Illinois. He has worked on many mainstream titles such as DC's *Magic of Shazam*, *Teen Titans*, *Young Justice* , IDW's *Transformers*, *GI Joe* and numerous others. When he's not creating for others he's busy building and destroying worlds in his mind, all in an effort to kill time until the Zombie Apocalypse. When that day comes, keep an eye out for him, he'll be the crazy bastard in a Batman shirt wielding an axe… not a crappy wood chopping axe.. a battle axe, like He-Man's. Check out *evilby.me* for Zac's projects and random whatnots.

**Jean-Paul Csuka** is an illustrator, comic creator and painter. He graduated from the Alberta College of Art and Design with a Bachelor of Design. He currently colors the ongoing series *Bedlam* from Image Comics. *cargocollective.com/jpcsuka*

**Nick Filardi** was born and raised in New London, Connecticut on a steady diet of Batman the animated series. A graduate of SCAD in 2004, he got his start with Lee Loughridge's Zylonol Studios before striking out on his own. You can find Nick's work in *Powers*, *Helheim*, and *Atomic Robo*. When he isn't coloring comics, you can find him flipping cards on MTGO. *twitter.com/nickfil*

**Nathan Fox** was born in 1975 in Washington DC. Raised from the age of five on the suburban outskirts of Houston, an early addiction to cartoons, commercials and video games led to a lifelong exploration of narrative art and the over-stimulation associated with his generation. His work has appeared in *The New York Times* newspaper and magazine, *Interview*, *The New Yorker*, *Rolling Stone*, *Wired*, *ESPN Magazine*, *Print*, *Entertainment Weekly*, *Mother Jones*, *Spin*, *Mad Magazine*, MTV Store windows and t-shirts, Burton US Open 2009,

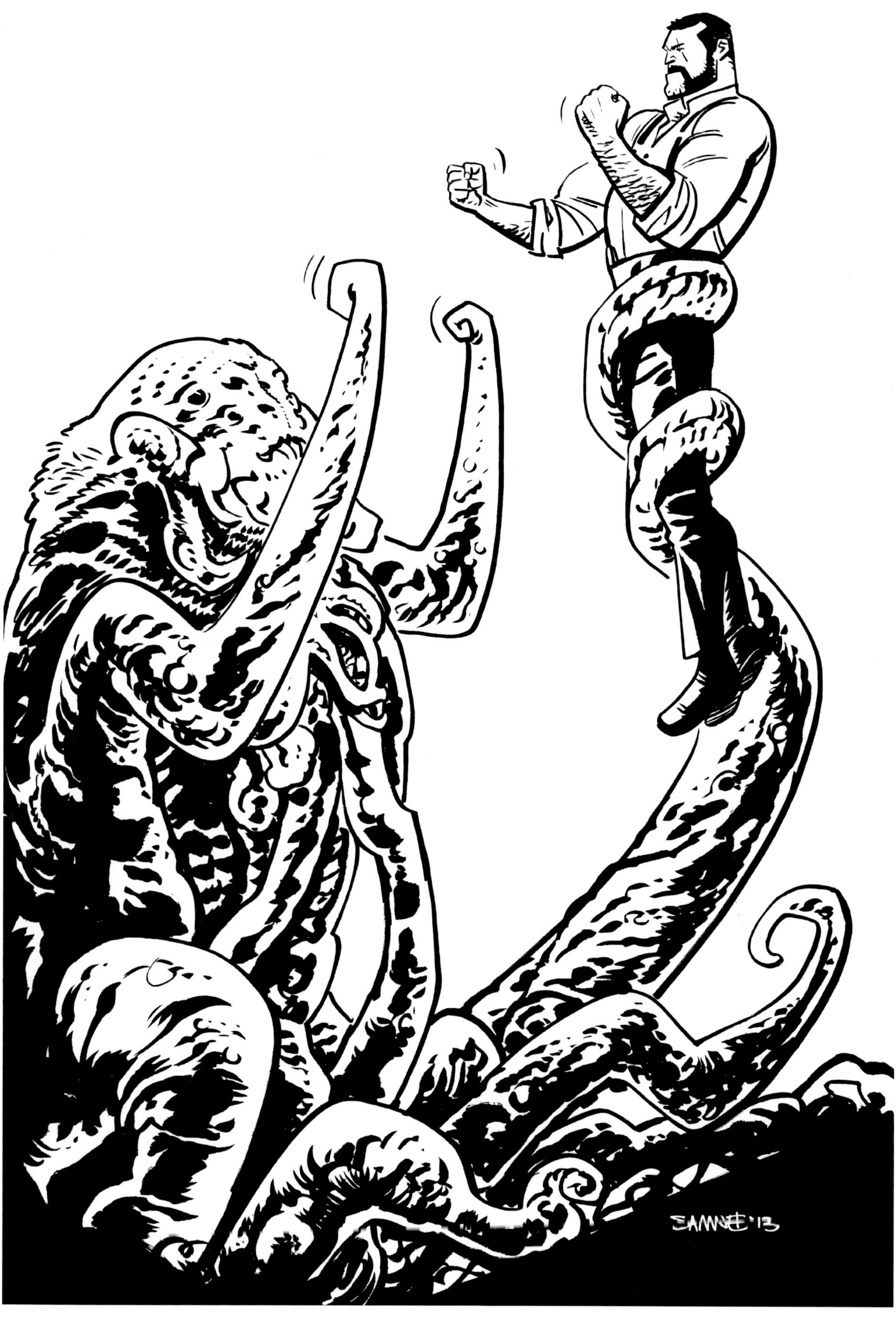
SAMNEE '13

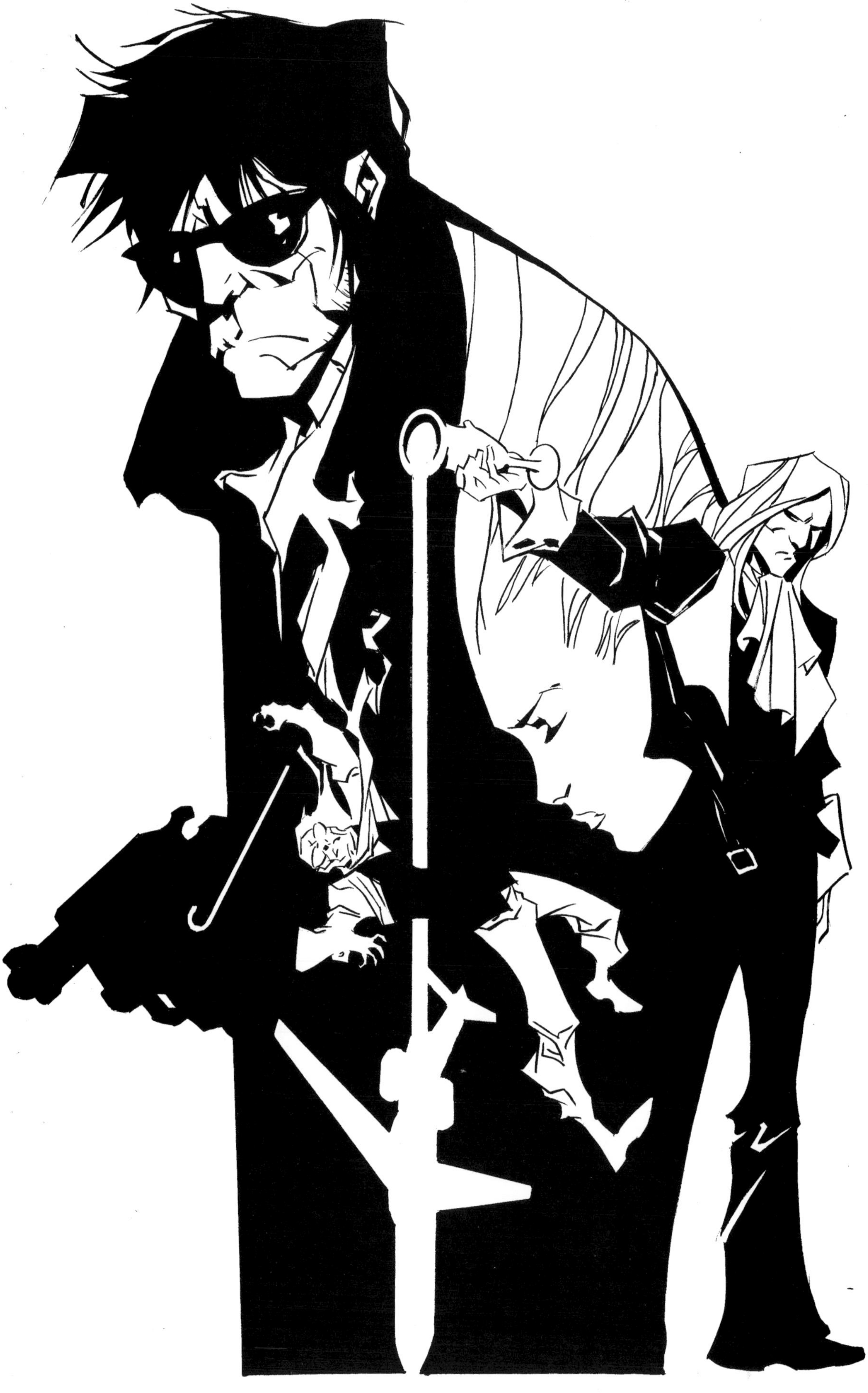

Instant Winner and REAL Skateboards, DC Comics, Vertigo, Dark Horse Comics, Marvel and many other publications and mediums. In 2011, Nathan designed the curriculum for a new low-residency graduate program in visual storytelling called MFA Visual Narrative for the School of Visual Art in NYC. In 2012, Nathan Fox moved back to New York and became Chair of the MFAVN program—a fully accredited MFA degree program which begins in June of 2013. *foxnathan.com*

Philip Hester has been writing and drawing comics for over two decades. Past work includes the Eisner Award nominated series *The Wretch*, and a long run as penciler of DC's *Swamp Thing* and *Green Arrow*. He wrote *The Coffin* with artist Mike Huddleston, and *Firebreather* with artist Andy Kuhn, which became a television feature for Cartoon Network. Phil currently writes *Invincible Universe* for Robert Kirkman's Skybound Entertainment.

Shaky Kane has been both delighting and confusing comic book readers, in equal measure, for the best part of 25 years. His sporadic output has appeared in numerous pivotal publications over the years, including *NME*, *Escape* magazine, *Revolver*, *Speakeasy*, *Deadline*, *2000AD* and *Judge Dredd the Megazine*. In more recent years, defying all logic, Shaky has reinvented himself as the artist behind the critically acclaimed Image series *Bulletproof Coffin*, in collaboration with David Hine, has entered into an ongoing collaboration with Richard Starkings on *Elephantmen*, and is currently drawing, again with David Hine, *Cowboys and Insects* for David Lloyd's *Aces Weekly*.

Brian Koschak is a professional comic book artist/ writer out of Springfield, Missouri. He illustrated Oni Press' *Narcoleptic Sunday* as well as a handful of *Star Wars* graphic novels for Dark Horse Comics. He has also self published the almost completely unknown underground classic comick series *The Eavesdropper Cafe* in addition to *Back Alley Hero* and *Battle of the Sea Titans*. He is currently working on writing and drawing *The Ballad of Louis Sweet*, and is the creator and caretaker of *headmedicine.blogspot. com*, an online resource of only the highest quality brainfood available.

Andrew R. MacLean is a Salem, Massachusetts based up-and-coming comic creator. He writes and draws *Head Lopper* and *Snip Snip* while lending his art to *Department O*, *Colonial Souls*, and *Meatspace*. Andrew also founded and contributes to the artist collective Brand New Nostalgia. Find him on Twitter, Tumblr, Facebook, DeviantArt, and Instagram.

Dave Lanphear Best-known for award-winning lettering and cartooning, Dave Lanphear is also an animation storyboard artist (*Ultimate Spider-Man*) and transmedia producer (*War of the Nephilim*, *Northland Frail*). Look for *77 Hero Plaza* with Troy Peteri at Thrillbent.com in 2013, some shorts on YouTube, and the usual passel of extraordinary comics and graphic novels like this one you're holdin'. Tweet him @artmonkeys and Like his facebook page to hear more.

Thomas Mauer has been working in comics as a letterer and graphic designer for many years. He's had a hand in a number of award winning and nominated books including Archaia's *Awakening*, Image Comics' *Popgun* anthology series, and the webcomic *The Guns Of Shadow Valley*. His current work includes Archaia's *Strange Attractors*, Image Comics' *Graveyard Of Empires* and *Undertow*, MonkeyBrain Comics' *Knuckleheads*, and the action figure tie-in webcomic *Armarauders*, which he letters in five different languages. You can find him on Twitter at @thomasmauer and see more samples of his work at *thomasmauer.com*.

Kevin Mellon is a graduate of the Kubert School. His first book *Gearhead* (with Dennis Hopeless) was released in 2007 and he has gone on to do a plethora of comic books since, including *LoveSTRUCK* (also with Hopeless), *Heart* (with Blair Butler), and *American Muscle* (with Steve Niles). He is currently storyboarding on FX's *Archer* for Floyd County Productions as well as working on new comic book projects. *kevinmellon.com*

Christopher Mitten Originally from the cow-dappled expanse of southern Wisconsin, Christopher Mitten now spends his time roaming the misty wilds of suburban Chicago, drawing little people in little boxes. He has contributed work for Dark Horse, Oni Press, DC Comics, Wildstorm, IDW, 44FLOOD, Image, and Simon & Schuster. He can be found online at *christophermitten.com* and followed on Twitter at @chris_mitten.

Troy Peteri has lettered a million things from *Amazing Spider-Man* to *Witchblade*, as well as written the mini-series *Abattoir* for Radical Comics. He's currently writing a webcomic entitled *77 Hero Plaza* for Thrillbent.com and a graphic novel that he can't speak of yet. Sometimes he tires of lettering other people's words and wishes he could write more, but then he remembers what it was like unloading trucks at 6AM in a Wisconsin winter and it puts things in perspective. Hooray, comics!

John Rauch is an American comic book colorist whose credits include *The Darkness, Invincible, Teen Titans: Year One, Patsy Walker: Hellcat*, and a bunch of other stuff not worth bragging about. He enjoys speaking about himself in the third person and pretending he is more talented and relevant than he really is in order to help fight off bouts of depression.

Cory Smith is a comic and commercial artist living and working in New York City. His clients include Nickelodeon, Hasbro, Dreamworks, Crayola, and more recently Aspen Comics. He's worked on Aspen titles such as *Fathom, Broken Pieces*, and *Legend of the Shadow Clan*. It's a good bet he's drawing as you read this...

Amber Stone is a freelance illustrator and artist. Her primary works are for the company 5finity. She has a degree in graphic design with an emphasis in fine art and she has studied calligraphy at Gakushuin Women's College in Tokyo. You can find her most recent offerings at *halloweenacademy.com*.

Mike Tisserand is an animator and artist with credits on shows such as *Teenage Mutant Ninja Turtles, Transformers* and *My Little Pony*. He resides in Vancouver, Canada. *miketisserand.com*

Tigh Walker ('76, *Lost Girl*) is a Toronto-based artist who enjoys grilled cheese sandwiches. He has worked in the comic/animation/film/video game fields and has a beard named Sparkplug.

Shane White has a varied artistic background in the entertainment industry. He's the author an illustrator of *North Country* and *Things Undone*, his first two graphic novels. He's worked in video games and film as a director, camera operator, editor, concept designer, and storyboard artist. When he's not painting or hiking around the world with his wife he makes his home in the often gray Shangri-La of the Northwest. You can see more of his work at *shanewhite.com* and *studiowhite.com*.

Nolan Woodard In 2006, Nolan gave up a lucrative career as a retoucher for Nike, Starbucks, and EA to dive back into comics, his first love, as a professor of Sequential Art at SCAD-Atlanta. During that time he also cultivated a career as a colorist working for BOOM! Studios, Dark Horse Comics, Image Comics, Marvel Comics, Thrillbent.com, and Oni Press. Today, he colors comics full-time and has begun developing his own OGNs on the side. Nolan might be a shade nuts. *nolanwoodard.com*

Rus Wooton is a comic creator best known for his lettering work on books like *The Walking Dead, Invincible, Super Dinosaur, The Manhattan Projects, Sex, Non-Humans*, and countless others from Marvel, Image, Dark Horse and Radical. An artist for as long as he can remember, Rus achieved Bachelors degrees in Fine Arts and Art Education from the University of South Florida in 1996 and then went into freelancing. He then went to work as Wizard's web designer for three years, then to freelancing again. He's been lettering since 2003 and draws and writes whenever he can. He is fueled by coffee, Dr. Pepper, spicy Korean noodles, and rock 'n' roll.

Frank Zigarelli My bio's not that deep. I've done books for Image and Red5 Comics. If my life were a Wiki entry, it would probably say, "Stubbed for rudimentary information". I'm in a transitional stage. The only thing I post to is *facebook.com/zigarf* and *xantumal.deviantart.com*.

Rafael Albuquerque *rafaelalbuquerque.com*
Ryan Browne *godhatesastronauts.com*
Burt Bucher *burtbucher.wix.com/printmaking*
Mark Englert *tacobelvedere.com*
Francesco Francavilla *francescofrancavilla.com*
Jenny Frison *jennyfrison.com*
Tony Harris *artandskulduggery.blogspot.com*
Brian Hurtt *thehurttlocker.blogspot.com*
Rebekah Isaacs *rebekahisaacs.com*
John Lucas *johnlucasart.wordpress.com*
Paul Maybury *paulmaybury.com*
Scott Morse *scottmorse.blogspot.com*
Ben Passmore *benpassmore.blogspot.com*
Eric Scott Pfeiffer *ericscottpfeiffer.com*
Robbi Rodriguez *frankiegetyourgun.com*
Chris Samnee *chrissamnee.com*
Evan Shaner *evanshaner.com*
Ron Salas *ronsalas.com*
Matthew Dow Smith *matthewdowsmith.com*
Ben Templesmith *templesmith.com*

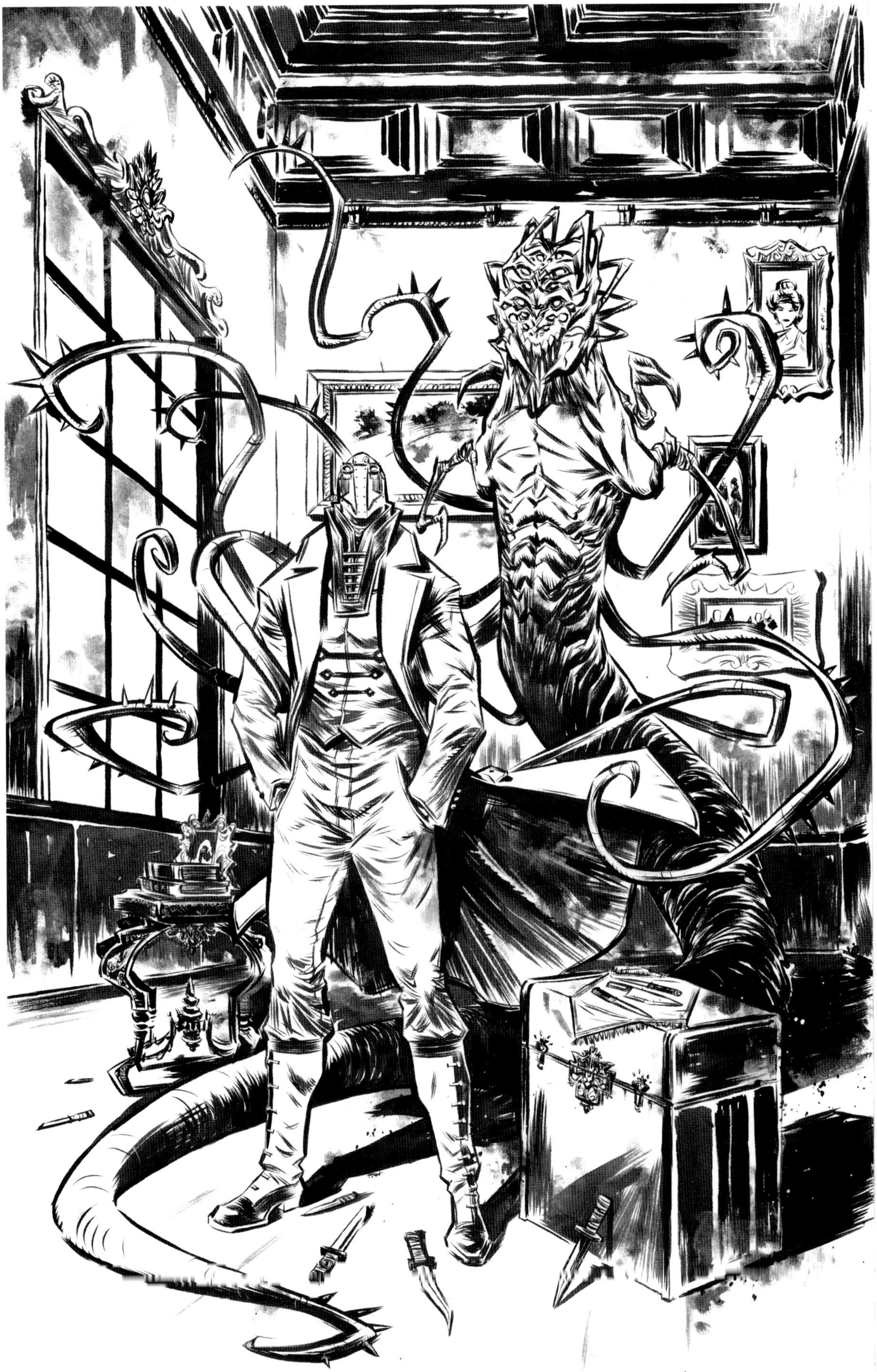

# DONORS

BAD KARMA wish to thank the backers of this project, without whose generosity this book would not have been possible.

| | | | |
|---|---|---|---|
| 44FLOOD | Johannes Braun | Donald Claxon | Tymothy Diaz |
| Ian A. | Brent | Alison Clayton | Doctor Spaceman |
| Jason Aaron | Bob Bretall | Matthew Clement | Doug Dorr |
| Edward Ainsworth | Jack Briglio | Zachary Clemente | Mathieu Doublet |
| Sal Aldana | Katherine Britt | Taylor Clements | Pete Dragasakis |
| James Allan | Patrick Brower | Justin M. Cline | Robin Draper |
| Jose Alva | Scott Brown | Ryan Closs | Leandro Moreira Duarte |
| David Anaxagoras | Ryan Browne | CMD | Robert Duckworth |
| Derek Anderson | Craig Browning | Shaun Cobble | Roxanne Duncan |
| Psyril Apacible | Rob Browning | Jorge Coelho | Anthony Eager |
| Gary Arkell | Pascal Brugger | Taylor Cohen | Bramble Eagle-Jack |
| Jason Arnett | Tyler Bruni | Robert Coleman | Dain Eaton |
| Stephen Aryan | Richard Bruning | Justin Comparetta | eatyourchildren |
| Janelle Asselin | Bruno | Chris Congiardo | Ryan Edgerley |
| Mathieu Auverdin | Marc Bryant | Bo Conroy | Matthew Edwards |
| Michael Avolio | Luke Buchanan | J. Cebron Cook | Alex Edwards |
| Lance Roger Axt | Alec Burkhardt | Rick Cortes | Steve Ekstrom |
| Evan Baier | Ryan Burniche | Clinton Cowen | Nathan Ellis |
| Glenn Bain | Jim Burzelic | Roy Cowing | Karen Enno |
| Balda | Hunter Bush | Jason Crase | Sebastien Fabre |
| Matt Baldwin | Kurt Busiek | Chad Crawford | Aaron Fader |
| Matt Baum | Ty Buttars | crazylikeafox11 | John Falcon |
| Thorsten Becker | Cian Caball | Michael Creasey | Steve Falcon |
| Max Beckman | J.D. Calderon | Daniel Crosier | Danny Feliciano |
| Reed Beebe | Charlie Caliano | Jason Crossman | Joseph Fernandes |
| Matt Bell | Chris Call | Vincent Cu | Belinda Fernandez |
| Paul Benjamin | Tim Callahan | Russ Cundiff | Sam Finley |
| Jeffrey Bennett | Chris Campbell | Shawn Curtis | Jean Fischer |
| John Berkenkopf | Alex de Campi | demifiend | Stephen Fisher |
| Todd Bialas | Richard Carbonneau | Christopher D. Ennis | Rick Flack |
| Cody Bland | Anthony Carpenter | Michael D. | Steve Flack |
| Hallis Blaney | Rob Casteel | Joe Dallacqua | Tony Fleecs |
| Andy Blase | John Celi | Thibauld Dallenne | Chuck Fletcher |
| Evan Blasor | Chris Chambers | Keith Daniels | Margaret Fletcher |
| David Blomquist | Steven Earl Chambers | Zach Darnell | Jason Fliegel |
| Mary Blomquist | Stephanie Chavarria | Brendan Dawson | Kevin Fong |
| Robb Boswell | Jason Chen | Marty Day | Christina Ford |
| Jeff Bouchard | Jack Chen | Jason DeMotte | Forgerelli |
| Fred Boulos | Ryan Jabba-San Cheshire | Dustin Dean | Nathan Fox |
| Mathilde Sachiko Bouhon | Denis Chistyakov | J.R. Deans | Michael Fralin |
| Daniel Bowling | Michael Chovanes | Paul Deatherage | Tyler Frazee |
| Bret Boyer | Iris Chu | Turner Dehn | Daniel Freedman |
| Matthew Bramante | Terence Chua | Vito Delsante | Mind Frell |
| Aaron Brame | Alex Chung | Jim Demonakos | Ryan French |
| Brandon | Shane Clark | Race DiLoreto | Paul Fricke |
| Ivan Brandon | Thayne Clark | Alejandro Diaz | Leo Frollini |

Courtland Funke
Alexander Beowulf Galer
Antonio Garcia
Ashley Garren
Chad Garrett
Enzo Garza
George Gatewood
Jason W. Gavin
Rèmi Gèrard-Marchant
Moutaz AL Ghussein
Logan Giannini
Dan Gibson
Kieron Gillen
Aaron Gillespie
Xhevat Gjokaj
Kari Goebel
Caleb Goellner
Clark Goetzinger
David Golbitz
Wayne Goldblatt
Hilary Goldstein
Nikki Gonzales
Gary Goodrich
Gord
Steven E. Gordon
Sean Gramoll
Philip Grecian
Brian Griesbach
John Grigas
Chris Grine
Joey Groah
Mike Grove
Sean Gruosso
Alexander Gudenau
Ant H.
Paul M. H.
Till H.
Ernie Hacks
Shannon J. Hager
Darrin Halsey
James Hancock
Derek Handley
Phillip Hanlon
Garrett Hanna
Ding Hao
Alan Harris
Marlan Harris
Jonathan C. Hart
Fiona Hartman
Paul Hartshorne
Nate Hartz
HassanT
Daniel D. Hastings

Simon Hausner
Curtis Hawkins
Morgan Hay
Shane Heckethorn
Erica Heflin
G. Hendroff
Anita Hensler
Link W. Herrman
Del Hewitt Jr.
Steve Higgins
Chad Hindahl
Adam Hines
Brett Hinton
Drew E. Hinton
Shannon Ho
Bob Hodges
Bryan Honda
Bryce Hopkins
Martin Hopkins
Matt Hopkins
Sean Hopkins
Jeff Hotchkiss
Dustin Hovatter
Don Howard
Chris Hughes
Brian Hunt
John Hunt
Doug Hurley
Jason A. Hurley
Hurley's Heroes
Hung Huynh
Hyathin
Saoud Nasser J.
Magnus Jacobsson
Brandon Lloyd James
Doak Jantzen
Harper Jaten
Michele Jeleniewski
Dennis Foged Jensen
Brad Johnson
Chris Johnson
Cory Johnson
Jeff Johnson
William Johnston
Justin Jordan
Matthew Kaczynski
Aaron Kafton
Kat Kan
Mark Katzoff
Joe Keatinge
Edward Keener
Andrew Keller
Conrad Kelley

Rob Kelly
Ken's Lil' Sister
Mike Kennedy
Luke Keppler
Arafaat Ali Khan
Navid Khavari
Joshua Kilzer
Jun Bob Kim
Das Kindt
Aaron King
Andy King
Matt Kliemann
Keith Knudsen
Jared Koon
Matt Kozera
Justin Kramer
Karin S. Ku
Gregory Kushlan
Theron Kusulas
Emmo Lütringer
Maxwell LaChance
Mark J. Lacey
Courtland LaVallee
Patrice Lalonde
Sean Lambert
Hunter Lambright
Addison Langford
Lachlan Larsen
Jonathan Larson
Legend Comics and
  Coffee
Will Lentz
Leroy
Andrew Leslie
David Levine
Craig Lewis
Sean Lewis
Jesse Lickman
Little Foot
John Littrel
Jordan Liv
Marty Lloyd
Local Heroes
Jose Loeri
Stephen Loiaconi
Pat Loika
Nate Lovett
Adam Luptak
Peter Lust
Michael Lutes
Roy MacKenzie
Marcel Mack
Chris Makarsky

Kara Malcolm
Michelle Manning
Ben Markwardt
Kevin J. Maroney
David Marquez
Radley Masinelli
Jono Matusky
Thomas Mauer
Dave Maulding
Bryan Mauney
Robert Mayland
Katherine Mays
Ronnie Mays Jr.
Ian McAllister
Kevin McAninch
Michel McCammon
Ronan McDermott
Blake McLean
Jason McRoberts
Barry McWilliams
Evan Meadow
Tim Meakins
Manny Mederos
Melissa
Mike Meltzer
Dennis Menard
Digger T. Mesch
Matthew Meylikhov
Benjamin Mialot
Noah Miller
Rian Miller
Scott Milstein
Christopher Mitten
Billy Mizrahi
Stephen Molnar
Adam J. Monetta
Philippe Montplaisir-
  Morissette
Christian Moore
Gibbs Moore
Hansel Moreno
Christian Morgan
Morki
Brad Morris
Lucas Morris
Craig Morrison
Alfred Moscola
Joshua Mote
Mouse
MrEvilStevo
Jonathan Muckala
Colin Murchison
Trista Musco

Mike and Barb Myers
Ken Nagasako
Casey Nakata
Nathan
Chris Nazareno
Chris Neseman
Greg Newman
Son Nguyen
Joel Niddrie
Joe Nozemack
Meredith Nudo
Jay Nystrom
Janna OíShea
Craig Okita
Eirik Skâr Olsen
Jason Oren
Julian Orr
Ramon Ortega
Out of Step Arts
Erech Overaker
Kristopher Owen
Dorothy P.
Eric Palicki
Dan Palmer
Jim Palmer
Jimmy Palmiotti
John Parkin
Ande Parks
Hywel Parrington
Rose Pascoe
David Pasquino
Kevin Pass
Paul Patane
Mark Paterson
Joe Patrick
Jorge Garcia Pavon
Josh Peck
Terry Peck
Mark Pengryn
Troy Peteri
Eric Peters
Tony Peterson
Michael Pettipas
Will Pfeifer
Eric Scott Pfeiffer
Denise Pirko
Dustin Pitre
Dan Pittman
Ernest Plange
John Popa
Craig Popplewell
Andrew Porwitzky
Caleb Potratz

Daryl Praeker
Eric Prestianne
Ione Priest
Jason Prince
Dave Punk
Kristy Quinn
Gary Rabuzzi
John Rauch
Kyle Rechsteiner
Rick Remender
Bertrand Renard
RetroFanatik
Rafael Reyes
Chris Rhodes
Justin Riddle
Erik Rinard
Jeffrey Rinvelt
Jeremy J. Rivera
RKDN Studios
Josh Roberts
Charles Robinson
Terry Rossiter
Jeff Rougvie
Geoff Rousseau
Christopher Rowley
Carlos Gabriel Ruiz
Christopher Ryder
Katherine S.
Mark Sable
Filip Sablik
Jorge Santiago Jr.
Rob Schamberger
Brandon Schatz
Cody Schibi
Lance Schibi
Scott R. Schmidt
Christopher P. Schmitz
Adam Schoenbart
Sthefan Schultz
Mike Scigliano
Jesse Scoble
Tim Segbert
Doug Shank
Douggie Sharpe
Jim Sharpnack
Andrew Shaw
Stephen Shayler
Desiree Shelton
Avner Shiloah
Andrea Shockling
Jason Shtrax
Jacob Shumaker
Austin Simmons

Steve Simmons
Joeseph Simon
Mark Simon
Tore Simonsen
Jeff Simpkins
Subrata Sircar
Robyn Sitz
Sketchbook Comics
Michael Anton Smid
Joshua Smith
Judy L. Smith
Mark Andrew Smith
Nolan Smith
Phil Smith
Randy Smith
Jake Soeldner
Ed Soto
Jason Southworth
Brie Spielmann
Brian Stello
Jeff Stephens
Ben Stephenson
Scott Steubing
Kyle Stevens
Dave Stokes
Amber Stone
Kyle Strahm
Summer Suzuki
Carlos T.
Jimmy T.
Jocelyn Talureau
Roderick Taylor
Darrell Taylor
Ben Templesmith
Brooks Terry
Phil Thomas
Brian Thompson
Kate Tillotson
Bryan A. Timmins
Top Moose
J. Torres
Chadwick Torseth
William Tournas
David Townsend
Pascal Tremblay
Robert Triplett
Brian Truitt
Paul Tucker
Brad Turner
Joshua Turner
Henry Van
Joseph Van Allen
Jamie Vann

Simon Varley
Steve Vaughn
Trinity Vaughn
Gabriel Velarde
Michael Vergalla
Will Vesely
Royce Viso
Gray VonFriedly
Richard Vu
Cody Walker
Heather Walker
Dan Wallace
Desmond Walsh
Big Mike Walton
Matthew Wang
Stanley Wang
Kyle Warnick
James Watson
John Wayda
James Welch
Brad Weller
Roxane White
Taylor Whittemore
Barry D. Willingham
Sam Wilson
Brian Winkeler
N.C. Winters
Dan Wisniewski
WJC
Stacey (Moore) Wohlford
Morgan Wolman
Wong Kum Yew
Jason Wood
Randy Wood
Michael Woods
Martyn Woodsford
Rus Wooton
Jefferson Workman
Reegan Worobec
Nathan Wright
John Wriston
Stella Wu
Jesse Young
Kurt Young
Ahmed Yousif
Craig Zablo
Andy Zeigert
Matt Zitron

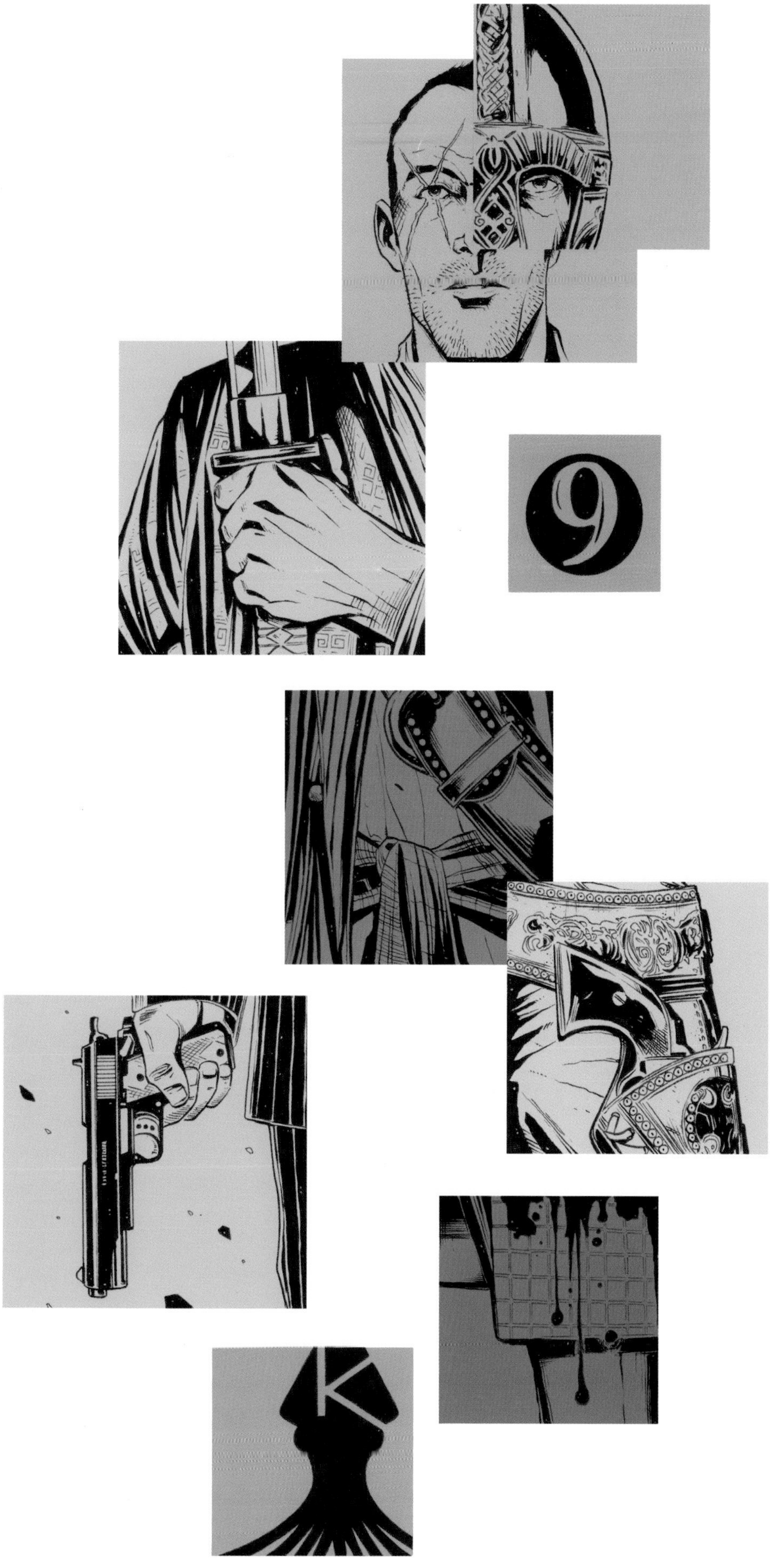
9